Eisenhower and Adenauer

Alliance Maintenance under Pressure, 1953–1960

Steven J. Brady

LEXINGTON BOOKS
A division of
ROWMAN & LITTLEFIELD PUBLISHERS, INC.
Lanham • Boulder • New York • Toronto • Plymouth, UK

Published by Lexington Books
A division of Rowman & Littlefield Publishers, Inc.
A wholly owned subsidiary of The Rowman & Littlefield Publishing Group, Inc.
4501 Forbes Boulevard, Suite 200, Lanham, Maryland 20706
http://www.lexingtonbooks.com

Estover Road, Plymouth PL6 7PY, United Kingdom

British Library Cataloguing in Publication Information Available

Library of Congress Cataloging-in-Publication Data

Brady, Steven J., 1967–
  Eisenhower and Adenauer : alliance maintenance under pressure, 1953–1960 /
Steven J. Brady.
      p. cm. — (Harvard Cold War studies book series)
  Includes bibliographical references and index.
  ISBN 978-0-7391-4225-7 (cloth : alk. paper) — ISBN 978-0-7391-4227-1
(electronic)
  1. United States—Foreign relations—Germany (West) 2. Germany (West)—
Foreign relations—United States. 3. Eisenhower, Dwight D. (Dwight David),
1890–1969. 4. Adenauer, Konrad, 1876–1967. 5. United States—Foreign
relations—1953–1961. 6. Cold War—Diplomatic history. I. Title.
  E183.8.G3B726 2010
  327.7304309'045—dc22   2009025627

Printed in the United States of America

For William, Matthew, and Lydia Grace

And

For Monica

With Love

Amor magnus doctor est

Contents

Acknowledgments

I owe a tremendous debt to Rev. Wilson D. Miscamble, CSC, who mentored me for many years, both actively and by example. I don't know how many dissertation advisers sit down with their students and read every sentence of their manuscripts aloud in order to catch every last error. I suspect that the number of *Doktorvaters* who do this is small; perhaps as small as one. Bill was present at the creation. Indeed, more than merely "present," he has been indispensable as a colleague, and even more so as a friend.

I would not have come upon the topic of this book were it not for a graduate-seminar review that I wrote on Thomas Alan Schwartz's *America's Germany*. I still have a copy of the review, and it appears that I praised the book unreservedly. I hope that he will find this reassuring. Ever since he read my dissertation, he has generously shared his time and knowledge with me. My colleague A. James McAdams, of the Department of Political Science at Notre Dame, gave the original version of this book a mind-bogglingly insightful read. His capacity for seeing what historians cannot see in their own work has been applied to my manuscript. It is far better for his suggestions. Rev. Thomas Blantz, CSC, gave his characteristically close read to the first draft of what is now this book. His careful reading produced his (equally) characteristically wise suggestions and corrections. I believe that I incorporated every one of them in this book.

My graduate education was enriched by a number of my professors. In particular, Alan Dowty inspired me to try to think originally about international relations theory and security issues. I feel particularly lucky to have worked with him. Prof. Laura Crago kindled in a young U.S. diplomatic historian a fascination with European diplomacy and learning languages.

She then convinced him not to, quote, jump ship, but rather to make it his specialty to study the connections between the two. Vincent P. DeSantis began teaching at Notre Dame in the late 1940s. He still teaches a course every fall, thus stretching the word "dedication" to its outermost limits. For teaching me to read Russian and French, thanks go out to, respectively, Tom Marullo and Pat Martin. At Roosevelt University, I was inspired by a number of teacher/scholars, especially David Miller, Daniel Headrick, Dennis Temple, and Farhang Zabeeh.

Many thanks as well to my colleagues and friends at Notre Dame's First Year of Studies, who have always blurred the line between "colleague" and "friend." Dean Holly Martin was my mentor at FYS. I sincerely hope that my shortcomings are, in the words of my patron saint, not laid to her charge. Special thanks to Dean Eileen Kolman, who was among the first people to encourage me to finish this manuscript. For this I am especially grateful. Dean Hugh Page—a veteran of academic publication—patiently answered my questions as I worked my way through the publication process. Finally, Sandy Tompkins deserves many, many thanks for making sure that the Coleman-Morse Center is always one of the most attractive spaces for our undergraduates, as well as for their faculty.

Friends from graduate school who have helped me in many different ways include Tim Schorn, James Old, Kevin Krause, John Quinn, Bob Shaffern, Jeanne Petite, Dan Graff, and Sean Brennan. Prof. Kathleen Cummings has managed to accomplish the impossible, and the sense of wonder among her friends is profound. V. Bradley Lewis listened patiently to my homilies on Wittgenstein without audibly snickering once. Brad is more than just a "clean-cut guy in a pink dress shirt," no matter what the *Washington Post* has reported. If it's related to the military, and I know it, it is probably because of Duane Jundt. At the Department of History, Myrtle Doaks, Jeanette Torok, and Tori Davies have been both helpful and great fun to be around. Anyone who considers their work valuable must view the work of those who make this work possible to be equally valuable, and I thank them for helping me to do what I do.

From back home in Chicago, special thanks to my longtime friend Dan Berger and his family. In my adopted home town, many thanks to John Soares. One is accustomed to reading in book acknowledgments that the book in question "would have been impossible" without this person or that. In this case, it is quite literally true that the book would never have seen the light of day without the patient assistance of series editor Mark Kramer of the Harvard Project on Cold War Studies and his gifted assistant Sylvana Kolaczkowska. They have encouraged me throughout the publishing process; been quick with answers to pesky questions; and more than tolerant of my tendency to use e-mail as a way of keeping myself entertained. I'm sure that their patience with me is more than I deserve.

Sidney Stein has been one of my closest friends through some difficult times ever since we met in Russian History I in the fall of 1986. Sid and I have sought to encourage each other as we make our way through the historical profession, and I suspect that he will be one of the people most pleased with the publication of this book. Prof. Michael Knock of Clarke University is likewise one of the most important friends that I have ever known. Because fulsome praise embarrasses small-town Iowans, I will end my acknowledgment of his friendship with a simple "Thank you, Mike."

My introduction to the history of European-American relations came from Stable Sgt. Francis J. Brady, American Expeditionary Force, 33rd Infantry ("Prairie") Division, 108th Engineers (France, May 1918–May 1919: Second Somme, Meuse-Argonne). Grandpa Harm "Harry" Veldman was the first person to take me to Cantigny, perhaps to compensate for Dutch neutrality during the Great War.

I hope that the Chicago Schopens know how much they mean to the South Bend Bradys. Thanks to Eileen and Keith, and to their wonderful children, Drew, Tom, Hannah, and Jenna. An earlier version of this work was dedicated to the memory of my parents, Aylward J. and Marie Alice Brady. Some lessons one learns too early. I will always be grateful to them. And for them.

The deepest thanks go to the four people who share my home and my life. William, junior scientist extraordinaire, reminds me every day of how my life changed when I became "Dad." The nights we spend "dozing with the dinosaurs" on the floor of the Field Museum are among the greatest experiences of my life. Matthew has taught me so much about trains in the last three years that I think my next book will have to be about railroads and international relations. Then Matt and Dad can snuggle up together and read it. Lydia Grace proves that my father was right when he said that every dad thinks that his daughter is the most wonderful little girl in the world. He'd be pleased to learn that I'm the dad who is right. To Monica I owe more than I can say. I would have nothing without her. Her love and patience are the greatest gift that one person could ever give to another. Thank you.

1

Introduction: Issues, Events, and Personalities

For forty years the Atlantic Alliance stood at the forefront of the West's Cold War strategies. At the heart of that alliance was the bilateral relationship between the United States and the Federal Republic of Germany. Considered from the perspective of postwar power politics in the Atlantic region, this simply made sense. Likewise, a "community of political ideals" in Western Europe—following Charles S. Maier's recent analysis—helped convince significant numbers of American policy makers that American security interests were best served by active support of moderate governments in Western Europe. Faced with a challenge from radical, ideological regimes, the United States could not afford to remain neutral, let alone isolated.[1]

For these reasons—and perhaps as much from growing used to things as they have been—the Atlantic Alliance has come, over the course of half a century, to seem an almost natural phenomenon. Yet if one takes a longer, historical view of trans-Atlantic relations, the cementing of a political and military alliance between the American and German governments must seem a hugely unlikely occurrence. For well over a century, relations between the United States and Prussia—and then the united German empire—had been primarily occupied by trade between the nations, as well as emigration of Germans to the United States. American policy makers early on perceived important interests depended upon a cordial relationship with Berlin. But formal alliance of the two nations would have served no purpose in the nineteenth century. Political and military issues became decisive for the relationship only when the nations came to fight each other in the following century's world wars. A German-American alliance must have seemed farther away in 1945 than it had a century earlier.

1

Yet a remarkable transformation in U.S. policy toward Germany occurred between 1945 and 1953. By launching the poorly timed Berlin Blockade in 1948, Soviet Premier Joseph Stalin managed in fact to give impetus to a policy shift that was already well underway: the growing sense in Washington that the western occupation zones of Germany would need to be revived. An unavoidable element of such a policy was the integration of the nascent West Germany into the security structure that was taking shape around twin pillars of European unity and American involvement.

Indeed, it would have been hard to predict that, in 1953, the engineer of victory over Germany in the west would enter the White House unambiguously committed to building a powerful West German state, and fully integrating it into the West. Common values and security interests gave alliance members continuous incentive to maintain unity. During Dwight Eisenhower's years in office, they would need it. As Geir Lundestad notes, even in the "golden years" of the Atlantic Alliance during the Cold War, conflict—even crisis—among the allies was a routine occurrence.[2] This is a book about the challenges, difficulties, and crises that the German-American alliance faced during the 1950s. In retrospect, the 1950s have sometimes been remembered as the most shining of the alliance's golden years. Yet these were, in fact, years of considerable turmoil. Thus this book makes an effort to investigate the ways in which the governments in Bonn and Washington managed to maintain a productive relationship in the face of international pressures. Strains arose from issues directly connected with Germany's anomalous postwar situation—for example, the Berlin Crisis of 1958–1959—as well as from those that had little to do with the "German Question"—such as the Suez Crisis of 1956. Given the challenges that imposed themselves upon the alliance, the results were better than they might have been. Indeed, better than they should have been, comparing the cohesion and cooperation within the bilateral relationship to what would come later.

This is thus a book about an alliance that lay at the heart of the Cold War in Europe. It is the story of how policy in that alliance was made. The bilateral alliance between the United States and the newly formed Federal Republic of Germany (FRG) proved to be a major force in the shaping of Western policy in the protracted East-West conflict in Europe. Germany's geographic centrality was replicated on the level of policy making. For policy makers in the United States, Germany held the unique position of being both a "problem" and also a tremendous potential resource in the struggle with the Soviet Union.

This book examines the interrelation of two groups of policy makers—one on the Rhine, the other on the Potomac—and seeks to shed light on the development of the alliance, the way in which policies were formulated, and the mutual interaction of this alliance and the wider European

Cold War. As Melvyn Leffler has recently remarked, "No question was more important than the future of Germany" to postwar Washington. Similarly, Geir Lundestad found, when assessing U.S. policy toward postwar Western European integration, that "Washington's abiding concern about the role of Germany" was "perhaps the most striking thread" of his narrative.[3]

Recent work on the Cold War in the 1950s, including Leffler's, has considered the possibility that the East-West conflict might have ended much earlier than it did. Perhaps all that was required was for certain decisions, at a specified point in time, to be made by leaders in Washington and Moscow. Yet such speculation clarifies why an understanding of the U.S.-FRG relationship is crucial. An early end to the Cold War would have depended upon a workable solution to the problem of the divided German nation. Cold War "hot-spots" would flare up in various regions of the globe over the course of the forty-year conflict. But the problem of German power and proclivity remained. A unified Germany would give a tremendous advantage to the bloc with which it was aligned. Germany divided meant the continued East-West rift in Europe. Indeed, a divided Germany was a precondition for the European Cold War. Yet recent history had almost certainly precluded a settlement that left a unified, unaligned Germany once again at the center of Europe. The question at the heart of Leffler's study is "why . . . did the Cold War last as long as it did?"[4] This book helps to explain why.

The Washington-Bonn nexus became a formal alliance in 1955, when the Federal Republic entered the North Atlantic Treaty Organization. But even before this formalization, Washington had been treating West Germany as a valued partner. Policy makers in both the Truman and Eisenhower administrations presumed "that the two sides of the Atlantic would continue to share the most basic interests."[5] In addition, the Americans sought to help, induce, and even pressure the Western Europeans into actively seeing to their own unity, prosperity, and security. As a result, the Atlantic Alliance was composed of allies, in the true sense of that word. There is no question that the United States planned on playing the role of leader in the alliance. This role, however, left substantial room for the "junior partners" to influence alliance policy, including policy emanating from Washington. It was not the case that the United States could simply dictate policies to its European allies.[6] Rather, they maintained a voice at the table; often, as we shall see, a cacophonous voice. West Germany, in particular, rose to the status of a valued partner. Questions of alternate possibilities cannot be understood from the perspective of the Washington-Moscow relationship alone. Nor can diplomatic historians understand what *actually* transpired in this relationship without frequently coming back to the interaction of the Germans and these superpowers.

Past studies of America's bilateral relationships have contributed greatly to our understanding of the development of the North Atlantic pact, as

well as to the events and decisions that gave shape to the Europe in which
the leaders of key North Atlantic nations found themselves operating.
Three studies that I have relied upon heavily for historical background on
the formation of the U.S.-FRG relationship are: James McAllister's study
of America's German policy under President Harry S. Truman; Thomas
A. Schwartz's work on John J. McCloy's term as high commissioner; and
Wolfgang Krieger's book on Lucius Clay and the American occupation of
Germany after World War II.[7] Obviously, the focus of much scholarly interest thus far has been on the critical immediate postwar period; that is, upon
the Truman administration and its attempts to determine how the defeated
Germans fit into American plans for postwar Europe. The question of how
Germany—or at least part of Germany—rose from the status of despised
enemy to invaluable ally in such a short period of time has for good reason
attracted substantial scholarly interest, since it must rank among the most
stunning national turns-of-fortune in contemporary history.

There is need for a study of this two-sided alliance during the crucial years
that followed. This book fills that gap.[8] During the Truman administration,
the relationship between the United States and the Federal Republic of Germany was established, and a democratic West Germany achieved central
importance in American policy planning. The question for the 1950s, then,
was how did this alliance work? The Americans sought to integrate West
Germany into Europe, and to use its economic and human capital to build
a political and military force strong enough to resist the East. *How, then, did
they pursue this goal, and how did the West Germans influence American plans
to achieve this goal?* And what were the consequences for the European Cold
War of this bilateral diplomacy?

The study begins with the remarkable year 1953, when Stalin's death and
Konrad Adenauer's re-election triumph, together with the arrival in Washington of the first Republican administration in a generation, suggested that
the Cold War between East and West might, at the very least, turn down a
different path. It takes the narrative to the end of the "Ike Age"; that is, to
a time of increased anxiety following Khrushchev's decision to challenge
the West in Berlin, leading, in a disappointing anticlimax, to the Soviet
decision to walk out of the Paris summit conference. This event put an end
to Eisenhower's dream of capping his life of national and international
service with an East-West nuclear test ban agreement prior to leaving the
White House.

Central to any understanding of the development of the Cold War in
Europe is the fact that both the United States and the Federal Republic
considered their mutual relationship vital to their success—and in the
Germany's case, its very survival. The Bonn regime considered this its *most
important international relationship*. The American position was, not surprisingly, complicated by the multinational nature of U.S. plans for West

Europe's security. The Eisenhower administration had to balance between important European allies when they came into conflict over policy. Yet, over the course of the decade, the administration came clearly to consider the FRG America's most important ally on the European continent; in that sense, a first among equals in the eyes of the western superpower. Tracing this development in the American attitude toward, and engagement with, the Federal Republic is a central part of this study.

A number of episodes from the period have generated much high-quality scholarship, and in German and French, as well as in English—party politics, German elections, the Geneva Summit, the Suez Crisis and the Atlantic Alliance, the "German Question," the Berlin Crisis of 1958–1959. All of these issues exerted an influence upon this bilateral relationship. The reader will find that each is addressed in this book to the extent that it affects the primary issue, which is the bilateral attempt to work out a functioning policy for the U.S.-FRG relationship, which was so central to the West's Cold War strategy.

Individuals matter to this story. As its title suggests, Eisenhower and Adenauer—as well as John Foster Dulles, whose name did not make it onto the book's cover—play a major part in this narrative. The importance of the German-American relationship was so significant, in the minds of the two heads of government, that they spent considerable time and energy on its development. This is especially true on the German side, where Adenauer kept the reins of relations with the Americans firmly in his own hands. The story of postwar West German diplomacy with the United States cannot avoid being, to a large extent, the story of Adenauer's handling of that diplomacy. A close treatment of these key individuals shows how policy within this alliance was made.[9]

While this book focuses on the U.S.-FRG connection, it also contributes to the wider understanding of the Cold War's development in 1950s Europe by consciously placing this central bilateral relationship within the context of the broader European context in which it developed and functioned. The Bonn-Washington alliance both affected and was affected by: changes in Soviet foreign policy after Stalin's death; East German relations with the Soviet Union; the East German policies of the West; military policy within NATO; French and British foreign policies; and U.S. and European policies for promoting European unification.

There have been confrontations, and even crises, in U.S.-FRG relations almost since the Federal Republic was conceived. Certainly, the political and security alliance binding the U.S. and FRG has never been free of disagreements. The 1950s provide us with no exception to this pattern. Historians have been studying and debating unpleasant episodes in the Atlantic Alliance for years. One needs to write only two words—"agonizing reappraisal"—to call to the Cold War scholar's mind a raft of citations.[10] And yet historians and political scientists should avoid following the TV news maxim "If it bleeds, it leads." Studying an alliance relationship that was successful is as worthy an endeavor as studying one that broke down under pressure. This book assesses a bilateral relationship that was, on balance, quite successfully managed during the 1950s. This was so, furthermore, not because the times were easy for this alliance, but because both sides had concluded that this alliance was vital to their respective nations—and not least because both sides generally possessed the diplomatic skill to manage conflicts that did arise.

This study thus addresses one of the misunderstandings that distorts the general, educated public's perceptions of post–Cold War international relations, at least in the United States. Namely, there is in the public conversation on American foreign relations a notable sense that Cold War policy formulation was somehow easy. That objectives were almost always clear. That threats were easily understood and agreed upon by allies, both as to their provenance and as to their danger. And most remarkably, that alliances functioned more or less as natural phenomena, thriving on their own, with minimal care-taking from the governments bound by relevant treaties. A close study of the relationship between Bonn and Washington during the 1950s demonstrates that alliance maintenance was by no means easy and decisions by no means clear, even if the principals did a better job, and attained better results, than has been the case with some of their successors.

It is tempting, after so many years have passed, to look back on the early Cold War period as a "Golden Age" in trans-Atlantic relations, and especially U.S. relations with its German ally. The reader of this study will not encounter this rosy picture. Again, the alliance was never free of friction or mistrust. And in the context of the European Cold War, and changes in Soviet leadership, the alliance in fact came under a significant amount of pressure from outside the Bonn-Washington nexus. Yet while the alliance did not always run smoothly, the stresses and conflicts within it were managed better than one might have predicted, given the pressures that the two sides found themselves under during rather turbulent times. It is this "alliance maintenance under pressure" that provides a significant chapter in the way the West waged the Cold War.

The alliance had emerged out of the American commitment to liberate Europe from totalitarian domination by committing large numbers of troops to the European continent. Ironically, that decision had been taken by Franklin Roosevelt, Henry Stimson, and their subordinates in order that Anglo-American and Russian power—*together*—might drive into the heart of Europe to crush the military power of Germany. The transformation in the European situation that ended this Grand Alliance and ushered in the Cold War has been the subject of continuous study for decades, much of it focusing upon the key issue of Germany. Eisenhower—the soldier and then the president—is never far off when this topic arises. As Thomas A. Schwartz has said, Eisenhower was "deeply involved" in the "extraordinary change that took place in American foreign policy toward Germany in the years after 1945."[11]

The Grand Alliance was showing cracks before what was left of Nazi Germany capitulated to the Allies. It was thus impossible for the Supreme Commander of Allied Forces in Europe to avoid forming an opinion about Soviet actions as the Red Army pressed westward toward its final goal, Berlin. Eisenhower sensed, as the war went on, that the Soviet Union "had no intention of continuing its policy of friendship, even on the surface."[12] This was, at any rate, how he remembered matters a decade and a half later. Perhaps he was recalling his own frustration at the time, which was certainly quite real. Yet Eisenhower continued to plug optimistically for American cooperation with the Soviets as postwar army chief of staff. In addition, he was vocally opposed to any talk within the Truman administration of the "inevitability" of a postwar war; the view, that is, that the Soviets would soon launch a military attack into Western Europe. Biographer Stephen E. Ambrose paints a picture of a reluctant Cold Warrior, who only gradually—over the course of two years—gave up on the hoped-for peacetime cooperation with Moscow. Even then, he never converted to the belief that the Red Army tanks were likely to pour through the Fulda gap at some point in the near future.[13]

Events in the world, and especially events in Europe, finally brought him around to the harder line toward Moscow. The Greco-Turkish Crisis of 1947, the Prague Coup, Berlin Blockade, and Hungarian coup (all in 1948), seemed to Eisenhower to signal the demise of Soviet-American cooperation in matters of postwar European politics and security. Eisenhower followed rather than led the Truman administration's overall trend toward a harder line in Soviet policy during the immediate postwar years. When in 1947 Truman and his advisers began to work out a general policy for countering the perceived threat—the policy eventually labeled "Containment"—Eisenhower was a willing participant in its *implementation*. Yet he could not have been impressed with the success of Containment in those last years of the 1940s. China was "lost" to Mao's Communists and then the Soviets broke the American atomic monopoly in 1949. It had been "year of tragedy," according to Eisenhower.[14]

Tragedy is sometimes a matter of perspective. For the former Lord Mayor of Cologne, Konrad Adenauer, and his political associates, 1949 had been rather a year of triumph. By then, the Western occupying powers had largely given up on East-West cooperation in Germany. Faced with what they took to be Soviet intransigence upon German economic revitalization and other key issues, France, the United Kingdom, and the United States moved decisively in the direction of helping to establish a German government for the western zones of occupation. The Berlin Blockade helped hustle this move along. So too did British and French fears that any conceivable East-West agreement on German unity would have meant, at that time, an American military withdrawal from Europe. Paris had a particular interest in the long-term fate of postwar Germany. From the French perspective, it was better to have a *West* German state under three-power occupation than a united Germany and American withdrawal.

Thus, the western Big Three made saltatory progress during 1949 on the creation of the "Federal Republic of Germany," even though French support for this project must have seemed absurdly unlikely even to those who were watching it happen. By September, a government was formed under the leadership of Konrad Adenauer. It was this Christian Democrat–led coalition in the Bundestag that elected Adenauer chancellor—by the margin of one vote, Adenauer's own.[15] At the time, Adenauer hardly seemed poised to dominate West German politics for a decade and a half. He had been born in 1876, and thus was seventy-three years old when he assumed the chancellorship. But his advanced age was, ironically, one of the reasons for his longevity: Had he been a younger and seemingly fitter man, it is hard to imagine that the Nazis would have let him live. True, his external features—disfigured in an automobile accident during the First World War—helped contribute to the outward appearance that this was a man whose better days were well behind him. But like the famous cathedral of his native Cologne, one had to look carefully before making presumptions regarding his age.[16] Like that landmark, he came out of the war physically damaged, but fundamentally intact. American policy makers would thus be dealing with *der Alte* ("the Old Man") in Bonn for the entire formative period of the U.S.-FRG relationship.

Eisenhower was able to follow the events of 1948 and 1949 from the relative tranquility of Morningside Heights in New York City. In 1948, he had accepted the presidency of Columbia University, which was seeking to add to its endowment the prestige and prominence of the Supreme Allied Commander of Allied Expeditionary Forces. "Ike" was a national hero, and would bring attention—and money—to any institution fortunate enough to land him as its president. He was thus in a good bargaining position, and was able, as Ambrose neatly summarizes, to stipulate that as president, he would have "no involvement in purely academic matters, no responsibility for fund raising, no extensive entertaining, and no burdensome administrative details."[17] It's nice work if you can get it, and Eisenhower was one of a very few men who could—which was precisely why he was so attractive to the university's trustees. (More heavy lifting would be required on the Rhine than on the Hudson at decade's end. Adenauer was, for example, giving an average of four speeches per day during the Bundestag election campaign of 1949.)

The Atlantic Alliance was simultaneously moving at a "leisurely" pace. But like the leisurely pace of Eisenhower's life at Columbia, the sense that the Western Europeans had "breathing space" came to an abrupt end with the outbreak of war in Korea.[18] The invasion of South Korea by the communist North was a Cold War watershed. The invasion provoked panic in Western Europe, especially since it was widely assumed—correctly as it turned out—that Stalin had approved the military aggression in advance. The presumed imprimatur from the Kremlin struck the West Germans as particularly ominous, since the parallels in the status of the two divided nations were impossible to ignore, particularly if one happened to reside in the Federal Republic. Stalin could not have had any illusions about American interests in West Germany. But he had nevertheless made two very significant miscalculations: first, he assumed that Washington would not fight to maintain the anticommunist government of South Korean strongman Syngman Rhee; second, he did not foresee that the European members of the newly formed Atlantic Alliance would interpret the Korean invasion as a test run for a similar action in Germany.[19] The crisis atmosphere and the events that followed also helped to convince important Americans that Adenauer was a reliable ally, "even if an obstinate and difficult man." His supporters now included Secretary of State Dean Acheson and the American High Commissioner John J. McCloy.[20] This increase in support from Truman and his aides was certainly a result, in part, of the changed context in which Adenauer now pursued his policies. The chancellor had been anxious to rearm Germany quickly *prior* to the invasion of South Korea. In 1948–1949, a German calling for rapid rearmament could be viewed in the West as somewhat worrisome. After June 1950, the same German struck some key players instead as prescient.

In Washington, the need for a stronger military component to containment was no longer such a hard sell, and the militarized version of American containment envisioned by National Security Council Paper 68 now became a blueprint for administration policy.[21] In the wake of the eruption in Korea, Truman made the decision that significant numbers of American troops should be deployed to Europe in peacetime. By doing so, he also committed to the appointment of an American supreme commander. This step was a sign of American seriousness for the concerned Europeans, as well as a political necessity to gain domestic support for the deployment. The commander of Atlantic pact forces would have to be someone of great stature, and would ideally be a soldier well known to the political leaders of the European nations. There was one clear choice for the job. "Eisenhower's appointment as commander of NATO forces . . . made him a clear embodiment of the American rejection of isolation and commitment of the long-term containment of communism." The president informed Eisenhower that America's North Atlantic allies unanimously wanted him to take command of the forces that NATO would now build. In October 1950, he accepted.[22]

It has been said that the war in Korea put the "O" in "NATO," which had previously been more of a paper alliance and a statement of united resolve directed against an unspecified threat. NATO was now to become a military pact capable of defending Western Europe against a Soviet-led attack. But as the atmosphere of immediate crisis abated, Eisenhower was compelled to spend a considerable portion of his time trying to convince the European allies to spend the money and raise the force levels necessary to reach stated goals. American intervention in Korea could only be interpreted in Moscow as unambiguous proof that the United States would fight to preserve West Germany.[23] This reassurance had undermined the Europeans' resolve to substantially build up their armed forces even before Eisenhower officially took command. The supreme commander, like High Commissioner John J. McCloy, realized that success in burden-sharing was a key element in moderating domestic criticism of America's participation in a peacetime military alliance in Europe. The powerful Ohio Republican, Senator Robert A. Taft, publicly raised doubts about the strategic utility of a large American ground presence in Europe. And he mused that "France cannot be defended by us, unless it shows a great interest in a strong army of its own." Eisenhower, like Taft's most recent biographer, could dismiss much of the Ohioan's thinking on world affairs as dated and not relevant to the postwar situation.[24] He nevertheless had to have a budget and troops, and so he had to address the issues that concerned Congress.

Yet Eisenhower, the epitome of the staff officer, recognized that he had no chance of raising the forty divisions (ambitiously) called for in North Atlantic Council plans if the West Germans were not brought in. The soldier who organized the Normandy landings knew how difficult it would be for Germany's neighbors to accept German rearmament. But his conclusion was practical: the alliance had no other option. The Soviet manpower advantage could not be counterbalanced if Germany remained demilitarized. In addition, Truman administration officials considered a buildup of European forces to be a key element of countering "defeatism" and rebuilding Western European self-confidence, and thus a key element in combating any neutralist tendencies. And there could be no question as to which partner nation could *not* be allowed to choose a path of neutrality between East and West.[25]

The new government in Bonn recognized the leverage that, as if by some miracle, they now possessed. NATO needed a significant German contribution, and Adenauer was willing to use this fact to gain concessions from his allies, especially on the matter of German sovereignty. Marc Trachtenberg emphasizes this leverage as one of the most important arguments in favor of a potential go-slow policy toward rearming the FRG. In addition to provoking the Soviets, a rapid buildup of German forces could "put the Germans in the driver's seat and encourage them to pose political conditions, and the allies might end up having to give them too much political freedom too soon."[26] It was hardly a surprise, then, when Adenauer made it known to the Western high commissioners at the end of 1950 that "the German public" could not accept participation in a common defense framework without a guarantee that their soldiers would not "fight under less favorable terms than the contingents of other peoples."[27] This would not be the first time that the German public conveniently "demanded" what Adenauer wanted. General Eisenhower was sometimes frustrated, sometimes angered by what he perceived as manipulation. But again, as a general with an army to build, he saw no alternative to German rearmament, and viewed continuing integration of the Federal Republic into the community of Western Europe as a stabilizing factor in that vital region.[28]

One of the most significant issues with which the supreme commander would have to wrestle was the European Defense Community. Conceived as a vehicle for bringing German soldiers into the NATO force structure, while simultaneously reassuring Germany's neighbors by placing those soldiers under a multinational command, the EDC represented to Washington policy makers a kind of alchemy that could transmute French fears into German divisions. The story of the EDC is well known to historians and to political scientists who study European security and integration.[29] The proposal had germinated out of a trans-Atlantic deadlock over the framework, pace, and extent of German rearmament within the North Atlantic security framework. The French were rather understandably the most reluctant of all the Atlantic allies to see a German national army begin to arise a half-decade after the liberation of Paris. As a result, Premier René Pleven proposed in October 1950 that a European army be established under the political umbrella of a transnational political structure. Pleven foresaw the European Army falling under the direction of a European defense minister—who, one assumes, would not be a German. In addition, all nations that participated would also be able to maintain parallel national armies; all but one, that is. The most significant component of this plan, in the eyes of the French Assembly, was that it would preclude the creation of a German general staff.[30]

The multinational force concept had one implication—though not actually part of the plan—that made it even more attractive, especially in Paris: The Pleven Plan held out the possibility of "infinite delay in rearming Germany."[31] This tacit understanding made the plan palatable to the Assembly, which voted for it by a wide margin. But the fact that the French policy community had proposed and then approved a plan for German rearmament that they expected would never come to fruition put the entire idea of a multinational force on the road to a crash.[32] Problems would necessarily arise with the Americans, who were by then fully committed to integrating a German military contribution into NATO. And they would arise with the

Germans, who perceived military integration into EDC as a significant step on the road to regaining sovereignty and achieving equal status among the Western allies.

The Germans became increasingly invested as the EDC plan, which evolved out of the proposal for a European army under a single command, became legally tied up with the so-called "Contractuals." Adenauer and his aides seized upon the French-inspired proposal for EDC as a tool to exert leverage on the NATO powers. The chancellor made it known that Germany was willing to contribute to the defense forces of that alliance, but only under condition of nondiscrimination. The Federal Republic must be treated as an equal. This meant that the status of West Germany's relationship with the three occupying powers would have to change fundamentally. The occupation regime imposed upon Germany would have to be replaced, said the chancellor, by a mutually agreed set of contractual agreements.[33] The adoption of the EDC was thus to become linked with the concession of full sovereignty to the Federal Republic. From the beginning, then, the EDC's political implications took precedence over its military implications, especially in Bonn. For as long as the EDC remained a potential but unrealized defense option for NATO, the political status of occupied West Germany would remain on ice.

Initial American hesitancy about EDC was thus frustrating and discouraging for the Bonn regime. It is worth noting here that the vital push for American acceptance of the EDC formula for German rearmament came from General Eisenhower. The supreme commander lent his substantial prestige to the idea of a European army, as opposed to simply national contingents within NATO, in June 1951. Eisenhower had come to favor German rearmament within the European framework. Like McCloy before him, he had come to see increasing European unification as a:

> skeleton key, unlocking the solution to a number of problems at once, and most important, providing a type of "dual containment." The Soviet Union could be kept out, and Germany kept in Europe, but with neither able to dominate the Continent.[34]

"Ike's" prestige was great at this time, and thus when he spoke on military issues, he could expect to carry the day. Advocates of the European framework concept for the German military were now in the position to take the initiative. For a time, German rearmament seemed on the move again; and in step with it, it seemed, would come the political rehabilitation of Germany.

Eisenhower's intervention in the EDC matter brings up one final point on the EDC history. Eisenhower would run for the presidency on a platform that sought to distance himself and his party from the containment policies of Truman. But in large measure, President Eisenhower and Secretary of State John Foster Dulles continued the policies of their predecessors. This was true specifically in the area of German policy. Eisenhower's thinking on the German issue, in fact, deviated not one whit from the official policy of the Truman administration, despite his attempts during the 1952 presidential campaign to distance himself from "Containment" and its authors. In February 1951, the State Department set out its "Policy Statement" on Germany. Through integration of Germany into the Western community of nations "on the basis of substantial equality"; the pursuit of reunification on terms favorable to the West; fostering the capacity of the Bonn regime to "resist attack" from enemies of democracy, both foreign and domestic; the quick recovery of the West German economy[35]—Eisenhower shared all of these goals as supreme commander, and would carry them intact with him into the White House.

Adenauer may not have appreciated the extent of continuity between the outgoing and incoming American administrations on matters regarding Germany. He certainly was willing to use fears that Dulles sympathized with the "Asia-First" Republicans in the U.S. Senate to gain votes in the Bundestag for the Contractuals.[36] Yet on his first visit to Europe as secretary of state, Dulles evinced no interest in blazing new trails in America's German policy. Before departing, he told High Commissioner–designate James B. Conant that his meeting with the chancellor "would be a courtesy visit." His reason for going to Bonn soon after taking office was "to accumulate information from those who were already on the spot to ascertain the political trend in Germany."[37] The Bonn government was in fact becoming aware of the degree of policy continuity that they could anticipate even before Dulles alighted in Europe. Otto Lenz, state secretary in the chancellery, reported that around 8 January he received "reliable reports" from the office of the American high commissioner that the new administration "would completely retain the course of the Truman administration in foreign policy." He noted as well that the new administration issued "quite unambiguous statements" to this effect soon after taking office.[38]

Writing twelve years after the fact, Adenauer makes no mention of his early fears regarding Dulles's reliability. He does, however, recall that he was concerned about elements of Dulles's Republican Party, including the supporters of Senator Robert Taft of Ohio—who was thought to be a representative of prewar isolationism—and also about the "China Lobby."[39] While Adenauer was aware that the new president was not in the isolationist camp, he was concerned about the role of congressional and public opinion in determining the success of the European policies inherited from Truman. He realized that the Europeans themselves would have to work assiduously to maintain American interest and confidence in the European democracies. In addition, the nations of Western Europe would have to demonstrate progress toward integration: political, economic, and military. For the Federal Republic, pursuit of *Westbindung*—the integration of Germany into the western community—was the "policy of most limited risk; there was no policy without risk."[40]

Given the risks, Adenauer must have been pleased to discover that Dulles and his boss had accepted the policy of *Westbindung* wholeheartedly, even if they called it by other names. When the topic of the military arose, Dulles emphasized to Adenauer that there was particular need for "fusion" (*Verschmelzung*, in Adenauer's rendering) of French and German forces. For this reason, EDC had to be passed by the would-be members, and then implemented. "Germany must become strong," Dulles was supposed to have said. Then, Russia would no longer be in a position to "blackmail" the Germans. Thus, military strength would make reunification *more* likely. Since this was the line that Adenauer had taken, he must have found his conversation with Dulles very reassuring. "I was in complete agreement with Dulles's view," he recalled. As for Dulles, he came away from the meeting optimistic that the Bonn government was in the hands of an executive who would press ahead with EDC and the Contractuals.[41]

There was at one time a tendency to make much of the "friendship" that developed between Dulles and Adenauer.[42] Yet the two worked well together primarily because they were so similar in their views of the realities and demands of international politics. As Hans-Jürgen Grabbe has noted, friendship for Adenauer meant "being akin in substance," and the two statesmen "believed in the same basic values."[43] What struck Adenauer about Dulles, upon first meeting with him, was that the new U.S. secretary of state "was governed by the idea of an inexorable deepening of the East-West conflict."[44] The two also shared a common prescription for the long-term treatment of this problem: Further integration of Germany into the West and the concomitant strengthening of the "free world," economically, psychologically, and, not least, militarily. In practice, this also implied American leadership of the West, which Adenauer took to imply America's continued commitment to Western Europe.[45]

The problem for Adenauer, Eisenhower, and Dulles, was that the success of their planned program was highly dependent upon the perception in the West of a threat from the East. The situation was not all-or-nothing: When the sense of crisis abated in the West after June 1950, the perception of threat from the Communist world did not simply evaporate. But one might have expected that, to the extent that fear of the Soviet Union diminished, the willingness of Western European voters to build and sustain high troop levels would also diminish. Even more worrisome was the consequent likelihood that American voters and their representatives in Congress would begin asking why the United States needed to defend Europe when the Europeans saw no need to defend themselves.

The death of Joseph Stalin on 5 March, 1953, thus threatened—potentially—to undermine the policy of German remilitarization and integration, and harbored the potential to put EDC on permanent hold. Again, this threat to agreed policy was entirely potential at this point. Much depended upon what Stalin's death meant for East-West relations *in practical terms*. This, in turn, depended upon what happened next in Moscow. The West now had to seek to decipher what it meant that Stalin was no longer on the scene, and how the subsequent jockeying for position in the Kremlin would affect the Cold War.

Eisenhower was unsure what Stalin's death portended. But, characteristically, he displayed a cautious optimism in a number of internal administration discussions. Dulles responded with more skepticism, and in that sense reflected the presumptions about the world that he and Adenauer shared. For Adenauer did not think that the peril faced by the West was lessened by the marshal's death. Stalin's death, rather, made world politics even more precarious, and thus increased the threat faced by the West, at least temporarily.[46] Better the devil you know, apparently.

The situation faced by the new U.S. administration thus appeared fluid, and the continuing ossification of the Cold War could not be taken as unavoidable. The Eisenhower administration now had to decide whether significant improvement might be possible in the East-West relationship, and if so, how much risk was involved in pursuing that possibility. That Stalin would die at some point was foreseeable. That he would die just weeks after Eisenhower took office, and that his successors would take the opportunity to launch a "Peace Offensive," was not. In 1952, the Republicans had waged a campaign for the White House based in part upon Truman's alleged weakness in the face of the Soviet Union. Now sitting in Truman's chair, Eisenhower found himself wondering how "soft" he should be.

NOTES

1. Charles S. Maier, "Privileged Partners: The Atlantic Relationship at the End of the Bush Regime," in Geir Lundestad, ed., *Just Another Major Crisis: The United States and Europe since 2000* (Oxford: Oxford University Press, 2008). Quotes from 22; 29.

2. Ibid., Lundestad, "Introduction," 9. See also Lundestad, chapter 15, "Conclusion: The United States and Europe: Just Another Crisis?" 298.

3. Melvyn Leffler, *For the Soul of Mankind: The United States, the Soviet Union, and the Cold War* (New York: Hill and Wang, 2007), 8; Geir Lundestad, *"Empire" by Integration: The United States and European Integration, 1945–1997* (New York: Oxford University Press, 1998), 4.

4. Leffler, *For the Soul of Mankind*, 4; and see also 6.

5. Lundestad, *"Empire" by Integration*, 54.

6. This point has been convincingly made about Franco-American alliance relations by Michael Creswell. For a summary of Creswell's argument that the United States was inclined to act unilaterally in imposing policies on Paris, see *A Question of Balance: How France and the United States Created Cold War Europe* (Cambridge, MA: Harvard University Press, 2006), viii–ix.

7. James McAllister, *No Exit: America and the German Problem, 1943–1954* (Ithaca, NY: Cornell University Press, 2002); Thomas A. Schwartz, *America's Germany: John J. McCloy and the Federal Republic of Germany* (Cambridge, MA: Harvard University Press, 1991); Wolfgang Krieger, *General Lucius D. Clay und die amerikanische Deutschlandpolitik 1945–1949* (Stuttgart: Klett-Cotta, 1988). And see also: Michael Creswell, *A Question of Balance*; Irwin Wall, *The United States and the Making of Postwar France, 1945–1954* (New York: Cambridge University Press, 2002).

8. The most recently published study of U.S.–West German relations during the time when the "Ike Age" coincided with "die Ära Adenauer" is Detlef Felken, *Dulles und Deutschland: Die amerikanische Deutschlandpolitik, 1953–1959* (Bonn: Bouvier, 1993). A very useful dissertation on the topic unfortunately remains unpublished. See Jill Davey Colley Kastner, "The Ambivalent Ally: Adenauer, Eisenhower, and the Dilemmas of the Cold War, 1953–1960" (PhD dissertation. Department of History, Harvard University, 1999).

9. For a synopsis of Adenauer's attractiveness to many American policy makers in the 1940s and '50s, see Jeremi Suri, *Henry Kissinger and the American Century* (Cambridge, MA: Belknap/Harvard University Press, 2007), 81–86.

10. For recent examples, see: Creswell, *A Question of Balance*, 133–35; Kevin Ruane, "Agonizing Reappraisals: Anthony Eden, John Foster Dulles and the Crisis of European Defence, 1953–54," *Diplomacy & Statecraft* 13/4 (December 2002), 151–85.

11. Thomas A. Schwartz, "Eisenhower and the Germans," in Günter Bischof and Stephen E. Ambrose, eds., *Eisenhower: A Centenary Assessment* (Baton Rouge: Louisiana State University Press, 1995), 207.

12. Dwight D. Eisenhower, *The White House Years*, Vol. 1 (Garden City, NY: Doubleday and Co., 1963), 80.

13. Stephen E. Ambrose, *Eisenhower*, Vol. 1, *Soldier, General of the Army, President Elect: 1890–1952* (New York: Simon and Schuster, 1983), 447–52.

14. For the gradual development of the Containment policy under Truman, see Wilson D. Miscamble, CSC, *From Roosevelt to Truman: Potsdam, Hiroshima, and the Cold War* (New York: Cambridge University Press, 2007), chapters 7 and 8; quote from Eisenhower, *White House Years*, 81.

15. The coalition governed with a somewhat greater parliamentary margin, but a few Christian Democrats did not cast a ballot in the vote for chancellor. Ronald Irving, *Adenauer* (London: Pearson, 2002), 76.

16. Construction began on Cologne's stunning Gothic cathedral in the mid-1200s, but stalled for four centuries before being resumed in the 1800s. The façade was, however, built according to the original medieval plans, giving a decidedly ancient look to a building that was actually completed when the city's future mayor was a four-year-old.

17. Ambrose, ibid., 471.

18. Lawrence S. Kaplan, *NATO and the United States: The Enduring Alliance* (Boston: Twayne, 1988), 40.

19. For Stalin's thinking, see Vladislav M. Zubok, *A Failed Empire: The Soviet Union in the Cold War from Stalin to Gorbachev* (Chapel Hill: University of North Carolina Press, 2007), 78–81. On the impact of the outbreak of war in Korea on NATO and the West German political leadership, see Schwartz, *America's Germany*, 124–27.

20. Quote from Irving, 101.

21. See Steven Casey, "Selling NSC-68: The Truman Administration Public Opinion, and the Politics of Mobilization," *Diplomatic History* 29/4 (September 2005), 655–90.

22. Peter G. Boyle, *Eisenhower* (London: Pearson, 2005), 40; Herbert Parmet, *Eisenhower and the American Crusades* (New York: Macmillan, 1972), 35; Ambrose, *Eisenhower*, 495; Kaplan, *NATO*, 46–47.

23. Melvyn P. Leffler, *A Preponderance of Power: National Security, the Truman Administration, and the Cold War* (Stanford, CA: Stanford University Press, 1992), 383.

24. For McCloy's assessment, see Schwartz, *America's Germany*, 128–29; information on Taft is from Clarence E. Wunderlin, *Robert A. Taft: Ideas, Tradition, and Party in U.S. Foreign Policy* (Lanham, MD: Rowman & Littlefield, 2005), chapter 5; quote from 169.

25. Leffler, *Preponderance of Power*, 384.

26. Marc Trachtenberg, *A Constructed Peace: The Making of the European Settlement, 1945–1963* (Princeton, NJ: Princeton University Press, 1999), 109.

27. Konrad Adenauer, *Erinnerungen, 1945–1953* (Stuttgart: Deutsche Verlags-Anstalt, 1965), 400–401.

28. Ambrose, 504; 508.

29. This summary relies on a number of sources, but my interpretation of these events is influenced significantly by the work McAllister and of Trachtenberg. See McAllister, *No Exit*, 192–208; Trachtenberg, *Constructed Peace*, 110–25.

30. *New York Times* (Hereafter *NYT*), 26 October, 1950, 3; Schwartz, *America's Germany*, 141; Creswell, *A Question of Balance*, 29–33.

31. McAllister, 193.

32. McCloy perceived this problem immediately, and wondered about French sincerity. See Schwartz, *America's Germany*, 143. The French were far from united on an approach to German rearmament and the EDC proposal, however. See Adm. Marcel Duval, "La Crise de la CED (1950–1954)," in Maurice Vaïsse, Pierre Mélandri, and Frédéric Bozo, *La France et l'OTAN, 1949–1996* (Armées: Éditions Complexe, 1996), 192–97.

33. See McAllister, 201.

34. Schwartz, "Eisenhower and the Germans," 215.

35. National Archive and Records Administration (Hereafter NARA), State Department Central Decimal File, 611.62/2-151.

36. Hans Peter Schwartz, *Adenauer*, Vol. 2, *Der Staatsmann, 1952–1967* (Munich: Deutscher Taschenbuch Verlag, 1994), 36; Otto Lenz, *Im Zentrum der Macht: Das Tagebuch von Staatssekretar Lenz, 1951–1953* (Düsseldorf: Droste, 1989), 474–75.

37. Dulles/Eisenhower Library materials: Telephone Conversations, Box 1, Folder 4. John Foster Dulles Papers, Seeley G. Mudd Library, Princeton University (hereafter Dulles Papers).

38. Lenz, 517.

39. A useful summary of the China Lobby and its impact on Congress is Warren I. Cohen, "China Lobby," in Alexander DeConde et al., eds., *Encyclopedia of American Foreign Policy* (New York: Scribner's Sons, 2002), 185–91. See esp. 187–90.

40. Adenauer, *Erinnerungen, 1945–1953*, 553; 557.

41. Adenauer, ibid., 552–59; Telegram, Dulles to Eisenhower, 6 February, 1953, *Foreign Relations of the United States* (hereafter *FRUS*), *1952–1954*, Vol. 5, Part 2, 1572.

42. See, e.g., the remembrances of the State Department's Berlin desk officer, Dulles's sister Eleanor Lansing Dulles, "Adenauer und Dulles," in Dieter Blumenwitz et al., *Konrad Adenauer und Seine Zeit: Politik und Persönlichkeit der ersten Bundeskanzlers* (Stuttgart: Deutsche Verlags-Anstalt, 1976), 377–89.

43. Grabbe, "Konrad Adenauer, John Foster Dulles, and West German-American Relations," in Richard Immerman, ed., *John Foster Dulles and the Diplomacy of the Cold War* (Princeton, NJ: Princeton University Press, 1990), 111. Creswell points out that Adenauer fully expected his allies to "put their own interests first," instead of being moved by international affections. This was nothing other than what he planned on doing for Germany, and to his credit he did not hold Washington to a different standard. *A Question of Balance*, 37–38.

44. My analysis of the Adenauer-Dulles relationship is influenced by Felken, *Dulles und Deutschland*. See esp. 148–49; quote from Waldemar Besson, *Die Aussenpolitik der Bundesrepublik: Erfahrungen und Maßstabe* (Munich: R. Piper and Co. Verlag, 1970), 143.

45. That the Union Parties saw the reunification of Germany, and the subsequent end of the East-West duel, as a long-range goal and not an immediate possibility, see Clay Clemens, *Reluctant Realists: The Christian Democrats and West German Ostpolitik* (Durham, NC: Duke University Press, 1989), 28–30.

46. Adenauer, *Erinnerungen*, ibid., 559.

2

"Confined to the Smallest Number of Powers": The Peace Offensive after Stalin

In the weeks and months that followed the death of Joseph Stalin, the West grappled with the changes that were taking place in Moscow. The United States, Germany, and their allies now wondered whether meaningful changes in Soviet foreign policy were possible, even likely. Faced with a changing leadership in the Soviet Union, Bonn and Washington must have wished for some time to assess the importance of Stalin's death. The new leaders in the Kremlin gave them less than ten days. As a result, these two governments, together with their allies, were forced to make policy as they went along. Desire to explore new options clashed with unwillingness to imperil existing policy.

MOSCOW'S PEACE OFFENSIVE, SPRING 1953

On the occasion of Stalin's funeral, the chairman of the Soviet Council of Ministers, Georgi Malenkov,[1] gave an oration praising the marshal and the state which he had helped to create. Veritably hidden among the paeans to the departed leader and the exhortations to continue his work were two paragraphs concerning a foreign policy for peace. The Soviet foreign policy was directed at the prevention of war, and sought "international cooperation and development of business relations with all countries." Malenkov did not stress the inevitability of conflict with the West, for Soviet foreign policy was based upon the Lenin-Stalin premise of the possibility of "prolonged coexistence and peaceful competition of two systems, capitalist and socialist."[2]

Malenkov's need to stress continuity with Stalin's policies during his funeral eulogy prevented his statements on cooperation from achieving any impact. If a "policy of peace" meant a continuation of Stalin's policies, then this was not an olive branch. The American chargé d'affaires, who was present at the funeral, noted in retrospect, however, that Malenkov, Vyacheslav Molotov—Stalin's foreign secretary, known more for his obsequious devotion to Stalin than for the originality of his diplomacy—and Lavrenti Beria—the dreaded head of Stalin's secret police—"got off to a good start in the first speeches at Stalin's funeral: no mention was made of the United States which had been under bitter propaganda attack only a week before."[3]

Days later, Malenkov introduced his new cabinet to the Supreme Soviet. In the course of doing so, he signaled to the world that the new masters in the Kremlin might be interested in a significant departure from the confrontational policies of their immediate predecessor. The significance of the new premier's words was impossible to ignore.

After stressing Moscow's intention to continue to "strengthen the ties of fraternal friendship and solidarity" with the People's Republic of China—and thus asserting his Marxist-Leninist good faith—Malenkov turned to the question of East-West relations. Stalin's successor said that:

> There is no disputed or outstanding issue at the present time which cannot be settled peacefully on the basis of mutual agreement of the countries concerned. This refers to our relations with all States, including those with the United States. Countries interested in preserving peace may have confidence both now and in the future, in the lasting peace policy of the Soviet Union.[4]

These words were seized upon immediately, unlike those of the funeral oration, as a sign that Moscow might now be willing to enter into serious and productive negotiations on significant outstanding issues in the East-West conflict.[5] "One of the most experienced diplomats in Moscow" told the *New York Times'* Harrison Salisbury that "he regarded the statement as a virtual invitation to President Eisenhower to enter into negotiations with Mr. Malenkov with a view to removing world tensions."[6] Beam, the American chargé, noticed changes in atmosphere which coincided with Malenkov's suggestion of a change in policy. Soviet officials became more accessible, and "[h]arassment of foreigners abated." Most important from Washington's perspective, Beam detected "intimations that the Soviet government was willing to help with the signature of an armistice in Korea."[7] Eisenhower was happy to receive such intimations, having made the conclusion of the war in Korea a central element of his election campaign.

"Far earlier than anyone had expected," Eisenhower later noted, the new Soviet leaders began a campaign which seemed designed to bring about the first thaw in the Cold War. The American president viewed Malenkov's actions as "startling departures from the ways of his predecessor."[8] In public, however, the president was more cautious. At his 19 March press conference, Eisenhower stated that the Soviets "will never be met less than halfway."[9] He said nothing of "startling departures," but displayed the cautious optimism that was characteristic of him.

Dulles evinced less optimism, telling a 20 March press conference that "we have evaluated these speeches [from Moscow], but we do not receive any great comfort."[10] Dulles's critics have read much into his response at this key point in time, pointing to his inflexibility and obsession with Marxist-Leninist ideology. "In an important sense," sneered Townsend Hoopes, "Stalin did Dulles a philosophical and practical disservice by dying, but Dulles retaliated by continuing to act as though the death had not occurred."[11] Yet what of substance had the Soviets offered? Words from Moscow were well and good, but only when they were translated into real progress on substantial issues could their merits be assessed. Issues such as control of atomic weapons, the Austrian treaty, German unification, and an end to the Korean War would be the test of the sincerity of the new Kremlin leadership. One might well ask: "How then can we believe these fair words until there are concrete actions and deeds to back them up?"[12] That these were the words, not of a reactionary secretary of state, but of the liberal *New York Times*, indicates that Dulles was simply not out of the mainstream of American thinking on this issue; *all* were waiting for words to give birth to deeds.[13]

As Nikita Khrushchev's foreign affairs adviser, American-educated Oleg Troyanovsky, reminded readers decades later, relations between East and West had reached a terrible state of tension prior to Stalin's death. "The new leadership replacing Stalin received a grave foreign policy inheritance. The 'Cold War' was reaching its apogee. If the level of international tension could have been measured in detail," the Cold War would have been quite hot, indeed.[14] It should have been no surprise, then or now, that the new American administration chose to be cautious. Yet there is, in retrospect, one very surprising fact about Washington's response to Stalin's death.

The shocking fact about American foreign policy at the time of transition from Truman to Eisenhower was that those responsible for formulating policy had not planned for the eventuality of Stalin's death!

> To Eisenhower's distress, he discovered that Truman and his national security managers had given hardly any thought to these [Kremlin transition] issues. The CIA had not prepared a single intelligence estimate that took into account that Stalin would not live forever.[15]

In fact the Soviets were far better prepared than the West for the marshal's inevitable death: as Vojtech Mastny notes, Stalin's successors acted quickly to clarify their roles in the new regime, and to put an end to the Korean

War, "which by then hardly anyone but the deceased dictator had wished to continue."[16] This lack of contingency planning gave additional incentive to respond with caution. As Klaus Larres indicates in his superb study *Churchill's Cold War: The Politics of Personal Diplomacy*, there was a certain ambiguity to the Eisenhower administration's assessment of the significance of Stalin's death and replacement. After all, Stalin was a known quantity. "His much less familiar potential successors" presented an intelligence and analytical difficulty for Washington.[17]

For its part, the government in Bonn was unwilling to take the Soviets at their word. Too much had transpired in recent years for that. And it was not simply about the past: too much was now at stake. Adenauer wanted to integrate Germany into the Western community of nations as a means of rehabilitating Germany—at least the Western half—and thus taking a step toward equality. This meant that the Contractuals had to be approved, and thus allow a German military contribution to the new EDC. As the chancellor put it in a June interview, Germany "must not fall between the two millstones, because then it would be lost."[18] Then, too, there were the general elections. That September, the West Germans would again elect a government. Adenauer thought that he needed to take a hard line with the Soviets. The socialist opposition disagreed. Could the chancellor afford, in an election year, to hand the opposition such an important issue?

PREPARATION FOR TRIUMPH

Adenauer's first visit to the United States, in April 1953, would have been an extraordinarily significant event, even had the Moscow peace offensive not occurred. Bonn and Washington now had the additional task of attempting to clarify the situation in light of developments in Moscow. Additionally, Adenauer now had to seek "once and for all to guarantee that a settlement [*Ausgleich*] between East and West would not occur at the expense of Germany." The response to the Soviet peace offensive in Paris would certainly have exacerbated Adenauer's fears. As Georges-Henri Soutou notes, there was a tendency among "many French politicians" to be tempted by the potential for a "final negotiation with Moscow on the German question before resigning themselves to the EDC." Official Paris had not surrendered the idea that France and Russia had a shared interest in avoiding "a German-American understanding that was becoming too close."[19] Most importantly, Herbert Blankenhorn, head of the Office of Political Affairs in the West German Foreign Office, noted in his diary, the chancellor sought to make certain that "Germany not fall back into a new isolation. His concerns, which he openly expressed, were especially great in this regard. The conciliatory gestures of the new Soviet policy had, in addition, strengthened [these concerns] considerably."[20]

Adenauer put great stock in this visit, both for reasons of atmosphere and for reasons of policy. Aware as he was of the "mistrust and antipathy"[21] with which many in America still viewed Germany, he hoped to "further cultivate the trust in us," believing that "liking and trust in reliability" between peoples plays an important role in international relations.[22] A favorable reception of him by the American people, furthermore, could only help him politically at home.

Adenauer, never a devotee of diplomacy's "proper channels," sent Blankenhorn ahead to meet secretly with former high commissioner John J. McCloy.[23] (McCloy responded as Adenauer must have hoped, and forwarded Blankenhorn's comments directly to Dulles.) Adenauer was faced with the third reading of the Contractual agreements in the Bundestag in four days. Now was the "last clear chance for the establishment of a solid European Defense Community." He was convinced that he could gain approval from the Bundestag and, after returning from America, the Bundesrat. By late April or early May, he estimated, Germany would have completed ratification.

Yet he was not so certain that other nations—especially France—would follow up so rapidly. This was especially troublesome, since the heavily armed "police" forces of East Germany, the *Bereitschaften*, were rapidly becoming "a people's army." Adenauer thus proposed that: (a) immediately after ratification by Germany, a German force of roughly 100,000 men be raised, in accordance with "EDC formulas"; and (b) the United States diplomatically support the proposition that the Contractuals should go into force upon German ratification, instead of after all parties had ratified.[24]

Washington clearly expected nothing so breathtaking to come from the conference. The State Department indicated to the high commissioner on 23 March that "As far as we [are] concerned, we may well wish [to] present U.S. views or have brief high-level discussion of certain problems such as Saar or German (*financial*) [emphasis added] defense contribution." But discussions of these questions would be such that State saw "no reason for [the] Chancellor to prepare himself particularly for any such subject or bring along qualified experts."[25]

In part, at least, because of Adenauer's reluctance to use the high commission[26]—which had the functional, though not legal, position of an American embassy—HICOM found it difficult to brief the State Department on Adenauer's intentions for the coming visit.[27] When the Americans learned of Adenauer's intentions, they were taken aback. High Commissioner James B. Conant, a former president of Harvard University, cabled to Washington on 24 March a summary of the chancellor's proposed list of subjects, which

Conant had just received. This list reinforced what Blankenhorn had told McCloy: Adenauer wanted parts of the Contractuals to go into effect prior to ratification by all parties; he wanted to begin training West German troops "prior to EDC ratification"; and he proposed an upgrade of the status of the West German mission in Washington, making it an embassy.[28]

The German Affairs bureau of the State Department responded negatively to all three of these propositions. Invocation of "certain provisions" would have to wait until France had ratified the accords, while premature training of German forces "would seem certain to impair French ratification prospects." Finally, "any change in status [of the] German mission here would be subject to tripartite agreement."[29] The high commission seems, however, not to have passed this information on to the Bonn foreign office. Blankenhorn, meeting on 29 March with James Riddleberger, director of the German Affairs bureau, once again advanced the proposals he had made to McCloy on the 16th, and presented Riddleberger with a draft proposal by the chancellor regarding the return of German sovereignty in case of delayed ratification. Adenauer also proposed the upgrading of the missions of both countries, and the training of "up to 100,000 men. These reserves would then be ready when the EDC comes into effect." Blankenhorn portrayed these steps as important for Adenauer's political viability. "Because of the elections in Germany this summer, the chancellor is most insistent in requiring certain solutions" with regard to the Contractuals. "The Chancellor feels most strongly that he must have something concrete in hand when he returns to Germany from this trip."[30]

But, as Adenauer was soon to find, Germany's American allies often set priorities which diverged from her own.[31] One of the American administration's dearest priorities was the ratification of the EDC agreement by all parties concerned. For the administration, it was "the acid test of Western cohesion." Dulles instructed Riddleberger to tell Blankenhorn that "it would be exceedingly unwise, if not disastrous, at the present time to imply in any way that the EDC treaties would not be ratified." Adenauer, added Riddleberger on his own, "would be well advised to continue on his present clear and consistent line of ratification of the treaties."[32] The American administration did not even want whispers of Adenauer's proposals to reach the public.

This time, the message seems to have gotten through. Adenauer met with Conant on the 30th, two days before boarding the boat that would take him to New York. Adenauer's memorandum for Conant said nothing about America unilaterally announcing that the Contractuals should go into force. Rather, the chancellor would merely like to "discuss which joint measures could be taken even before coming into force of the treaties" so that delayed ratification would not adversely affect "Western defense preparedness." He also meant to learn the administration's view of the "repercussions" of Stalin's death. Hesitant to grant that real change might be occurring in Moscow, Adenauer nevertheless was willing to admit that the West might be able to exploit the flux in leadership. "If it is assumed that because of momentary feeling of insecurity Soviet side is prepared to make certain tactical concessions," the chancellor proposed, then the West might want to test Soviet goodwill by raising the issue of German detainees in the Soviet Union.[33] Success on this issue, of course, would help Adenauer domestically. The domestic ramifications of his visit to the United States seem to have been foremost on his mind at this time. Adenauer stressed to Conant the "importance of real accomplishment [on] his trip in connection with the forthcoming elections," especially in light of his view that "the opposition party was not in a condition to take the responsibilities for government either internally or externally." If no progress was made on the question of German sovereignty, Adenauer feared "serious political consequences for future of government."[34] Adenauer continued to use the alleged weakness of his domestic position as a means of exerting leverage over his more powerful ally. But Eisenhower and Dulles were unwilling to endanger French cooperation in European integration. As the Eisenhower administration saw it, Bidault's government in Paris was far shakier than Adenauer's in Bonn. If concessions were to be made to allied public opinion, then it was to be the French that would be placated. No one, thus, could even imply that EDC was not going to be passed.

Adenauer had, in any event, missed the true significance of his visit to the United States. Regardless of whether he came to any substantive agreements with the Americans, the journey to the United States was bound to be a victory—both for West Germany as a whole, and for Adenauer. Americans could perhaps not perceive the significance of the visit of yet another head of government to Washington. But no one in Germany could overlook its importance: their chancellor was greeted as an equal, as a valuable friend and ally, by the most powerful nation in the Western world. The symbolism of his reception by the general who had eight years before led his forces into the heart of Germany served to heighten the symbolic impact of the event.[35] The playing of the "German national anthem at the soldiers' cemetery in Arlington was an experience which one did not easily forget. It helped Adenauer to achieve the first decisive breakthrough in public opinion."[36] In the opinion of one of Adenauer's high-ranking diplomats, it was with his triumphal return from America that the "Adenauer Era" began.[37]

ADENAUER'S VISIT: APRIL 1953

The Eisenhower administration was also concerned with Adenauer's prospects for re-election. If they could not say so officially, Eisenhower and

Dulles, nevertheless, were "firmly, albeit unofficially committed" to helping the chancellor win in September.[38] With Adenauer came a guarantee of stability and continuity in German foreign policy. And Washington had to do little other than receive him with honor and respect to achieve this goal.[39]

Adenauer was seeking to reassure his electorate that he had the stature necessary to make Germany's voice heard. Did he, did the FRG, carry sufficient weight in Washington to prevent America from pursuing policies detrimental to West Germany's vital interests? This became an especially pressing question in light of the Soviet peace offensive. On the day of his arrival in New York, Adenauer's press aide, Felix von Eckardt, briefed the chancellor—who did not read English—on reports in the American press regarding U.S.-U.S.S.R. relations. Adenauer must have found the summary disturbing. The "main press theme [was] the Russian peace offensive." The American press speculated as to the possible ramifications of a change in Soviet policy for numerous issues, "above all the possibility of an agreement in Korea"—which, any German would note, took precedence in American eyes over German unification. The American press was quite concerned about the "stronger and stronger effect of the Russian action on the European and American general publics." The newspapers predicted that this public interest in the Soviet peace offensive would cause "difficulties for the Eisenhower government." It would be difficult to get acquiescence to foreign military aid, and by implication, German rearmament, if "the sense of direct threat from the Russians were lost."[40]

This was the real threat: the Russian peace offensive was having "a very strong effect on the American general public," particularly since it implied the possibility of an end to America's stalemated sacrifices in Korea.[41] Even a skeptical von Eckardt had to admit that the Korean question now seemed to be in motion.[42] The Germans could not ignore the response of the American people to Soviet propaganda.[43] Nor could the American administration. Von Eckardt told Adenauer of a good deal of "excited bustle [*aufgeregte Betriebsamkeit*] behind the scenes" in Washington. "Eisenhower and Dulles have in their statements, in spite of all the skepticism, left the door wide open."[44] The Soviet "propaganda machine" was at work in the United States, and "things had changed" with the change of administrations in Washington. The Eisenhower administration was more receptive to Soviet moves. "Even the new foreign minister, John Foster Dulles . . . appeared to be somewhat influenced by the Soviet 'peace offensive.'"[45] Adenauer's concern that America might deal with the Soviets without consulting him must have been reinforced by such news.

Adenauer thus had a dual task to perform in Washington. He had to assess the American attitude with regard to Soviet policies and intentions, and at the same time, continue to stress his own convictions that the West must hold to the path it selected before Stalin's death. He had to emphasize the need to stay the course, without seeming to be out of step with the times—inflexibility of mind often being attributed, in any event, to men in their late seventies. The chancellor, in fact, thought that he did understand the American mood: "The American families wanted their sons to come back from Korea. One was tired of the war and the tensions."[46] This did not mean that Adenauer had to agree with rosy interpretations of Soviet intentions, only that he had to be all the more careful to avoid giving the impression that *Bonn* was the impediment to peace.

After a meeting in New York with McCloy—who told the chancellor of his belief that Malenkov and Beria might well be willing to discuss the German question[47]—Adenauer was off to Washington.[48] From the airport, Adenauer and his team were taken directly to the White House for a meeting with Eisenhower. As mentioned above, Adenauer was sensitive to the American public's concern regarding Korea. He thus attempted publicly to link the Federal Republic with America's fighting forces by offering to send a German field medical unit to Korea. Eisenhower thanked the chancellor, noting that the offer "showed that Germany and the United States had the same problems"—exactly the sort of interpretation which Adenauer must have desired.[49] The president and secretary of state stressed to Adenauer America's interest in European unification in general, and EDC in particular. They were especially concerned that the issue of the Saar be solved, so that it did not hinder French ratification of the Contractuals. Adenauer "indicated that he [was] at [the] full disposal [of the] U.S. Government" on this issue, and hoped that it could be solved.[50]

Turning to the Soviet peace offensive, Eisenhower expressed "hope that as a result of new developments, we may succeed in lessening some of the world's tensions and burdens."[51] Dulles preferred to emphasize the lessons, rather than the opportunities, which the changes in the Soviet Union offered to the West: the "obvious lesson to be drawn from the present is [the] necessity for us to continue strong constructive policies which evidently [were] now inducing latest Soviet moves. Settlements with Soviets [were] best obtained through strength." If the West "held its course," Dulles told the chancellor, it could attain its desiderata: "German reunification, a State Treaty for Austria, and a peace settlement in Korea and Indochina."[52] Dulles asked Adenauer whether Soviet peace feelers would have an effect upon the German public and the prospects for EDC ratification. Adenauer responded that the Americans need not worry. The Germans would not "grow weak." Given German experience with the "way of thinking" of totalitarian regimes, the Germans would not be lulled into neglecting their contribution to western defense—"even though there may be some Germans with such tendencies."[53]

Meeting with Dulles that afternoon, Adenauer raised the specter of certain Germans with "such tendencies." Elections were coming up in

September, the chancellor reminded Dulles, and opposition from the Social Democrats was "intense." Yet it was "absolutely necessary that current policies be continued for four more years, above all with regard to the EDC." If public support for Adenauer's policies was to be maintained, however, the West Germans would have to see some sign that *Westbindung* was yielding results. Would it not be helpful, then, if the high commissioner were to be given the rank of ambassador prior to the ratification of the Paris agreements?[54] This represented a significant scaling-down of his proposals to which Dulles had previously evinced such a negative reaction. Clearly, Dulles had been successful in his attempt to keep off the agenda any issues which might inflame relations with France. Dulles now pronounced that the United States was "sympathetically disposed to such a proposition," but would have to take the matter up with the British and French.[55] He suggested that they avoid giving advance publicity to the issue, and the chancellor agreed.[56] The Eisenhower administration was willing to do what it could to help Adenauer politically, unless such help implied harm to America's relations with France, and, thus, harm to the prospect of EDC ratification. At this point, Washington was far from seeing German rearmament as a potential alternative to attempting to please the difficult French.[57]

Dulles then asked Adenauer to give his assessment of post-Stalin Moscow. Adenauer responded that he agreed with Eisenhower and Dulles, and understood them to mean that they were quite skeptical about the chance for any real change. As the chancellor saw it, "the recent peace feelers were simply evidence that the death of Stalin had caused instability within the Soviet Union. There was no indication that the Soviet Union was diverging from its previous policies." One could debate the significance of the change of leadership inside the Kremlin. But, according to the German, one ought not to overstate its import for Soviet foreign policy. "The Chancellor was firmly convinced that the Russians were not ready for any just solution of the problems in Central Europe, but rather sought to torpedo the western defense community."[58] He admitted that the Soviets might propose "a peace offer which could be acceptable to the West." The West must, however, continue to build its strength, "since the only way to negotiate with a totalitarian country was to negotiate from strength."[59] "If the Soviet Union offers something concrete," Adenauer told Dulles, "one should accept it." But otherwise, the West should stay the course.[60] Under no circumstances, moreover, should one seek to settle any of the outstanding questions *before* EDC was ratified.[61]

Essentially, this was the position presented in the official communiqué on the talks, which contained nothing surprising, and had in fact been largely worked out by von Eckardt and Eisenhower's press aide James Hagerty before the talks had begun.[62] Bonn and Washington offered the

Soviets an opportunity to demonstrate their earnest desire for a peaceful settlement: they could release the German detainees being held in Russia, and allow free elections in East Germany.[63] The former condition was met more than two years later, when Adenauer himself went to Moscow. The latter would have to wait until the Soviet Union itself disintegrated.

BEYOND WASHINGTON: ADENAUER AND AMERICA

Even after the official meetings with members of the American administration had ended, the chancellor's work in America was far from over. The Germans were not merely anxious for a good hearing from official Washington; the chancellor also had to be "sold" to the American people, in the words of his press aide, von Eckardt. Aware of the residual suspicions of Germans dating back to the war, and conscious of the "reserved," if generally friendly, treatment of Adenauer in the American press, the German delegation put much work into "popularizing" the chancellor. They even went so far as to hire Roy Bernard, an American public relations firm, to help them sell their product, namely Konrad Adenauer.[64] As it turned out, they were good marketers, and he was a good product.

On his hectic first day in Washington, the chancellor received an honorary doctorate at Georgetown University. In his acceptance speech, Adenauer called his listeners' attention to the "great clash [*Auseinandersetzung*]" which was then occurring between the "constructive forces of the free world and the destructive powers of godless totalitarianism." Détente with the Soviets seemed far from Adenauer's mind, as he urged the Jesuit university to educate young men's minds and souls to resist the lure of the "ideology of totalitarianism."[65]

The following day, Adenauer spoke before the National Press Club. This event was absolutely crucial to the German attempt to gain sympathy in America. Von Eckardt informed Adenauer that the American press was more skeptical of Soviet peace moves than was the American public.[66] Here, then, was a fine opportunity to receive a sympathetic hearing.

Adenauer took the opportunity to beat the drums for a wary response to Moscow. He reminded the American press of certain "irrefutable and unalterable facts" which had to be taken into account when making policy decisions. First and foremost was the role the Soviets had played in world affairs since the Bolshevik Revolution. Since 1918, the Soviets had considerably strengthened their position, both militarily and economically.[67] Now their reach extended into the "heart of Europe," and they intended to "expand it farther still." West Germany was "the most important objective of the Soviet-Russian expansion policy," and for that reason, the chancellor found it necessary to clarify these realities for the American people. Aware

that American public opinion was responsive to Soviet "peace-feelers,"
Adenauer urged "caution. The West can on no account lend a hand to a
possible attempt to weaken the West vis-à-vis Soviet Russia." Aware also of
the strength of isolationist sentiment in certain segments of the American
public, the chancellor stressed that peace, freedom, and unity in Western
Europe were "also in the interest of the United States," and that they "could
not be achieved without the help of America."[68]

The Germans were aware of the significance of this speech—as well as
Adenauer's meetings with the Council on Foreign Relations, the publisher
of the *New York Times*, and the Senate Foreign Relations Committee—as
a means of influencing opinion in America. The German delegation, as
mentioned earlier, sought to sell their chancellor; to win "the whole nation
for him and the cause which he represented. The general impression of the
listeners was doubtless that the Federal Republic, and with it an important
part of Europe, lay in good and certain hands with Konrad Adenauer."[69] The
chancellor and his advisers, as these incidents make clear, were attempting
to convince the American public—especially elite opinion—as well as the
American government that West Germany would be a reliable and valuable
partner in the Cold War struggles that lay ahead. One must note, however,
that the German delegation connected inextricably the effort to "rehabili-
tate" Germany to the effort to "sell" Adenauer personally. Americans could
trust the Federal Republic, because the Bonn government was in the hands
of Adenauer, whose reliability was beyond question. To no small extent,
they were successful in this effort. To the American people, and to the Eisenhower administration, West Germany *was* Konrad Adenauer. In one sense,
this merely reflected the realities of policy making in Bonn, where Adenauer
in fact approached the status of the unmoved mover of German foreign policy. Yet this "sale" of Adenauer in America was an attempt to shape events,
as much as to reflect them. The incarnation of German foreign policy in the
person of Adenauer was designed to pay big dividends for the chancellor
both at home and abroad—success at home, in fact, *due to* success abroad.

The reception that the chancellor received in America was quite gratify-
ing. So, too, was the "triumphal" reception in Germany when he returned,
bleary-eyed and exhausted, to Hamburg on 19 April.[70] Adenauer emphasized the significance of the meeting—*his* meeting—with Eisenhower. The
friendship treaty and the trade and shipping agreements provided concrete
evidence of the success of his journey. On the major issue of the day, the
Soviet peace offensive, however, things remained murky.

CHANCE FOR PEACE, AND FOR CONFLICT

As Adenauer and his lieutenants suspected, the American administration
felt pressured to respond to the Soviet peace offensive. One reason for this

was rather clear. Eisenhower was unwilling to let Moscow steal a march on the West in the ongoing propaganda war. The British prime minister, as it turned out, was also anxious to see if circumstances after Stalin's death were favorable to a western peace offensive. Larres emphasizes Churchill's eagerness to take advantage of a potential thaw with Moscow at this late point in his career: "In view of his age and the increasing pressure on him to retire, Churchill felt that Stalin's death presented him with his final opportunity to engage in summit diplomacy" and to play the role of "peacemaker."[71] Too rapid a move in that direction, however, would be certain to undercut the foreign policy that Bonn had been conducting since 1949. Adenauer could not view these developments with equanimity. Generally speaking, the State Department shared this apprehension, fearing especially any weakening of Western unity on the anticipated European Defense Community.[72]

In the days following Stalin's death, certain members of the Eisenhower administration were reluctant to advise the president to deliver a "big speech" on world peace. Presidential speech writer Emmet John Hughes reports that he, Undersecretary of State Walter B. Smith, and State Department Counselor Charles Bohlen—who, after 27 March, was America's ambassador in Moscow—all rejected the "big speech" as amounting merely to "a shallow kind of verbal improvisation, in lieu of serious national policy."[73] Bohlen and Smith were not philosophically opposed to a peace initiative, but wanted to wait until more facts were in. Dulles's opposition to a strong peace feeler was more pronounced. According to Ambrose, Dulles "did not believe a word of what Malenkov was saying."[74] According to Immerman, Dulles's suspicions were in fact quite strong. But Immerman, characteristically, gives a nuanced portrayal of the secretary of state. Dulles did in fact sympathize "emotionally and philosophically" with the desire to improve relations with the Soviets after Stalin's death. But, as will repeatedly be seen, he was concerned about the effects of an overly solicitous American move "on the strength and cohesion of the Western coalition."[75] Dulles was not advocating obstruction but prioritization for American policy.

Whether he "believed a word" or not, the trend was clear; significant members of the State Department and the White House staff opposed a precipitous, grand American response to Soviet peace moves. "Hard-line" cold warriors were not alone in urging caution. As Hughes asked of the potential "big speech": "Will it be aimed at Soviet satellites, to stir their insurrection? Or quite the contrary: will it be aimed, over their bowed heads, to Moscow, to bring the Soviets into a field of East-West negotiation. It cannot aspire to do *both*."[76] Thus, one might well have thought it better to decide what the strategic objective of American foreign policy was, before one began planning the "big speech."

In deciding how to respond to the Soviet peace offensive in the short term, decision makers in Washington found themselves faced with two very important questions. First, how serious were Malenkov, Beria, and Molotov about their expressed desire for a settling of the outstanding disputes of the Cold War? Was Soviet rhetoric just rhetoric; just one more shot in the battle for international public opinion? Or could the West expect real results if it engaged in serious negotiations?[77] Second, how much of an impact did Moscow's profession of interest in peace—whether earnest or otherwise—have upon public opinion at home and abroad? Could the West afford to allow the Soviets to cast themselves as the force of peaceful change and diplomatic settlement?

It was this second question, at least as much as the first, which drove American policy in these crucial weeks. Eisenhower was concerned that America was offering nothing positive to a world that so desperately wanted peace. He was tired of the angry words of denunciation directed at the Soviet Union from Washington. Whether his impatience extended to his secretary of state, he did not say. But he did tell Hughes that America could not sit passively while the Kremlin put its best foot forward. In mid-April, he explained:

> Look, I am tired—and I think everyone is tired—of just plain indictments of the Soviet regime. I think it would be wrong—in fact, asinine—for me to get up before the world now to make another one of those indictments. Instead, just *one* thing matters: what have *we* got to offer the world? What are *we* ready to do, to improve the chances of peace?

If America could not give specifics of its desires for the world, "then we really have nothing to give, except just another speech. Malenkov isn't going to be frightened with speeches. What are *we* trying to achieve?"

Eisenhower then told Hughes exactly what it was that he wanted to achieve: an end to the arms race, which could lead "at worst to atomic warfare. At best, to robbing every people and nation on earth of the fruits of their own toil." Disarmament was to be the goal America put before the world, without "double-talk," "sophisticated political formulas," or "slick propaganda devices." He would not issue new indictments of the Soviet government. Both Washington and Moscow were, in 1953, under the leadership of new men. "The slate is clean. Now let us begin talking to each other." The president dismissed the objections which Dulles had expressed to Hughes and others. "If Mr. Dulles and all his sophisticated advisers really mean that they can *not* [sic] talk peace seriously, then I am in the wrong pew," cracked a clearly exasperated Eisenhower. "Now either we cut out all this fooling around and make a serious bid for peace—or we forget the whole thing."[78]

Eisenhower proceeded to call a meeting, at which he, Foster Dulles, and Dulles's brother—CIA Director Allen Dulles—met with Hughes and C. D.

Jackson, Eisenhower's other main speech writer.[79] Their goal was not to devise a plan for peace, but to "think toward specific actions to fit the spirit of [Eisenhower's] intent," as outlined above. Secretary Dulles, uninspired by the effort, contributed only his "dry and dubious acquiescence that [the president's speech writers] draft such a speech as Eisenhower proposed." Jackson, Hughes reports, was even more skeptical, believing the Soviet leaders would not be influenced at all by "genial bourgeois talk about schools and hospitals for the ignorant and sick." Eisenhower's thinking on the Soviets lacked clarity at this point. But he did not think that the United States could be as dismissive of the peace offensive as Jackson suggested. Hughes, who was in synch with Eisenhower on this issue, sought from the beginning to limit the influence of the Dulles brothers and Jackson on the drafting process. With the help of Truman administration hold-over Paul Nitze, director of the State Department's policy planning staff at the very beginning of the Eisenhower administration, and Eisenhower himself, Hughes completed a draft of what came to be known as the "Chance for Peace" speech. The speech carefully avoided any mention of "liberation," and gained the president's approval despite Dulles's "delicately muted opposition" and a climate in Washington which seemed to militate against such a speech.[80] The State Department sent a summary text of the speech to Bonn, as well as to Paris and London. Adenauer's government did not—could not—raise objections. Churchill advised the Americans to hold off for a time, a suggestion which some interpreted as an attempt to "reserve for himself the initiative in any dramatic new approach to the Soviet leaders."[81] Eisenhower approved the speech, and delivered it to the American Society of Newspaper Editors on 16 April.

The contents of this speech are sufficiently well known, and do not require lengthy recapitulation here. Eisenhower lamented the arms race which the Cold War had engendered. Spending on new weapons represented a "theft" from the needy. "This is not a way of life at all, in any true sense," the president insisted. "Under the cloud of threatening war, it is humanity hanging from a cross of iron." He then appealed to Stalin's heirs, whose "links to the past, however strong, cannot bind [them] completely." Both camps now had the chance to change the world, to save humanity from its cross of iron.

This did *not* mean, however, that the West was abandoning its Cold War policies. For the free world had learned certain lessons from "the bitter wisdom of experience." Two of these lessons prove relevant to this discussion. First, the West knew "that the defense of Western Europe imperatively demands the unity of purpose and action made possible by the North Atlantic Treaty Organization, embracing a European Defense Community." In addition, America and her allies had learned "that West Germany deserves to be a free and equal partner in this community [EDC] and . . . that this, for Germany, is the only safe way to full, final unity." This assertion of the necessity of progress on the EDC and West German integration into the western security alliance, together with a notably muted statement of interest in an *eventual* reunification of Germany, represented no change at all from existing American policy on these issues. Rather, the president was calling for a sign from Moscow that their rhetoric was backed by a real desire for settlement of those issues which could be settled in short order. These were predictable: an Austrian treaty, release of World War II detainees, and, above all, an armistice in Korea. Settlement of these issues would be taken by the West as signs of a serious desire on the part of the Soviets for a broader settlement. If East and West could satisfactorily set these problems aside, then the "wider task" of overcoming the division of Europe— including Germany—could be addressed. The world could pull back from the brink. A comprehensive disarmament agreement might then be reached. This would simultaneously eliminate the fear of nuclear war and allow resources to be spent on the needs of people throughout the world.[82]

Eisenhower's "Chance for Peace" speech had little new to offer in terms of concrete proposals for the amelioration of Cold War tensions. He asked the Soviets to take action on a set of issues which were important to the West in general, and America in particular. Only by helping to achieve a settlement in these areas—and Korea especially—could the Soviets convince the West of their sincere desire to depart from the course of Cold War. Only after it was convinced of Soviet sincerity could the West turn with confidence to the issue that was most important for the future of humanity. All of this had been said—far less eloquently—before. It is noteworthy, too, that Eisenhower had given a speech calling for a new era of cooperative relations between the blocs *without proposing a meeting* of the leaders of the Soviet Union and the West. Had he desired a summit, this would have been the time to propose it.[83]

Yet what the speech lacked in concrete proposals, it made up for in that intangible currency of diplomacy: atmosphere. Eisenhower had indicated to the world that the United States was not committed to a purely negative policy of denunciation and armed peace. America was not willing to continue "down a dread road with no turning."[84] The Soviets had said that the outstanding conflicts were negotiable. Eisenhower responded for the world to see with a resonant "Agreed!" He went, moreover, beyond that expression of goodwill, for he laid out America's vision for the future of the world should East-West détente succeed. The U.S. government saw détente as serving the goal of disarmament. Disarmament, in turn, would allow a refocusing of resources in order to reduce the suffering of humanity.

By making this speech, Eisenhower had also given a clear answer to Hughes' question concerning whom the president's "big speech" would address. He made it clear that he was speaking to the Kremlin, and not to the peoples of Eastern Europe. There was no trace of "liberation" to be detected. Settlement would come as the result of Western negotiations with Moscow, and not by Western intrigues in Warsaw or Budapest. Thus, well before the Hungarian uprising of 1956, and even before the Berlin uprising of June 1953, the American president refused to act according to the more aggressive implications of liberation rhetoric.[85] At this time of confusion in Moscow, America sought to negotiate with the new lords of the Kremlin, rather than to exploit the opportunity to promote centrifugal tendencies within the bloc. An agreement on the reunification of Europe, if it were to come at all, was to result from great power negotiation, and not from the overthrow of local communist governments.

The implications of Eisenhower's words for Adenauer's government in Bonn were ambiguous. The chancellor held little hope for any agreement with the Soviets which did not reflect the realities of power politics in Europe at the time. Given this assumption, a settlement of Europe's bifurcation could occur only as the result of a comprehensive peace settlement among the Great Powers. True, Adenauer feared a second Potsdam—a Great Power conference which made decisions for the German people without seeking their input. But the key to avoiding another Potsdam was to make sure that the German voice, represented by Bonn, was heard in the councils of the West. Germany would, in point of fact, undermine its chances of having an impact on Western policy if it gave the impression of unwillingness to pursue any sort of détente with Russia. While Adenauer's foreign policy presupposed a strong and firm stance against Soviet pressures, to avoid undercutting its own influence, Bonn had to give the impression of flexibility.[86] Adenauer recorded the Chance for Peace speech in his memoirs without comment.[87] He appears at this time to have realized that he had to allow Eisenhower to lead.

Yet Churchill soon gave Adenauer cause for concern. On 11 May, the aging prime minister delivered a peace speech of his own to the House of Commons. Behind this address lay Churchill's very real fear of nuclear war, and his desire—expressed in April to JCS Chairman Arthur Radford—for "conversations at the centre" of the Cold War, rather than conflict at the peripheries.[88] One might also speculate that Churchill did not want to sit on the sidelines while the most momentous events of the postwar world unfolded before him.[89] Clearer than his motivation was his determination to press ahead with his plan for "conversations at the centre." Toward the end of his long monologue on foreign affairs, the prime minister turned to "the change in attitude and, as we all hope, of mood which has taken place in the Soviet domains and particularly in the Kremlin since the death of Stalin." He spoke for all in Britain in welcoming the "amicable gestures" which the Soviets had made since interring Stalin. These gestures could not, alas, be reciprocated, since they "have so far taken the form of leaving off doing things which we have not been doing to them." They were, nevertheless, amicable gestures, and indicated real change.

This change opened up the possibility for settlement of numerous issues. Like Eisenhower, Churchill considered Korea and Austria to be conflicts which might be easier to solve in this new atmosphere. But Churchill's proposals went beyond Eisenhower's. The prime minister recalled his days as chancellor of the exchequer in the 1920s. In those days, the days of Gustav Stresseman, Austen Chamberlain, and Aristide Briand, the European powers had united in the Locarno Pact. "I do not believe that the immense problem of reconciling the security of Russia with the freedom and safety of Western Europe is insoluble," Churchill told his colleagues. A mutual security agreement along the lines of Locarno could guarantee security to the Soviets, who had "a right to feel assured that as far as human arrangements can run the terrible events of the Hitler invasion will never be repeated." The Locarno-like pact would, at the same time, guarantee the policy objectives of the West. Without saying so outright, Churchill implied that this meant an end to the puppet status of Poland.

In order to get things moving in the right direction, Churchill called for "a conference on the highest level" which should "take place between the leading powers without long delay." He put his prescription for a successful conference in his own inimitable words, which are presented here verbatim:

> This conference should not be overhung by a ponderous or rigid agenda, or led into mazes and jungles of technical detail, zealously contested by hordes of experts and officials drawn up in vast, cumbersome array. The conference should be confined to the smallest number of Powers and persons possible. It should meet with a measure of informality and a still greater measure of privacy and seclusion. It might well be that no hard-faced agreements would be reached, but there might be a general feeling among those gathered together that they might do something better than tear the human race, including themselves, into bits.

What could we lose by calling a summit? Churchill asked. In the worst case, it would merely allow for "more intimate contacts" between the participants. There was no reason, the redoubtable Briton argued, why a Great Power summit ought not to occur soon, without a fixed agenda. Who, after all, wanted to tear the world into bits?[90]

SETTLEMENT OR SETTLEMENTS?

What did these "big speeches" by the American and British heads of government mean for the government in Bonn? These policy statements raised certain issues which Adenauer could not ignore. In the first place, he may well have wondered whether his policy of meeting Soviet challenges with Western strength was being undermined by Western leaders vying for the title of peacemaker. If so, his own vision of the road to reunification was called into question and with it his political viability. Also in question was Bonn's ability to influence events; Germany, East and West, was certain to be excluded from a conference limited to "the smallest number of powers possible." Who could then be relied upon to speak for the interests of the Germans? The ostensible differences between Churchill's proposals and Eisenhower's also gave Adenauer cause for concern. Churchill apparently wanted a conference without a set agenda as soon as possible. Washington wanted to avoid such a conference. Perhaps the Soviet peace offensive had already succeeded in creating fissures in the Western alliance.[91]

At the root of these issues was a fundamental difference among the Western allies as to the strategic goal of a policy of peace. The view of détente implied by Eisenhower in his Chance for Peace speech is an empirical one. The West, said the president, was not yet sure that the Soviet leadership was earnest in its professed desire for a settlement with the West. America and its allies could accept that the Soviet professions were made in good faith *only if the Soviets first provided them with evidence* that this was the case. "We care nothing for mere rhetoric," said Eisenhower. "We are only for sincerity of peaceful purpose attested by deeds." These deeds, for instance the release of detainees, or the signature of an Austrian treaty, could be performed *now*, insisted the president, since their performance "waits upon no complex protocol but upon a simple will to do them."[92] Apparently, a new Locarno was superfluous for the resolution of these issues. At his 14 May press conference, Eisenhower was noncommittal about Churchill's proposal for a summit. But he did want a signal from Moscow that a conference could lead to tangible results. "I believe," he said, "that the dignity and the self-respect of the United States demands . . . that we have some reasonable indication that progress can be made. I don't insist upon full progress, or any great blueprint to come out of such a conference for the peace of the world, just something that could be called progress by all of us." Therefore, before he could commit the United States to participation in a summit conference, he wanted "something that would be an earnest of good faith all around." As of the present, he had seen "nothing that you could really point to as definite evidence of good faith."[93] Eisenhower and Churchill agreed that the Soviets had to take the first step. Churchill thought that they already had. Eisenhower was not so sure.

The American concept of détente, as articulated by the president, went from the specific to the general. Détente was not a matter of a one-time, general settlement of the conflict with the Soviet Union. Far less was it an atmosphere of goodwill and pleasant words which replaced the hostility and acid rhetoric of the last eight years. The thaw which interested America was one built up, block by block, by means of settling certain outstanding, individual issues. Settlement of, for example, the Korean War would be partial indication that an improved atmosphere in East-West relations *already existed*. Once this was in evidence, the Powers could then go on to address trickier issues, most notably arms control. The culmination of détente was to be an arms reduction agreement which would allow the West to refocus its resources upon alleviation of human suffering.

The trouble was that Eisenhower's vision of détente differed not only from Churchill's, but also from Adenauer's. And this disagreement adds a key piece to the debate over whether Eisenhower squandered a chance to end the Cold War at this time. The response to the Soviets would have to come from *the West*, not from Washington alone. American security policy relied heavily on the trans-Atlantic political-military alliance. There could be no unilateral initiative from Washington on questions that fundamentally affected the future of America's European allies. But since those allies had come to differing, and sometimes antithetical, conclusions about what the Soviets were up to, only patient diplomacy among the members of the Atlantic Alliance could yield a united response. This was not likely to occur quickly. Yet the window of opportunity for an East-West settlement—and especially a settlement on the future of Germany—was opened, if at all, only for a very brief time.[94] Any approach to this issue that neglects the multilateral context of American policy making on Atlantic-area issues neglects influences that help to explain American policy. The case of the Federal Republic is illustrative.

The German chancellor's conception of a desirable thaw between the blocs was in fact very different from that of the American president. The cooperative and generally friendly tone of German-American relations in the 1950s helped to mask the difference. So did Adenauer's realization that Germany must avoid being perceived as the obstacle to peace. But differences there were. Eisenhower's image of détente, built upon a guarded optimism about the Soviet Union, was cautious and piecemeal. Adenauer's image, based on extraordinary distrust of Soviet motives, was ironically far more ambitious.

The chancellor's position was, theoretically, well grounded. The East-West conflict was not a basket of separate conflicts which, when tallied, equaled the Cold War. It was, rather, one large conflict between two systems, two views of humanity, two irreconcilable ways of life. Only if the fundamental underlying hostility between the two systems were set aside could real progress be made on separate issues. After all, the individual disagreements in the Cold War were merely manifestations of the foundational conflict in world politics. "I was of the opinion," Adenauer wrote a dozen years later:

that the political tension between the Soviet Union and the Western powers did not rest on individual differences; individual differences of opinion or individual claims or counter-claims. It was rather a matter of *one* great tension between the two power groupings, inside of which, at any one time, now this point, now that point would be manifest more strongly, according to the will of the Soviet Union.

Adenauer could almost never bring himself to say that Eisenhower was wrong. Perhaps he himself failed to recognize that this was exactly what he was doing. The "area of conflict" between the Great Powers "would certainly not be capable of solution in the first stage by negotiations on individual problems. The resolute will must first of all be present on all sides to completely put aside this area of conflict and to create a real peace."[95] Here he clearly expressed his disagreement with Eisenhower's step-by-step approach to détente. Resolution of individual problems was the basis of a peace plan for Eisenhower. Adenauer considered this approach to be seriously flawed; it was like removing tumors without treating the cancer.

Of course, Adenauer's more ambitious plan for rapprochement was not motivated by idealism or optimism which surpassed Eisenhower's. On the contrary, the chancellor was very pessimistic about the possibility of real change in the Kremlin. At an informal press conference on 8 May, a journalist asked Adenauer whether he thought that the policy of integrating the Federal Republic into the West by means of treaties—presumably EDC was on the reporter's mind—would lead the Soviets to propose "real compromises in the German Question." Adenauer responded with an explication of the motives behind Soviet policy. The Kremlin wanted to get hold of the Federal Republic "intact, by means of the Cold War." If they should succeed in this, then France and Belgium would not be able to resist for very long. When the Soviets then came to control the French and Belgian industrial resources, "the industrial potential of the Soviet Union, when it comes to coal, iron, and steel, would be greater than the present industrial potential of the United States." Eisenhower professed to see in recent Soviet behavior a chance for peace. Adenauer, in contrast, saw "nothing other [than measures] which serve the goal, which I just outlined briefly," of making the Soviet Union as strong as possible for a future conflict with the United States.[96]

Adenauer was motivated by an extraordinarily pessimistic view of Soviet ambitions. The Soviets had no interest in what Eisenhower had termed a "just and lasting peace." Their objective was still conquest; conquest of West Germany, to be followed by domination of the rest of Western Europe. Dulles also had remained characteristically skeptical about the good faith of the Kremlin's interest in peace. Yet even the Eisenhower administration's most prominent hard-liner had to admit that Communist leadership was making concessions which, though minor, were "not without significance. They suggested to us that the time had come to launch a true peace offensive." The Soviets could prove their goodwill by ending their attempts at subversion of noncommunist governments.[97] According to Adenauer's analysis of the situation, however, this would never happen. The overthrow of the noncommunist governments of Western Europe *was* the goal of Kremlin foreign policy, a goal which the peace offensive was meant to serve. Adenauer was convinced that only when the Soviet Union had given up on this desideratum—that is, only when East and West had reached a comprehensive settlement of the Cold War—could one speak of a détente worthy of the name. The real advantage of his plan for one comprehensive settlement, vis-á-vis the Eisenhower-Dulles vision of numerous discrete settlements, was that it would put aside the root causes of the Cold War, rather than treating its symptoms. The sole disadvantage was that this could never happen.

Adenauer's version of the West's policy toward Moscow in fact amounted to a continuation of the policy of negotiation from strength. First, the West had to impress the Soviets with its own unity and resolve. Then, the Soviets would be forced by their "domestic economic difficulties . . . to negotiate with the West. Soviet Russia had very great internal economic worries." The Soviets would change their policy at this time, presumably realizing the futility of their plans to dominate the democracies of Western Europe. Only then would it be possible to forsake the policy of strength for another policy "such as the one which President Eisenhower had proposed in this speech of 16 April, 1953." Implicit in this assessment was a criticism of Eisenhower's peace feeler. This was especially evident when it came to the thorny question of disarmament. The president planned to leave this question aside until the East-West rapprochement was in full bloom. Then, a comprehensive disarmament agreement could be negotiated as the culmination of the new atmosphere of cooperation. Adenauer could not have disagreed more: disarmament was a precondition for a thaw, and not a result of it. Only when all sides had demonstrated their will to participate in "controlled disarmament" was their any hope of settling the "individual questions" which the Cold War had raised.[98]

Adenauer did not say outright that America's professed interest in a piecemeal settlement of Cold War conflicts would undermine Western unity. But he clearly saw a danger in Churchill's proposal of a four-power conference without an agenda and without concrete expectations of success. "Fundamentally," the chancellor claimed, "I was for a four-power conference." But prior to any such meeting, one *had* to be certain that the meeting "promised at least some positive results. I considered a four-power conference which was nothing but a 'palaver' to be dangerous." A conference which produced nothing but talk "would allow the countries which were not well-disposed to Germany to put off the European unification plan."[99] Given Adenauer's conviction that strength through unity was the only means of achieving Western objectives, a four-power talkfest would be at best counterproductive, at worst suicidal. There was no logical contradiction between the call for a comprehensive settlement—a *Gesamtlösung*—with the Soviets and his stern warning to avoid a conference aimed at just that sort of solution. After all, EDC had yet to be ratified, and until the West was unified militarily, economically, politically, and—this was key for Adenauer—contractually, negotiations had no prospect for success. "Der Alte" thought at this point that "not much has come of this whole peace offensive,"[100] and had absolutely no interest in slowing the pace of Western consolidation by one day in order to pursue it further.

But opposition to Eisenhower's or Churchill's proposals had to be finely calibrated, or better yet, left to others. Public opinion in the West had been animated by the fair words coming out of London, Washington, and Moscow. Bonn would only give further ammunition to those "countries which are not well disposed to Germany" if the German federal government were too visibly to play Cassandra. Herbert Blankenhorn noted in his diary on the day after Churchill's Commons speech that:

> I believe it is not useful to treat this speech too negatively from our, the German, side. In English public opinion, but also in other countries of the European Continent, the speech has been positively received, since it gives the peoples some hope of emerging from the ossified situation of the Stalinist epoch.[101]

Germany simply could not be the nation which splashed cold water on such hopes.

But all was not lost. Blankenhorn, for one, was convinced that the Americans were not as enthused about Churchill's proposal as were Churchill's countrymen. He found David Bruce, America's ambassador to the European Coal and Steel Community and observer to the EDC Interim Committee, to be quite skeptical. Bruce's attitude toward Churchill's proposal of a four-power conference was "disapproving. He feared Soviet acceptance of the Churchill proposal, and then a phase of prolonged, fruitless discussions, which in the final result would work to the disadvantage of European unification."[102] Alexander Wiley, chairman of the Senate Foreign Relations Committee, echoed this less than enthusiastic response. The senator "asked for positive proof of Soviet peace intentions" before calling a meeting of the type proposed by the British prime minister.[103] This was, in fact, the essence of Eisenhower's proposals: the United States would be willing to negotiate with the Soviets *after* the Soviets provided evidence that their intentions were sincere.

The general sense in the Eisenhower administration appeared to be that it would be "imprudent" to press for a summit at that time. Talks were already taking place in Korea, and West and East had recently agreed to hold talks on the Austrian question. The administration was unwilling to put at risk progress on these issues for the sake of a conference which might lead to nothing concrete. The *New York Times* endorsed Eisenhower's step-by-step approach to rapprochement with the Soviet Union. If Moscow agreed to a settlement of the Austrian question, then "a Big-Power meeting might become the logical step toward further settlement." But should the Soviets "continue to frustrate agreement on the issues which are overripe for agreement, then there would be little hope of settling the bigger and more difficult problems."[104] Bonn could be reasonably confident that America would not be stampeded into a summit which would delay, and possibly kill, EDC. If Adenauer disagreed with Eisenhower's approach to détente, he nevertheless could not object to his timing. The piecemeal approach adopted by the Americans made it rather unlikely that a summit would be held before EDC was ratified.

"BETWEEN THE GRINDSTONES":
REDUCED TENSIONS, INCREASED WORRIES

Adenauer was concerned that premature rapprochement between East and West—rapprochement, that is, which preceded significant unification of Western Europe—would serve the Kremlin's long-range policy of dividing the West, in hopes of ruling it. Western unity could not be sacrificed for the pursuit of the détente will-o'-the-wisp. Real peace with the Soviets required strength. Strength required unity.

How upset the chancellor must have been then when "big speeches" by Eisenhower and Churchill brought to the fore differences between the English-speaking powers concerning the single most important issue in world politics. Adenauer met with America's NATO ambassador, William Draper, in early May when he stopped in Paris on his way to London to meet with Churchill. Undersecretary of State Walter B. Smith reported the results of this meeting to Eisenhower. Adenauer was, according to Draper, distressed by "recent signs of disagreement" between London and Washington. He planned on pointing out to Churchill the "vital importance of continued unity among the Western Powers in dealing with the Soviet Union."[105]

Adenauer's concern was punctuated by the Labour Party's response to Churchill's words. The media had noted potential conflicts between the proposals of Churchill and Eisenhower.[106] But it was Labour leader Clement Attlee's speech on the day following Churchill's that pointed to the possible extent of the rift between London and Washington. Attlee said that he did not want his words to make anyone think that "I am in any way anti-American." Some of my best friends are Americans, said the former prime minister. But he had to make clear his criticisms of the way the United States was conducting foreign policy. The American system of foreign policy making was different from the British way, he reminded his colleagues. The American Constitution was "framed for an isolationist state," and thus is not "particularly well suited to a time when America has become the strongest state in the world and has to give a lead." For his part, Attlee had trouble figuring out "where effective power lies" in Washington. Sometimes he wondered "who is more powerful, the President or Senator McCarthy."

Attlee was quite upset by America's seeming tendency to want to settle Asian questions alone, without bothering to consult her allies. He was disturbed "that negotiations in Korea were taking longer than necessary." He also reminded the House of Commons that Eisenhower could not guarantee acceptance by the Senate of the results of the Conference proposed by Churchill. Had the Europeans not seen what happened to Woodrow Wilson when he returned from Paris? Attlee supported Churchill's proposal. But he questioned America's will, portraying the United States as a less-than-reliable ally.[107]

Adenauer arrived in London with this Anglo-American friction still hanging in the air. As Eisenhower had learned from Draper, the chancellor went to London with a desire to impress upon Churchill the need for allied unity. Adenauer was also aware of his own disagreements with Churchill. In this atmosphere, he found it necessary to press Churchill for assurance that the western powers would not come to an agreement with the Soviets without consulting Bonn on questions affecting Germany. Adenauer faced a dilemma at this time. Too little allied unity would undermine the policy of strength which he advocated. Too much unity on the part of Germany's allies might lead to an agreement to settle with the Soviets, Bonn be damned. In this meeting with Churchill, the chancellor sought to prevent either of these extreme situations from coming to pass.

Despite his protestations of sympathy for Churchill's proposal, Adenauer was fundamentally opposed to the calling of a four-power conference at that time. According to Adenauer, the new leaders in Moscow had given the West "no special sign of a readiness of the Soviet Union for a restoration of German unity in freedom. Regarding German unification, not even the simplest terms were clarified, since Moscow described its system in the Soviet Zone [of Germany] as a system of freedom and our system in the Federal Republic as a system of bondage. I saw no basis to believe that a four power conference could lead to a positive result." The Soviets continued, he said, to refer back to the Potsdam Accords, which Adenauer labeled his "nightmare." The Soviets viewed these accords as "an eternal Morgenthau Plan of the Four Powers." Moscow wanted to revive the idea of a settlement of the German situation "behind our [the Germans'] backs." The Kremlin was saying to the West: "let us unite with each other at Germany's expense." Adenauer was determined to do everything in his power to prevent this from occurring. "Germany," the chancellor insisted, "must not fall between the grindstones; then all would be lost."[108]

Adenauer's report of his meeting with Churchill suggests complete unanimity between the two on all significant points of discussion. This could hardly have been the case. Bonn and London disagreed strongly on the fundamental question facing them, namely, to what extent was the post-Stalin Kremlin leadership willing to seek genuine settlement of disputes with the West? Adenauer's unvarnished assessment is presented above. But he—and von Eckardt, Hallstein, Blankenhorn, and diplomat Hans von Horwath, who all accompanied him to London—found the British assessment to be quite different. Churchill believed that "a change in the Russian attitude had really taken place." The British people, in any event, were anxious that the government should pursue this possibility. The chancellor could not have missed the point. He wanted to stress the need for unity while he was in London. Yet he and Churchill were far apart when it came to the first premise of the West's Soviet policy. The chancellor told Churchill that, in his opinion, his meeting in the United States had confirmed that the "present policy . . . must be continued." Churchill, however, emphasized that "all efforts must be undertaken in order to come to an understanding" with the Soviets.[109] Adenauer simply had nothing to gain by stressing the extent of the disagreement. But his untroubled reportage of a dozen years later cannot retroactively dismiss the problem that he and his government faced.

In fact, the Germans found that Churchill himself was cause for worry. Blankenhorn discovered that Churchill "had really aged; he often comes across as absent-minded [*er macht oft einen abwesenden Eindruck*]. When he asks questions, these sometimes miss the point." Like many people of his age, Blankenhorn remarked, the prime minister was often on the verge of tears.[110] Only two years Churchill's junior, the chancellor lacked this age-induced sentimentalism. He was not in London to debate Russian psychology. He was there, rather, to stress the need for allied cohesion, and to seek reassurances that the British would not—whatever their assessment of Soviet intentions—seek a settlement similar to that reached at Potsdam. Churchill repeatedly assured the chancellor that the British would never come to an agreement behind Germany's back; that "the Federal Republic would be consulted if her political interests were directly affected" in future negotiations with the Soviets. Adenauer claimed he was reassured by this promise, as he had been by similar assurances made in Washington one month before. "I returned to Bonn from London," he noted, "with the certainty that Great Britain would not negotiate over the head of Germany."[111]

But his other goal, that of cementing allied unity, continued to haunt him. Adenauer attempted to convince Churchill that Eisenhower's Chance for Peace address "corresponded in many fundamental questions" with Churchill's House of Commons speech.[112] But Attlee's words still hung in the air. Perhaps had it been only the opposition leader who expressed misgivings regarding American leadership, things would not have been so tense. But Churchill himself seemed obsessed with blaming the current world situation on the weakness of America's leaders in 1945 and 1946. It was he, Churchill told Adenauer, who had wanted in those days to stand up to the Soviets.[113] He was, in effect, telling Adenauer not to worry: *he* had always been realistic about Soviet intentions, even if the Americans had not.

Still, Adenauer worried. On the first day of June, Blankenhorn catalogued in his diary the litany of the chancellor's apprehensions. He was "seriously concerned" about "certain British-American differences of opinion in the assessment of the new Soviet trend in foreign policy, especially with regard to the idea of an eventual four power conference." He fretted, too, about the mood in the United States itself, "which reacts increasingly nervously and impatiently to the delay of the mechanism of European unity."[114] Nor, despite his attempts to convince Churchill of the opposite, did he think that London and Washington agreed on the approach to be taken toward the Soviets. On 29 May, Bruce reported to Conant on a meeting he had had with Hallstein earlier that day. The chancellor, Bruce informed Conant, was in fact "somewhat disturbed by his conversations with Churchill. He thinks Churchill unrealistic about the benefits for [the] West that might be derived from [a] conference with [the] Russians." Viewing with a cold and calculating eye what Churchill's misty eyes failed to see, Adenauer criticized the prime minister's hubris. Adenauer thought that Churchill "mistakenly considers himself [the] man who can accomplish personal wonders with [the] Russians and overestimates his own and British Empire's influence in Russian political circles." Since "the existing East-West tensions involve Germany more than they do any other power," Adenauer felt compelled to send Blankenhorn to the president himself, in order to present Eisenhower with a special message, indicating the seriousness with which he viewed the situation.[115]

Blankenhorn's special mission reveals much about German thinking on foreign affairs at this time. The *means* by which Adenauer conducted diplomacy in this matter indicates his lack of confidence in High Commissioner Conant. He feared leaks from the high commission, but also simply thought the commissioner to be the wrong man for the job. Blankenhorn went so far as to tell Dulles that Adenauer "felt the need of someone in Bonn with a greater background than possessed by President Conant."[116] The *timing* of the trip was motivated in part by allied plans—later put off—to hold a three-power conference in Bermuda in a few weeks. Adenauer clearly wanted to impress upon Eisenhower the extent to which Great Power decisions affected Germany, and to do this *before* the Bermuda conference took place.

But he was also motivated to send a personal envoy to Eisenhower at that time as a result of the shocking words of Senator Taft on 26 May. At a meeting of the National Conference of Christians and Jews in his home town of Cincinnati, Ohio, Taft's son Bob delivered an address which his father had written. The elder Robert Taft was at the time hospitalized with an unknown illness, which was in fact the cancer which would soon kill him.[117] Terminally ill and racked with pain, the senator was nonetheless in fighting spirits. He asked of NATO whether "this policy of uniting the free world against communism in a time of peace [was] going to be a practical long-term policy," adding "I have always been a skeptic on the subject of the military practicability of NATO. I am no military expert, but I have never heard an argument that impressed me attempting to show that United States ground forces could effectively defend Europe." Taft called on the Europeans to provide, instead, for their own defense.

Just as unsettling as his call to rethink America's military commitments was his assertion of allied unreliability. France and Britain were "more than anxious to settle with Russia and resume as much trade as possible, which means that as long as Russia talks nicely the whole military alliance against Russia is weak."[118] Biographies of Taft and Eisenhower stress the surprising extent of cooperation between the two after Eisenhower's inauguration.[119] But Taft's willingness to work with the new administration on budget and labor issues was of little interest in Bonn. His suggestions that America needed to cut commitments to allies whom he deemed unreliable hit like a sledgehammer. Blankenhorn considered the senator's speech as one of the primary goads which induced Adenauer to send him to Washington on 2 June.[120] Adenauer claimed to have been reassured, "somewhat," by Eisenhower's response to Taft's speech at his subsequent press conference.[121] He nevertheless dispatched Blankenhorn.

The Eisenhower administration sought to dampen Adenauer's Potsdam fears. Dulles instructed the high commission, on 4 June, to make clear to the chancellor that the purpose of the Bermuda meeting was "a general exchange of views rather than to make detailed decisions on a variety of problems. . . . While it is obviously impossible to talk about European affairs without references to German problems, [the] President would like to assure Adenauer that no decisions affecting Germany will be taken without full consultation with Adenauer."[122] Meanwhile in Washington, Blankenhorn found the atmosphere to be quite congenial. Dispatched to Washington in large part to make known Adenauer's grave reservations regarding a four-power summit, Blankenhorn found that his American counterparts at the State Department were also "skeptical with regard to a four power conference with the Soviet Union. It is not believed that such a conference can be avoided, but it is desired that it begin only on the basis of clear planning coordinated with the other western powers."[123] This accorded precisely with Adenauer's belief that negotiations with the Soviets could only be successful "if the West knew clearly and unambiguously what it wanted, and expressed this clearly before the start of possible negotiations with Soviet Russia."[124] Churchill's call for talks without an agenda—without, in fact, any definite goals—had received criticism in Washington as well as in Bonn. Blankenhorn found in Washington "concern" about Churchill's "unconventional wishes." Dulles added to the appearance of harmony between the American administration and the German government. He told Blankenhorn, on 2 June, that he too was "concerned regarding the position of the American Congress," a not-so-veiled reference to Taft's speech.[125] Eisenhower once again reaffirmed his assurances that America would not act on questions which affected Germany "without full consultation" with the chancellor. Eisenhower cabled this assurance on 4 June, and Adenauer received the news with gratitude, announcing the contents of the cable at a press conference the following day.[126] Yet the president was reluctant to accept certain of Adenauer's suggestions for America's future German policy. While Eisenhower did not reject Adenauer's request—made via Blankenhorn on 4 June—that a West German observer be present at any four-power conference, he indicated that he thought this plan to be problematic. After all, the presence of an observer from the FRG would "certainly result in [the] Soviet[s] having [an] East German observer present." And no one wanted this. Then, too, he was reluctant to accede to Adenauer's wishes that the United States put into effect certain provisions of the Contractuals before ratification by all signatories.[127]

This was to be a contentious issue between Bonn and Washington for the next year, even if Bonn, perforce, could not press the issue too hard. Blankenhorn was quite mistaken when he recorded in his diary that his conversation with the president "revealed Eisenhower's complete agreement with the opinions of the chancellor."[128] The discussion in fact revealed the limits of Adenauer's influence in Washington. Eisenhower was concerned with British and French reactions to American decisions. More than anything else, his administration sought cooperation among its European allies which would lead to ever-increasing unity among them. At this touchy point in the history of European integration, Eisenhower had no intention of pressing forward with policies which Bonn favored, but which would make dealings with other capitals—particularly Paris—more difficult.[129] The Federal Republic, although quite important to Western security policy, had yet to attain the status of America's paramount European ally. German interests could still be subordinated, by Washington, to French sensibilities.

NOTES

1. For analysis by Russian scholars of the maneuverings for position within the Kremlin leadership, that began before Stalin was even pronounced dead, see Zh. A. Medvedev, "Zagadka Smerti Stalina," *Voprosy Istorii* (1/2000); 83–91; and Vladislav Zubok, " 'Unverfroren und grob in der Deutschlandfrage . . .' Berija, der Nachfolgstreit nach Stalins Tod und die Moskauer DDR-Debatte im April-Mai 1953," in Christoph Kleßmann and Bernd Stöver, eds., *1953—Krisenjahr des Kalten Krieges in Europa* (Cologne: Böhlau Verlag, 1999), 31–34.

2. *Current Digest of the Soviet Press*, Vol. 5, No. 7, 9. As William Taubman has recently noted, the new Soviet leaders—including Malenkov—were interested in recasting "the Stalinist image of the outside world" in part due to the demands of *domestic* policy. In the midst of an agricultural crisis, the new men in Moscow needed options. The myth of an "irredeemably hostile" capitalist world tied their hands. Taubman, *Khrushchev: The Man and His Era* (New York: W. W. Norton, 2003), 260.

3. Jacob Beam, *Multiple Exposure: An American Ambassador's Unique Perspective on East-West Issues* (New York: W. W. Norton, 1978), 33–34.

4. *Keesing's Contemporary Archives*, Vol. 9 (1952–1954), 12869. For an analysis of the developments in Moscow immediately after Stalin's death, see Melvyn P. Leffler, *For the Soul of Mankind: The United States, the Soviet Union, and the Cold War* (New York: Hill and Wang, 2007), 84–93.

5. Henry Kissinger is correct in saying that "Malenkov made no concrete proposals" in this speech, probably because the Russians themselves were unsure what they should do. This did not, nevertheless, detract from the significance of Malenkov's words. Henry Kissinger, *Diplomacy* (New York: Simon and Schuster, 1994), 505.

6. *The New York Times*, 16 March, 1953, 1.

7. Beam, 34. Public sources also pointed in this direction. For example, *Pravda* editorialized, on 11 April, that the "broad public circles in all countries are increasingly manifesting a desire for a peaceful settlement of the Korean question," and noted that the "U.S.S.R. government invariably supports all steps taken to end the Korean war." *Current Digest of the Soviet Press*, Vol. 5., No. 12, 4.

8. Eisenhower, *Mandate for Change*, 148–49.

9. *Public Papers*, 1953, 31.

10. Hoopes, 171. On the contrast between Eisenhower and Dulles on this matter, see especially McAllister, 227–30. McAllister judiciously avoids overstating the practical impact of this difference of opinion on the administration's European policy.

11. Hoopes, 171.

12. *NYT*, 16 March, 1953, 18.

13. For a contemporaneous, and highly insightful, observation of the significance of these changes, see Raymond Aron (Georges-Henri Soutou, ed.), *Les articles de politique internationale dans Le Figaro de 1947 à 1977*, Tome I, *La Guerre froide* (Juin 1947 à mai 1955) (Paris: Éditions de Fallois, 1990). According to Aron, "there is no reason to think that Stalin's successors, who where his comrades, have become at one blow less hostile to the West. Their objectives remain the same and their strategy, as for the main points, has not changed; but the change of tactics is evident" (1017).

14. Oleg Troyanovsky, *Cherez gody i rasstoiania: Istoriya odnoi sem'i* (Moscow: Vagrius, 1997), 173–74.

15. Robert R. Bowie and Richard H. Immerman, *Waging Peace: How Eisenhower Shaped an Enduring Cold War Strategy* (New York: Oxford University Press, 1998), 109–10.

16. Vojtech Mastny, "The Elusive Détente: Stalin's Successors and the West," in Klaus Larres and Kenneth Osgood, *The Cold War after Stalin's Death: A Missed Opportunity for Peace?* (Lanham, MD: Rowman & Littlefield, 2006), 4. For details on the division of labor reached by Stalin's successors, see Mark Kramer, "The Early Post-Stalin Succession Struggle and Upheavals in East-Central Europe: Internal-External Linkages in Soviet Policy Making (Part 1)," *Journal of Cold War Studies* 1/1 (Winter 1999), 7–8.

17. The quote comes from Larres, *Churchill's Cold War: The Politics of Personal Diplomacy* (New Haven, CT: Yale University Press, 2002), 188. The "fresh dynamic" that Stalin's death brought to international politics was naturally disconcerting to an administration in its first weeks in office (189). See also ibid., 109, on the "deep divisions" within the administration on this issue.

18. Manfred Görtemaker (Trans. Terence M. Coe), "Germany Between the Superpowers, 1948–1968," in Detlef Junker, ed., *The United States and Germany in the Era of the Cold War, 1945–1990: A Handbook*, Volume 1, 1945–1968 (Cambridge: Cambridge University Press, 2004), 114. Görtemaker rightly concludes that Adenauer's fears of drastic "experiments in German policy" were overblown by 1953.

19. Georges-Henri Soutou, *L'alliance incertaine: Les rapports politico-stratégiques franco-allemands, 1954–1996* (Paris: Fayard, 1996), 14.

20. Herbert Blankenhorn, *Verständnis und Verständigung: Blätter eines politischen Tagebuchs, 1949 bis 1979* (Frankfurt am Main: Verlag Ullstein, 1980), 145–46. France also had fears of being left out as the major decisions regarding Europe were made, and feared "more than anyone else a separate bargain between Germany or the United States and the Soviet Union." Françoise de la Serre et al., *Les Politiques étrangères de la France et de la Grande-Bretagne depuis 1945: L'inévitable adjustement* (Paris: Presses de la Foundation Nationale des Sciences Politiques, 1990), 33.

21. Ibid., 146.

22. Adenauer, *Erinnerungen, 1945–1953*, 564.

23. Even though Dulles was a critic of the Truman foreign policy, he held McCloy in some regard, and respected his advice on German issues. See particularly Schwartz, 280.

24. *FRUS, 1952–1954*, Vol. 7, 405–7. For the third and final reading of the Contractuals in the Bundestag, see *Verhandlungen des Deutschen Bundestages* (1. Wahlperiode 1949: Band 15, 255. Sitzung), 19. März 1953. Adenauer argued during the debate that Stalin's death had "certainly not reduced" the dangers of the international situation. His death increased the "delicateness of the world situation," at least until his heirs had consolidated their hold on power. For that reason, the West should use this "breathing space" [*Atempause*] to build up West Europe's defenses. In seeking to attain ratification, Adenauer had committed himself to an interpretation of events in the Soviet Union which ran counter to détente hopes; Stalin's death in fact *required* of the West a military buildup. 12301–2.

25. Telegram, Department of State to Hicog Bonn. NARA, State Department Central Decimal File, 611.62a/3-2053.

26. See James G. Hershberg, *James B. Conant: Harvard to Hiroshima and the Making of the Nuclear Age* (New York: Alfred A. Knopf, 1993), 658–59.

27. See telegrams on 16, 20, and 23 March: NARA, State Department Central Decimal File, 611.62a/3-1653, 611.62a/3-2053, and 611.62a/3-2453 respectively.

28. NARA, State Department Central Decimal File, 611.62a/3-2453.

29. State Department to HICOG Bonn, 25 March, 1953: NARA State Department Central Decimal File, 611.62a/3-2453.

30. Memorandum of a conversation, Riddleberger and Blankenhorn, *FRUS, 1952–1954*, Vol. 7, 413–16.

31. Hans-Jürgen Grabbe, *Unionsparteien, Sozialdemokratie, und Vereinigten Staaten von Amerika, 1945–1966* (Düsseldorf: Droste Verlag, 1983), 194–95.

32. Mastny, "The Elusive Détente," in Larres and Osgood, *The Cold War*, 6; Memorandum of conversation between Riddleberger and Blankenhorn, 29 March, 1953, *FRUS, 1952–1954*, Vol. 7, 416–17.

33. *FRUS, 1952–1954*, Vol. 7, 421–22.

34. Telegram, Bonn to State, 30 March, 1953. NARA, State Department Central Decimal File, 611.62a/3-3053.

35. Felix von Eckardt notes that "the reader will hardly be able to feel with the same intensity what the first personal meeting with the president meant for us Germans." How amazing it was that now the German chancellor was being greeted in the White House by "the American hero of the Second World War." Von Eckardt, *Ein unordentliches Leben* (Düsseldorf: Econ-Verlag, 1967), 211.

36. Besson, 144. Grabbe notes Adenauer's desire to use the trip to America "propagandistically, to the advantage of the CDU/CSU," by showing that "the West course had brought dividends." The result was a "considerable effect upon the domestic political scene." *Unionsparteien, Sozialdemokratie*, 194. For Adenauer's trip to America, see Köhler, *Adenauer*, 767–71.

37. Wilhelm G. Grewe, *Deutsche Aussenpolitik in der Nachkriegzeit* (Stuttgart: Deutsche Verlags-Anstalt, 1960), 137.

38. Hershberg, 654.

39. The German press watched Adenauer's reception in America that April, and reported back to the Federal Republic that Bonn "had won considerable prestige and respect in its most important partner country." Blankenhorn, 147.

40. "Pressebericht für den Herrn Bundeskanzler, 6.4.53": Nachlaß von Eckhardt, I-010-004/1, Archiv der Christlich-demoktatische Politik (ACDP).

41. Memorandum for the chancellor of conversation with American journalists, 5 April, 1953: Nachlaß von Eckardt, ACDP, I-010-004/1.

42. Von Eckardt, 213. On his skepticism with regard to the Soviet peace initiative, see 206. In von Eckardt's opinion, the peace offensive was really a "campaign . . . against the European Defense Community," as well as an attempt to buy time. After Stalin's death, "conditions under his successor Malenkov were still so little stabilized that one did not need any foreign complications."

43. Adenauer in fact recognized the effects quite clearly: "It appeared as if a great segment of the American public opinion was only too ready to succumb to the allure of a détente, which for the present, however, was only a pipe-dream [*Wunschtraum*]." *Erinnerungen, 1945–1953*, 564–65.

44. "Pressebericht für den herrn Bundeskanzler, 6.4.53," Nachlaß Lenz, ACDP.

45. Von Eckardt, 206.

46. Adenauer, *Erinnerungen, 1945–1953*, 565.

47. Ibid., 209. Anastas Mikoyan confirmed in his memoirs that these two Stalin heirs had "arranged" between them to take a critical stance toward the German Democratic Republic. He quotes Beria as declaring that " 'We should not cling to the GDR: What sort of socialism can be built there?' and so on." *Tak Bylo: Razmyshleniya o Minuvshem* (Moscow: Vagrius, 1999), 584. See the discussion of the Beria affair in Taubman, chapter 10.

48. In terms of symbolism, his reception at the airport was itself a great victory. Two years before, as he landed in Paris, no French official of cabinet rank condescended to meet his plane. The snub was obvious. Now in Washington, he was greeted by the vice president, and the secretaries of state, defense, and the treasury. Adenauer received a reception reserved for only a few—very important—foreign dignitaries. On the 1951 trip, see Christian Hacke, *Weltmacht wider Willen: Die Aussenpolitik der Bundesrepublik Deutschland* (Frankfurt am Main: Ullstein GmbH, 1993), 64. On the 1953 reception, see von Eckardt, 210; Adenauer, *Erinnerungen, 1945–1953*, 566–68.

49. See Adenauer, *Erinnerungen, 1945–1953*, 568–69; "United States Delegation Minutes of First Meeting of Chancellor Adenauer and President Eisenhower," 7 April, 1953: *FRUS, 1952–1954*, Vol. 7, 426.

50. State Department Telegram to HICOG, Bonn, 8 April, 1953: NARA, State Department Central Decimal File, 611.62a/4-853; *FRUS, 1952–1954*, Vol. 7, 528; Adenauer, *Erinnerungen, 1945–1953*, 569–70.

51. NARA, ibid.

52. NARA, ibid.; Adenauer, *Erinnerungen, 1945–1953*, 570.

53. Adenauer, *Erinnerungen, 1945–1953*, 570; NARA, ibid. The perpetually anxious chancellor at this time found himself trying to ease the fears of his American allies. Such was the administration's commitment to EDC as the key to a secure, friendly Europe. See McAllister, 237–38.

54. Adenauer, ibid., 571–572; NARA, ibid.; "United States Delegation Minutes of the First General Meeting of Chancellor Adenauer and Secretary Dulles," 7 April, 1953: *FRUS, 1952–1954*, Vol. 7, 431–32.

55. The British likewise responded favorably to the suggestion. See Telegram number 5489, from London to State: NARA, State Department Central Decimal File, 611.62a/4-953.

56. *FRUS, 1952–1954*, Vol. 7, 432–33.

57. The State Department quickly became aware of the mixed reaction in the French press to reports of Adenauer's talks in Washington. Gaullists seemed upset that Adenauer blamed Paris for failure to solve the Saar question, while centrist papers noted Adenauer's hard-line attitude toward the Soviet peace offensive. Reportedly, Adenauer found "Americans too confident in Russian peace overtures." See Telegram, Paris to State Department, 9 April, 1953: NARA, State Department Central Decimal File, 611.62a/4-953.

58. Von Eckardt, 213.

59. *FRUS, 1952–1954*, Vol. 7, 434–35.

60. Adenauer, *Erinnerungen, 1945–1953*, 573.

61. Von Eckardt, 213.

62. See von Eckardt, 214–15.

63. *FRUS, 1952–1954*, Vol. 7, 453; see also Adenauer, *Erinnerungen, 1945–1953*, 579. The British also expressed their agreement with these priorities in London's "Official Comment on Recent American-German Talks." The British government insisted that "there can be no lasting solution of the German question short of reunification of Germany in freedom." The Churchill government also endorsed "the emphasis which the joint American-German communique lays on the urgency of early ratification of the EDC Treaty." Foreign Service Dispatch, American Consul General Singapore to State Department, 16 April, 1953, NARA, State Department Central Decimal File, 611.62a/4-1653.

64. See von Eckardt, 204–6.

65. Adenauer, *Erinnerungen, 1945–1953*, 581–82.

66. See "Pressebericht für den Herrn Bundeskanzler 6.4.53": ACDP, Nachlaß von Eckardt, I-010-004/1. The press summary quotes *US News and World Report* as opining that "nothing has changed in Moscow."

67. The emphasis upon Soviet economic strength was out of character for Adenauer. As the 1950s progressed, he increasingly attributed Soviet actions to domestic economic weakness.

68. Adenauer, *Erinnerungen, 1945–1953*, 583–84. On American isolationism, see a memorandum of a conversation with American journalists, mistakenly labeled "5. April, 1952," in ACDP, Nachlaß von Eckardt, I-010-004/1. The Soviet peace offensive was undermining the willingness of the American people to pay taxes and support foreign aid in order to maintain the "political and military strength of the West." Days later, while the German delegation was in Chicago—residing, oddly, at the Bismarck Hotel—von Eckardt informed Adenauer that Senator Styles Bridges was calling for a cut in foreign aid. Additionally, the American press was concerned about the possibility of unilateral American disarmament. Would America, they asked, be capable of providing the aid and leadership that NATO allies expected if such trends continued? (13.4.53 Presse Übersicht, Nachlaß von Eckardt, ACDP.)

69. Von Eckardt, 233.

70. Von Eckardt, 237; Lenz 613.

71. Larres, *Churchill's Cold War*, 188.

72. Leffler, *For the Soul of Mankind*, 101–2.

73. Emmet John Hughes, *The Ordeal of Power: A Political Memoir of the Eisenhower Years* (New York: Athenaeum, 1963), 102.

74. Ambrose, *Eisenhower: The President*, 92. Ambrose's evidence on this point is not altogether clear. Dulles's suspicions regarding the new Soviet leadership are, however, easily documented. Bohlen, for one, recalls that Dulles did not approve of any face-to-face contacts between the ambassador and Soviet leaders, since "he believed that if Americans were seen in friendly conversation with Russians, the will to resist Communism would be weakened throughout the world." Although he disagreed with the secretary's attitude, Bohlen did not see his instructions as having any practical consequences. Bohlen himself "could not see much value in attempting to cultivate" the Soviet leaders. Charles E. Bohlen, *Witness to History, 1929–1969* (New York: W. W. Norton, 1973), 343–44.

75. Immerman, *John Foster Dulles*, 53.

76. Hughes, 102.

77. Soviet Foreign Minister Molotov expressed his opinion on this question that summer, indicating to the CP Central Committee that the Peace Offensive was meant to cause "confusion in the ranks of our aggressive adversaries." Mastny, "The Elusive Détente," in Larres and Osgood, *The Cold War*, 5–6.

78. Hughes, 104–5.

79. On the ambivalent Allen Dulles/CIA assessment of the post-Stalin Kremlin, see Mark Kramer, "Introduction: International Politics in the Early Post-Stalin Era: A Lost Opportunity, a Turning Point, or More of the Same?" in Larres and Osgood, *The Cold War*, xiv–xv. Considering Kramer's portrayal, Allen Dulles may serve as a synecdoche for much of the administration. No one expected significant departures from Stalin's hostility toward the West. Yet some sensed that things were now meaningfully different in Moscow.

80. Hughes, 105–9. Hughes quotes Dulles as saying that he was "grow[ing] less keen on the speech, because I think there's some real danger of our just seeming to fall in with these Soviet overtures. It's obvious that what they [the Soviet leaders] are doing is because of outside pressures, and I don't know anything better we can do than to keep up these pressures right now." One must keep in mind that at this time Washington was also the stage for the acrimonious debate over Bohlen's appointment as ambassador to the Soviet Union. The appointment became the focal point of the debate about America's policy toward the communist powers. Hard-line Republicans like senators Styles Bridges and William Knowland, and Democrats like Senator Pat McCarran were concerned that Bohlen represented a "soft" line toward Moscow. Thus, Eisenhower was bucking a significant trend, both with his speech and with the appointment of a pragmatist like Bohlen. See Bohlen, chapter 18.

81. Hughes, 110–11.

82. *Public Papers, 1953*, 179–88. The Soviet leaders indicated their interest in the speech by allowing it to be printed in full by *Pravda*.

83. Geneviève Maelstaf, *Que Faire de L'Allemagne? Les responsables français, le statut international de l'Allemagne et le problème de l'unité allemande, 1945–1955* (Paris: Imprimerie Nationale, 1999), 394.

84. Von Eisenhower, *Mandate*, 145.

85. The Eisenhower administration never formally rejected "liberation." Yet even early on, as administration security policy was being formulated, it was clear that Eisenhower and Dulles had in mind a "psychological," not military, approach to the doctrine. See Gaddis, *Strategies*, 155–56.

86. Von Eckardt, 244–45.

87. Adenauer, *Erinnerungen, 1953–1955* (Stuttgart: Deutsche Verlags-Anstalt, 1966), 203–4.

88. Martin Gilbert, *Churchill: A Life* (New York: Henry Holt and Co., 1991), 925.

89. This, at least, was Adenauer's assessment of Churchill's motives. See Konrad Adenauer, *Teegespräche, 1950–1954* (Berlin: Siedler Verlag, 1984), 467. Adenauer thought that Churchill reflected the British people in general, who did not want to be left out of major developments in East-West relations. Rather, they sought to demonstrate that "they themselves had something to say."

90. *Parliamentary Debates: House of Commons, Official Report (Hansard)*, Volume 515: 11 May, 1953, 899–902.

91. The cautious approach that Molotov and the Soviet foreign ministry took in response to Churchill's proposal would have reassured Adenauer more, had he known of the inner workings of Kremlin foreign-policy making after the Beria purge. Molotov saw no good that could come from a summit with Eisenhower and Churchill. In general, "he was clearly unwilling to depart from a Stalinist foreign policy." Derek Watson, *Molotov: A Biography* (New York: Palgrave, 2005), 247. Watson's endnotes and bibliography are an invaluable guide to the Russian-language sources that are currently available to scholars of the Cold War. The author wishes to acknowledge his debt to Watson for this assistance.

92. *Public Papers, 1953*, 50.

93. *Public Papers*, 284–85.

94. Kramer has made this point in his introduction to Larres and Osgood, *The Cold War*, xiv, xx.

95. Adenauer, *Erinnerungen, 1953–1955*, 209–10. Adenauer did not, in this instance, consider reunification to be a special case. Settlement of this issue, too, would have to wait until the basic conflict had been set aside.

96. Adenauer, *Teegespräche, 1950–1955*, 447–48. See also Adenauer, *Erinnerungen, 1953–1955*, 211.

97. "The First 90 Days: Address by Secretary Dulles," *Department of State Bulletin* (*DSB*), Volume 28, Number 72 (20 April, 1953), 607.

98. Adenauer, *Erinnerungen, 1953–1955*, 209–11.

99. Ibid., 211.

100. Adenauer, *Teegespräche, 1950–1954*, 448.

101. Blankenhorn, 149. On the British response to Churchill's speech, see *New York Times*, 12 May, 1953, 1.

102. Ibid., 149.

103. Quoted in *New York Times*, 12 May, 1953, 1.

104. *New York Times*, 12 May, 1953, 1, 10; and 13 May, 1953, 28.

105. DDEL, Whitman File, International Series: Box 14, File: Germany 1953(3). This memorandum bears no date, but Adenauer's presence in Paris dates his meeting with Draper at no later than 13 May.

106. See, e.g., *New York Times*, 12 May, 1953, 9.

107. *Hansard*, Volume 515, 1065–75.

108. Adenauer, *Erinnerungen, 1953–1955*, 215–16. Adenauer was quite taken by the irony of Moscow's oft-repeated declaration that his was the dictatorial, and theirs the democratic Germany. He had already faced a close election, and was set to go to the voters again in the fall. On the other hand, he would publicly repeat, the GDR government had the support of perhaps 10 percent of its population. See A. M. Filitov, "SSSR i GDR: god 1953–i," in *Voprosy Istorii* (7/2000), 135.

109. Ibid, 205.

110. Blankenhorn, 150–51. After the meeting, Hallstein told Bruce that Adenauer "found Churchill in a variable state of mental agility depending on the time of day." Telegram Bruce to HICOM, 29 May, 1953: *FRUS, 1952–1954*, Volume 7, 457.

111. Adenauer, *Erinnerungen, 1953–1955*, 206; 207; 209.

112. Blankenhorn, 150.

113. Adenauer, *Erinnerungen, 1953–1955*, 207; 208.

114. Blankenhorn, 152.

115. Telegram, Bruce to HICOM, 29 May, 1953: *FRUS, 1952–1954*, Vol. 5, 457–58.

116. Memorandum of a conversation between Blankenhorn and John Foster Dulles, 3 June, 1953: DDEL, Whitman File, International Series, Box 14, File: Germany 1953 (5). See also Hershberg, 658–659.

117. Patterson, *Mr. Republican*, 601.

118. *New York Times*, 27 May, 1953, 6.

119. Patterson, 591–98; Ambrose, *Eisenhower*, 118. See also Eisenhower, 218–22.

120. Blankenhorn, 152.

121. Telegram from Bruce to HICOM, 29 May, 1953: *FRUS, 1952–1954*, Vol. 7, 458.

122. Telegram, Dulles to Samuel Reber (Director of Political Affairs, Office of Political Affairs, U.S. High Commission, Bonn), 4 June, 1953: NARA, State Department Central Decimal File, 611.62A/6-453.

123. Blankenhorn, 153.

124. Adenauer, *Erinnerungen, 1953–1955*, 203.

125. Blankenhorn, 153.

126. Telegram, Reber to Dulles, 5 June, 1953: NARA, State Department Central Decimal File, 611.62A/6-653; Telegram, Dulles to HICOM, ibid., 611.62A/6-653.

127. Telegram, Dulles to HICOM, ibid.

128. Blankenhorn, 154.

129. On Eisenhower's sympathy toward the French position, as well as the limits of EDC's ability to reassure them, see McAllister, 236.

3

"There Is No Other Foreign Policy": The Road to Berlin

In June 1953, Soviet actions seemed to speak louder than words. The suppression of the workers' uprising in East Berlin and elsewhere in East Germany reinforced in the minds of many in the West the impression that Moscow was unwilling to make any real concessions that might help to mitigate the tensions between the superpower blocs. The Kremlin, in sending tanks into the streets, had indicated the limits of their flexibility. They would under no circumstances allow a popular movement in East Germany to topple the communist SED (Socialist Unity) regime in East Berlin. Washington and Bonn took this as evidence that the Kremlin feared the erosion of other puppet governments in the East. Whatever Stalin's death meant in Moscow, it clearly did not extend to the loss of Russia's sphere of influence east of the Elbe. How, then, was any meaningful settlement to be reached with the Soviet Union? The fault line of the Cold War ran through Germany. And if the Soviets pursued an intransigent policy with regard to Eastern Europe, East and West would, it seemed, have no recourse but to face off across the divide that had once been "Central Europe."

But matters were not so simple. In the first place, Washington still had not abandoned all hope that a compromise on Europe could be had with the Soviets. Granted, the Kremlin was not willing to allow the East Germans to topple the Ulbricht regime. But perhaps they would be willing themselves, under the right circumstances, to sacrifice the SED government. Vladislav M. Zubok has recently reconstructed the "patchy evidence" that has survived regarding the Soviet Presidium's thoughts and actions regarding unrest in the German Democratic Republic. According to his reconstruction, the Soviet leaders "considered a radical change in German policy" in late May and early June 1953. This willingness to consider abandoning the Ulbricht regime was not limited to Beria, as had previously been believed.[1]

Perhaps if the West could offer Moscow an acceptable proposal for the resolution of the German question—one which took into consideration the Soviet Union's security interests in Eastern Europe—the Soviet Union might allow the East German government to expire.

Others, both in Washington and in Bonn, held little hope for a resolution along these lines. Adenauer, for one, remained convinced that the Soviets sought to divide the West and, thereby, to gain time to regroup before embarking upon a further wave of expansion. Now, after the Soviets had crushed the aspirations of eighteen million Germans for freedom and self-determination under the treads of the Red Army's tanks, was there room for doubt?

Yet with an election approaching in September, and with his major allies seeking an agreement with the Soviets on issues ranging from German unification to a settlement in Austria and arms control, the times called for more from Bonn than passive expressions of worry and intransigence. The chancellor sought increasingly to inject his voice into the discussions in the West. As 1953 wore on, his efforts were rewarded with increasing success.

The Soviets crushed the uprising in the East to a large degree because Moscow had become convinced that its European policy could not survive unless its German client regime remained in place; unless, in fact, socialism were shown to work in the German Democratic Republic.[2] Ironically, parallel developments in the Western alliance increased the bargaining power of the Bonn regime. For America too was convinced—after Adenauer's sound re-election, and especially as the French dragged their heels on EDC—that Germany had become indispensable. If American security policy were to succeed in Europe, a strong and, equally importantly, *reliable* ally would have to be found. Paris had made it clear that France was not such an ally. Adenauer went to great pains to prove to Washington that the Federal Republic was. It was his task to demonstrate to Washington that Germany, not France, was America's primary ally—her junior partner—on the Continent.

17 JUNE, 1953: THE WEST DOES NOTHING[3]

In negotiations and exchanges with the Soviets, Adenauer and his Western allies insisted that no settlement of the German question would be acceptable if it did not achieve unification though the holding of free and open elections across the entire nation. The 17 June uprising in East Germany was, thus, a watershed in the search for a settlement of Europe's division which was acceptable to both blocs. For the workers' uprising in East Germany meant different things to West and East. In Bonn, the uprising provided graphic evidence of how necessary free elections were. The Bonn government had no choice, after 17 June, but to press the issue of free elections, and to place greater emphasis on reunification as a *stated* goal of the Adenauer government. For the Soviets, the uprising provided stark evidence of the frailty of the East German government, and reinforced the Kremlin's commitment to shoring up the SED regime. Ironically, the uprising resulted in the *strengthening*—at the hands of the Soviets, of course—of the position of the East German communist government. In addition, the Soviet assumption that the West lay behind the uprising "portended ill for the prospects of détente."[4]

The administration of the eastern zone of Germany had brought discontent long before the summer of 1953. After the war the Soviets had been interested in keeping Germany weak, and in rebuilding the war-torn Soviet economy with equipment taken from the Soviet sector. Thus, Moscow had contributed significantly to the failure of the East German economy to thrive after the war. So too did Walter Ulbricht's program of rapid "socialization" of East Germany, which outpaced even Moscow's desires. In the spring of 1953, the Soviet Presidium was too busy dealing with the aftermath of Stalin's death, with each member jockeying for position. Once stability was restored, however, the Soviet leadership soon came to a consensus in favor of drastic changes in their East-Central European policies:

> Although Soviet leaders differed slightly in their views about some aspects of intrabloc relations, they increasingly agreed on two fundamental points: (1) that sweeping political and economic reforms were needed in East-Central Europe; and (2) that the Soviet Union should exert strong pressure on East European officials who tried to resist reforms.

The "New Course" in SED policy came too late, however. The unrest only increased, as frustrated workers now sensed that the Ulbricht regime was faltering. Faced with an abnormally low standard of living and a government beholden to Moscow, the workers of East Germany had had enough when the SED regime imposed further hardships on 28 May. Walter Ulbricht's government on that day increased laborers' production quotas while simultaneously reducing wages.[5] The people of East Germany took to the streets.

"The uprising in the Soviet Zone had the effect," the chancellor later declared, "to those of us in Germany . . . of a signal which indicated that force could not suppress the will to freedom."[6] But if force could not extinguish the will to freedom, it could nevertheless prevent those so disposed from doing anything about it. Soviet tanks reclaimed the streets of East German cities for the Ulbricht regime. The United States watched passively. The desire for freedom, the "profound ill-will [*abgrundtiefe Mißstimmung*]" against the Soviet-sponsored regime and the Red Army, proved impotent in a battle that pitted rock-throwing demonstrators against Soviet tanks.[7]

Adenauer's first step was to call a meeting of his aides, at which the chairman of West Berlin's CDU was also present, in order to devise a quick response to the crisis.[8] The chancellor never wanted to speak ill of the American administration. Yet he was convinced that the Eisenhower-Dulles rhetoric of liberation was to blame in large measure for the disaster. Michael Lemke has noted an important, easily overlooked element of Adenauer's German policy: his caution. He spoke frequently of the desire for all Germans to live in freedom, and expressed sympathy for the East Germans, who lived under a foreign-imposed tyranny. But he also took for granted that any type of insurrection against the Soviet-sponsored regime "would not only be in vain, but also, if the case arose, would end bloodily." Because of this conviction, Adenauer's policy "had avoided, as far as possible, any encouragement of the East Germans to revolt by force against the Soviet presence" in Germany.[9]

He did not think that Eisenhower and Dulles had shown the same rhetorical prudence. Rather than saying so himself, Adenauer quotes approvingly in his memoirs a lengthy analysis of the causes of the uprising from the Swiss *Neue Zürcher Zeitung [NZZ]*. This newspaper concluded that "international politics," and not domestic economic reforms, were the root cause of the uprising. "Tens of thousands of East German workers had believed," the *NZZ* opined, "that the American President Eisenhower, who came to power in January 1953, would translate into action the program of liberation of Eastern European peoples announced in the election campaign."[10] Without question, the proclamation by the new president and secretary of state that the "negative" and "bankrupt" policy of containment must give way to an active policy of liberation inspired many captives of the East Bloc to believe that America sided with them. Yet the overwhelmingly proletarian composition of the demonstrators indicates the role that economic hardship played, for it was the workers who had to bear the brunt of the new production demands without benefiting from economic reforms.

Adenauer nevertheless had come face-to-face with the limits of the Republicans' 1952 campaign pledge. When "liberation" brought America directly into conflict with the Soviet Union, the Eisenhower administration was unwilling to pursue its declared policy. And any attempt to liberate the 18 million East Germans from Soviet control was bound to result in such conflict.[11]

INITIATIVE FROM BONN: DOMESTIC AND FOREIGN POLICY[12]

The developments in East Germany were of unquestionable significance. But they did not stop the world. A meeting of the foreign ministers of the three Western powers had been planned for Washington beginning 10 July. Despite the objections of the State Department, which wanted to see progress on the Korean and Austrian negotiations prior to a high-level meeting, Eisenhower had insisted that a conference should be held.[13] Adenauer, in the wake of the uprising of 17 June, was even more concerned than usual to have the German voice heard when the Atlantic allies met in Washington. He would soon face an election. In the coming campaign, he sought to use the smashing of the Eastern uprising to gain public support for *Westintegration* and the policy of strength; that is, for his chosen course. Soviet tanks had demonstrated what Moscow had in mind when it raised the prospect of a neutralized, reunified Germany.[14] But in pressing this line, he needed to demonstrate that his government was nevertheless doing everything that it could to aid the countrymen who had been so brutally put down in the cities of the East. For this reason, Adenauer weighed in with an unsought proposal to get the German question in motion. It was a risky move, and it worked.

Adenauer was less than thrilled by the prospect of a four-power conference when Churchill had proposed one in May. He thought it a bad idea and had at first shied away from it. The chancellor's difficult position was well understood in the governing circles of the West, even if Churchill was willing to discount Adenauer's concerns. In February, British Foreign Secretary Anthony Eden had himself emphasized, in a letter to the prime minister, that a four-power conference that "discussed Germany's future without [Adenauer] being present must do him great harm."[15]

The uprising in the East Zone of Germany changed Adenauer's outlook on the wisdom of holding East-West conversations in the near future. Adenauer saw the uprising as "present[ing] an opportunity emphatically to make the demand for reunification in peace and freedom the center point of a four-power conference."[16] Why this was desirable now, the chancellor failed to make clear. What had changed as a result of the 17 June uprising? Adenauer had always seen the prospects for a negotiated settlement of the German question to be rather close to nil. And even if the uprising brought home to the Western powers the importance of the German issue, it also— by making clear the Soviet commitment to the preservation of the Ulbricht regime—indicated that Adenauer had a point. Why then, after certain illusions about the extent of Soviet readiness to compromise were shattered, was the chancellor willing, even anxious, to convene a summit?

The record shows that Adenauer was motivated primarily by a desire to outflank the Social Democrats in an election year. The suppression of the uprising intensified the already strong desire on the part of West Germans to find a settlement that would allow their countrymen in the East Zone to escape oppression. Adenauer, by clearly and publicly pressing the allies for a summit, would be seen as the champion of German unity in the Western alliance. This role, furthermore, was denied to the socialists. The opposition had no opportunity to publicly press Germany's case with the West. That electoral considerations played a major role in the Bonn government's response to the Soviet peace offensive at this point in time is unquestionable, and was well known in Washington. On 9 July, Hallstein and Blankenhorn met with David Bruce, the American ambassador to the European Coal and Steel Community (ECSC), and made all of this very clear. Adenauer was "absolutely certain [that] the Russians would shortly make a new move designed to defeat him in the German elections. . . . He believes, therefore, he should take the initiative so as to exclude the possibility of the Russians being the first to offer a plan that would appeal to German public opinion regarding the reunification of the two parts of the country."[17]

Adenauer was also determined to play as significant a role as possible in allied deliberations on German policy. There was to be no new Potsdam. If the allies were determined to have a four-power conference—and uprising or no uprising, they seemed intent on moving along that trajectory—then the chancellor would do his best to make certain that the interests of his state and of his government were always at the forefront of Western discussions.[18]

He began immediately to implement that plan. Faced with the impending foreign ministers' conference in Washington, Adenauer "held it necessary to report unambiguously to the three foreign ministers concerning the German views" about the issues that were to be discussed at the conference. The uprising and its suppression had "presented an opportunity" to the West. They could use this event to press the Soviets, at a four-power conference, on the question of "reunification in peace and freedom." Thus Adenauer, who had "shied away" from a four-power conference when Churchill proposed one on 11 May, now became an advocate of such a meeting.[19] Adenauer may well have believed that in addition to giving the reunification question additional urgency, his shift also gave West Germany leverage. Bonn could now advance its interests on this topic. Germany's allies, now more aware of the importunateness of the question, would be more likely to listen to the voice of the Germans.[20] The upcoming foreign ministers' conference gave Adenauer and his government an opportunity to test just how much leverage they could now exert.

There was a problem, however: the Germans were not invited to this conference, nor was their input desired. Adenauer was not deterred by such niceties. Rather, he was convinced of the need to be seen as an important player in the debate about Germany's future. On 8 July, he met with his chief foreign affairs aides at his retreat at Bühlerehöhe. The chancellor quickly jumped on a proposal by Hallstein that Germany take the initiative on the German question. He must have been thinking along the same lines already, for he quickly dictated to his aides the rough draft of a letter that he wanted delivered to Dulles, the chairman of the tripartite conference.[21] Reflecting the 10 June statement of the federal government on the question of

German reunification,[22] the letter proposed that a "four power conference concerning the German question should meet in autumn at the latest." The coincidence of the conference and the German elections hardly needs to be mentioned. The conference would come after the elections, but the public would go to the polls knowing that a conference was coming soon.

Adenauer boldly went on to lay out the basis for the discussion at a conference to which he was not invited. The first condition for a successful settlement was to be the holding of "free elections in all of Germany," the freedom of which was to be guaranteed by "international control"—there would be no trusting of the Soviets on this issue. The elections were to lead to the "formation of a free government for all of Germany."[23] A final peace treaty was to be concluded with this regime, and with this regime only. All outstanding territorial questions were to be settled by this treaty.

The next two points were particularly problematic, if the goal was actually to gain acceptance of this plan from the Soviets at a future quadripartite conference. First, almost as an afterthought, the chancellor advocated "the securing of the freedom of action for an all-German parliament." A seemingly unobjectionable proviso in and of itself, in the context of the reunification issue this was clearly meant to guarantee that the new government would have the freedom to continue its membership in the Western political-military alliance. *Westbindung* did not, in Adenauer's mind, exist merely to serve the end of reunification. While he proclaimed that unity with the West was the only route to reunification, he clearly intended that the government of the reunified Germany would continue the same policy. His next point makes it clear that this was in fact what he had in mind. "The European Defense Community," he insisted, should be the "point of departure for a security system which takes into account the security needs of all European peoples, including the Russian people."[24] No one could doubt the response of the Russians to such a proposal—and certainly not Adenauer, who assumed that the Soviet peace offensive was designed to derail progress toward EDC ratification.

But Adenauer was determined to submit this proposal for the consideration of the Western foreign secretaries. In doing so, he also demonstrated his desire to elbow his and the Federal Republic's way into a conference of the Powers. The chancellor insisted that Blankenhorn fly to Washington to deliver the missive personally. He lamely defended his decision in retrospect by pointing out that the Federal Republic's highest-ranking representative in Washington, Heinz Krekeler, did not hold the rank of ambassador, but was merely head of mission. Given Adenauer's proclivity for bypassing the "normal channels," this assertion is less than convincing. Nor did Blankenhorn, Adenauer's designated messenger, find the chancellor's directions to be advisable. "I fought strongly against these ideas," he confided to his diary, "because I knew well that a renewed appearance of my person in the background of this important conference would be gladly seen by none of the conference partners. It [his appearance in Washington at the time of the conference] would seem obtrusive [*aufdringlich*], it would also give rise to the impression that Germany intended to push its way into this conference."[25] Blankenhorn's arrival in Washington gave rise to just such an impression, because this was precisely what the German chancellor was seeking to do. Against Blankenhorn's protestations that he did not want to be the "uninvited guest at the table," Adenauer's response was curt: "It's no use. You have to go."[26]

Ronald J. Granieri, in his study *The Ambivalent Alliance*, rightly points to a certain cageyness in Adenauer's diplomatic methods. *Der Alte* had diplomatic objectives, to be sure. What was unsure was the leverage that Bonn could exert in the Western alliance, and particularly upon the Americans. As a result, he sought to insulate himself from possible rebuffs, and thus to protect the image of international influence that he cultivated at home. The secret Blankenhorn mission allowed him to test the limits of West German influence "without public embarrassment. Once he reached those limits, he adjusted his [public] statements to shape expectations."[27] In this way, Adenauer could use his high-profile diplomacy with the Western alliance to his political advantage, while suffering no disadvantage from the unavoidable limits imposed by the Federal Republic's position as a postulant rather than a full member of that congregation.

In Washington, Blankenhorn's reception was predictably cold. He met with James W. Riddleberger, the director of the State Department's German Affairs bureau. Riddleberger was, according to Blankenhorn, "deeply astounded by my visit, almost indignant." Conant had already given a thorough explication of Adenauer's wishes. But "then comes the special emissary with additional requests, which required additional decisions by the American government."[28] Blankenhorn, clearly embarrassed by his mission, nevertheless did what was expected of him. He delivered Adenauer's letter to Dulles, and stressed to Riddleberger the chancellor's fears "that the Soviets would make important moves to defeat him in the [September] election." He claimed to have information from the East SPD that Soviet High Commissioner V. S. Semyonov had been holding discussions with Moscow on just such a proposal.[29] Thus in discussions with both David Bruce and Riddleberger, Adenauer's emissaries presented the German proposal more as a requirement of *domestic* politics in the Federal Republic than as a proposal designed to overcome the international stalemate which left Germany divided. Blankenhorn emphasized in his discussion with Riddleberger that Adenauer's "whole position is in danger because of the prevalence of the idea that he is somewhat against German unification. Therefore, the chancellor must demonstrate his support of German unification and he would very much like to publish eventually the letter which he has addressed to the Secretary."[30] Riddleberger showed Blankenhorn a copy of the tripartite draft that the State Department planned on producing at the upcoming conference.[31] Blankenhorn emphasized that the declaration was "not strong enough to meet the problem of public opinion in Germany," which seemed to require an invitation to a four-power conference. Blankenhorn "emphasized that the Chancellor's proposal was a tactical move designed to improve his position in the election campaign and that our proposed declaration did not go far enough in meeting the problem that the Chancellor was not sincere in his desire for German unification [sic]."[32]

Thus, the Germans told Bruce and Riddleberger—and presumably Conant[33]—that Adenauer thought he needed to make this proposal now, before the Soviets beat him to the punch. The change in Adenauer's position on a four-power conference—from opposition to advocacy—seems to have been motivated by a sense of the inevitable. If he did not propose such a conference, the Soviets would. If he acted quickly, however, he could cast himself as a peacemaker in the coming election, while hopefully exerting some influence over the West's preparations for the conference. The latter consideration caused him to send Blankenhorn to Washington. In any event, the secretary of state had planned to issue a declaration very much along the lines adumbrated in Adenauer's letter. The 10 June resolution of the Bundestag, with its emphasis on free elections as the only possible basis for reunification, had been accepted by Washington prior to the convening of the conference. Whether the foreign ministers' conference would produce an invitation to the Soviets remained to be seen.

ASSESSMENTS AND POLITICS: THE SOVIET UNION, GERMANY, AND THE WASHINGTON CONFERENCE, 10–14 JULY, 1953

As the Western foreign ministers prepared to meet in Washington, news of a significant change in the Kremlin was filtering out. Lavrenti Beria, it seemed, was being ousted from the post-Stalin triumvirate which had ruled in Moscow since March. The reception of this news in the West was at least partially influenced by the widespread impression that Beria's advocacy of a looser imperial policy and negotiation with the West had contributed to his downfall.[34] In fact, the inclination to seek a settlement of the German Question had been rather broad within the Presidium, until the June uprisings brought the "New Course" idea to an end. Khrushchev and his allies then used the East German revolt in their purge of Beria, laying responsibility at his feet.[35] Much of this information comes from very recently available sources, none of which could have been known to the Western leadership.

At the very opening of the first plenary session of the foreign ministers' conference, Dulles raised the Beria purge as an issue which the ministers had to consider. On 10 July, the day before the official opening of the conference, *Pravda* reported that Beria had been stripped of his offices, and that the Supreme Court of the Soviet Union was going to look into charges against him. Dulles compared this development to the great purge of the 1930s, when Stalin had eradicated all opposition in a series of staged "trials." Dulles was unsure how the current Kremlin leaders could level "anti-foreign charges" at Beria—as Stalin had done to Trotsky and Nikolai Bukharin—and still reconcile those charges with their policy of a "peace offensive."[36] Dulles revealed that he did not see this particular situation, at least, in black-and-white terms. "If the past is any guide to the present," he offered, "we may have to anticipate some hardening, rather than a general softening, of Soviet policies." But he immediately added that "we should not count upon the future being a precise repetition of the events of fifteen years ago."[37]

Dulles's response to the Beria purge was no more "hard-line" than anyone else's at the time. In the West it was well known that Beria had advocated some greater degree of cooperation with the West than his rivals. Thus there was some reason to speculate that this had been a major reason for his ouster. Nor should his concern about the Beria purge be taken to mean that he was making more out of the issue than was warranted by the purge of a functionary who could not rival Khrushchev in the black arts of Kremlin infighting. "Beria's fall was to be the end of the first triumvirate," an event of no small significance, increasing as it did the "prestige and authority of Khrushchev, the organizer of the anti-Beria plot."[38] French Foreign Minister George Bidault echoed Dulles's concern and confusion about what recent events might mean. As far as the French knew, "there had been some enthusiasm in Russia for the new policy of moderation, but . . . more extreme elements felt that things had gone too far so brakes must be applied."[39]

The Acting Foreign Secretary of the United Kingdom, Lord Salisbury, also thought that "the bad results of the milder policy might have been responsible" for Beria's downfall. Then, too, "domestic considerations" may have played a role as well.[40] The general consensus among the three was, to use Salisbury's words, that the changes in the Soviet Union "should not . . . cause us to alter our policies."[41] This consensus meant that the West would proceed with the process of ratifying and then constructing EDC, as part of the broader plan for European unification. Up to this point, Adenauer's priorities conformed to those of the three Western powers. But differences in emphasis and timing arose between the French, British, and American representatives which, had the chancellor known of them, would undoubtedly have caused him concern.[42]

Adenauer's about-face on the question of the four-power talks was, as has been noted, a result largely of his assessment of the mood of the German electorate. Ironically, the British had also moved away from their advocacy of a quick quadripartite conference since May, due to similar considerations. Concerned that "immediate 4-power talks would provoke uncertainty in Germany which might impair Adenauer's chances" for re-election, Britain "as of today . . . was not pressing for talks on Germany." The British were still interested in talks, but did not want to press the issue, for fear of derailing German support for Adenauer.[43] The situation was almost comical: London and Bonn had switched roles, with Adenauer seeking to speed up the invitation to the Soviets in order to help himself domestically, and the British hoping to slow the process down, in order not to hurt Adenauer domestically.

The Anglo-German disagreement centered on the issue of timing, and the conflict was not irreconcilable.[44] In the end, the British agreed to issue an invitation to the Soviets *before* the elections to a meeting to be held some weeks *after* the elections. From the beginning, Salisbury had no objection to making an announcement that "4-power talks would be held when practicable." Dulles told his French and British counterparts of the letter which Adenauer had sent, and of the German's desire that a four-power meeting should be announced for the autumn. Salisbury continued to believe that any announcement of a meeting with the Russians which was made prior to the September Federal Republic elections would hurt Adenauer, and added that he did not think that a meeting should be held with the Russians prior to the integration of the German military into EDC. Were a meeting to be held before this occurred, London feared that the Soviets would use the conference as a means of destroying EDC by presenting a plan for German unification which prohibited German integration into the Western security apparatus.[45] In such a manner, the Soviets could attain their desired goals—killing EDC, preventing German remilitarization and alliance with the West, and derailing West European integration—without paying any price themselves.

Bidault and the French disagreed and said so. The French foreign minister was convinced that "a 4-power conference was the only way to prove to the French people the necessity for the EDC."[46] He did not say why, but his statements of the previous day shed some light on his thinking. Bidault had implied on 10 July that public opinion, and not foreign office wishes, would determine the timing of a four-power conference. The Frenchman, while admitting that delaying such a meeting "might be advantageous to the West," noted that these were not "the days of Metternich. . . . Because of the strong pressures in Western Europe for having these talks and because it was difficult to continue with rearmament of the West until all possibilities had been exhausted in this field, we should talk with the Russians." Bidault clearly did not want to put EDC before the French Assembly if he could not make the case to the French public that the government had first made a serious attempt to discuss the European situation with the Soviets.

There were dangers in this approach, and Bidault was quick to point them out. Particularly troubling was that a face-to-face meeting with the Soviets would make obvious the "abyss" that lay "between Adenauer's five points and the Russian view." But the "psychological attraction" of four-power talks outweighed the disadvantages to the West of holding such talks prior to EDC ratification. In fact, the "political-military integration of Germany into the West will not be accepted until the Soviets are faced squarely across the table and it is evident that a solution cannot be reached by negotiation." Had he been so inclined, the foreign minister might have added that German integration would not be accepted *by the French* until a meeting with the Soviets had occurred. Dulles, however, was not sympathetic toward the French, who were moving much more slowly on this issue than other Western allies. The secretary was expecting relatively rapid progress on ratification in Brussels, Rome, and the Hague, all without any promises of a meeting with the Kremlin's leaders.[47]

What was one to make of the French argument? In a sense, Bidault was taking the same line as Adenauer, namely, for domestic political reasons it was necessary to call a quadripartite meeting in the near future. So far, so good. But Adenauer's interest in a Western meeting with the Soviets was clear as crystal: he wanted to present himself to the West German electorate as a peacemaker interested in reunification. As he made clear in his letter to Dulles—and just about everywhere else[48]—the German chancellor was committed to the ratification of EDC. No doubt Bidault, when speaking of the "abyss" which separated Bonn and Moscow, had in mind the problems of reunification, the timing of elections, composition of a provisional government, and so forth. Still, the West German determination to enter the Western security community via EDC widened the gulf considerably. Adenauer's commitment to EDC was strong, and Adenauer wanted to smuggle the defense pact into four-power discussions as the basis for a Europe-wide security arrangement.

The French commitment to EDC was, on the other hand, always subject to doubt,[49] and with good reason, as it turned out. Paris's reasons for desiring a meeting with the Soviets in the near future were bound to raise concern. One had always to suspect that the French were looking for a way to avoid ratifying the defense pact, and thus acquiescing in the rearmament of Germany. Dulles harbored these concerns and suspicions, and sought clarification of the French position. Dulles asked Bidault if he had said "that such talks [with the Soviets] might demonstrate that radical solutions such as the EDC were not necessary, or rather that the failure of such a meeting

to produce results would show that EDC was essential." Bidault replied
that the Soviets might, at a future conference, "make tempting proposals"
regarding Germany—exactly what Adenauer feared would occur. Yet the
foreign minister denied that he was "attempting to find excuses for abandoning European integration." This seemed to satisfy Dulles, who assumed
that the French "would not go into [a four-power meeting] with the idea
that the EDC was up in the air."[50] This was no minor point. The United
States, like Germany, viewed EDC as an integral step toward European
unification, an achievement valuable both in and of itself,[51] and for the
contribution that it would make toward containment.[52] Immerman summarizes the president's view of Western collective security in stark language:
"The alternative to collective security was nuclear holocaust." Thus, the
United States had to focus on strengthening the Western alliance, in terms
of military ability, alliance unity, and morale.[53]

Thus the intricate interplay between East-West détente and European integration—manifested, respectively, by a four-power meeting and
EDC—came to be a central point in allied discussions. As indicated by the
above discussion of the Powers' conflicting positions on the question of
chronology—that is, should a quadripartite conference precede or follow
EDC ratification—the issue of timing was considered important in all three
capitals, and Bonn as well, for reasons of domestic politics in France and
in the German Federal Republic. With regard to France, the three foreign
ministers could do little. Washington and London sought, for more than a
year after the Washington conference, to placate the French on the question
of EDC and German rearmament, all to no avail. In the end, a four-power
foreign ministers meeting occurred before the French Assembly considered
EDC, just as Bidault had advocated. The Assembly nevertheless rejected the
defense community.

West German domestic politics, however, was a very different matter.
Faced with the prospect of Adenauer's loss to the Socialists in September,
the Western allies resolved to use the question of a conference with the
Soviet Union as a campaign device to help ensure Adenauer's re-election.
This is what Adenauer had asked of them. This had motivated him to send
Blankenhorn to Washington. And there is no question that he exerted an
influence. Ironically, by stressing his own weakness—his allegedly shaky
electoral prospects—he was able to exert a far greater influence on allied
deliberations than had his re-election been a foregone conclusion.

That Washington wanted Adenauer's re-election is generally assumed.
What has been less clear until now is the extent to which the Eisenhower
administration was willing to go to help Adenauer prevail in September.
Officially neutral toward the results of the coming election, the administration was in fact anything but disinterested, and sought to engage in collu-
sion with the Christian Democrats to aid them in their re-election bid. The

administration was willing to enmesh itself secretly in domestic, partisan politics in Bonn, in order to see its candidate through to victory.[54]

On 18 July, 1953, Otto Lenz, chairman of the CDU foreign policy committee, reported to Adenauer an interesting conversation which "friendly" sources—whom Lenz does not identify—recently had with Conant. The high commissioner told Lenz's source that his instructions from Washington were "in every respect to do everything which could be done on the American side, in order to assure a victory by Adenauer in the election." Conant then asked "which sort of measures on his [the American] side would likely have a favorable effect, whether for example new concessions in the war criminals question or whatever." "I would be grateful to you," Conant continued, "if you would perhaps name for me—completely informally and privately—. . . some points or measures which appear possible and desirable for the American side in the sense of supporting the position of the chancellor."[55] In other words, the United States was putting the American office of the high commission at the disposal of the Christian Democrats' re-election campaign. Conant's instructions were to find out ways that HICOM could help Adenauer's election prospects, and then to use the high commission to advance this purpose.

Two days later, the chancellor responded to Lenz. Adenauer already knew that Conant had received "other instructions," but he does not make clear how he knew this, or whether the proposition had already been put to him. Tersely, the chancellor informed Lenz that the war criminals question was already being dealt with, and that he wanted the high commission to deal with labor legislation. It would be a benefit to him if this matter were "taken care of as soon as possible."[56] If this did not seem like much to ask, one must keep in mind that, more than anything else, Adenauer wanted Washington to invite the Soviets to a conference. This, as we shall see, he received. What is significant is the extent to which the Eisenhower administration was willing to go in its support of the chancellor.

This interest in materially affecting the outcome of the German elections was clearly visible in discussions at the Washington foreign ministers conference, and no one made any attempt to hide this fact. On 13 July, Dulles suggested that the foreign ministers turn their attention to the invitation to the Soviets. The importance of positively affecting German and French public opinion seems to have convinced Salisbury to drop his objections to this invitation. Again, Dulles made it quite clear that he was glancing with one eye at the September German elections. After the ministers had cleared the note with their governments, Dulles thought that the draft "should then be sent to Chancellor Adenauer to make certain that it would be helpful to him in his present political situation." For this reason, Dulles suggested that the publication of the invitation to the Kremlin might be delayed for three or four days after the end of the conference.

Bidault objected to this delay, ostensibly because the invitation was the only truly new result of the conference. He "could not go back after these lengthy talks in Washington and present something to his government which represented only affirmation of a constant policy, and not something new and constructive." He pointedly added that failure to bring something "new and constructive" back with him to Paris would further damage the chances of EDC ratification. Dulles saw no reason why the text might not be sent to Adenauer "immediately," with the caveat that "slight changes" might later be made to it. This would obviate the need to delay its issuance. Dulles refused, however, to acquiesce to Salisbury's request that the invitation be ambiguous as to the level of the proposed conference. The secretary insisted that the note make clear that the "the U.S. could not agree to extending an invitation for a four-power meeting except in terms of a Foreign Ministers' meeting." He commented that President Eisenhower "will not attend a meeting to discuss such matters as Germany and Austria." Clearly, Eisenhower wanted to see some evidence of progress on these issues at the ministerial level before committing himself to a summit, for Dulles quickly added that Washington was not ruling out a future summit, if the foreign ministers meeting "produc[ed] results which would justify a higher level meeting."[57]

By 14 July, Adenauer had already been informed of the contents of the invitation by the British high commissioner, Sir Ivone Kirkpatrick,[58] as well as by Blankenhorn, who had remained in Washington for the duration of the conference, and was informed of developments by Riddleberger.[59] Adenauer once again took the opportunity to inject himself into the conference proceedings, making it clear that he wanted the allies to act in a way that would aid his electoral prospects. It was important to Adenauer that the Western powers issued an invitation to the Soviets anticipating a quadripartite conference. It was equally vital that the West German electorate recognized that Adenauer played a significant role in this decision. Hence, "for electoral reasons" he suggested that the communiqué make clear that the proposal had Adenauer's support and that it indicate that this decision had been taken " 'in consultation with the German Federal Government' rather than 'after consultation,'" as the communiqué had initially read. Adenauer hoped this wording would imply a greater level of German involvement in the decision-making process. The wording of the communiqué was altered accordingly. Adenauer also objected to the proposed conference date of 15 September. Coming only days after the German election, a mid-September conference would not give him enough time, said the chancellor, to form his cabinet before the conference began. The allies agreed to retain rather more vague wording in the communiqué—the conference was to take place, according to that document, in "early autumn."[60]

How should one assess the Adenauer-Blankenhorn intervention in the Washington foreign ministers' conference? For his part, the chancellor viewed this odd episode in diplomatic history as an unmitigated success. He noted in his memoirs that his letter "had an active effect on the course of the conference. . . . The final result was that all three foreign ministers agreed upon the claims [*Forderungen*] which were contained in my letter."[61] One might add the caveat that Adenauer—clearly impressed by his own success at shaping the results of a conference to which he had not been invited—tended to overstate the extent to which his letter had caused an about face in mid-July. At the 31 July meeting of the CDU leadership, the chancellor proclaimed that "at the Washington conference, no one wanted a four-power conference. . . . But Dulles then made his [Adenauer's] letter known and decided in favor of the four-power conference."[62] This was hardly the case. In fact, *no one* had been opposed to the convening of such a conference, and Bidault had stressed in Washington that a conference ought to come sooner rather than later. Adenauer exerted influence primarily on the question of timing. This, however, was no small feat. Because the three foreign ministers tended to downplay the likelihood of successfully resolving the German Question at a four-power conference—Bidault, for example, thought that holding four-power talks with the Soviets soon would quickly "demonstrate the impossibility of this approach" as a solution to the German problem[63]—timing became quite important. The West sought to send a signal by means of the invitation, and the chronology of a quadripartite meeting and EDC ratification was an important part of that signaling.

What is perhaps most significant is the role that considerations of Adenauer's own political future played in the discussions of the timing question. It is impossible to know whether French interest in an early conference with Moscow would have carried the day had Adenauer not intervened with a call of his own for an autumn conference. In any event, the participants in the Washington conference reacted favorably to Adenauer's ideas, if not to the means by which he chose to advance them. Adenauer intervened in the conference with the claim that the foreign ministers' actions would concretely affect the CDU/CSU chances for re-election. The foreign ministers then proceeded to debate the invitation to the Kremlin in exactly these terms. Most important, as we have seen, was Dulles's championing of Adenauer's cause by unabashedly advocating steps which would aid the chancellor in his bid for a second term of office. In this manner, Adenauer was clearly able to influence the actions of his Great Power allies on a question of vital importance to both his country and his government. That he was able to do so essentially by playing upon his own alleged domestic weakness is one of the ironies of alliance diplomacy.[64]

Adenauer was pleased with the results of Blankenhorn's mission, describing them in terms of purely domestic politics. "My step had worked excellently," he later recalled. "Henceforth we had the official resolution of the three foreign ministers: A four-power conference in the autumn. That was a resolution which just knocked the wind out the SPD, since they constantly accused the federal government of hindering a four-power conference."[65] Even Adenauer's reluctant messenger, Herbert Blankenhorn, wrote in his diary that the Western offer to the Soviets was "unobjectionable."[66] On this question, Adenauer had achieved his purpose and helped himself significantly.

The second issue on which Adenauer attempted to exert his influence was EDC. Specifically, he sought to make sure that any agreement with the Soviets on the question of European security would be an *addition*, not an *alternative*, to EDC. This formulation, the chancellor observed, was at first difficult for London, Paris, and Washington to understand. Yet they came, in the course of the conference, to understand what Adenauer had in mind.[67] Implicit in this description of events is the chancellor's presumption that, once the allies understood what he wanted, they gave it to him.

Occam's razor, however, helps to clarify the question of Adenauer's influence on the EDC question at the Washington conference. The Americans, and Dulles in particular, were so strongly committed to the defense community that had Blankenhorn never been dispatched, the conference would no doubt have affirmed the Western commitment to EDC.[68] "There was total unanimity of opinion between Dulles and Eisenhower . . . on the question of the rearmament of Germany," and the need for EDC, as R. F. Ivanov rightly concludes in what is up to this point the only full biography of Eisenhower from the Russian side. James McAllister discerns a relevant nuance that does not, however, contradict Ivanov's strong description of administration commitment to EDC. The two Americans had differing reasons for this commitment to EDC: Dulles wanted to rearm West Germany in a context that would place limits on German power. Eisenhower wanted a militarily strong Western Europe that could do without a large American troop presence.[69] But both president and secretary perceived the need to establish EDC as the framework for the German contribution to the defense of the West.

The impact of the German intervention on this issue at the Washington conference can thus fairly be called negligible, the Germans having argued for a position which was never in question. As we shall see, it was only as French and German priorities came more clearly into conflict that the United States found it necessary to decide between Germany and France. For the present, all were agreed that EDC ought to be ratified, even if French agreement came with qualifications.

RUSSIAN RESPONSES AND GERMAN VOTES

As 1953 wore on, and as the German election approached, the Eisenhower administration continued to evince its interest in both the Federal Republic and in the Adenauer government. The partisan preference bestowed upon the Union parties by the free world's leading power did not escape the notice of the German opposition. Conant informed Dulles on 27 July that "[t]he German reaction to the U.S. is at the present heavily conditioned by the forthcoming election." (The high commissioner failed to note the irony that the reverse was also the case.) What was this response? The response from the Social Democrats was predictable. "The S.P.D. leaders," Conant informed the Secretary, "cannot help regretting the obvious fact that the U.S. Government had taken actions which help Adenauer's election and some are inclined to be bitter on this point. Comments by American newspaper correspondents to the effect that the United States is actively assisting Adenauer's campaign by such means as insisting on postponing any four-power conference until late September may have intensified [this] feeling." Adenauer, while not broadcasting the American offer to use HICOM to help him gain votes, was nevertheless "not worried about the possibility that the opposition will throw in his face the fact that he is clearly the candidate favored by both the British and American Governments." HICOM was "officially, of course, doing all we can here to preserve neutrality in this campaign."[70] Conant's choice of adverb here is instructive. "Officially," the Eisenhower administration had to remain neutral. In reality it slanted its foreign policy in ways that helped the chancellor.

The desire to keep Adenauer in office was rooted in the conviction that Adenauer, better than anyone else on the scene in Bonn, would carry out policies which Washington thought vital to European security and development. Personal regard for the chancellor most likely played little role in American considerations. Adenauer's bumptiousness at the time of the Washington conference did not earn him any friends. And the vaunted Dulles-Adenauer relationship had not yet blossomed—though given the personalities of these two statesmen, it is highly unlikely that either would have allowed friendship to interfere with calculations of national interest.

Thus it was a harmony of thought on concrete policy questions, rather than personalities, which lay at the root of American attraction to Adenauer and the Union coalition. Eisenhower and Dulles put the highest priority upon European integration in all of its possible permutations: economic, political, and military.[71] These three, in fact, went hand-in-hand, for economic integration would curb Germany's independent war-making capacity, while military integration, via EDC, would foster political cooperation. Integration meant security against a revival of German militarism, as well as against Soviet expansionist aims. A precondition for the successful integration of Western Europe was significant reconciliation between Bonn and Paris. The administration considered the current initiatives to be the best manner for achieving integration, particularly since they originated with the often hesitant French themselves. And they saw in Adenauer a German who shared their commitments.

This assumption was correct. Adenauer was committed to European integration, in part for the same reasons as Eisenhower and Dulles, in part for his own reasons. "Cooperation on the joining together of the European nations" was the self-declared "central element [*Kernstück*] of the first Federal Government's efforts in foreign policy."[72] The impetus, of course, came from Adenauer, whose desire for European unity was traceable to a complex of personal, historical, and strategic reasons which all pointed him toward the West. The westward orientation of the Rhineland was an article of faith for Cologne's longtime mayor. So too was the conviction that Germany—or at least West Germany—must place herself squarely in the camp of the *"christliches Abendland,"* the Christian West. This was all well and good from the point of view of Washington. But Eisenhower and Dulles were more impressed by Adenauer's unanimity with them on a more concrete, realpolitik basis. Helga Haftendorn, though writing more broadly about West German–American relations, describes the Adenauer-Eisenhower dynamic quite well: "For the West German sector [*Teilstaat*], close relations with the U.S.A. became a 'reason of state.' In return for the promise of military protection Washington expected burden sharing and accommodation to its guidelines."[73]

Briefly, Adenauer's longing for a unified Europe was traceable, first and foremost, to his perception that only by the integration of Western Europe would it be possible to stave off Soviet expansionism.[74] The Americans agreed completely. Adenauer also understood that European integration meant, first of all, a break with the historically antagonistic relations between Germany and France. Due to France's understandable "security complex," this step in turn meant that whatever German military forces would arise in the future must be put under credible restraints[75]—which for Adenauer, Eisenhower, and Dulles was another way of saying that EDC must be passed. For Adenauer, the Franco-German relationship was central to the whole plan. For this reason Adenauer bore considerable domestic pressure—including attacks from within his government—in order to placate French sensitivities on the Saar question.[76] If Berlin had not been able to establish good relations with France, Bonn would give it a try.

The Eisenhower administration's commitment to this aspect of Adenauer's foreign policy agenda reinforced its desire to see the Union defeat the Social Democrats. Washington was convinced that the SPD opposed these goals, and that their coming to power would undermine the very basis of America's security policy. The Social Democrats had lost their redoubtable leader, Kurt Schumacher, in August of the previous year. Schumacher had survived imprisonment and torture at the hands of the Nazis, and had emerged, physically broken but spiritually unbowed, as the most impressive spokesman of German socialism. His low regard for Adenauer was not reciprocated: Adenauer recognized in him a worthy, if totally mistaken, adversary. He knew Schumacher's socialism was of a nationalist, and not a Soviet, kind.[77]

But the differences between the two on international policy were legion, and provoked severe disputes. Schumacher, motivated above all by his nationalism, sought in his last years to press the issue of German reunification, as opposed to European union. His nationalism brought with it a strong aversion to rapprochement with Paris, which wanted, as far as he could tell, to "keep Germany down, to paralyze it, to make it impotent."[78] Attempts to tie Germany to such a questionable ally came, furthermore, at the price of a hardening of the division of Germany.

In this sense, Schumacher missed a rather significant, and quite valid, point recently raised by B. V. Petelin. "Adenauer's critics have called his German-Policy 'empty chatter.'" But Adenauer's approach to the Saar question supports a contrary interpretation. "Where it was possible, Adenauer strove for results in the matter of unification of the country." The return of the Saar to West Germany was a significant result, it meant progress toward the unity and integrity of the German state, and "it is unlikely that this event would have occurred without his participation."[79] Adenauer's policy of *Westbindung* was bringing results for German unification in the only realm where the chancellor thought results could be had.

But cultural factors, and not just diplomatic issues, played a significant role in Schumacher's critique of Adenauer's expansive approach to *Westbindung*. His socialism and Protestantism significantly influenced his thinking on the government's foreign policies. A union between Germany, France, and the Benelux states meant that the western *Länder* would find themselves increasingly integrated into a conservative, capitalist-oriented, and Roman Catholic–dominated community of states. This was Schumacher's dreaded "Europe of the four Cs:" conservatism, capitalism, clericalism, and cartels. Rather, he wished to look northward, to Protestant lands and an economic "middle way"—a policy doomed from the start by lack of interest on the part of the United Kingdom and the Nordic countries.[80]

Schumacher's successor, Erich Ollenhauer, was simply not a leader of the caliber of Schumacher.[81] He did not, moreover, share Schumacher's contempt for any whisper of German neutralism—the western hobgoblin—and his party moved increasingly toward the idea of a collective security system which would include the Soviet Union.[82] The CDU, on the other hand, rejected neutralism outright in its campaign, adopting as one of its campaign slogans "Germany, social *Rechtsstaat* [state under the rule of law] in the united Europe."[83] The Allies naturally felt sympathetic toward the

CDU. Adenauer was aware of the benefits he gained from the Allies' positive disposition toward him, and he wanted to make the most of it.

He expressed this awareness on 15 July, at a meeting with the federal CDU leadership. Adenauer told his colleagues that the Allied insistence, at Washington, upon EDC and upon the "political community of Europe . . . absolutely contradicts" the SPD's position. That London, Paris, and Washington repudiated the foreign policy conceptions of his domestic opposition was, according to Adenauer, "the great positive result of this conference"—more important, apparently, than the French commitment to press ahead with EDC. The Washington conference, he continued, was "exactly and very clearly" in line with the positions which the Union had been advocating up to that point. The result was that "we can, in the entire area of foreign policy, chalk it all up to us as a coalition, and the Social Democratic party, on the other hand can chalk nothing at all up to themselves." Washington showed clearly that "there is no other foreign policy" than that pursued by the government.[84] Unlike Schumacher and the early West German socialists, Adenauer viewed rapprochement and integration with Germany's western neighbors—and especially France—as an "aim and purpose" of Bonn's diplomacy. Under Adenauer, the Union Parties argued that the cultivation of closer ties with the Western democracies could eventually return to Germany the status of an equal partner. The socialists, on the other hand, sought equality and unification as a precondition for European integration. This was a significant difference indeed.[85]

The German Socialists were not alone in sensing an increased coziness between Washington and Bonn. The French, too, had noted the shift. But American favoritism toward the governing party in Bonn registered in Paris as a shift in favor of Germany vis-à-vis France. On 30 July, C. Douglas Dillon, the American ambassador to Paris, went to the Elysee Palace for tea with President Vincent Auriol. Dillon had brought his father along to meet Auriol, no doubt expecting a quiet exchange of chat and pleasantries. Instead, Dillon's father found out how difficult the job of an ambassador can sometimes be. Upon the Dillons' arrival, President Auriol "launched immediately into a lengthy and quite violent diatribe on the German question." Clearly, the Eisenhower administration's spirited advocacy of EDC, and thus of German rearmament, was causing profound anguish in Paris. Auriol felt the need to intervene. He reminded Dillon, "at some length," of the suffering that German militarism had inflicted upon the French. The president then observed with regret:

> that the U.S. was at present apparently favoring Germany over France, and that this policy was hurting the French very deeply. I [Dillon] explained that this was most certainly not the case, that while we were obviously interested in

helping the Germans stand up to the Soviets, and while we felt that Germany must be integrated as a part of Western Europe, we very definitely did not favor Germany over France.

Auriol was not convinced by American intervention in the last two wars with Germany. America's "present policy certainly gave the appearance of being oversoft toward Germany, if not actually favoring her against France." This, the president added, "was certainly not good for Franco-American relations." Dillon came away from the meeting convinced that Auriol had wanted his sentiments to be reported back to Washington.[86] Dillon obliged. But the fact remained that a fundamental cleavage was opening between Washington and Paris on the issue of the means, timing, and extent of German rearmament. And since both states viewed the question as inextricably intertwined with vital national security interests—European integration, including military integration, had become "a sort of dogma with the Republican administration," in the assessment of one French scholar[87]—the split was bound to grow. A dressing-down delivered to a diplomat could not bridge the gap.

Almost lost in all of this wrangling was the fact that the Washington conference had produced a note, made known to the Kremlin on 15 July, which proposed a four-power conference to deal with the German question. The Soviet response came in the form of a pair of notes sent to the United States, Britain, and France, on 4 August and 15 August, respectively. The Soviets did not reject the idea of a meeting with the three powers of the West. But Moscow indicated, in the first note, a reluctance to participate in a conference limited to the question of German reunification. The Kremlin, rather, thought it advisable for a foreign ministers' conference to be convened, which "considered the question of measures which promote a general lessening of tension in international relations, including questions of reduction of armaments and the impermissibility of foreign military bases on territory of other states." Given the significance for world peace of an Asian settlement, Moscow thought it wise to include the People's Republic of China in the discussions. One must be rather imaginative to think of conditions which Washington would have found less appealing.

The Soviets then went on take a subtle—for them—swipe at the German chancellor. As stated above, Adenauer had pressed for wording in the Washington communiqué which indicated that the decisions made had been taken "in consultation with" him. Too bad, said the Kremlin. The West's proposal for internationally supervised elections throughout Germany was "humiliating" for the Germans. The West's plan for German reunification was a nonstarter. "If all this is conducted in agreed consultation with the Bonn Government," the 4 August note continued, "then this can only destroy completely the confidence of the German people in such a government."

Despite all of this, however, the Soviets indicated that they attached great importance to German reunification. For that reason they proposed a foreign ministers' conference, which would: (a) consider the broader question of measures designed to lessen "tensions in international relations"; and (b) consider the questions of German unity and a German peace treaty, as well as a state treaty for Austria. Overall, the tone of the note was milder than usual. Some elements, furthermore, pointed to the possibility of negotiated settlement. Perhaps, then, this note indicated a certain amount of Soviet flexibility.

The second note was harsher in tone, and one cannot help but conclude that it was meant to influence the thinking of the West German electorate, set to vote in three weeks. The Kremlin stressed the need for a German peace treaty, and the insincerity of the Western powers which claimed to seek reunification of Germany, while propounding policies meant to solidify Germany's division. The note's authors blame America in particular. Washington was seeking to militarize the Federal Republic to turn West Germany "into a weapon for the implementation of the plans of [the Western] bloc." The conclusion was obvious: the Western powers and Adenauer were colluding on a policy designed to keep Germany "divided into parts for many years." American calls for free elections did not fool Moscow.

The Soviet condemnation of Adenauer could not have been stronger. The Adenauer government, which claimed partial parenthood of the 15 July note:

> serves the interests of the greatest capitalist monopolies of Western Germany, [it] more and more unleashes the hands of yesterday's Hitlerites and open fascists for the suppression of German democratic forces, [it] represents the mouthpiece of extreme German nationalists and revanchists, who are striving for the rebirth of German militarism for new and aggressive wars.

One may be forgiven, then, for being surprised by the Kremlin's conclusion that peace and unity for Germany could come only by means of the merger of this neo-Hitlerite parliament with that of the German Democratic Republic for the purpose of forming a provisional government. This, nevertheless, is what the 15 August note suggests. To this end, the Soviets proposed the convocation of a conference of the powers and representatives of both Germanies—including, apparently, the militaristic Nazi revanchists—within six months' time.[88]

The reaction to the first note can justly be called "mixed," with a certain optimism prevailing in Washington and skepticism in Bonn. Blankenhorn claimed to see in the first note a clear attempt "to drive a wedge between the United States on one side and Great Britain and France on the other side." The more moderate tone of the note was directed to play on the sentiments of the British, as expressed by Churchill in May. Meanwhile, dire warnings concerning EDC were meant to play to a broad audience in France.[89] Many French shared the Soviet fears of German rearmament. Adenauer in his memoirs describes the first Soviet response to the 15 July note as "positive in principle." He notes, however, the problem caused by Soviet wishes to invite Chinese participation.[90]

In Washington, one of the administration's coldest of Cold Warriors was busy trying to make sense of the Soviet position. C. D. Jackson was one of the initial skeptics with regard to the Soviet "new course." But the first Soviet note had caught his interest. He reported to Dulles that the Soviets seemed to him to have undermined their bargaining position through their brutality in Berlin. Now, they were forced to accept the West's "principle of a four power proposal" as the framework for dealing with the outstanding conflicts in Europe. Certainly, they hoped to use the opportunity to play off desires for reunification against plans for EDC and rearmament. The Soviet note nevertheless "is sufficiently serious and plausible to make a reply of ours which simply referred them back to the previous notes, and did not move a little forward, at least by intimation, appear arbitrary and unimaginative if we are really sincere in our expressed desire for a German and Austrian solution." As Jackson saw it, the Soviet note "calls for our most thoughtful reconsideration of our German position. . . . Does it have to be EDC, unification, free elections or else?" To continue insisting on all of these terms from the Soviets was tantamount to seeking "unconditional surrender." That was not the way to go, if one wanted results. To impose such a situation on the Soviets was just fine with Jackson, "if we really have the leverage to bring it about. But we haven't, and they know it." In lieu of total victory, perhaps there was an "acceptable interim move."[91]

But the search for middle ground did not in any way imply that American commitment to the Adenauer government was to be attenuated. Jackson reported that he had seen a cable "from Germany saying Adenauer hoped we would not be too hasty in our reply, in order to avoid the possibility of upsetting his election apple cart." For that reason, Jackson recommended that the United States follow Russia's lead of delaying its reply "to show that we have our pride too." Were the administration to do this, "the reply could easily be postponed until after the German election."[92] The reply was not delayed this long, however. In a note sent to the Soviets on 2 September—just five days before the election—the United States reiterated its invitation to the Soviets to participate in a conference. The note emphasized the need to "concentrate in the first instance" on free elections in Germany. The other goal of the conference was to make progress on Austria. Hence, the United States made no significant new demands in this note.[93] Nothing contained in the note, it would seem, could upset Adenauer's "apple cart."

Both in America and in Germany, the second of the Soviet notes played to a tougher audience. Washington and Bonn noted the harsh tone and apparent inflexibility. Acting Secretary of State Walter Bedell Smith contrasted the second note with the first. The 15 August note was, in his estimation, "directed at Germany," in an attempt to undermine support for EDC and to divide the West. Equally important, the second note "aims directly at influencing the Bundestag elections to Adenauer's detriment." Smith asked Conant to "check with Adenauer and informally with Ollenhauer to ascertain their positions" on these issues.[94]

The timing of the notes and responses, however, meant that final decision as to if and when a four-power conference would take place came after the West German elections. On Sunday, 6 September, Adenauer went to bed early after leaving instructions that he should be awakened at about half past seven the next morning.[95] Computer forecasting and sophisticated exit polling had not yet transformed election-day news. In the early fifties, one still had to wait for the votes to be counted. Von Eckardt phoned him the following morning. The news, as it turned out, was better even than the CDU's own polls had projected. The CDU/CSU had won over 45 percent of the votes cast, a colossal increase over the 31.2 percent that they had won in the 1949 election. More importantly, due to the intricacies of German election law, the Union Parties now had an absolute majority of the seats in the new Bundestag. There was now no question of the SPD—which had suffered a slight loss, and now held only 31 percent of the Bundestag mandates—derailing Adenauer's foreign policy by holding up treaties in the Bundestag.[96] The landslide confirmed in Adenauer's mind the correctness of his foreign policy. Buoyed, to the extent that he was capable, by his stunning victory, the chancellor told his audience at a reception in Bonn that evening that now "one does not have to speak of reunification, but rather of the liberation of the eastern territory."[97] Adenauer was never given to "agonizing reappraisals" of his decisions. Now he felt that he had external confirmation for his chosen course. He was, furthermore, well aware that the world had been closely watching Germany on 6 September. For their part, the new Soviet leadership was severely disappointed by the Union Parties' stunning victory.[98]

It is impossible to say how many votes Adenauer garnered through his foreign policy. There were other reasons for supporting the government, most notably the beginnings of the "economic miracle" that was to transform West Germany in the 1950s. But von Eckardt's assessment that Adenauer's foreign policy line brought "good, visible results" defies contradiction. As von Eckardt notes, Adenauer's pursuit of European integration, as well as his policy of *Westbindung*, "led the Federal Republic out of complete isolation in Europe and the world. The new state had, with modest limitations, won back its sovereignty."[99] Against this, the Social Democrats had little to offer but a resounding "*Nein!*" Then, too, the opposition claims that Adenauer was a tool of the Western allies did not stick.[100] Adenauer was aware that foreign policy had helped him domestically. He was also aware that his domestic victory could help him on the world stage. His now undeniable hold on the reins of government in West Germany made him a force to be reckoned with, and he was not the type to waste such an asset.

Dulles—who had abandoned all pretense of neutrality with regard to the election results days before the vote[101]—agreed that the election considerably increased Adenauer's standing in the West. The secretary told Conant, only two days after the election:

> Now that the election is over and [Adenauer] has won such a smashing victory, I imagine that his personal influence will be enhanced to a point where it will be very difficult—and perhaps undesirable—to deal with the German problem except on the basis of treating him as a full partner.

Yet it will not do to overstate the case. Adenauer's electoral triumph was not the philosopher's stone which could turn domestic support into an equal measure of international influence. By the middle of November, Dulles was still instructing Conant to press Adenauer—allegedly Dulles's "full partner"—to "give on the Saar until it hurts."[102] The election returns helped to ratify an existing trend in administration thinking. They did not drastically alter the course of American policy on Germany.

BERLIN: "THE BEST STALINIST TRADITION"

The anfractuous history of the notes exchanged between Washington and Moscow in the summer and fall of 1953 finally ended with an agreement to convene a foreign ministers' conference in Berlin on 25 January, 1954. Following Washington's wishes, the conference was to deal with German and Austrian affairs, and not the broad range of topics outlined by the Soviets in their August 1953 notes. Few assumed that the conference would produce final agreements on these two topics. Khrushchev's foreign affairs advisor, Oleg Troyanovsky, suggests in his memoirs that a "dead-end situation" had been the predictable result in Berlin on the German, Austrian, and collective-security problems. It was not on Central Europe, but on the Far East, that the diplomats in Berlin could hope for meaningful steps toward a negotiated settlement.[103]

On the American side Livingston T. Merchant, assistant secretary of state for European affairs, claimed after the conference that the "original assumption" of the American delegation was "that we would not get any progress on the German treaty, and that it was improbable that we would get the Austrian state treaty signed." For that reason, the purpose of the conference was "to sufficiently explore and expose and probe the Soviet position as to make plain to the world, and particularly to Western Europe public opinion, that the 'new look' since Stalin's death in Soviet policy [*sic*] was strictly cosmetic, that it didn't go any deeper than the skin."[104] Dulles echoed this assessment. Two days after the end of the conference, Adenauer came to Washington to hear the postmortem first hand. Dulles told Adenauer that America was aware that the chancellor had wanted the conference to demonstrate "that the Soviets were unwilling to compromise." Adenauer responded that Berlin had been "useful," since it had demonstrated that Western strength was the key to future negotiations with the Soviets.[105]

Yet despite their claims of cynicism, the Western delegates to Berlin had not anticipated the complete roadblock that Berlin became. On questions relevant to this study, no progress whatsoever was made during more than three weeks of meetings with the Soviet foreign minister and his entourage. And, despite coming "within an inch of an agreement on Austria,"[106] Soviet unwillingness to compromise on key points precluded agreement on the Austrian treaty. The barrenness of Berlin reinvigorated skeptics in the West, who saw the Soviet "new look" as hollow. Prospects for a détente looked worse in February 1954, than they had before the two blocs had sat down to talk with each other.[107]

Dulles officially expressed this disappointment in his closing remarks on the final day of the conference. The secretary said that he "cannot but record a large measure of regret. We have failed to satisfy the hopes which many throughout the world placed in us." The reason for this was clear. "We encountered a fundamental difference between the views of East and West."[108] That there was a "difference of views" could not have come as a surprise. That differences defied all attempts at rational compromise *was* a bit surprising. On numerous issues related to the German question, the Soviets simply asserted views which were unacceptable to the West—the FRG included.

First, the Soviets refused to accept the Western schedule for unification. The British proposed a "Plan for German Reunification in Freedom" on 29 January. This plan called for free elections as the first step toward the formation of an all-German government. The Soviets continued to resist holding elections before the formation of an interim government, and rejected the idea of strict international oversight of any elections that did occur. Eden's proposal, said Soviet Foreign Minister Molotov, "showed distrust of democratic forces and too much concern with supervision and preparations and carrying out of elections by foreign powers."[109]

Second, as hinted in the second of the August notes, the Soviets would not budge from their assertion that the Yalta and Potsdam agreements

should continue to be the model for the settlement of the German question. The West, and the United States in particular, rejected the application
of the principles of these wartime conferences. Things had changed too
much to insist upon the relevance of decisions reached eight or nine years
before.[110] On a related topic, the Soviets declared that the eastern border of
a reunified Germany had been set in Potsdam. The West was not willing to
settle this issue permanently until a peace treaty could be negotiated with
an all-German government.[111]

The Soviets, in addition, pressed repeatedly for the inclusion of the two
German governments in the conference. The West refused to be lured into
legitimating the GDR government. Inclusion of the Ulbricht regime, furthermore, could only delay any possible settlement.[112] The Soviet delegation also aimed severe attacks against German "militarism," and against
the "aggressive" EDC and NATO alliances. Yet Molotov was unable to
provide alternatives to these organs when asked repeatedly to do so by the
Western delegates.[113] The Soviets, finally, proposed a security agreement
for Europe which would implicitly have required an American retreat
from the continent, confining them to the "role of observers." Neither the
Americans nor the Western Europeans were willing even to consider an
American withdrawal.[114]

Nor is the above catalogue of disputes exhaustive. Disagreement on
the Austrian question also consumed a considerable amount of time.
The tripartite powers and the Soviets did agree on holding a five-power
conference—including China—later that year. But an agreement to hold
another conference provided little evidence that East and West could
settle their differences at meetings such as this. All the evidence seemed
to point in the opposite direction. As Dulles observed, the "fundamental
difference" between Soviet and Western positions on the German issue
were huge, and seemed unbridgeable.

The Soviets, it seemed to the American, British, and French participants,
had not altered their substantive positions since Stalin's death.[115] What was
new about the "new look" in Soviet policy was the affectation of amiability.
All three of the foreign ministers noticed this trend in Berlin. "Molotov,"
according to Dulles, "shows [an] obvious desire [to] appear reasonable
to [the] extent of making tactical concessions without substantive concessions."[116] Without substantive concessions, East and West could not settle
the German question. And they did not.

The immediate result of this failure was a reassessment in the West of
the new approach in Soviet foreign policy. Those who had shown some
willingness to give the Soviets the benefit of the doubt during the note
exchange now reconsidered their positions. C. D. Jackson, author of the
quite conciliatory August note to Dulles, thought that Berlin removed "all
question marks" regarding Soviet policy. Molotov, said Eisenhower's Cold

War policy adviser, "chose to take the most extreme position that could be taken." As a result, the Soviets set "absurd conditions for what they call relaxation of tensions." State Department Russian desk officers, assessing Jackson's letter for Dulles, agreed that the Soviet position in Berlin was "in accord with the best Stalinist tradition." The only change, they opined, was cosmetic.[117]

The response in Germany was the same. Adenauer told the press that Berlin demonstrated "that all of the reflections which were placed in the newspapers of various nations since Stalin's death concerning the end of the Soviet course [in foreign policy] were dreams, which did not correspond to reality."[118] Krone thought that Molotov had made clear at Berlin the Soviet Union's perfidious intentions. The Soviets demonstrated that reunification would occur only on their terms. This meant beginning with neutralization. "In the end, Germany was to become a satellite state." One thus had to maintain one's guard, and not be fooled into relaxing one's "mistrust and watchfulness" with regard to Soviet intentions.[119]

The German people had expected results, and were disappointed by the conference. Perhaps even Adenauer, who always maintained that he had expected nothing from the Soviets, shared in the "feeling of grief over the results." Grewe returned periodically to Bonn from Berlin to report to the chancellor about the conference. At one point, Adenauer lay down in a room next to his office, listening to Grewe's report with closed eyes. When Grewe was finished, Adenauer began to tell him of "his worries for the future of his people, for whom he had taken on the responsibility."[120]

Berlin produced no concrete results on issues affecting Germany. In the sense that it led to disillusionment with, and cynicism toward, the new Soviet diplomacy, one might even categorize the whole episode as counterproductive. Yet from the point of view of the West German–American relationship the upshot of Berlin was not so negative. Bonn was especially pleased that the Western allies had demonstrated unity in the face of Soviet pressure. Western unity, and thus Western strength, was always a key element in Adenauer's foreign policy. He interpreted Berlin as confirming both the appropriateness and the feasibility of the policy of strength and unity. Berlin, moreover, helped to dispel some of his Potsdam fears. The West had met with the Soviets, and refused to come to an agreement about Germany so long as a freely elected all-German government was not at the table. Equally as important, the American delegation consulted with representatives of the FRG government throughout the conference. The implication was clear: there would be no German settlement without German (i.e., Bonn's) input.

Even the French, about whom the "Chancellor of Worry" worried considerably, were not captivated by the Soviet proposals at Berlin. Bidault and his team saw in Molotov's concatenation of proposals an attempt to test the unity of the West, and to undermine the support of the French public for the EDC. In the former, the Russians failed. In the latter, however, they succeeded, at least to the extent that Bidault felt the need to clarify publicly that it had not been the EDC issue that prevented peace and reunification deals at Berlin. The problem, rather, was the poverty of the Kremlin's vision: They had offered nothing but the same tired formulas that the Western democracies had already rejected in Stalin's last year of life. Or, as the foreign minister himself put it: "One cannot break the bank with 50 kopeks." That, apparently, was the value of Molotov's proposals.[121]

Adenauer told reporters at his 19 February press conference that "something good" had come from Berlin. "That is the solidarity of the free West." According to the chancellor, "never before has western solidarity manifested itself so clearly, never before has [Western unity] thus withstood—so honorably withstood—the temptations of Soviet Russia."[122] Merchant likewise indicates in his notes from Berlin that the "Big 3 unity of delegations [was] greatly reinforced. Worked together + held common front."[123] Both Bonn and Washington were pleased by the unity displayed by the allied delegations.

Just as important to the Germans was the extent of German participation at the margins of the conference. As indicated earlier, the Western powers refused to allow direct German participation at Berlin. The Americans, however, initiated the practice of inviting German observers to come to the conference location, and to consult with the American delegation on questions that directly affected Germany. Dulles himself was instrumental in this decision, for policy and—he claimed—personal reasons. Dulles did not believe "that an arrangement which is imposed upon the Germans against their will, which made them into a second-rate country, would be in the interest of peace." While Adenauer remembered Potsdam, Dulles was haunted by an older conference. "I have one such effort slightly on my conscious [conscience?] as a result of my participation in the Treaty of Versailles, and I don't want to have the second one." Thus on his watch decisions regarding Germany would be made in consultation with the freely elected German rulers in Bonn. "Germany is not technically a member of this [Berlin] conference. . . . But the views of Chancellor Adenauer which will be fully reported to us here will also carry great weight."[124]

Adenauer's views were to be reported to the Americans by Blankenhorn and Grewe. On a daily basis, the Germans received reports from the American delegation.[125] Blankenhorn and Grewe also met with members of the Western delegations on a frequent basis to present Bonn's position on allied proposals affecting Germany. In particular, the Germans met several times with the "tripartite working group," composed of high-level representatives of the three powers, including State Department counselor Douglas MacArthur II. Adenauer had no bombshells to drop, as he had the previous summer. But his representatives were nevertheless at the conference, consulting with the allies and making sure that Bonn's voice was heard.

The result of Blankenhorn's and Grewe's efforts was often relatively minor changes to a proposed Western draft.[126] Yet the Germans were not complaining. Grewe himself summarized the real significance of the FRG's active participation in Western deliberations at Berlin. "The very inclusion of a German representative meant something new," in contrast with the occupation, during which the three Western powers had faced the Germans as a unit. But the West was seeking to make Germany a partner, and perforce could no longer treat the Germans as one would treat a defeated enemy. Grewe noted this change in the tone of the discussions with the tripartite representatives. "I was accepted completely as a partner to the discussions; the barriers of the occupation mentality . . . disappeared more and more."[127]

The contrast with the Washington conference was there for all to see. At Washington, the Germans had to elbow their way into the conversation. At Berlin, they were invited guests. The West still denied Bonn a full place at the table, but only because of divided Germany's peculiar situation. Adenauer and his nation could now claim to be significant, if junior, partners of the American superpower. Things had changed so much in such a short time.

NOTES

1. Zubok, *Failed Empire*, 88–89.

2. Leffler, *For the Soul of Mankind*, 148.

3. The starting point for any investigation of the 1953 East German crisis is Christian F. Ostermann's multilateral document collection, with commentary. Ostermann, *Uprising in East Germany, 1953* (New York: Central European University Press, 2001).

4. Mastny, "The Elusive Détente," in Larres and Osgood, *The Cold War*, 11. See also Kramer's introduction in ibid., xiv.

5. Quote from Kramer, "Early Post-Stalin Succession Struggle," 22. The above discussion of East Germans' response to the "New Course" follows Kramer, 40–41. On the difficulties of the "construction of socialism" in East Germany, see A. James McAdams, *Germany Divided: From the Wall to Reunification* (Princeton, NJ: Princeton University Press, 1993), 38–39. On Soviet occupation of Germany in the 1940s, see especially Norman M. Naimark's authoritative *The Russians in Germany: A History of the Soviet Zone of Occupation, 1945–1949* (Cambridge, MA: Belknap Press/ Harvard University Press, 1995). On Soviet frustrations with Ulbricht, see Kramer, ibid., 24–28, 31–33; also Gaddis, *We Now Know: Rethinking Cold War History* (Oxford and New York: Oxford University Press, 1997), 130. For an early assessment based on newly available archival materials, see Christian Ostermann, "New Documents on

the East German Uprising of 1953," *Cold War International History Project Bulletin* 5 (Spring 1995), 10–21.

6. Adenauer, *Erinnerungen, 1953–1955*, 220.

7. On the rhetoric and reality of "rollback" and the East Berlin crisis, see David G. Coleman, "Eisenhower and the Berlin Problem," *Cold War Studies* 2/1 (Winter 2000) 9–19. Quote is from Blankenhorn, 156.

8. Blankenhorn, 156.

9. Michael Lemke, "Konrad Adenauer und das Jahr 1953. Deutschlandpolitik und 17. Juni," in Christoph Kleßman and Bern Stöver, eds., *1953—Krisenjahr des Kalten Krieges in Europa* (Cologne: Böhlau Verlag, 1999), 151.

10. Adenauer, *Erinnerungen, 1953–1955*, 221.

11. Von Eckardt argued that the feeling of betrayal felt by many West Germans as a result of Western inaction resulted from misunderstanding of the nature of allied commitments to the Federal Republic. "Our allies," said the press chief, "had assured us by treaty that they would support us in the reunification policy. They had and have never promised to use military means to attain this goal. . . . The German treaty and the treaty concerning the European Defense community—which, incidentally, was not in force—says not a single word promising a military intervention [*verspricht mit keinem Wort ein militärische Eingriefen*] in East Berlin or the [East] Zone. There were in the broad public opinion many unclear ideas about the facts in this case, which hardened into reproaches against the non-intervention of the western allies." Von Eckardt, 255–56.

12. On the interconnection between foreign and domestic politics in postwar West Germany, see, e.g., Thomas A. Schwartz, "The United States and Germany after 1945: Alliances, Transnational Relations, and the Legacy of the Cold War" (1995 Bernath Lecture), *Diplomatic History* 19:4 (Fall 1995), 561.

13. Initially, a three-power heads-of-government meeting had been scheduled for Bermuda on 29 June. But Churchill became too ill to travel, and the conference was downgraded to a meeting of the foreign secretaries and rescheduled for Washington in July. Although the serious nature of Churchill's condition was not made public—he had suffered a stroke, his second—the prime minister personally informed Eisenhower of his condition. Peter G. Boyle, ed., *The Churchill-Eisenhower Correspondence, 1953–1955* (Chapel Hill: University of North Carolina Press, 1990), 80–84. See also "Editorial Note," *FRUS, 1952–1954*, Vol. 5, 1710–11. On the U.S.-UK bilateral discussions held after Churchill's illness was announced, see ibid., Telegram, Dulles to U.S. embassy, Paris, 27 June, 1953, 1582–83.

14. Lemke, 152.

15. Larres, *Churchill's Cold War*, 195.

16. Adenauer, *Erinnerungen, 1953–1955*, 224.

17. The quote comes from Bruce's diary. Adenauer's representatives, in attempting to sell the chancellor's plan to Bruce, stressed the point that EDC ought not to be sacrificed in order to get Soviet agreement to a conference. Bruce advised Washington that Blankenhorn was on his way, and advised Hallstein to take the matter up with Ambassador Conant in Bonn. Bruce notes that he was forced to report the discussion in "guarded language, since our telephones are undoubtedly tapped both by the French and Germans." *FRUS, 1952–1954*, Vol. 7, 484–85. See also Blankenhorn, 160; Schwarz, *Adenauer: Der Staatsmann*, 85.

18. Hans-Peter Schwarz considers this to be one Adenauer's great achievements at the Washington conference, the other being the aid which it gave him in the election. As Schwarz notes, no one would, in the future, "attempt to push him [Adenauer] to the side at preparatory conferences concerning the German question," as had been attempted in Washington. *Adenauer: Der Staatsmann*, 89.

19. Adenauer, *Erinnerungen, 1953–1955*, 224.

20. It should be added that the Bonn regime was also concerned that the Soviets might take the initiative on the reunification issue, in the shadow of 17 June. This they would do, in Blankenhorn's assessment, to "exert influence on the Bundestag elections." Blankenhorn, 158.

21. See Blankenhorn, 159.

22. See *Verhandlungen*, Band 16, 273. Sitzung, 1953, 13250–59.

23. The order of these first two was, as we shall see, to be a major problem in the negotiations. The Soviets, for their part, wanted to cobble together an interim regime out of the *existing* governments in Bonn and East Berlin. Only then, they said, could all-German elections be held. This was not acceptable to Bonn.

24. Both Adenauer and Blankenhorn reproduce the letter to Dulles. Adenauer's copy is more complete than Blankenhorn's, and thus it is the source of the above quotes. Adenauer, *Erinnerungen, 1953–1955*, 225–26.

25. Adenauer, *Erinnerungen, 1953–1955*, 225; Blankenhorn, 159.

26. Adenauer, *Erinnerungen, 1953–1955*, 225.

27. Ronald J. Granieri, *The Ambivalent Alliance: Konrad Adenauer, the CDU/CSU, and the West, 1949–1966* (New York: Berghahn, 2003), 60–61.

28. Blankenhorn, 160.

29. *FRUS, 1952–1954*, Vol. 5, 1606.

30. Ibid., 1607.

31. The declaration protested officially the "oppression" in the East Zone and in East Berlin which led to the uprisings, and called for reunification via the program set out by the Bundestag on 10 June, 1953. The note encouraged the Soviet Union to take steps toward liberalizing the occupation regime in their zone of control, but stopped far short of calling for a quadripartite conference at anything higher than the level of the high commissioners. It is worth noting that Dulles, in transmitting this note to Conant, instructed him not to discuss the draft declaration with Adenauer. Ibid., 1601–2.

32. Ibid., 1607. Riddleberger no doubt meant that Blankenhorn thought the declaration did not deal sufficiently with the *perception* that "the Chancellor was not sincere in his desire for German unification."

33. Hallstein may have met with Conant after he (Hallstein) and Blankenhorn were adjured by Bruce to do so, but I have found no record of this meeting.

34. Amy Knight, *Beria: Stalin's First Lieutenant* (Princeton, NJ: Princeton University Press, 1993), 191–94; Vladislav Zubok and Constantine Pleshakov, *Inside the Kremlin's Cold War: From Stalin to Khrushchev* (Cambridge, MA: Harvard University Press, 1996), 159–63. See also Georg von Rauch, *Geschichte der Sowjetunion* (Stuttgart: Alfred Kröner Verlag, 1990), 497–500.

35. Zubok, *Failed Empire*, 88–93.

36. Given what Dulles knew at the time, this was a valid point. As R. Craig Nation indicates, Malenkov had advocated "a more moderate foreign policy" since the

early 1950s. He nevertheless escaped Beria's fate. *Black Earth, Red Star: A History of Soviet Security Policy, 1917–1991* (Ithaca, NY: Cornell University Press, 1992), 204.

37. *FRUS, 1952–1954*, Vol. 5, 1609–10.

38. Mikhail Heller and Aleksandr Nekrich, *Utopiia u Vlasti: Istoriia Sovetskogo Soiuza s 1917 goda do nashikh dnei,* II (Frankfurt am Main: Interchange, 1982), 274.

38. *FRUS, 1952–1954*, Vol. 5, 1612. On Dulles's response to news of Beria's ouster, see especially Bohlen, 356.

39. Ibid., 1613.

40. Ibid., 1612–13.

41. Adenauer claims in his memoirs to have had at least a general awareness of this problem at the outset of the Washington conference. "It was known to me," he recorded, "that the United States, Great Britain and France did not wholly agree in their views about the advisability of a four-power conference." *Erinnerungen, 1953–1955*, 226.

42. *FRUS, 1952–1954*, Vol. 5, 1613.

43. Churchill had indicated his awareness of the situation in the Federal Republic in a "Dear Ike" letter on 1 July. Churchill "had never thought of a Four Power meeting taking place till after E.D.C. was either ratified or discarded by the French," and considered November to be the right time. "Adenauer and Bonn," he added, "seem to be moving towards a united Germany and now they speak of a Four Power Conference with approval." Boyle, 83.

44. *FRUS, 1952–1954*, Vol. 5, 1618; 1625–26. This was certainly the reason for Churchill's statement to Eisenhower that no conference should come before the French had decided on EDC. This fear comports with Molotov's statement to a plenary meeting of the Party Central Committee (on 2 March, 1954) that scuttling EDC had been one of his primary goals at Berlin. Leffler, *For the Soul of Mankind*, 142.

45. "McBride Minutes" [Minutes of Second Tripartite Foreign Ministers Meeting], 11 July, 1953, ibid., 1622.

47. Ibid., 1614; 1622. For a very clear and frank assessment of Bidault's line at Washington, see Victor Rosenberg, *Soviet-American Relations, 1953–1960: Diplomacy and Cultural Exchange during the Eisenhower Presidency* (Jefferson, NC: McFarland, 2005), 38–39.

48. Hans Edgar Jahn recalls that "up until the early days of 1954" he had never heard Adenauer even hint that he had doubts about EDC ratification. "He had identified himself completely with the EDC." Jahn, *An Adenauers Seite: Sein Berater erinnert sich* (Munich and Vienna: Albert Langen Georg Müller Verlag, 1987), 249.

49. Bruno Bandulet accurately describes French policy toward EDC and European union at the time as having entered a "phase of ambivalence." Originators of both the Schuman and Pleven Plans, the French nevertheless could not commit themselves to the latter, insofar as it meant a rearming of Germany. Bandulet, *Adenauer zwischen West und Ost: Alternativen der deutschen Aussenpolitik* (Munich: Weltforum Verlag, 1970), 117.

50. *FRUS, 1952–1954*, Vol. 5, 1627. Dulles was probably convinced, at least, that Bidault desired ratification of the defense pact, since this is what Bruce, who was America's observer to the EDC interim committee, was telling him. Yet he could not have forgotten Bruce's observation that a "large majority of foreign office officials advising [Bidault] are violently opposed to EDC." Telegram, Bruce to Department

of State, 12 March, 1953; *FRUS, 1952–1954*, Vol. 5, 766. Churchill, for his part, thought that Bidault was anticipating the failure of a four-power meeting to generate results, in order to give him leverage in the fight over EDC. Boyle, 86.

51. Dulles in fact stressed the need for EDC in its own right at the tripartite meeting on 13 July. He insisted that *only* if EDC were recognized as valuable in its own right did it have a chance of being ratified. Viewed only as a means of countering the Soviets, its ratification could easily be prevented by Moscow, which need only feign relaxation of tensions to undermine Western support for EDC. Minutes, Third Tripartite Foreign Ministers Meeting, 13 July, 1953, *FRUS, 1952–1954*, Vol. 5, 1662.

52. There can be no more forceful or authoritative expression of American commitment to EDC than that made by Eisenhower to the British prime minister on 6 July. The president warned Churchill that "[I]f the French parliament should reject [EDC], I cannot possibly over-emphasize the adverse effect such action would have on public opinion in this country. Our people and our Congress are getting exceedingly tired of aid programs that seem to them to produce no good results. They believe earnestly that only closer union among the nations of Western Europe, including West Germany, can produce a political, economic and military climate in which the common security can be assured. Personally, I think our people are right on this point . . . [I]f they find their judgments and convictions completely ignored by the principal NATO country in Western Europe, it will indeed take a genius to keep our people from washing their hands of the whole affair. To my mind that kind of a result would be catastrophic for us all." Boyle, 85. Eisenhower did not use the phrase "agonizing re-appraisal" in this letter, but his assessment was no less dire.

53. Immerman, *John Foster Dulles*, 79.

54. While the literature in this area indicates U.S. interest in Adenauer's re-election, the extent of America's attempts to influence German voting has not been the focus of much attention.

55. "Nachlaß Lenz," I-172-58/2, ACDP.

56. Ibid.

57. Minutes, Fourth Tripartite Foreign Ministers Meeting, 13 July, 1953; *FRUS, 1952–1954*, Vol. 5, 1672–74.

58. Minutes, Fifth Tripartite Foreign Ministers Meeting, 14 July, 1953: ibid., 1691.

59. Blankenhorn, 161.

60. *FRUS, 1952–1954*, Vol. 5, 1691–92. The relevant section of the communiqué can be found in ibid., 1705.

61. Adenauer, *Erinnerungen, 1953–1955*, 226.

62. Lenz, 674–75.

63. *FRUS, 1952–1954*, Vol. 5, 1626–27.

64. This episode is fascinating, too, in that it closely parallels contemporaneous developments in the GDR-Soviet "alliance." Hope M. Harrison's studies of bargaining power in the relationship between these two states show that the Ulbricht regime was able to use its own domestic weakness to gain leverage with its superpower sponsor. This was true particularly after the Berlin uprising and the Beria purge. See Harrison, "Soviet-East German Relations after World War II," *Problems of Post-Communism* 42:5 (September–October 1995), 12–13. See also Harrison, *Driving the Soviets up the Wall: Soviet-East German Relations, 1953–1961* (Princeton, NJ:

Princeton University Press, 2003), especially 40–48. McAdams notes the extent to which Ulbricht's grip on power in East Berlin was actually strengthened as a result of the uprising. *Germany Divided*, 40–41.

65. Adenauer, *Erinnerungen, 1953–1955*, 226–27. Conant agreed with this assessment. He reported to Dulles that "there can be no doubt that the Chancellor has scored a considerable political advantage and for the time being at least has fairly well spiked the Opposition's claim that he was not doing all he could to bring about German unification. I think everyone must admire the skillful way in which he has turned the flank on the SPD." Letter, Conant to Dulles, 17 July, 1953, *FRUS, 1952–1954*, Vol. 7, 487–88.

66. Blankenhorn, 16.

67. Lenz, 675.

68. See especially *FRUS, 1952–1954*, Vol. 5, 1622–23. On Eisenhower's and Dulles's commitment to European unification and EDC, see, e.g., Pascaline Winand, *Eisenhower, Kennedy, and the United States of Europe* (New York: St. Martin's Press, 1993), 34–38.

69. R. F. Ivanov, *Duait Eizenkhauer: Chelovek, Politik, Polkovodets* (Moscow: IPO Poligran, 1998), 237. McAllister, *No Exit*, 224–25.

70. Telegram, Conant to Dulles, 27 July, 1953, NARA, Department of State Central Decimal File, 611.62a/7-2753. In a related telegram Dulles informed Conant "that any concession given Adenauer between now and date [of] German elections should be carefully examined lest it boomerang." Apparently both Conant and Dulles feared that American support of Adenauer was walking the line between effective and obvious. If American support were to become any more obvious, it might "be interpreted as interference in elections." Telegram, Dulles to office of the United States High Commissioner, 30 July, 1953, *FRUS, 1952–1954*, Vol. 7, 499.

71. Eisenhower's devotion to the idea of a unified Europe dates back to the years prior to his taking of the White House. As supreme commander of NATO forces, Eisenhower had thought that a European federation would "instantly . . . solve the real and bitter problems of today. . . . So many advantages would flow from such a union that it is a tragedy for the whole human race that it is not done at once." With regard to EDC, the SACEUR came to the conclusion that "there is going to be no real progress towards a greater unification of Europe except through the medium of specific programs of this kind." Ambrose, *Eisenhower*, Vol. 1, 508.

72. "Tätigkeitsbericht der Bundesregierung für das Jahr 1951," quoted in Herbert Müller-Roschach, *Die Deutsche Europapolitik, 1949–1977: Eine politische Chronik* (Bonn: Europa Union Verlag, 1980), 11.

73. Helga Haftendorn, *Deutsche Außenpolitik zwischen Selbstbeschränkung und Selbstbehauptung, 1945–2000* (Stuttgart: Deutsche Verlags-Anstalt, 2000), 96. Instructively, Haftendorn goes on to note that the successive governments of West Germany continued to seek expansion of their own freedom of action within the bilateral alliance, while seeking to avoid the burden-sharing responsibilities that came with that freedom.

74. See Hans-Peter Schwarz, "Adenauer und Europa," *Vierteljahrshefte für Zeitgeschichte* 27:4 (Oktober 1979) 475–77. See also Bandulet, 121. According to Bandulet, Adenauer thought that "the [Western] European nations in isolation did not have at their disposal the potential to be able to effectively look after their interests." Such potential could come only through amalgamation.

75. Schwarz, ibid., 477–78.

76. See, e.g., Richard Hiscocks, *The Adenauer Era* (Philadelphia and New York: J. B. Lippincott, 1966), 75–76.

77. Adenauer's comments at 22 May meeting of federal CDU leadership, printed in Günter Buchstab, ed., *Adenauer: "Es mußte alles neu gemacht werden." Die Protokolle des CDU-Bundesvorstandes, 1950–1953* (Stuttgart: Ernst Klett Verlag, 1986), 527. Cited hereafter as *Protokolle, 1950–1953.*

78. Schwartz, *America's Germany*, 55.

79. B. V. Petelin, "Konrad Adenauer: Patriarch germanskoi politiki," *Novaia i noveishaia istoriia* (3/2006), 155.

80. Klaus-Peter Schulz, *Adenauers Gegenspieler: Begegnungen mit Kurt Schumacher und Sozialdemokraten der ersten Stunde* (Freiburg: Verlag Herder, 1989), 139–40. In German all four horrors begin with "K," but this alliteration translates well into English.

81. On 22 May, Adenauer told his party leadership, almost gleefully, that "Social Democracy went into a blind alley with the illness of Herr Dr. Schumacher," and had "no great prospect—if any at all" of winning the autumn elections. *Protokolle, 1950–1953*, 529.

82. Schwarz, *Die Ära Adenauer*, 191.

83. Hans-Otto Kleinmann, *Geschichte der CDU, 1945–1982* (Stuttgart: Deutsche Verlags-Anstalt, 1993), 156, 159–60.

84. Adenauer's comments at the 15 July meeting of the federal CDU leadership, *Protokolle, 1950–1953*, 584–85.

85. Haftendorn, *Deutsche Außenpolitik*, 62.

86. Telegram, C. Douglas Dillon to Dulles, 30 July, 1953, NARA, State Department Central Decimal File, 611.62a/7-3053.

87. Yves-Henri Nouailhat, *Les États-Unis et le monde au XXe siècle* (Paris: Armand Colin/Masson, 1997), 199.

88. Both Soviet notes are reprinted in full in *Department of State Bulletin (DSB)* 29:741 (7 September, 1953), 352–56.

89. Blankenhorn, 163.

90. Adenauer, *Erinnerungen, 1953–1955*, 244.

91. Memorandum, C. D. Jackson to John Foster Dulles, 8 August, 1953, JFD, DDEL Files, White House Memoranda Series, White House Correspondence—General, Box 1, file 1953 (2). Dulles's response to the memorandum was brief, noting only that "I think it contains some good thoughts on the German situation and the Russian note." Ibid.

92. Jackson to Dulles, ibid.

93. *DSB* 29:742 (14 September, 1953), 351–52.

94. Telegram, Walter Bedell Smith to HICOG, n.d. (September(?) 1953), International Series, Whitman File, Box 14, File: Germany 1953(2), DDEL. Adenauer, for his part, was predictably concerned by the second note's invocation of Potsdam. On Adenauer's concerns about Soviet invocations of Potsdam, see *Teegespräche, 1950–1954*, 476–77.

95. Schwarz, *Adenauer: Der Staatsmann*, 103.

96. Data on the election returns are taken from Gerhard A. Ritter and Merith Niehauss, *Wahlen in Deutschland 1946–1991: Ein Handbuch* (Munich: Verlag C. H. Beck, 1991), 100.

97. Lenz, 692.

98. See comments to the German Federal Cabinet on 8 September, ibid., 693; Gerhard Wettig, *Bereitschaft zu Einheit in Freiheit?: Die sowjetische Deutschland-Politik 1945–1955* (Munich: Olzog Verlag, 1999), 270.

99. Von Eckardt, 261.

100. See, for instance, a January 1954 poll conducted by the CDU's public opinion research arm. Seventeen percent of respondents said that they thought that Adenauer was pushing for German rearmament "in the interest of foreigners," while almost half (47%) thought he was doing this because "he thinks it is best for Germany." Nachlaß Lenz, 172–38, folder 2, ACDP.

101. In reply to a question at his 3 September press conference, Dulles said that failure to reelect Adenauer would be "disastrous" for Germany and for the prospects of German unification. On the eve of the election, Adenauer thanked Dulles for his comments, assuring him that "the vast majority of the German people agreed with your remarks." See *New York Times*, 4 September, 1953, 1; Editorial note, *FRUS, 1952–1954*, Vol. 7, 532–33.

102. Telegram, Dulles to Conant, 20 November, 1953, Subject Series, International Subseries, Box 8, Folder 13, Eisenhower Library Files, JFD.

103. Troyanovsky, *Cherez godi i rasstoiania*, 179. Nouailhat makes a similar point in *Les États-Unis*, 200. For an excellent, concise summary of Molotov's proposals at Berlin, and the reasons for their rejection by the Western delegates, see Maelstaf, *Que Faire L'Allemagne?*, 452–60.

104. Address to National War College, 12 March, 1954, Livingston T. Merchant Papers (LTM), Correspondence and Related Material, 1954–1957, Box 2, File: Re: Berlin Conference, Seeley G. Mudd Library, Princeton University.

105. Memorandum of Conversation, Dulles and Adenauer, 20 February, 1954, *FRUS, 1952–1954*, Vol. 7, 1209. On 4 February, Dulles had already indicated to Blankenhorn that he expected the conference to fail due to the question of free elections in Germany. Blankenhorn, 185.

106. Bohlen, 362.

107. Wilhelm Grewe, head of the legal affairs division at the German foreign office and a West German "observer" of the conference, thought that now "the last illusions concerning a change in Soviet policy after Stalin's death were scattered." *Rückblenden, 1976–1951* (Frankfurt am Main, Berlin, Vienna: Propyläen, 1979), 186.

108. Telegram, U.S. Delegation at the Berlin Conference to Department of State, 18 February, 1953, *FRUS, 1952–1954*, Vol. 7, 1172.

109. For the text of the Eden Plan, see ibid., 1177–80. See also minutes of first session of foreign ministers' meeting, 25 January, 1954, 813, ibid. On Molotov's criticisms of the British plan, see telegram, U.S. Delegation to Department of State, 30 January, 1954, ibid., 893–94.

110. The Yalta and Potsdam accords "point out the path to be taken by the Berlin conference in the interests of European security," according to Molotov. Minutes, first session, ibid., 815. See also Molotov's statement on 26 January, ibid., 825. For the Western response, see especially Dulles's statement on 26 January, ibid., 829. Dulles argued that the situation had changed since the end of the Second World War, and one must no longer hold to "the cruel decisions which hatred and bitterness occasioned."

111. For the Soviet proposal on German borders see "Soviet Government's Draft Peace Treaty with Germany," ibid., 1184. For the Western position, see tripartite "Declaration of Intent Regarding German Peace Treaty," ibid., 1181.

112. On East German/Soviet attempts to include the Ulbricht regime in the Berlin talks, see, e.g., Telegram, U.S. delegation to the Department of State, 26 January, 1954, ibid., 836. Minutes of 29 January session, ibid., 874. Dulles "doubted that two sets of representatives so diametrically opposed in their views [as Bonn and East Berlin], would set a helpful tone to the discussions." Ibid., 875.

113. Molotov claimed that EDC and the Bonn and Paris accords were "part of a larger American military plan in which France and Italy were being used as implements of American policy. These new agreements would make Germany into [a] base of preparation for [a] new war." Minutes, 2 February session, ibid., 913. See also report of Eden's dinner with Molotov, 3 February, ibid., 936.

114. Nouailhat, *Les États-Unis*, 200; A. M. Filitov presents the Soviet perspective on this issue in "SSSR i germanskii vopros: Povorotnye punkty (1941–1961 gg.), in N. I. Egorova and A. O. Chubar'ian, eds., *Kholodnaya voina. 1945–1963 gg.: Istoricheskaia retrospektiva* (Moscow: Olma Press, 2003), 248–49. For a text of the Soviets' European security proposal, see *FRUS*, ibid., 1189–90.

115. The Germans, too, saw nothing new here. Blankenhorn wrote Adenauer on 2 February to inform him of Molotov's speech of the previous day. Molotov's statement—stressing Potsdam and an end to *Westbindung*—was merely a repetition of the 1952 Stalin note. The Soviets, he thought, had no will for peace. Blankenhorn, 183. Adenauer viewed Molotov's remarks as so "diametrically opposed" to what the Allies and the FRG were proposing that he did not see how it would be possible to get an agreement. Nachlaß von Eckardt, "Informationsgespräch mit Adenauer: Thema—Erklärung Molotov," 2 February, 1954, I 010-007/2, ACDP.

116. Telegram, Dulles to Eisenhower, 1 February, 1954, *FRUS, 1952–1954*, Vol. 7, 917. On Eden's and Bidault's observations of this phenomenon, see telegram, U.S. Delegation to Department of State, 26 January, 1954, ibid., 835.

117. "Post-Berlin thoughts on the Current Soviet Psyche," prepared by C. D. Jackson, 22 February, 1954, Administration Series, Whitman File, Box 22, File: Jackson, C. D. 1954 (1), DDEL. "Comments by State Department Russian Desk Officers," 3 March, 1954, ibid., File: Jackson, C. D. 1954 (2).

118. *Teegespräche*, 529.

119. Nachlaß Krone, I-028-001/2, ACDP.

120. Grewe, 186–87.

121. For Bidault's conclusions regarding Berlin, and his subsequent actions, I rely on Maelstaf, *Que Faire L'Allemagne?*, especially 459–60.

122. *Teegespräche*, 530.

123. Loose note cards (LTM summary, Berlin Conference), Correspondence and Related Materials, 1954–1957, Box 2, File: Re: Berlin Conference, LTM.

124. Background briefing to press, n.d., Correspondence Files—Alphabetical Files, Box 78, File: Re: Berlin Four-Power Conference of Foreign Ministers, JFD.

125. Blankenhorn, 185.

126. See, e.g., Minutes of a Meeting of the United States Delegation, 29 January, *FRUS, 1952–1954*, Vol. 7, 867–68.

127. Grewe, 175–77.

4

"The Year Things Began to Get Unstuck": 1955

The year 1955 was marked by extraordinary activity. It was the year in which Germany was admitted into the Atlantic Alliance as an equal partner. It was the year in which the Soviets and the West united to end the division of Austria, and in which Moscow reversed Stalin's policy toward Yugoslavia. This was also the year in which the leaders of the Big Four sat down together for the last time before the Soviet Union and the United States began holding summits of two.

Since one of the most pressing differences between the superpower blocs was German policy, the events of this year thoroughly engaged the West German government in Bonn. Adenauer realized that much could be lost or gained in the events of this remarkable year. Predictably, he and his lieutenants did not sit idly by while the powers sorted out the world situation. Rather, he did all he could to make certain that his allies did not negotiate Germany's fate without Bonn's input. It was a busy time for German-American communication.

Adenauer's position was strengthened when, in May, the Federal Republic entered NATO. During the previous year, the governments of the Western powers had done little to explore the possibilities of détente, in order not to disrupt EDC's chances for ratification. But the French National Assembly rejected EDC in late August 1954. A bath ostensibly saved Western defense policy: Eden reports having hit upon his plan for the revivification of the Western European Union in the tub. This was, if true, the most important ablution in the history of the Federal Republic. The WEU had been devised in 1948 to shield Germany's neighbors from further German militarism. In 1955, the moribund union was revised in order to *allow* West German rearmament, within, of course, the NATO context.[1] Adenauer now saw his primary task to be assuring the acceptance of West Germany's NATO entry, first in his own country, and then abroad.[2]

MUCH DEBATE, LITTLE SUBSTANCE: JANUARY–MAY 1955

It had been a tumultuous year within the Western alliance. From the West German point of view, the results had been on the whole positive. Adenauer had expressed to Churchill a desire to see West Germany "take its place among the leading powers of the free Europe."[3] He wrote these words after the French had rejected the European Defense Community pact. The decisions of the next few weeks resulted in the "inclusion of Germany, based on partnership, in a community of reasonably-cooperating western democracies."[4] ("Germany," of course, excluded the eastern sector.) According to CDU whip Heinrich Krone, the Berlin conference had sufficiently demonstrated that reunification could occur only if *Soviet* preconditions were met. "The neutralization of Germany is to constitute the beginning of this policy. At the end, Germany is to be a satellite state."[5] Thus Bonn felt the pressing need for unambiguous, legal inclusion in the Western alliance.

For the Americans, the autumn of 1954 had also been instructive. American frustration with France was nothing new. And every discussion of Eisenhower's European policy must mention Dulles's "agonizing reappraisal" speech. Yet the "two years of prophecy from Washington that a rejection of the EDC would destroy the Western Alliance proved far from accurate," notes a perceptive student of French policy. In fact, the death of EDC at the hands of the French was ultimately beneficial to the cause of German rearmament, forcing as it did Prime Minister Pierre Mendès-France to actively seek an alternative. By this time, any viable alternative was destined to include a West German national army.[6]

The (for Eisenhower and Dulles) obnoxious action of the French parliament also enhanced the value of Bonn's stock in official Washington. By rejecting EDC, Paris did not simply pave the way for German integration into NATO. The sorry episode gave a final impetus to Washington's tendency to view West Germany as America's most reliable partner on the European continent. Eisenhower had once told Adenauer to give on the Saar "until it hurts." Now, by the end of 1954, the president had reversed himself. In a conversation with Dulles on 14 December, 1954, Eisenhower indicated his concern over this issue. "He felt we could not desert the Germans on this issue. We could get along without France but not without Germany."[7] This conversion had little to do with the merits of the Saar question, and everything to do with the perception that Germany—*Adenauer's* Germany—and not France would pursue policies in Europe which reflected America's preferences. The burden of proof now lay with France.

In this sense, and perhaps counterintuitively, the EDC episode damaged Franco-American relations more deeply than relations between France and the FRG. Bonn had too much to gain from economic diplomacy with France to allow rapprochement across the Rhine to falter over EDC or the unclear future of the Saar—itself a potential engine of Franco-German economic integration in the mining and metallurgy industries. As a result, Adenauer did not bother to snub the Frenchman who had failed to put his weight behind EDC when the chips were down. Instead, he met with Mendès-France to discuss economic and trade issues when in Paris a matter of weeks later for the signing of the Paris accords.[8]

On a third front, the Soviets followed the proceedings in London and Paris with a great deal of concern. Critics of the Kremlin's European policy—this author included—need not exculpate Soviet policy makers for their very real crimes in Eastern Europe, Germany included. But we do need to remind ourselves of the perspective that the Soviet peoples gained from recent experience. Writing several years after the fall of the Soviet Union, R. F. Ivanov reminds his readers that the Second World War in Europe was experienced differently, depending on who and where one happened to be at the time.

> The monstrous atrocities of the fascists left their horrible mark on the entire course of the war, compelling each one of its participants, regardless of ideological and political orientation, to draw a conclusion about the fascistic and military leadership of Germany . . .[and about the atrocities they committed] during the course of the war, and in the occupied countries.

Postwar attitudes toward a revival of Germany would depend, at least in part, on the experience that a nation had had during the war. Ivanov calls attention to the fact that Eisenhower—uniquely among Western leaders, one might add—had been in the position at war's end "to see with his own eyes what the Germans did with Soviet prisoners of war." These firsthand observations of the horrors inflicted by the Nazis had initially caused him strongly to desire significant punishment for the violators of the laws of war. Ivanov then expresses a Russian's sense of surprise that this same soldier, "a short time after the end of the war . . . exchanged wrath for mercy (*smenil gnev na milost'*) . . . Eisenhower's metamorphosis was rapid and revealing."[9] Revealing of what? This is left to the reader.

Ivanov's discussion of Eisenhower points up two matters worth considering about the Soviet position at Geneva. The first will be nothing new to anyone with even a glancing familiarity of twentieth-century Russian history. Moscow feared a revived Germany, and doubly so one that it could not in any way control. Historical memory is not simply a perception; it is a construct. And the Soviets had constructed recent history in such a way that they were the aggrieved victim of foreign aggression. Moscow's interpretation would no doubt be met with incredulity in other national capitals, or would-be capitals—Warsaw, Helsinki, Vilnius, Grozny, and others have very different interpretations of the role of the Soviet Union in the late 1930s and the 1940s. But the diplomatist gains no credit for the ability to debate, seminar-style, another nation's conception of itself and its past. What was significant for the Western leaders going into the Geneva summit was simply an understanding of the way that Russia saw the world.

The second point is revealed, piece-by-piece, through recently available Russian sources, both primary and secondary. This piece of the puzzle concerns Soviet attitudes toward Eisenhower, the first-among-equals of the Western delegations. From Moscow's perspective, Eisenhower's "metamorphosis" on the German question presented an analytical challenge, to say the least. Eisenhower had waged war on the Nazis. He had "deliberately" (his words) visited the sites of the worst Nazi atrocities, so that he might observe them "with his own eyes" (Ivanov's words). After witnessing the gruesomeness of Nazi occupation, he wrote his wife: "I never dreamed that such cruelty, bestiality, and savagery could really exist in this world!" His most important biographer writes twice, in this context, of the general's deepening "hatred" for the Germans.

Ivanov may thus be correct that the Soviets were unsure of the measure of the man who could perceive things in this way, only to reverse himself within a decade. There is no question that a transformation had occurred in Eisenhower's thinking on Germany in the time between the liberation of the death camps and the meeting in Geneva's Palais des Nations. Unfortunately, Soviet planners did not have access to Ambrose's two-volume biography, and thus could not read the passages that hint at the reasons for Eisenhower's transformations. *President* Eisenhower, unlike *General* Eisenhower, was aware of the atrocities committed by the Soviet Union during and immediately after the war.[10] He was also far more inclined than the Kremlin leadership to accept the historical interpretation of the 1930s and 1940s—thus that of Warsaw, Helsinki, Vilnius, Grozny—that portrayed the Soviet Union as anything but an innocent victim. For him, the "Great Patriotic War" was set in motion by the Molotov-Ribbentrop Pact, and not by Operation Barbarossa. Ivanov rather caustically assesses his transformation as flowing from a failure to understand that the viewpoint of the Soviet Union resulted from the suffering of the Soviet people at the hands of the Germans. "A logical, thinking person, Eisenhower must have understood [this] position of the Soviet Union. . . . However this did not occur."[11] Perhaps he was not logical? Or thinking?

Ivanov conducts his discussion without reference to Soviet policy in the territories the Soviet Union occupied as a result of the war. As unfortunate as this is for the historian working in the limited Soviet sources that are now available, it gives insight into the position of the Moscow delegates at Geneva. In addition, it helps to explain the seemingly maudlin decision to bring Ike's old comrade-in-arms, General Georgii Zhukov, to Geneva for discussions with the president; perhaps the "old" Eisenhower of 1945 could be rallied to the flag once again by the presence of another commanding general from the war against Hitler.[12]

What one can say with certainty at this point is that Moscow delivered two official notes to the West in autumn 1954. The first was sent on 23 October, and the second on 13 November.[13] In von Eckardt's asessment, the notes demonstrated that the Soviet Union had come to accept NATO's existence.[14] Given that the Soviets decried in both notes the "aggressive" nature of the Atlantic Alliance, this might seem an odd conclusion. The Soviet opposition to NATO had not abated. Rather, as von Eckardt astutely noted, their emphasis had shifted. The main point of the notes was not to launch another broadside against NATO, but against West Germany's military integration into that alliance.

The reason for this shift in emphasis may simply be that the London conference took the Soviets by surprise. Given the acrimony in the Western alliance after the French rejection of the EDC treaty, the Soviets might well have expected the recriminations and multilateral hostilities to drag on for the foreseeable future. Then came Eden's plan in London, and the remarkable rapidity of its acceptance by all, including the French. If Washington and Bonn failed to anticipate how easily this seemingly intractable problem could be solved, Moscow must be forgiven for the same lack of clairvoyance. As of November 1954, the Kremlin was faced with a new situation. Instead of attempting to prevent, or at least slow, the integration of German units into EDC, the Soviets now faced the reality that there would be "created in the very near future a West German army of 500,000 men with its own sizable air force, tank formations, and military staffs."[15]

The Soviet response, as reflected in the November note, indicated that Moscow was no longer focusing its attention on the alliance itself. Rather, in von Eckardt's assessment, the Soviets "concentrated more and more on the German defense contribution, which is judged to be the resurgence of German militarism."[16] The November Soviet note makes numerous references to "Hitlerite" Germany and its depredations upon Europe. Moscow indicated that it had already warned the West about the "serious danger connected with the rebirth of militarism in West Germany and with the drawing of the latter into military groupings." This was a process which would lead to confrontation, hostility, and "in the final reckoning, to war."

As a way out of this dire situation, the note called for a conference to take place on 29 November, in Paris or Moscow, to decide upon a "system of collective security" for all of Europe.[17]

Adenauer had recently indicated what he thought of Soviet collective security schemes. He had returned to the United States in October 1954. On the twenty-ninth of that month, he gave an address to the National Press Club, in which he expressed his general skepticism with regard to negotiating reunification and collective security with Moscow. Twelve days before, he reminded his audience, the GDR had held elections. That country's Ministry of Information had predicted an SED victory with a narrow 97.3 percent of the vote. It must have come as quite a relief, then, when the communists won 99.3 percent of votes cast. This, the chancellor told America's journalistic elite, was "what the Soviets mean when they talk of free and democratic elections." With regard to plans for a collective security arrangement in Europe, Adenauer was equally skeptical. The Soviet Union had not changed its "main objective." From their point of view, the purpose of a Europe-wide security agreement was to "disinterest the United States in [the] European question and to eliminate Atlantic influence from European affairs." The Soviets intended to dominate the future collective security alliance.[18]

The chancellor could perhaps take comfort in the progress which the FRG was making toward NATO entry. The ratification of the Paris accords by the French assembly came on 30 December. The Bonn government was no doubt relieved by the decision. Yet the vote had been close, and the terms of the debate left bad feelings and worries. Blankenhorn gave credit where credit was due, indicating that Mendès-France had helped this time to push the accords through. But Blankenhorn could not ignore the evidence of the debate in Paris over rearming Germany. One had to conclude from the tight vote and the Germanophobic speeches that "the French people do not want an alliance with the Federal Republic."[19] Krone, too, expressed little joy over the ratification, recording in his diary that "for Germany and for France the European Army would have been the better solution."[20] Thus the year 1954 ended on a mixed note. The Paris accords, though well on their way, had not yet been ratified by the West German and American legislatures. And Adenauer's deep desire for a rapprochement across the Rhine had stumbled on French fears of a rearmed Germany. On the other hand, 1954 had seen the cementing of the U.S.-FRG relationship, a development helped along by American frustrations with France.[21] In Blankenhorn's assessment, "the chancellor succeeded in winning America for Germany. In the Democratic as well as in the Republican camp, one is beginning to see our country as the partner with whom cooperation is worthwhile." He added that "the relationship with the American president is marked by trust. One can count on Foster Dulles as one of the Chancellor's friends."[22]

Thus began the year which German diplomat Wilhelm Grewe labeled "the Federal Republic's best year."[23] The two Geneva conferences and Adenauer's trip to Moscow marked this year as one of extraordinary diplomatic activity, as did the progress made on the Austrian situation, culminating in the signing of a State Treaty on 15 May. It was this latter development itself, however, which led to significant tension between the West Germans and the Eisenhower administration. Throughout the 1950s, events from time to time cast doubt on Blankenhorn's rosy assessment of U.S.-FRG relations, and of the relationship between the leaders of those nations. This was one such time.

According to Hans-Peter Schwarz, through the winter of 1954 and into the spring of 1955, "neither Adenauer nor his closest advisers believed . . . that the time for productive negotiations with the Soviet Union had yet arrived."[24] Although Schwarz does not say why he believes this to be the case, he is probably correct. Blankenhorn, who was to be a major player in the months ahead, confided as much to his diary on New Year's Eve. "I believe," said Adenauer's close aide, "that the Soviet Russia of the New Year 1954/1955 is not so very different from the Russia of Stalin." The Soviet Union had changed its tactics. But when it came to concrete questions, "everything has stayed the same, and we will find that Russia, as at this year's Berlin foreign ministers conference, will also in the future keep the Soviet zone tightly in its hands."[25]

But prospects for settlement were not so bleak on all fronts. On 8 February, 1955, Molotov gave a speech to the Supreme Soviet which helped to put the Austrian question in motion again. Molotov's speech was confusing. In it, he reiterated the Soviet claim that no settlement of the Austrian question was possible independent of an agreement on Germany. For this reason, the State Department initially concluded that the "Molotov speech gives no basis [for] improved hopes for Austrian treaty."[26] But the Austrians were not willing to accept that assessment of Molotov's speech, and asked Molotov for clarification. On 25 February, Molotov told the Austrian ambassador to Moscow, Norbert Bischoff, that the "Soviet Union did not demand total agreement on [the] German question but wanted security that Anschluss would not take place now or in the future." Molotov told Bischoff that "if this was achieved [an] Austrian treaty could be concluded and evacuation carried out immediately."[27]

The Soviet line seemed to have departed from the tight linkage of the Austrian and German questions that, since Stalin, had been viewed by Moscow as leverage to "influence the German public and put pressure on the West to achieve a solution favourable to the Soviet Union."[28] If Austria could be neutralized, and prevented from ever aligning with Germany, then perhaps the Soviets would go along with an Austrian treaty after all. The

Vienna government reacted quickly, attempting to take advantage of the possibility for motion on the question.

The government of Julius Raab in Vienna—a "black-red coalition" which had come into office not long after Eisenhower—had since the beginning assumed that a settlement of the Austrian question would mean the withdrawal of all forces of occupation from Austria.[29] For the government of Austria, neutralization was an acceptable means of assuring the reunification of their country, even though this would mean that Austria could not take part in the Western defense alliance which West Germany was on the verge of joining.

Why Moscow was willing to acquiesce in Austrian reunification at this time is less clear. Perhaps, as was assumed widely in the West, the Soviets were trying to use their flexibility in the Austrian question, and their professed desire for a four-power conference, "as an instrument for preventing, or at least slowing down, the coming into force of the Paris treaties and thereby the entry of West Germany into NATO."[30] According to this interpretation, the Kremlin's new, reasonable approach to Austria was merely a last-ditch effort to avoid the dreaded rearmament of Germany.

But Günter Bischof's thesis that the new Soviet policy actually indicated grudging Soviet acceptance of the reality of the FRG military integration into the West must be taken seriously. According to Bischof, the conclusion of the Paris accords, along with the rise of Khrushchev in the Kremlin,[31] brought about a *real change* on the Austrian issue. The Soviets had seen their best efforts to prevent West German rearmament and alignment with the West backfire. Now, the Soviets feared that the same would be true of their policy toward Austria. If Moscow wanted to prevent Austrian integration into NATO, it made sense to decouple the Austrian and the German questions, and to gain an Austrian commitment to neutrality as quickly as possible. Additionally, progress toward an Austrian settlement could help Khrushchev "collect points" with Eisenhower, who demanded progress on specific issues like Austria before he would agree to a summit.[32]

Bischof's thesis has much to recommend it. From Bonn's perspective, however, it certainly looked as if the Soviets were once again attempting to stymie Adenauer's plan for German acceptance into the West, and for the return of sovereignty for Germany west of the Elbe. It is unlikely that the effects of Soviet moves on domestic politics in the Federal Republic were the result of mere serendipity. Nor is it hard to understand how one might interpret an initiative from Moscow in the middle of January as, above all, an attempt to forestall West German entry into NATO.

On 15 January, the official Soviet news agency, TASS, published a statement on the German question which was, more than anything else, an appeal to the German public to agitate against the ratification of the Paris accords. The Bundestag was set to vote on the agreements, and thus upon German entry into NATO, in February, and the TASS declaration represented Moscow's eleventh-hour effort to forestall that development. The Soviet statement decried the Paris agreements as a "contradiction to the interests of the German people, especially because they fix the division of Germany for long years." The accords were the pet project of those who desired a "rebirth of German militarism," and were willing to pay the price of reunification to achieve this goal. There remained, however, "unexploited possibilities" which might allow German reunification by means of free elections, if only the main impediment to these—"the plans for remilitarization of West Germany and its inclusion in a military grouping"—were set aside. If this were done, the two German governments could then together work out an election law which would give a free and unfettered vote to all, and allow "democratic parties and organizations" the right to run candidates. (The statement said nothing about which were the democratic groups.) The Kremlin made a concession on the question of international observation of these elections. If the two German governments could agree upon such a regime, then the Soviets, contra their August notes, would apparently allow some sort of *oversight*, although not necessarily *control*.

None of this was particularly new or bold. Nor was the repeated mention of the two German governments likely to be welcomed in Bonn. Toward the end of the TASS report, however, came a suggestion which elicited quite a reaction: "The Soviet Union maintains good relations with the German Democratic Republic. The Soviet Union is prepared, as well, to normalize relations between the USSR and the German Federal Republic."[33]

After the TASS declaration of 15 January, the chancellor found himself under heavy pressure from the opposition to hold off on ratification of the Paris accords until after reunification had been discussed by the Big Four. On 23 January, Adenauer received a letter from Erich Ollenhauer calling on him to pursue just such a policy. With reference to the TASS report, the head of the SPD reminded Adenauer that the "position of the Soviet Union shows, that negotiations concerning German unity will no longer be possible after the ratification of the Paris accords." In a pointed comment on Adenauer's policy, Ollenhauer expressed concern that, if Bonn did not make every effort to gain reunification at this point, then "the erroneous perception will persist abroad, that reunification in freedom is not viewed in Germany as the most pressing goal." It was the position of the Social Democratic Party that all possibilities for negotiation, *prior to the ratification of the Paris accords*, were not yet exhausted. For that reason, the SPD called upon Adenauer to, in turn, call upon the three Western powers to "negotiate with the government of the Soviet Union concerning the proposals in the statement of 15 January, 1955," and to begin these negotiations prior to ratification.[34] In his response two days later, Adenauer questioned whether Ollenhauer and his allies had a grasp of what was really going on. The

Soviets had not proposed conditions for reunification that were acceptable to the Federal Republic. In any event, whatever the Soviets had proposed on 15 January "can be negotiated just as well after ratification as before."[35] There would be no change in policy.

This was not the first time, nor the last, that Adenauer found himself swimming against the current of world politics. The Soviet announcement in May that they were willing to sign an Austrian treaty was viewed "in most of the world . . . as a deed auguring well for melting the Soviet ice that had frozen fruitful negotiations between East and West," according to Eisenhower.[36] But from the start, Adenauer harbored concerns. The parallels between the two divided, German-speaking former Axis members were too obvious to overlook. If East and West were willing to negotiate an end to Austrian occupation on the basis of mutual withdrawal, as seemed likely, why not do the same for Germany?[37]

Concerned about these developments, Adenauer gave Blankenhorn and Adolf Heusinger—Adenauer's military aide—the task of thinking over the German response. This episode has been exhaustively treated by Schwarz. Here it suffices to say that Blankenhorn, Heusinger, and Adenauer all agreed that neutralization was not an option for Germany. Implying, as it did, the withdrawal of American troops from the Federal Republic—and eventually from Europe altogether, the Germans concluded—neutralization would leave West Germany defenseless against Soviet depredations.[38] Bonn's conclusions were the opposite of those reached in Vienna; unity was not worth the price of the evacuation of Western troops. And since this was what the Soviets really wanted, "a successful four-power conference was, under these circumstances, not to be expected."[39]

Adenauer's meeting with Blankenhorn and Heusinger took place on 9 March. By 13 March Adenauer was making the Americans aware of his conclusions. On that date, Blankenhorn met with Elim O'Shaughnessy, director of the Office of Political Affairs at the High Commission. O'Shaughnessy had earlier asked Blankenhorn to solicit the chancellor's views on certain questions of interest to the high commission. Blankenhorn had in fact presented these questions to Adenauer. Before addressing these questions, however, Adenauer had one or two things, "general observations," which he would like to mention. According to Adenauer, "any negotiations with the Soviets would be very difficult. No guarantee which could be offered to them would satisfy them." The only thing that they would accept was "an Austrian-type solution, which the chancellor found completely unacceptable." Adenauer rejected out of hand any security agreement with Moscow which would not allow Bonn to raise and maintain the twelve divisions— 500,000 soldiers—foreseen by Heusinger. Additionally, the chancellor emphasized "that the Soviets' sole interest was the withdrawal of U.S. forces and bases from the European continent, and there can be no price for this.

He feels it essential that U.S. forces and bases remain." Asked if there might be "tactical advantages" in "appearing to be willing to discuss . . . a proposal for a quadripartite agreement to refrain from entering into one-sided military alliances with Germany," the chancellor had only two words: "Emphatically not." He also categorized a proposal for a demilitarization of the East Zone as "not an acceptable solution," since it would necessarily involve demilitarization of Poland and Czechoslovakia, and hence "a Soviet request for Allied withdrawal from Western Germany."[40] Adenauer was clearly on record with the State Department. Bonn opposed any plan which foresaw the withdrawal of American troops from West Germany.

The next two months were marked by little motion and much commotion, as Adenauer, despite considerable domestic turmoil, was able to steer German policy in the direction he had prescribed. The Bundestag approved the Paris accords on schedule. That was by no means, however, the end of debate on the German unification issue. Some of Adenauer's liberal partners, in particular, expressed dissatisfaction with the chancery's recent actions. Reinhold Maier, an important and rising Free Democrat who was then visiting the United States, complained to assembled members of the State Department on 10 March that Adenauer's approach to German rearmament was flawed. The rearmament discussion had awakened strong resentments in Germany, resentments which "transcended established party lines." Parliamentary approval did not translate into public acceptance, as much as Adenauer or anyone else might wish that it did. A large part of the problem, said Maier, was Adenauer himself. The chancellor preferred to act in an "autocratic fashion," making bipartisanship in foreign policy impossible.[41] Maier, in expressing his frustration with Adenauer's policy-making style, was echoing a common sentiment: the chancellor had too much control over foreign policy. Pressure mounted for him to hand the foreign affairs portfolio to someone else.

Bundestag approval left ratification by the French Council and the American Senate as the last significant legal hurdles. The French Council approved the treaties, to the relief of many. Ratification by the Senate came in early April, and was from the beginning a foregone conclusion.[42] But Adenauer continued to fear that the Federal Republic's entry into NATO, and the restoration of West German sovereignty could still be short circuited before they were to be consummated in May. He and his aides, therefore, continued to resist any new approaches to the German situation, and continued to reject any analogy between Germany and Austria. The chancellor achieved his goal in the middle of May, but at the cost of much domestic goodwill.

The debate within Germany over the relevance of Austria to Germany could only strengthen America's commitment to Adenauer. As far as the high commission was concerned, the Social Democrats had been taken in by the idea that the Austrian compromise could be applied equally well north of the Alps. The opposition showed signs of "preparing to go all out on the line that an Austrian solution is practical for Germany." Spokesmen for the SPD were arguing that "the Soviets apparently are now ready talk, that they are not nearly as intransigent as depicted by the Government." Inflexibility was, rather, a trait of the Adenauer government. The TASS declaration and the newly discovered Soviet flexibility on Austria hinted at an opportunity which one ought to investigate.

The government feared that the Soviets could exploit just such thinking. The Soviets, ever shrewd, had dropped "the bombshell of an Austrian settlement just prior to final culmination of the Paris treaties." Adenauer's response to the new situation was anything but imaginative. He kept insisting that the Soviets were bending to the Western policy of strength. By implication, the *last* thing the West should do now was to weaken its position by delaying German entry into NATO. In addition, Union spokesmen continued to reject the alleged similarity of the Austrian and German cases.[43] Krone responded to all the talk of German neutralization with a certain weariness. He had heard it all before.

> Where there is now so much talk that the Russians would move out of the [East] Zone if we only established a proper dialogue with them, I have to think about the observation, which someone made in Berlin when the Russians lifted the blockade in 1949: That was the beginning of the pullback, and soon the Russians would stand behind the Oder.[44]

Rumors arose in April that the government was softening its stand, and perhaps "regard[ed] the Austrian development as [a] possible first step toward general international detente [*sic*]," due largely to unclear statements made by von Eckardt at an 18 April press conference. The press chief had seemed to suggest that the Federal Republic's contribution to NATO was open for negotiation if Germany should be reunified. The "establishment of German divisions serves no aim of its own," he stated.[45] This certainly *seemed* to contradict everything the government had said up until 18 April. It is highly unlikely, however, that von Eckardt's statements represented a trial balloon, intended to test reaction to a change of policy. The Adenauer government did not rate the chances for reunification in the near term to be very good, and was not sure, beyond maintaining a "policy of strength," how to achieve it. Krone, for his part, thought that the Bonn government was simply unprepared for the beehive of discussion which followed the Western invitation to the Soviets. "Do we have a conception of reunification? I do not know," he wrote in his diary on 5 April. "Are we prepared for the conversations which are coming upon us?"[46] Against this background, it is likely that von Eckardt, always conscious of public perceptions, was at most attempting to give the impression of flexibility.

This impression was not universally welcomed, and the government found itself repudiating the ill-chosen words of Adenauer's spokesman. HICOM found that certain elements of the fractious FDP were completely nonplused by von Eckardt's statement. The government had given itself over to the "current neutrality psychosis," according to unnamed Liberals. The government reaffirmed its boilerplate responses on the subject—the Austrian settlement would be an "impressive success for [the] western policy of strength. But Germany is not Austria. . . . Neutrality is not the road to security, [a] reunified and neutralized Germany would be [the] first step toward loss of freedom as in present Soviet satellites"[47]—and made no further statements like von Eckardt's. The government's press office, meanwhile, issued a declaration labeling as "dangerous and unrealistic" any attempt to end the division of Germany by pulling the Federal Republic out of the Western defense alliance.[48] There was no sign here of the psychosis which certain Free Democrats perceived.

Washington must have been scratching its collective head at this point, since talk of a "third way," in between absolute alignment with the West and surrender to the Soviets, had recently been emanating from none other than the Free Democrats themselves. This vague idea—encompassing some undefined agreement to reunify Germany in the context of a broader security arrangement—began trickling out in mid-April.[49] In a meeting with Conant on 22 April, FDP leaders Viktor-Emanuel Preusker and August-Martin Euler—Housing Minister and deputy *fraktion* leader, respectively—sought to assure the High Commission that this was not, in fact, the policy of the FDP. The party leaders, Preusker and Euler pointed out, had yet to discuss this question among themselves. American withdrawal from Europe was, they assured Conant, "unacceptable," and "they believed [the] maximum concession which could be offered would be an agreement not to station troops in [the] present Sov[iet] zone" after reunification. They also suggested that it might be best if reunification talks were drawn out over a long time, so that the Paris accords could be implemented before the final settlement.[50]

The talk of a "third way," and the internal German debate concerning the relevance of the Austrian compromise for Germany, indicated that many in West Germany—including some in Adenauer's coalition—lacked the chancellor's confidence in the policy of strength. Reinhold Maier was correct: Parliamentary approval of Adenauer's program did not guarantee that the hearts and minds of the entire German populace would follow. This is not to say that the government lacked supporters. This is far from the case. But the confused debate of April 1955 indicated that not all was well within the ruling coalition. It demonstrated, too, that the policy of strength, regardless of its merits, was not psychologically satisfying to a large number of West Germans.

In the face of this, Adenauer and his lieutenants continued to assert the correctness of their approach. The debate engendered by the Austrian situation produced no change in the government's policy on reunification and *Westbindung.* The government continued to chant its mantra: Austria and Germany are not the same, no neutralization, integration of the Federal Republic into NATO. Much debate, but no concrete changes, were the result. The government did, however, have one advantage in this debate: they were right. Austria and Germany were not the same. Germany's location, power potential, and recent history made it a special case. The West feared Germany; hence "dual containment." And it was obvious that the Soviets, despite all their overblown rhetoric about "revanchism," harbored serious fears. Austria could be treated symbolically, as earnest money for future negotiations; as a propaganda tool; as an unwanted burden. But Germany was not a symbol. It was the concrete cause of so much violence and instability in Europe for thirty years. It is inconceivable that the German and Austrian problems could be treated as diplomatic twins.[51]

Yet Adenauer could not make this case too strongly, and here was a problem. Germany was *not* Austria, because the Soviets could never treat it like Austria. They could not do so, because they were terrified of it. But Adenauer's proposed course of action did not aim at reassuring the Soviets. Rather, negotiation through strength meant impressing upon the Soviets just how powerful their Western adversaries were. And a big part of this was the rearmament of the Federal Republic. Adenauer thus was forced to repeat over and over that "the Soviets do not fear . . . Germany but only the United States."[52] This was patently false, as Adenauer must have known. The Soviets wanted to get America out of Europe. But they *feared* Germany. Yet committed as he was to German integration into NATO, and claiming that this was a route to reunification, the chancellor continued to insist that Moscow was more or less neutral to the raising of a half-million man West German army.

FROM LONDON TO PARIS, AND THE LIMITS OF GERMAN INFLUENCE

With the ratification of the Paris accords completed, the May 1955 NATO ministerial meeting was destined to be a glorious day for the Federal Republic and its leaders. On 5 May, the western part of Germany was to regain its sovereignty and, simultaneously, become legally an equal partner in the Western alliance. These festivities were not, however, the only significant issue which faced NATO's Big Three and their new ally. In the previous year, Britain, France, and the United States had suggested a four-power meeting. But the desire to quickly replace the moribund EDC with German NATO membership had preoccupied Western policy makers through the final months of 1954 and into the spring of 1955. With that process well on its way to completion by April 1955, London, Paris, and Washington began to turn their attention back to the invitation. The decision-making process of the allies as they wrestled with the questions of when and on what level to hold a four-power meeting, and what to discuss when there, now demands attention.

France took the lead in calling for the West to actually propose a date for the four-power conference. On 6 January, Mendès-France wrote Eisenhower and Dulles to suggest that a four-power conference be set for May, the month when Germany was set to enter the Atlantic Alliance. The State Department registered strong objections to this plan. By refusing to meet unless German NATO membership were scrapped, the Soviets could exert an influence upon the French public. This might well harm the chances for ratification of the Paris accords. State also wondered whether Mendès-France really wanted to begin, at this time, complicated negotiations with the West Germans concerning a four-power conference. After all, the conference would not take place until after the FRG had attained sovereignty. And since "the subject matter of a conference [with the Soviets] would primarily be Germany," the sovereign West German government could not be excluded from the discussions.[53] Presumably, the Americans assumed that Mendès-France would not like the prospect of Bonn making its weight felt at this time. The United States continued for some time to resist the idea of a conference in the near future.

Britain seemed initially to be quite cautious as well. Churchill wrote Eisenhower on 12 January to assure him that he and Eden thought a four-power conference could come only after ratification of the Paris accords.[54] But Churchill was in fact very interested in the idea, not just of a conference, but of a summit. He had promised the increasingly impatient Anthony Eden on 8 March that he would retire on 5 April. But after receiving word that Eisenhower wanted to discuss a four-power conference at the upcoming Paris meeting, he rethought his departure from office. Perhaps he could get his friend Ike to agree to a June summit. If so, he reasoned, he probably ought to stay in office through June. This led to a rather unfortunate scene between the prime minister and his understandably livid foreign secretary.[55]

The whole episode was unfortunate, too, in that it was all based on a false premise. Eisenhower was *not* interested in a summit meeting, in June or at any point in the foreseeable future. At his 23 March news conference, the president declared that "there is no place on earth to which I would not travel" to promote "the general cause of world peace." The time for him to do so, however, had not arrived. Exploratory talks with the Soviets should begin after the Paris accords were ratified. And, as he saw it, "they would be

taken up at first on a different level from the chief of state." Nor was he sure
that the conference would take place on the foreign ministers level.[56] The
president, in his own words, was "determined, in the absence of tangible
evidence of Soviet sincerity, to avoid a premature meeting because of the
probability that failure to achieve worthwhile results would dash the hopes
of truly peaceful nations" and increase pessimism throughout the world.[57]
Eisenhower was not a big fan of summitry for its own sake. If there was no
good reason to expect concrete results from a meeting with Bulganin, then
he had other things to do.

On the other side of the Atlantic, however, a meeting with the Soviets
was looking quite attractive. Churchill finally retired on 5 April, at the
age of eighty, to be replaced by Eden. Eden soon called for the dissolu-
tion of parliament and the scheduling of new elections, in part because
he considered his parliamentary margin too narrow.[58] He must also have
wanted to win the prime ministership in his own right, to finally step out
of Churchill's shadow.

At this point, a common theme emerges: It was now London's turn to
seek the announcement of a four-power conference for domestic political
reasons. Such an announcement would help the Conservatives immeasur-
ably. But the foreseen meeting with the Soviets could not be just any conference, as Eden's new foreign secretary, Harold Macmillan, quite candidly
recalled. He realized:

> that in the fantastic atmosphere of party politics an immense distinction was
> going to be drawn between "top-level" and "not quite top-level" talks. Foreign
> Secretaries, it seemed, were regarded as very small beer in these high controver-
> sies. "Top-level" meant Heads of Government or Heads of State. This, of course
> was a legacy of Churchill's famous speech of 11 May 1953. In the atmosphere
> of an election the difference might prove vital.[59]

The British had evinced interest in a meeting with the Soviets since at least
May 1953. But, primarily for domestic political reasons, Churchill's velleity
was for Eden a matter of political life and death. To recognize this fact, one
need not assume that the new prime minister's motivations were purely
mercenary: Yvonne Kipp writes of "the British interest" in securing some
sort of four-power agreement in light of persistent worries about "a sudden
withdrawal of the United States from Europe and the continuing undeter-
mined state of affairs in the Federal Republic."[60] But although he insisted
in his 5 May letter to Eisenhower that "this is not a party question here,
but responds to a deep desire of our whole people," Eden was clearly influenced by the electoral time table. Eisenhower responded on the following
day that he and Dulles were "a bit surprised that you have gone so far in
your thinking as to present your idea as a definite proposal." Yet in spite of
this, they "appreciate[d] the importance to you of this project under exist-

ing circumstances," and so were disposed to help the new prime minister.[61] That "existing circumstances" meant "election" did not need to be specified. Eisenhower and Dulles assumed that the timing of the proposal, at the very least, was accelerated by the Conservative government's electoral interests.

London had raised the possibility of a meeting shortly before Churchill's resignation. On 28 March, the State Department sent a telegram to the American embassy in London discussing a paper recently received from London which proposed talks with the Soviets aimed at getting "results even of limited character."[62] As J. H. A. Watson, counselor at the British embassy, observed a couple days later in a meeting at the State Department, Eden would "be fighting for his political life" in the coming campaign. Hence, London was exerting pressure on Washington to get moving. In particular, the British wanted to convene a tripartite working group within a matter of days. This group could then begin planning for a meeting with the Soviets. The suggestion echoed one Adenauer had made in late January. But Adenauer's suggestion had included West German participation in the planning group from the beginning, and the Eisenhower administration expressed similar desires to the British. "Newly sovereign Germany," the State Department opined, "cannot be entirely excluded from initial phases" of the planning group meetings.[63] America was insistent, now and later, that the Germans be integrated into alliance planning. In his 6 May response to Eden's proposal for a summit, cited above, Eisenhower himself insisted that any announcement that the summit would treat of German reunification would have to "specify that Germany would be represented."[64]

Bonn wanted a meeting with the Soviets, or at least was not opposed to the idea. But Adenauer, to no one's surprise, had his own ideas about both the process and the substance of planning for the big meeting. He assiduously sought allied adoption of these points during the preparatory stages before the conference. Four items, in particular, stand out as Bonn's desiderata. First, Adenauer thought that any meeting with the Soviets must be prepared in detail. A conference, and particularly a summit, must not be merely an exchange of words and smiles (or barbs, if things did not go well). The chancellor pressed his allies to adopt a concrete agenda before holding talks with Moscow. Second, Adenauer thought that nuclear arms control was the key element to any successful lessening of world tensions. Agreement on this issue, he argued, must be part of any meaningful security agreement with the Soviets. Third, he was insistent that the German issue not be discussed in isolation from the larger context of the East-West conflict. Austria was clearly on his mind. From Bonn's vantage point, the Powers may well have treated Austria in an instrumental manner, settling the Austrian situation *in order to* improve relations between the blocs. The chronology of a German settlement, according to the chancellor, must be different. Reunification was to be a result of a comprehensive settlement, not a precondition. For this reason, he opposed a conference agenda which focused exclusively on Germany. After all, he noted, "all the tensions on Earth are innately connected with one another."[65] The German problem must be solved in this context. Finally, Adenauer was adamant about the continued need for German integration in the West. This meant NATO, as well as Western European integration. Even if the above-mentioned problem of a comprehensive settlement were somehow overcome, the government of a reunified Germany must retain the freedom to stay in NATO. The Western Powers had to resist Soviet demands that Germany be neutralized via the final German peace treaty. Adenauer categorically rejected the *Bündnisverzicht*, the renunciation of alliance membership. The all-German government of the future had to be free to choose. And Adenauer thought that he knew what the choice would be.[66]

These were the matters which Adenauer meant to stress throughout the planning of the four-power conference. Under pressure from allies—and after the French committed to a date for the deposit of the instruments of the ratification of the Paris accords—the Eisenhower administration accepted Eden's proposal for a working group. 27 April was set as the date when the working group would convene in London. In planning for the conference, Washington resolved to keep its cards close to the chest. The focal points of the conference would necessarily be Germany and European security. Yet the American delegation was instructed not to suggest any potential solutions for the security problem at London. Rather, "it should attempt to draw out the other delegations on the subject of European Security [*sic*] arrangements in general." In addition, it was the "basic position" of the administration "to maintain and strengthen NATO and Germany's association with the West through NATO. No proposal should be accepted which conflicts with this proposal."[67] This can fairly be read as a renunciation of any suggestion—bound to be raised at a four-power conference—that Germany be neutralized after unification. Important players in the State Department obviously agreed with Adenauer's fourth point mentioned above.

While American policy makers in Washington resolved not to accept a security arrangement that implied German neutralization, the Bonn government continued to stump for German rearmament.[68] In this quest, Adenauer faced domestic opposition, although that opposition was neither spirited nor unified enough to deflect the government from its course.[69] As Conant saw it, Adenauer was at the present not very interested in security arrangements in Central Europe, even if they met his criteria. During a conversation with the chancellor on 25 April, Conant gathered that Adenauer "feels that the time is not yet ripe to push forward with the real steps which will bring about German reunification and the creation of a more peaceful posture in Middle Europe." Adenauer was:

not at all desirous of trying to get a yes or no answer from the Russians on the question of German rearmament. Quite the contrary, he feels that if the subject must be discussed, the discussions must be kept going on in the broadest possible framework. In the meantime, I assume he would be prepared to go ahead with the rearmament of Germany.

This is probably a fair assessment of the chancellor's priorities at the time. The positive step Adenauer was willing—in fact anxious—to see at a four-power meeting was a nuclear arms control agreement. He repeated to Conant his extraordinary claim that the proposed twelve Bundeswehr divisions were of little interest to Moscow. What the Soviets feared was "American power and above all American nuclear weapons." Without a nuclear arms agreement the Soviets would never agree to German unity.[70]

Against this background, the London Working Group began consultations on the morning of 27 April. Jacob Beam of the State Department's Eastern Europe bureau headed the American delegation.[71] Prior to the meeting, the Americans had indicated that they supported full German participation in the planning group. During its first meeting, the Working Group accepted the U.S. suggestion that "the Germans attend as many plenary sessions as possible." Blankenhorn, the Federal Republic's incoming NATO delegate, was thus invited to London. It was decided, furthermore, to leave the question of German participation at a four-power conference to the FRG. Bonn must "take the responsibility" for this decision.[72] If Adenauer sent a delegation, then Moscow would certainly insist that the German Democratic Republic be represented as well. This, in turn, would grant legitimacy to the Ulbricht regime. The Western allies were no doubt certain that Adenauer could not accept this. But the conference was largely to focus on Germany. The responsibility for rejecting German participation in such a conference rested with Bonn itself. There could be no talk of a second "Potsdam." Still, this was an important occurrence. Bonn *could have* participated at the East-West summit. West German participation was, in the final analysis, not desirable. But this had nothing to do with those fears which plagued Adenauer, fears of another Potsdam. Rather, the West Germans were relegated to the edges of the conference by a political reality that weighed as heavily on Bonn as on its allies, if not more heavily. Bonn did not wish to compromise the *Alleinvertretungsanspruch*, its claim to be the sole representative of *all* Germans. Adenauer's allies harbored no intentions of cutting a deal with the Soviets behind his back.[73] The chancellor's "Potsdam nightmare" was quite at odds with reality.

The first piece of evidence which ought to have convinced Adenauer of this fact was allied acceptance of—and American insistence upon—West German participation at the London meetings. Blankenhorn's role in the

Working Group was limited. But the limitations were placed by Adenauer himself, who did not authorize the ambassador to "deal with any point of substance" before he himself met with Dulles at the NATO ministers' conference in Paris some days later.[74] He was, however, apparently authorized to raise some talking points. Adenauer must at this point have been preoccupied with the Austrian situation, since Blankenhorn felt the need again to emphasize Bonn's absolute rejection of German neutralization. The German federal government nevertheless thought that the Western allies might want to propose to the Soviets the creation of a "European security system." While Bonn had no proposal to make, Blankenhorn suggested some talking points, including nonaggression guarantees and arms limitation agreements. And, of course, American participation in the Europe-wide security arrangement was a must. The Germans and French, however, agreed that Moscow would probably decide that Germany should remain divided, especially if they could not secure American withdrawal from the continent.[75] The West Germans were determined to prevent this. Hence, the Adenauer government rejected the only plan for reunification which it thought the Soviets might accept. NATO was that important to Adenauer's policy.

It was exactly at this point in time that the Federal Republic was to begin contributing to NATO as a full member. This was the second piece of evidence to which Adenauer might have looked for reassurance that Germany's Western allies were not about to make a deal with the Soviets at Germany's expense. Washington had been campaigning for a substantial West German contribution to Western defense well before Eisenhower had entered office. In retrospect, it is impossible to imagine that Eisenhower and Dulles would have sacrificed their concrete victory some short weeks after it became a legal reality, in order to pursue a highly risky diplomatic initiative which directly contravened the wishes of America's valuable new ally. Von Eckardt seems instinctively to have grasped this. The Federal Republic's entry into NATO, the press aide correctly observed, was a "guarantee" against a Potsdam-like settlement between the Big Four.[76] Despite this, Adenauer continued to fret.[77]

These fears of Western, and particularly American, abandonment, mixed with what one scholar has with insight labeled Adenauer's "historical memory," to produce an "overriding foreign policy priority: integration within western economic, political, and security institutions."[78] The Germans, in fact, presented the political-military *Westintegration* that NATO entry brought as their overriding priority. Blankenhorn told the London working group that Adenauer was "determined to avoid at all costs giving any impression that the Federal Republic would waver in its allegiance to WEU and NATO."[79] He wanted, therefore, to "hold this course" until he had won the 1957 elections, by which time NATO integration ought to be irreversible. Thus, Blankenhorn asked his counterparts to "understand, certain questions of internal politics [were] more important than reunification immediately."[80] The domestic political questions were made more acute by those who thought that West Germany could get a good deal if it dumped NATO. Von Eckardt, at this point, thought that one of the "greatest dangers" faced by the Federal Republic, and the West in general, was:

> the position of public opinion in Germany and of the other western peoples, who time and again believed that the powerful men of the world need only sit themselves down at a table and then somehow peace would break out by itself.[81]

Because these ideas existed in the Federal Republic, Adenauer would have to continue to give rearmament in the context of NATO pride of position over reunification, at least in the short term. And it followed from this that he needed to stay in office to carry this plan to fruition.

NATO'S PARIS CONFERENCE: MEMBERSHIP AND OVERTURE

The Paris conference of NATO ministers was a milestone along the path toward Adenauer's goals, and, whether he recognized it or not, toward those of Eisenhower and Dulles. The two developments at Paris which are relevant to this study are (a) the Federal Republic's entry into NATO as a full partner and its simultaneous re-winning of sovereignty, and (b) the resolution to invite the Soviets to a four-power conference. The first development, though of tremendous importance, can be dealt with cursorily. The second development must be examined in greater depth for what it reveals about Bonn's influence upon American decision making at this time.

On 5 May, Germany was welcomed into NATO, a foregone conclusion since the instruments of the Paris accords' ratification had already been approved and deposited by West Germany's new allies. On this day, too, Conant, André François-Poncet, and F. R. Hoyer Millar, in Bonn, ended their service as high commissioners by proclaiming that "a new relationship" now existed between the Federal Republic, on the one hand, and the United States, France, and the United Kingdom on the other. As of noon, "the Allied High Commission and the Offices of the Land Commissioners in the Federal Republic are abolished."[82] On the same day, the German federal government proclaimed that the Federal Republic was "a free and independent state." In recognition of Adenauer's dogged attempts to reach this goal, the proclamation continued: "That which prepared itself for a long time on the basis of growing trust henceforth becomes a legal fact: We stand as free among the free, bound in true partnership to the erstwhile powers of occupation."[83] On this day, Bonn became the legal partner of Paris, London, and Washington.

But the meaning and extent of this partnership was immediately to be put to the test. The Paris conference was not meant merely to solemnize and celebrate the welcoming of a new and powerful ally into the alliance. The allies had serious work to do. The West was going to propose a four-power meeting before the foreign secretaries left Paris. But everything else—where and when to hold it, who should go, what should be discussed—remained to be settled. Thus the Paris meeting was a convenient time and place for the secretaries to attempt to reconcile conflicts over the four-power conference's level and agenda.

The most obvious conflict was that which had already emerged between London and Washington concerning the level of the meeting with the Soviets. Eisenhower had reiterated at his 27 June press conference that he saw "at this moment" no reason to hold a summit. The Austrian situation was a good sign, but apparently not enough evidence of Soviet goodwill to warrant a heads of government meeting.[84] But no number of like statements was enough to put off Eden. The prime minister wrote Eisenhower on 6 May, to advocate again the British proposal for a summit. Eden portrayed himself, in this letter, as very different from those naive individuals about whom von Eckardt expressed concern. Eden did not believe "that everything can be settled in a few hours or days of conversations." Rather, he saw a summit as providing an unmatched opportunity to decide upon a future program for discussion. The meeting would be "a starting point," and not a "final solution." He indicated, too, that this desire did not grow out of partisan politics, but out of the "deep desire of our whole people."[85] This last statement, Eisenhower knew, was less than candid. He indicated so in his response to Eden. Eisenhower and Dulles thought that a meeting held without adequate—that is, long—preparation would be a serious mistake. The foreign secretaries would have to discuss the question of a four-power conference's agenda before any decision was made. "I wonder," the president added, "whether such a scheme could be implemented without delaying too long the ability to issue the invitation, which delay might defeat the purposes you may be seeking."[86] The message was clear and unmistakable. Proper planning for a meeting with the Soviets took precedence over Tory political needs.

It was Dulles who first began to weaken in his opposition to a four-power conference at the heads of government level. With regard to a significant meeting with the Soviets, Dulles found "that there is a tremendous demand in [the] U.K. and France for something of this order." He still saw "serious disadvantages in any meeting of the President with the heads of the Soviet Union." But perhaps, if the meeting were to be of the sort that Eden proposed, an opportunity to talk without attempting to "reach any substantive decisions, probably the harm is held to a minimum."[87] Consequently, Dulles now advocated precisely the opposite case that Eisenhower had made to Eden only two days before. After consideration—and no doubt substantial pressure from the London delegation—Dulles concluded that a meeting without a thoroughly planned agenda was the least, and not the most, risky option for an expeditious summit. Dulles forwarded a U.S.-U.K. draft of an invitation to the Soviets in which the allies called for a heads of government meeting. The draft stipulated that the world leaders "should not undertake to agree upon substantive answers to the major difficulties facing the world."[88]

The president was patently not thrilled with the development, and insisted that the Big Four foreign ministers must meet to "canvass the field" before a summit. Dulles, in a letter to Eisenhower, reiterated his reservations. There was a "passionate eagerness here in Europe for a meeting of the Big Four, particularly on the Head-of Government level on the theory that this will produce some kind of miracle."[89] The Americans were very reluctant to hold a summit at which they felt pressured to work "miracles." Failure to resolve important questions at a summit could lead to disappointment, which in turn could engender the belief that America had not displayed enough flexibility. On the other hand, Eisenhower wanted Eden and Macmillan to know that he was aware of their domestic needs.[90] The key to resolving this dilemma was a summit of limited aspirations. The West could make clear as crystal that no one ought to expect anything concrete from the summit. The heads of government meeting would be the first in a series of meetings. These follow-up meetings of the foreign secretaries and experts would do the heavy lifting. The invitation to the Soviets, delivered on 10 May, said essentially this.[91]

This decision spoke volumes about a second question discussed at Paris and beyond, that of the substance of the discussions. London, Paris, and Washington united upon a formula which called for a conference without a concrete agenda. But resolve all they might to take no substantive steps at the summit, the Western heads of government could not foresee what the Soviets had planned. Nor could they guarantee that discussions would not go beyond what they initially foresaw. Since Germany had so much at stake at the summit, Adenauer thought that the West ought not to leave so much to chance. "In my opinion," wrote the chancellor, "this sort of important conference, as the imminent summit conference was supposed to be, had to be carefully planned, at least through prior arrangement of an agenda." To begin a conference without a concrete agenda in difficult times like these risked "great danger." Adenauer attempted to convince his allies of this in Paris. After all, he reports saying, he had shepherded the Paris accords through the Bundestag in part so that West German entry would cause Germany's uncertainty to dissipate, and would clarify the course for reunification.[92] At Paris, he had prevailed upon Dulles to take the lead in reunification.[93] Yet the Paris conferees delivered to Moscow an invitation which not only failed to propose a plan for overcoming German division. It failed, in fact, to even *mention* reunification as an issue for resolution. Perhaps Adenauer's Potsdam preoccupation was set off by this occurrence. He does not say. But the chancellor did record that "the failure to mention the German question in the invitation to the Russians was for me a grave disappointment." But "protests did not help."[94] Bonn's new allies had made their decision.

Nor could Adenauer count on a West German delegation at the summit to keep the discussions on track. The disadvantages of G.D.R. representation at the summit outweighed the benefits of having Blankenhorn, Hallstein, and Grewe attend. On 8 May, the chancellor informed Dulles that "he would prefer that Fedrep not participate if [this were] necessary to avoid D.D.R. [East German] participation." He still wanted Bonn "to be a full partner in preparing for such talks and closely consulted" during the summit.[95] But no Germans would sit at the green table.

As the previous chapter demonstrated, Adenauer was able to exert a certain amount of leverage in the allied discussions of the German question. He was not abjectly bound by the Federal Republic's singular status as occupied ally. Just as the Federal Republic became a full-fledged ally, however, the limits of this influence must have been depressingly obvious to the chancellor. Washington—the fulcrum of any leverage Bonn wished to exert in the alliance—had other allies with other demands. In attempting to compromise between Eden's needs and the administration's concerns, Eisenhower and Dulles agreed to a solution which was hard for Adenauer to swallow. Adenauer could, and sometimes did, get Washington to consider his government's position on issues of interest to West Germany. These concerns entered into the discussions of American policy makers. But as the invitation to the Soviets demonstrated, this influence was not a faucet which Adenauer could turn on at will.

His hands were tied, as well, by the political realities of the divided Germany. His determination to avoid granting legitimacy to the SED regime limited his diplomatic maneuverability. He could be reasonably certain that his allies would consult with him before and during the conference, as he had suggested to Dulles. But for the next few weeks, Adenauer faced the prospect of sitting on the sidelines at a Big Four conference that could determine the fate of Germany. And he worried.

"THE FIRE MUST BE KEPT BURNING": MAY AND JUNE 1955

As the summit approached, Adenauer's first fear was neutralization. Despite the generally good relations between Washington and Bonn, the strains of simultaneously seeking détente and rearming Germany in the context of

NATO began to take their toll. Bonn was constantly concerned that Eisenhower might sacrifice the latter goal in pursuit of the former. Washington's ambiguity—brought about by lack of coordination, more so than by any real interest in neutralization—culminated in a regrettable statement by the president at a press conference. The damage was severe, and Adenauer felt more alone than he had in half a dozen years. Even the friendship between the chancellor and Dulles fell victim to this "crisis."

The chancellor hardly needed his allies to call his foreign and German policies into question. He was getting enough of that at home. As elections approached in certain western *Länder*, the SPD had released its major report on foreign policy, which took the federal government to task for not doing enough to gain reunification. It was the "inescapable" (*unausweichlicher*) duty of all Germans to do what they could to gain reunification as quickly as possible. The West Germans especially needed to take action on this front. That this was one of the most important questions of *international* politics as well made it all the more "regrettable and incomprehensible" that the Adenauer government had yet to present a program. The SPD therefore presented a reunification program of their own.

The Social Democrats did not want to see the summit become another Berlin conference, at which the participants reiterated their old and incompatible positions. Such a result would leave Germany divided. Thus they suggested numerous points for the conferees to consider. The relevant points concern the "status of the reunified Germany" and the "European security system," for these proposals were most directly related to the neutrality issue. The Social Democrats fail to address the neutrality question in their discussion of the post-reunification status of Germany. This is quite an oversight, as well as a recognition of the difficult nature of the question. Ollenhauer and his lieutenants satisfied themselves with a hortatory statement that the question should be the subject of "rational (*vernünftige*) negotiations."

The opposition's position on neutralization becomes clearer in the next section, despite their best attempts to obscure the question. In addressing the European security system, the Socialists proposed that the reunited Germany should be a member of:

> [a] regional security system in the framework of the UN. At the same time it should be made clear that the reunified Germany does not have the intention of becoming a member of one or the other military bloc. That would, however, be neither neutralism nor neutrality, because it [Germany] would oblige itself through the raising of its own troops to cooperate in the guaranteeing and defense of security within the regulation of the United Nations.[96]

In point of fact, the SPD proposal *was* a proposal for neutralization of the reunified Germany. The opposition advocated the renunciation of alliance membership. This was the very core of the neutralization debate, which turned around whether a reunited Germany could continue to be a member of NATO. The SPD attempted to finesse the neutralization issue by claiming that an armed Germany, participating in a broad collective security arrangement, would by definition not be neutral. In fact, such a Germany *would* be neutral in terms of the East-West conflict. The SPD proposal is, rather, in line with the idea of "armed neutrality," which claimed some adherents at the time. The Social Democrats, nevertheless, continued to compare themselves and their ideas to the allegedly barren policy of the government.[97] Ollenhauer went on to elucidate his party's proposal for reaching a collective security agreement. On 17 May, he proposed in a radio address that the first step to be taken was the abrogation of the Paris and Warsaw treaty agreements, "insofar as they affect Western and Central Germany."[98]

Adenauer could well expect criticism from his domestic opposition. But he was nonplused when he perceived his American ally leaning in the direction of neutralization.[99] The most severe shock came when, at the end of his 18 May press conference, the president himself seemed to hint at the idea of "armed neutrality." In response to a question from Henri Pierre of the French newspaper *Le Monde*, the president spoke of "the thought that there might be built up a series of neutralized states from north to south through Europe." He added quickly that, although Austria and Switzerland were neutral, they were not disarmed. Switzerland would, he thought, "fight to the death" to preserve its independence. "That kind of neutrality," he concluded, "is a far different thing from just a military vacuum."[100]

Adenauer's response was intemperate, and, in retrospect, unwarranted by Eisenhower's statement. The president, in fact, *never mentioned Germany* in his response to Pierre's question, and said nothing whatsoever about German neutralization. The question itself was asked in the context of the Soviet-Yugoslavian rapprochement which was occurring at that time. The substance of the president's statement was that he had no objection to the neutrality of Switzerland, Austria, and Yugoslavia, as long as they could maintain their independence from outside domination. One might add that these three nations were in fact outside of the NATO–Warsaw Pact alliance framework, and that Eisenhower was thus saying nothing that Adenauer did not already know.

On the other hand, the president—whose mind clearly was not on Germany—failed to speak any word of reassurance to his ally, or to make clear that he was not referring to German neutralization. The Austrian settlement still weighed heavy on the minds of Adenauer and his colleagues.[101] Eisenhower's words, interpreted in this context by Adenauer, suggested that America was seriously considering the idea of a neutral belt in Central Europe, and that "the neutralization of Germany [was] a possible result of such considerations." The Soviets wanted nothing more than the withdrawal of American forces from Europe. He had said this time and again. But if Germany were neutralized, and America evacuated Europe as part of the settlement, then who was left to make sure that Moscow kept its end of the bargain? "The Soviet Union's breaking of treaties in the last decade did not encourage the belief that such a treaty would be in force for long." He instructed Ambassador Krekeler to make Bonn's objections known to Dulles.[102]

The chancellor was so disconcerted by Eisenhower's statement that he recalled his ambassadors from Paris, London, and Washington, with the goal of "killing once and for all" the idea of neutralization. His remarks at this meeting were quite extreme; he went so far as to suggest that Dulles was secretly working on a neutralization scheme. And after exerting so much effort over the past years to convince America of the Federal Republic's reliability, it seemed that the Americans had an historical memory of their own. "Germany was still the enemy. In spite of everything, they do not view us as a friend. They view us as necessary against Russia." If America could come to some sort of agreement with the Soviets, they might disregard Germany's interests. Adenauer thus set his aides to work to come up with a German initiative on the neutralization question.[103] His government also ratcheted up its press campaign, attacking the SPD and Ollenhauer in particular for allegedly sympathizing with the "neutral belt" scheme. The SPD responded that they too rejected the idea of a neutral belt in Central Europe. A neutral zone necessarily would be a buffer between two hostile blocs. This flew in the face of their desires for a collective security agreement for all of Europe. And in the opinion of the FDP press, the "coalition and opposition unanimously reject American-Russian speculation on a Middle European neutrality belt."[104] Adenauer could apparently count on significant domestic support against this new American initiative.

But, in fact, there was no new initiative, and the United States acted quickly to counteract some of the damage. In late May, Acting Secretary of State Herbert Hoover Jr. met with Krekeler—now back in the United States—in an attempt to reassure him that nothing was being done behind the chancellor's back. Krekeler reported that the chancellor was quite disturbed by the way in which the American press and populace had embraced the suggestion of a neutralized belt in Central Europe. Hoover assured Krekeler that public opinion in favor of a neutral belt was "probably due to ignorance. Americans have not yet realized the import of neutrality." Hoover instructed the Bonn embassy to "to take earliest possible opportunity to relieve Adenauer [of] his concern regarding any independent action by the U.S. Govt. Reassure Chancellor [of] our intention [to] consult his Government respecting any negotiations with Soviets concerning Germany." He added that the administration agreed wholeheartedly with Adenauer's opposition to German neutralization. "We have not worked for many years to reach solution permitting Germany [to] make appropriate contribution to Western defense only to jettison our recent achievements in this field," he stated categorically.[105] Krekeler indicated that the chancellor was no longer worried about the position of the American government on the neutralization issue, since Krekeler "had been able to reassure the Chancellor with regard to [the administration's] official position."[106]

During the 27 May Bundestag foreign policy debate, Adenauer likewise expressed his satisfaction that neutralization was not a goal of the Eisenhower administration.[107] The Bonn embassy, following Hoover's instructions, likewise attempted to repair the damage by convincing the German federal government that the United States had no interest in neutralization or withdrawal from Europe.[108]

Despite his professions of confidence in the Eisenhower administration, however, it is likely that the chancellor was not yet reassured of American intentions. Meeting with Dulles in Washington on 13 June—only a month before the summit—Adenauer raised the issue of Eisenhower's press conference statement. He indicated that in his opinion Dulles's State Department "at times did not participate in the formation of foreign policy." This left certain other, influential figures to meddle in policy making. These were: the president's brother Milton; the White House chief of Staff, Sherman Adams; Senate Foreign Relations Committee Chairman Walter George; and George Kennan. Particularly by his inclusion of Kennan, Adenauer evinced a certain lack of awareness of how American policy was actually made. Dulles stated that no one in Washington was making foreign policy "of which he was ignorant," nor was there any substance to these rumors of a White House foreign policy cabal.[109]

With regard to the approaching summit, now set for Geneva in mid-July, Dulles and Eisenhower also sought to reassure the chancellor. They indicated that "we must keep in extremely close contact with the chancellor before and during the Geneva meeting."[110] From Washington, it was on to Boston, where the chancellor was to receive an honorary doctorate from Harvard University. During his Harvard address, Adenauer called for patience at the Geneva conference. Indicating that he expected no quick results from a heads of government meeting, he noted that Geneva could actually be the beginning of a long process, "as far as I am concerned very long, . . . one, two years long. Still, such a long duration of the conference will bring détente with it." Hitting upon his perennial theme, Adenauer called on the Americans to take the lead on disarmament, "since there can only be a détente, if the U.S.A. and the Soviet Union agree upon a comprehensive disarmament plan."[111]

On his way home from America, Adenauer stopped off in London for a meeting with Eden. The prime minister also sought to assure Adenauer that the Western powers had no intention of neutralizing Germany. Eden told the chancellor that he was attempting to figure out how to reunify Germany without neutralizing it. In his opinion, it was possible:

> that the Russians did not want the reunification of Germany. If this were true, he hoped that [the Western delegates] would succeed in compelling the Russians at the Geneva Conference . . . to make known before all the world their insufficient readiness to realize the reunification [of Germany].

If the Soviets proved obdurate, and said "no" to reunification and a European security agreement, then at least one would know "clearly and exactly" where one stood. If, on the other hand, they agreed with the West on these issues, it would indeed be a fine day.

The chancellor thought that the West must present a *package deal*—presumably linking reunification with security and disarmament agreements—to the Soviets, which they then could accept or reject. Settlement of one issue in isolation was, by implication, a danger to the West, since "the goal of the Russians remained the same, namely, to drive the United States out of Europe." Yet, with this said, Adenauer thought that there was value in continuing the Geneva process. He expressed to Eden a "pressing wish": If the Geneva round of talks produced nothing concrete or desirable, he hoped that the West would not simply break off discussions. He desperately wanted to avoid the impression that the process of negotiating German unity and security had died. "The fire must be kept burning." Difficult questions had to be referred to "committees or working groups" for further discussion. In his opinion, "it would make an unfavorable impression, and raise the unrest and fear in the world, and harden the opposing fronts, if the conference led to a visibly negative result."[112]

From Adenauer's perspective, it seemed that the best possible summit would be one which walked the fine line between futility and overanxious agreement. The latter, of course, meant another Potsdam. But a conference that ended in nothing but harsh words and mutual blame was equally dangerous. Thus, the chancellor hoped that issues which were not decided at the summit could be referred to commissions, which could continue discussions. The point seemed not to be the reaching of agreements, but the ability to say that reunification, European security, and disarmament were still being actively negotiated by East and West. The summit held great dangers for Adenauer and his government. If the summit ended brusquely and with no hope of follow-up negotiations, the West German public might well conclude that reunification was a dead issue. No German government could allow such a perception. Far better to be able to say that the allies were still discussing that issue with Moscow. The summit need not succeed. But he ought to be able plausibly to deny that it had failed.

The related issues of disarmament and European security gained added poignancy in the days before the summit as well, due to an ill-timed NATO exercise called "Carte Blanche." This war game was designed to test NATO's ability to respond to a Pearl Harbor–like strike by the "eastern" forces. Well over 300 atomic bombs were "dropped" during the exercise, "killing" an estimated 1.7 million West Germans. The episode has been treated well elsewhere.[113] What is important for this discussion is the fact that Adenauer was put on the defensive on the security issue quite soon before the summit, and only weeks after the Federal Republic entered NATO.[114] Adenauer's assurances regarding German security in the days after Carte Blanche may have been "bland," as one scholar has labeled them.[115] But the chancellor had been championing nuclear disarmament in allied councils before Carte Blanche. The war game made clear to many Germans what ought to have been obvious: that being the front-line state in a nuclear standoff was incredibly risky business. The chancellor's repeated calls for arms control must have resulted in part from a realization that the West German press and people would eventually realize this in its full and horrific scope. And while Bonn's defense doctrine certainly wanted something in coherence, Adenauer *had* in fact taken pains to avoid giving the impression that he was unaware or unconcerned about the threats which nuclear weapons posed to Germany. This he did by attempting to keep the issue of arms control alive.

Adenauer had emphasized disarmament when he visited Washington, viewing "general disarmament as a framework within which chances for world peace, in general, and the reunification of Germany, in particular, can grow."[116] Weeks before, Dulles had told the National Security Council that "the subject of disarmament would be among the most important matters on which the United States must be prepared for discussions" at the four-power conference. Presidential adviser Harold Stassen had been working up a report on this very topic, to aid in preparation for the conference. Yet Dulles indicated that he thought that no substantive progress would be made on this issue at the summit. Rather, the conference "would be expected to explore ways and means by which the interested nations could proceed to deal with the problem."[117] In other words, discussion of disarmament at the four-power conference meant discussion of *the procedure for further discussion*.

In essence, this was the Eisenhower administration's prognosis for the summit. Washington expected literally nothing of substance to come from the summit. But the administration was hopeful that the heads of government could refer questions of substance to the foreign secretaries, to committees of experts, or some other—*proper*—forum. Insofar as this was possible, the Bonn government's goals for the summit would be met.

Dulles in particular was convinced that the conference ought to be devoid of substance. If it was important to Adenauer that the West make German reunification a top priority, it was, nevertheless, important to Dulles not to get into concrete proposals at Geneva. On 20 May, during a State Department meeting held to prepare for the four-power conference, Merchant presented the secretary with a paper which the European Affairs bureau had prepared on German reunification. Dulles responded that "the meetings of the Chiefs of Government would not deal with substantive issues. It would determine what issues the four powers would discuss and how, when and where they would be discussed." As for the German question, it would be "assigned to the Foreign Ministers as a problem for a subsequent meeting with the three Western Allies consulting fully with the Federal Republic during the course of the meeting, while the Soviets did the same with the representatives of the German Democratic Republic."[118] Eisenhower likewise wanted to limit substantive discussions at Geneva. In a telegram to the London embassy, the State Department clarified Washington's assumptions about the summit. Eisenhower "believes that the Delegations should be limited to reflect the purpose of the meeting not to engage in any substantive discussions of issues." Rather, the delegations should clarify the issues for further discussion, and then "agree on methods" for solving the problems.[119]

Scholars who have studied American participation at the Geneva summit seldom fail to point out that Eisenhower and Dulles approached the conference with very different attitudes. Eisenhower's disposition was characteristically sunny and optimistic, while Dulles was burdened with worries, even fearing that Eisenhower might give away the store.[120] But if their attitudes were different, their expectations were similar: neither thought that significant progress would be made on the *substance* of any important issue, although both hoped that *procedures* for solving the problems could be worked out.

Adenauer had not asked for much. More than anything, he wanted to be able to show the West German public that the Western allies were sincerely seeking an agreement which would unify Germany. A "visibly negative" end to the summit, he had told Eden, would be a grave danger to his government. The Americans were willing—in fact anxious—to continue discussions with the Soviets after the summit. Yet it was unclear whether their expectations for a substance-free conference would lead them to neglect Adenauer's domestic political needs. A decision to simply agree that the four powers would discuss Germany at some later date, without any attempt by the West to emphasize the importance of German unification, would be a disaster for Adenauer. The West Germans could not sit by and passively await the conference.

THE GENEVA SUMMIT OF JULY 1955[121]

As the summit approached, the Germans continued to press the United States to take seriously their concerns. Blankenhorn, now accompanied by Wilhelm Grewe, participated in the Western planning group meetings held in Paris and Geneva from 8 July until the eve of the summit. Not shy about advancing German interests, Blankenhorn bluntly told the working group on 9 July that the "West must be prepared to advance concrete ideas on German reunification and security system because of [the] public opinion factor." Public opinion demanded that the West attempt to press the Soviets hard on this issue. In addition, the Soviets had, on 7 June, invited Adenauer to Moscow. The chancellor would be in a difficult situation indeed if he were to arrive in Moscow in September without knowing what the West proposed to do about the German question. Anticipating the path that the Soviets would in fact take, Blankenhorn emphasized that the Western powers must not allow the Soviets to extract the German question from its four-power context. It could not be solved in bilateral negotiations between Bonn and Moscow, or, worse yet, Bonn and East Berlin. The Germans also insisted that the West do something to placate public opinion on the question of a plan for European security. Blankenhorn suggested that this need could be met by proposing "principles for [a] European security plan on [a] vague and general basis." This should be sufficient.[122]

The Federal Republic's intervention in allied discussions again bore fruit. Dulles, Joint Chiefs of Staff Chairman Arthur Radford, and Deputy Secretary of Defense Robert Anderson—a favorite of the president—met on the following day and discussed the working group's telegram. While the Americans had hoped to "restrict [the] Summit meeting to identification of issues and methods for dealing with them," Washington now faced the "strong likelihood [of] some more substantive discussion in deference to our allies, particularly Germans."[123] In the days leading up to the conference, leaders of the three Western powers evinced a quick learning curve on this issue. On 15 July, Macmillan essentially repeated Blankenhorn's above-quoted suggestion in a meeting of the three foreign secretaries. The British foreign secretary suggested that the West "should be vague within necessary limits but sufficiently precise to give satisfaction to Adenauer and the Europeans." Dulles agreed, noting that "we should consider what [the] West Germans needed by way of encouragement."[124] The West had made its decision, then. Due to the domestic needs of their German ally, France, the United Kingdom, and America would not simply relegate German unity and European security to future meetings between experts. This did not mean that they expected to *solve* these issues at Geneva. They did not.[125] But they were willing to act as if they thought these questions soluble, in order to affect German and European public opinion.[126]

The opening of the conference found Germans from both East and West present as observers. The delegates from the German Democratic Republic, it goes without saying, never met with the Western representatives. Nor, as far as Grewe could tell, did they confer very much with the Soviets. They seem to have been relegated to the sidelines. The West Germans also kept to the margins of the conference, and, according to Grewe, did not "play a meaningful role on the western side."[127] The West German observer delegation made clear in its final report that its members were not entirely satisfied with the experience. Their complaints were legion: Only rarely did all three Western powers report to them on discussions with the Soviets; reports from one ally from time to time differed in fundamental ways from those of another; some important developments went unreported; the Germans were rarely given access to conference documents; and so forth.[128] Blankenhorn's assessment was considerably less gloomy. Grewe compared Berlin to Geneva and found the latter disappointing. Blankenhorn noted that a major difference between Berlin and Geneva was Adenauer's geographical proximity to the summit. During the conference, Adenauer found himself in the mountains at Mürren, Switzerland, "where I spent a vacation," he added, apparently without intended humor. Adenauer was in "constant contact" by telephone and telegraph with the other delegations, especially that of the United States. He was thus able to receive detailed reports about developments at the conference.[129]

Von Eckardt, the third high-level observer at Geneva, took a reporter's attitude toward the question. "It must be said that we were well informed," he noted in his memoirs. The real problem was that the Bonn delegates were in Geneva only as observers. Hence they received all of their information secondhand, like the army of reporters which had gathered to cover the conference. Von Eckardt thought that the Western participants tried hard to keep the West Germans informed. But the secondhand reports were often hard to reconcile, and the Bonn delegation had to spend time trying to sift through the differing reports, in order to come up with a single report for the chancellor at the end of each day.[130]

The West German observers differed among themselves as to the quality of the information which they received. But it would be hard to argue that their role went much beyond that of observation and reporting, and in this Grewe is certainly correct. Bonn's influence on the Geneva conference was exerted primarily *before* the conference opened. Adenauer had insisted that the West make a show of their deep desire for German unity. After the delegates arrived and took their places, however, they requested little German input. Given that they had already agreed with Adenauer's two basic exhortations—that they talk of reunification as if they meant it, and that they do nothing to imply acceptance of neutralization or weakening of NATO—there was no reason for them to do so.

A meeting between Eden, French Prime Minister Edgar Faure, and Eisenhower on 17 June in Geneva served to confirm that Adenauer's two major desires for the conference were already official allied policy. Eden thought that the most important issue that the heads of state would have to deal with in the coming days "was the question of German unity and how we could help a friendly German government and make sure that the NATO front was firmly sustained." The prime minister was convinced that the Soviets would not want to talk about Germany at the Geneva conference. Yet such a discussion was important to the "friendly German government" which had urged its allies to press this issue at the summit. Eisenhower agreed with Eden that Germany was the "most important subject" which they faced, and hence that reunification had to be the subject of frank discussions between the powers. But any discussion of the German question need not have raised the specter of Potsdam. The president added that a "second point which should be developed [at Geneva] is that neutralization of Germany would be an impossible condition for us as a price for the restoration of German unity."[131]

Eden, in his opening remarks to the plenary conference session, devoted himself to the question of German reunification. While progress on the issue was highly unlikely, he and his allies would not let the German question die of neglect at the summit. In an effort to present something new to the world—something which might be labeled as "progress"—Eden deviated from the reunification plan he had proposed in Berlin a year and a half before. He now proposed a multilateral security agreement which would go into effect upon reunification. This concert of powers would bind the Geneva summit participants and the reunified Germans in mutual pledges of assistance. Should any one of the signatories come under attack, the others would come to its aid. Along with this, he proposed discussions of force and armament levels in central Europe. These discussions were to embrace "Germany and the countries neighboring Germany," in other words, certain Warsaw Pact states. Finally, he raised the possibility of "a demilitarized area between East and West." He hoped, he said, that the conference could come to some agreement on the outlines of that which he had suggested.

This was not to be. Bulganin spoke after Eden, and in his reply indicated that "any unity for Germany was a matter for a more distant future." The Soviets still saw German membership in NATO as the supreme obstacle to reunification, and wanted a much broader security guarantee than Eden had suggested. The Soviets continued to stump for "a system of collective security with the participation of all European nations and the United States of America." The final goal of negotiations would be the withdrawal of foreign troops from European states. Eventually, the United States would have to leave Europe.[132]

Dulles thought that Bulganin's speech had been consciously "moderate in tone." Yet to him it was clear that Moscow was seeking "to bury German unification under a mass of prerequisites."[133] While Eden pointed to the positive tone of Bulganin's remarks, it is clear that he saw things as Dulles did. He indicated at a heads of government session on 19 July that there would be a "great delay involved in reaching agreement on [a] security pact involving all Europe, U.S. and Canada. . . . He concluded, expressing deep concern on idea of postponing German unity while working out European security system." Bulganin continued to insist that reunification could not be achieved any time soon, and that it must come "gradually step by step."[134] It must have been clear to all conference participants at this point that initial predictions had been correct: There would be no substantive progress on the German question at Geneva.

Molotov, in fact, hoped that his Western counterparts would "drop entirely the matter of German unification and leave Adenauer without any hope on this subject except such hope as he may derive from his prospective visit to Moscow." This, at least, was how Dulles perceived the Soviet position.[135] The British, however, were not yet willing to call it a complete loss. Macmillan worried that if the allies dropped the topic at this point "the German reaction to the seeming failure of the Western powers to support their aspirations would be unfortunate." Without getting *something* from the Soviets at this summit, *some* indication of progress on German unification, the impression would arise that the West had now accepted the fact of German division.[136] This could not be allowed. (Troyanovsky reports that the stubbornness did not hurt Anglo-Russian relations all that much. "At that time the English leadership continued to follow a somewhat different policy from that of Washington," and thus Eden felt free to suggest that Khrushchev and Bulganin might want to pay an official visit to London. The Americans, and Dulles in particular, were not ecstatic about this news," in Troyanovsky's view. If he is correct, then Eden achieved at least one of his objectives at Geneva.)[137]

Yet despite continued efforts to raise the issue, and to impress upon the Soviet delegation the "urgency Western delegates attach[ed to] German reunification,"[138] the Soviet position remained unchanged: The German question could not be profitably discussed at this point. Until the preconditions—including a European security arrangement and a disarmament agreement—were met, there was simply no point in discussing Germany.

Dulles suspected that the Soviets wanted to avoid any substantive discussion of Germany with the Western powers now, so that Adenauer would go to Moscow with the knowledge that his allies had been unable to help him. This could give the Kremlin considerable leverage during the coming talks with Adenauer. His perception is reinforced by Molotov's insistence that German reunification should not even be "one of those topics designated for future study at this time."[139] Yet this was the absolute minimum which would be palatable to Adenauer. Under no circumstances could the Western delegates leave Geneva without an agreement to discuss Germany at some future, hopefully fixed, date.

Discussion of the German question continued along these lines. The delegates from the West insisted that leaving Germany divided would result in great instability and insecurity in Europe. The Soviets responded that reunification before a European security agreement was in force meant German membership in NATO, which they did not view as a contribution to the security of the continent.[140] The discussion was fruitless. Although Eisenhower, Eden, and Faure did not drop the topic, the summit moved on to other matters. (George-Henri Soutou writes that the French delegation did not even try to hide their satisfaction with the implications of Moscow's apparent commitment to a two-Germanies policy. This "would put off for an indefinite period [*renvoyait aux calends grecques*] all prospect of reunification.")[141]

The discussion moved on, though only into a different dead end. Eisenhower got the attention of the conferees and the world with his "Open Skies" proposal, which was meant to strengthen arm control agreements by allowing the Cold War adversaries to observe each other's armament efforts.[142] Immerman is convinced that "Open Skies was no mere psychological warfare initiative. Rather, the proposal reflected "genuine conviction that both because of and despite East-West distrust and hostility, the effort must be made to try to control nuclear weapons." He thus concludes that the president was genuinely disappointed that Geneva "accomplished so little."[143] But little was accomplished. Notably for this study, there were to be no stunning proposals, no surprising initiatives on the German question. East and West had reached an impasse over the connection between German unification and European security.

Assessment of the Geneva summit is a difficult business, because it depends so heavily upon the expectations which one brings to such an event. Eisenhower's speechwriter captures well the conflicting interpretations of Geneva. It was certainly significant that the meeting at Geneva "signalize[d] . . . the acceptance by the major powers of the common necessity to shun recourse to nuclear war."[144] Transcending the specifics of "Open Skies" or the final arms control directive was the "Spirit of Geneva," the atmosphere at the summit which seemed to bode well for the survival of the world. The Great Powers had set a precedent: the preferred method for settling East-West disputes was diplomacy, not war. This result of the conference was no less significant for having been symbolic.[145] Granted, the symbolism was not reassuring to all contemporary observers. Former U.S. ambassador to Moscow Averell Harriman viewed the Spirit of Geneva as a "smoke screen," before which the West would be lulled into complacency, thus preparing the way for future conflict.[146] He need not have worried, since the mostly atmospheric thaw of mid-1955 turned out to be "very fleeting and superficial."[147]

Anyone who anticipated progress on *specific* disputed questions, however, must have been disappointed by Geneva, a conference "whose only specific achievement consisted of an agenda of unresolved issues for future meetings of foreign ministers to leave still unresolved."[148] Yet Adenauer had wanted no more than this. A delay in answering the German question had been, for him, infinitely preferable to an overly hasty settlement reached by statesmen intoxicated by the Geneva spirit. This was easily avoided, because it was never a real possibility. The Soviets were reluctant at Geneva even to classify German unity as a question warranting further discussion at the ministerial level. Far better, Bulganin, Molotov, and Khrushchev had said, to put the German issue on hold. The Russians "left the conference without any agreements, yet with big sighs of relief." They viewed it as in their best interest to impress the Western leadership with their strength and unity in the post-Stalin period. Concrete issues could wait.[149]

The Western delegates managed, nevertheless, to include German unity in the Geneva directive as a topic for the foreign ministers to discuss in the autumn. The heads of state agreed in principle to German reunification by means of free elections, in the context of "the interests of European security."[150] Adenauer thereby dodged the other horn of the dilemma. As he had requested, his allies were persistent in raising the question of German unity with the Soviets. While Moscow would certainly have preferred to ignore the German question entirely, Eisenhower, Eden, and Faure tirelessly insisted that German unity was a prerequisite for lasting security in Europe. They had managed, at the end of the day, to garner Soviet agreement to continue deliberating the German issue. Most important of all, the Geneva directive preserved the status of the German question as a four-power issue. Adenauer was not to be cut adrift, and left to fend for himself when in Moscow. He could now credibly claim that it was not his lot to reach an agreement on reunification. Juridically, that question was for the ministers of the four powers to decide, *later*. Adenauer indicated at the end of the conference that he was satisfied with the results. The Western allies had "conclusively demonstrated their consideration of German interests."[151]

STALEMATE: BERLIN, MOSCOW, GENEVA II

Immediately after the end of the summit, Adenauer sent a letter to Dulles, thanking him for his and the allies' indefatigable work at Geneva. Adenauer noted that he considered it a "positive result" that the West had been able to arrange, for October, a foreign ministers conference with the same agenda as the summit. The chancellor assessed this result as a success, and he seemed to understand that it was not easily won. Yet he had a warning for the secretary: "We must now count, to an increasing extent, upon so-called détente maneuvers of the Soviets, which aim at misleading public opinion in our countries about the true goals of the Soviet Union." But the Soviets were limited in what they could do in the area of "détente maneuvers," for a reason at which Dulles hinted in his reply to the chancellor. The Soviets had refused to discuss German reunification at the summit, focusing instead upon the security issue. Dulles had come away from the summit, however, with the impression that security was not really their main concern. Rather, what most concerned them was "the political consequences of a liquidation of the GDR." The reunification of Austria and the about face on Yugoslavia—which Khrushchev and Bulganin had visited in late May—harbored risks for the Soviets. Now, Dulles thought, they would have to move very carefully on the German question. To signal that they were willing to abandon their ally in East Berlin might, in this context, shake the foundations of their satellite empire in Eastern Europe.[152] Dulles repeated this assertion a couple weeks later. In a letter to Adenauer, the secretary insisted that the Soviets were terribly concerned that if they let go of the German Democratic Republic, all of the Eastern Bloc would follow.[153]

His point was borne out before the Soviet delegation again set foot in Moscow. On their way home from Geneva, Khrushchev and Bulganin made a stop in East Berlin to show their support for the regime there. While in Berlin, the Soviet leaders propounded what became known as the "two Germanies" thesis. The "road to the solution of the German problem," the Soviet leaders proclaimed, must take account of "the actual conditions, in which there exist two German states . . . with differing economic and social systems." Regardless of what they had said just days before in Geneva, the Soviets now insisted that "the German problem cannot be settled without the participation of the Germans themselves, without a *rapprochement* between the German Democratic Republic and the German Federal Republic."[154]

Tacitly, the Soviets had abrogated the Potsdam treaty's recognition of four-power responsibility for German reunification. Now, reunification was to come, if at all, by the extraordinarily improbable means of inter-German dialogue. Dulles saw Khrushchev's and Bulganin's words in East Berlin as confirmation of his analysis. In a memorandum to the president, he noted that the Russians had "confirmed our judgment that the greatest obstacle to the unification of Germany is the effect upon other satellite governments if the GDR is liquidated."[155] Hamburg's highbrow, left-leaning weekly *Die Zeit* drew a conclusion not unlike that of the secretary of state's.

The Soviets never tire of declaring anew that they would like to keep the GDR, at all accounts, as a communist regime and a sovereign state. But that means: No reunification, unless as delineated by the east (*es sei denn unter östlichen Vorzeichen*).[156]

The Geneva-Geneva II process thus came to an end with the tacit ratification by all four powers of the security architecture designed and constructed in the previous year. Germany remained divided, with the West German state contained in, and contained by, the North Atlantic Treaty structure.

Marc Trachtenberg has addressed this development at length in *A Constructed Peace.* He points out the irony that the Soviets saw the dual containment provided by NATO as helping to guarantee their security against a revanchist Germany. Even if the Atlantic Alliance was directed at containing them, it nevertheless was also likely to "keep German power limited"; thus "the most basic Soviet interests would be protected." Moscow could accept this solution to the "German Problem." As we have seen, so too could Adenauer, who sought to anchor the Federal Republic in NATO in order to prevent it straying from the path of westward-looking liberal democracy and military integration. Membership in an institution such as NATO—as well as European institutions—allowed him to mitigate his propensity for worry: The septuagenarian Rhinelander could rest assured that his nation would remain within this institutional structure even after he had departed from the chancery.[157]

Adenauer's visit to the Soviet Union has been treated extensively elsewhere, particularly by Schwarz and Köhler.[158] For the purposes of this study, what is important to keep in mind is the fact that Adenauer held tight to the Western line while in Moscow, and gave no indication that he was interested in solving the problem of German division alone. If he had a "Potsdam nightmare," he was also aware of his allies' "Rapallo fears." In the United Kingdom such fears were especially pronounced, with the Foreign Office even giving over to some speculative anxiety about the commitment of Adenauer's potential successors to *Westbindung.*[159] The chancellor did nothing at Moscow to encourage these concerns. In late July, Adenauer's foreign minister, Heinrich von Brentano—who on 7 July had assumed this cabinet portfolio previously held by Adenauer—held a press conference in which he sought to impress upon the West Bonn's reliability. Reunification would be the main topic for discussion at Moscow, said Brentano. He could hardly have said otherwise. Yet he wanted to assure all listening "that the Federal Government would handle [this] problem with [the] same loyalty demonstrated by the Western Allies and in consultation with the West." The government would "strictly stick to its treaty obligations," added the foreign minister. "I can assure you [that the] Chancellor will not conduct informal negotiations."[160]

Again, Adenauer found himself in a difficult position. He had, on the one hand, to demonstrate his real commitment to the Western insistence that German unification was a matter for the four powers to resolve. He could not compromise his stand against reunification talks between Bonn and East Berlin. On the other hand, he could not let his recalcitrance give rise to the impression that he was not concerned about reunification and détente.[161] As promised, Adenauer did not sway from allied policy.[162] Yet he still returned home to great acclaim, having gained the release of ten thousand German prisoners of war, and begun the process of establishing diplomatic relations with Moscow. Both of these were significant developments.

The second, however, promised to cause problems for Adenauer's declared policy that states could not conduct official relations with the German Democratic Republic if they sought such relations with the Federal Republic. This is the so-called "Hallstein Doctrine": in Adenauer's words, to establish relations with the Ulbricht regime was "an unfriendly act," and would be treated as such by Bonn. Adenauer maintained that Moscow was the lone exception to the ban on "double representation," due to its unique status as a member of the quadripartite occupation and sponsor of East Berlin. His actions in Moscow had, nevertheless, established a precedent that other nations were highly likely to follow.[163]

It was, however, the visit of Khrushchev and Bulganin to East Berlin—and not Adenauer's journey into the very heart of the Soviet empire—that proved more significant. The words which they had spoken were meant seriously: As a result of Adenauer's Moscow trip, Bonn would soon have an ambassador in the Soviet Union. As a result of the promulgation of the "two Germanies" policy, Adenauer's diplomatic flexibility would significantly decrease.

More than a month before the foreign ministers met for Geneva II, Adenauer received a letter from Dulles which hinted at the path which Moscow would follow at the conference. The Soviets, he had no doubt, "will make a great play of their recognition of two Germanies as an argument for the rest of us to do the same."[164] Geneva directive and Potsdam Treaty aside, the Soviets no longer had any interest in treating German reunification as an issue for the four powers to resolve. Henceforth, the Soviets presented the West with two possibilities: (a) acknowledge the existence of two German states, which must resolve the German question in discussions with each other; or (b) drop the question altogether.

The second of these options had the added advantage of guaranteeing the continued existence of Moscow's German client state. For this reason, it seemed likely that the Soviets would exhibit at Geneva II continued reluctance to discuss the German issue at all. Dulles was well aware of this likelihood. At a cabinet meeting one week before Geneva II, Dulles noted "the probable Russian desire to avoid discussion of German unification. He believed the conference would be successful if it could achieve a discussion of this subject."[165] Apparently, after Geneva I and the Soviet leaders' remarks in Berlin, success meant simply getting the Soviets to *talk* about Germany.

Even by this modest standard, the second Geneva conference of 1955 must be rated as a failure. Geneva II, it quickly became apparent, was less a postscript to Geneva I than to Khrushchev's and Bulganin's East Berlin visit. The heads of state, in their directive, had called for reunification in the interest of the German people and the peoples of Europe. But, as the promulgation of the "two Germanies" policy indicated, Khrushchev was now thinking "only about the East German '*Volk*' and the communist 'peoples government'" of East Germany.[166] At Geneva, Molotov rejected Western plans for German reunification via free elections, and gave rather clear indications that the Soviets had no real interest in sacrificing their East German client to the cause of German unity.

The fact that the conference was going nowhere became clear early. Dulles telegrammed the State Department on 3 November that Molotov had "in effect served notice that Soviets will not risk jeopardizing their position in East Germany." He added that, in emphasizing the "social gains" achieved by the communist government of East Germany—a phrase which now began to appear in Soviet statements on the German question—as well as by "pointing out [the] contribution which free elections made to the rise of Hitlerism," Molotov was patently indicating that the Soviets had no interest in free elections in Germany.[167] The Soviets instead insisted that the two German governments must meet to begin bilateral discussion and cooperation on the issue.[168] Molotov insisted upon the two Germanies approach, and clearly was not interested in forwarding the goals of the heads of government directive. As the president saw it, the Soviets were basing their actions upon their fear that the loss of a "friendly" regime in East Germany would undermine their entire Eastern European empire.[169]

After clarifying the Soviet position on free elections, Molotov went on to reverse one of the hard-won gains which the West had made at Geneva I: the recognition of the inseparability of German unification and European security. After returning from a brief visit to Moscow, Molotov seemed even more determined to discard the Geneva I directive. The West's reunification proposals were "removed from the realities of life." It was a fact that there were now two sovereign German states. The Soviet Union was determined to continue conducting relations between itself and the German Democratic Republic on the basis of the cooperation treaty which the two states had signed in September. The Soviets simply could not, under these circumstances, accept "that it is impossible to bring about European security prior to reunification of Germany."[170]

Dulles found Molotov's graceless performance contemptible. It was "one of the most cynical and uncompromising speeches which I have heard."

Molotov had unilaterally repudiated important elements of the heads of government directive. Perhaps most importantly, he now rejected the idea of "all German elections," indicating that the Soviet Union would "never permit Eastern Germany to be reunified with Western Germany except under conditions which clearly implied the communization of all Germany."[171] Eisenhower responded to Dulles's report of the Soviet position by acknowledging the stalemate: "In such an atmosphere," the president cabled Dulles "there seems to be little value in dragging out the conference." Molotov's biographer also emphasizes the "inflexible" line taken by the foreign minister throughout this phase of East-West negotiation. As a result, he concludes, the conference was "a complete failure."[172]

In his closing statement to the conference, Dulles expressed his frustration at the lack of progress during the previous weeks. There was "little agreement to record." The Soviets had rejected all attempts by the West to reach an agreement on European security and German reunification, despite Western attempts to meet their security concerns. The Soviets had thereby demonstrated that "security is not the primary reason why the Soviet Union does not agree to the reunification of Germany." Rather, the "primary reason" why Germany now remained divided was that Moscow did not want to subject its East German client to free elections, which it would surely lose.[173]

The Geneva process had, in the end, done nothing to bring German unification closer. A summary written in an Italian foreign affairs journal a year and a half later laconically expressed the state of the German Question after Geneva II: "Today, the Soviet Union does not want German reunification on terms that are reasonable for the West . . . nor, moreover, do its interlocutors appear in fact ready to meet the needs of Moscow."[174]

Adenauer had urged his allies to continue discussing the German question after the summit. They had done so. Yet now, with the Soviets stalwartly adhering to the two Germanies doctrine, the Western program for German unification had taken a step backward. This left West Germany in a difficult situation. Eden recognized this, noting in his 17 November letter that the "worrying part of this business [i.e. Geneva II's failure] is its effect on West Germany."[175] This deadlock on the issue of German reunification caused Adenauer anxiety. He made clear to Dulles that things could not be left as they were when the conference ended. Dulles reported to the State Department in a cable which the acting secretary forwarded to Eisenhower himself that "Adenauer is very anxious there should be another conference so that he will not be left alone to deal with [the] unresolved problem of German reunification."[176] Adenauer perceived, apparently, that he had to keep the pressure on his allies to continue discussing reunification with the Soviets. Conspicuous recognition of the impasse with the Soviets threatened to make his policy of *Westbindung* and nonrecognition of East Berlin untenable.

In June 1955—that is, after the Austrian settlement, the Soviet thaw with Tito, the invitation to Adenauer to come to Moscow, and the agreement upon a summit—C. D. Jackson wrote his influential former boss to give him an assessment of the state of the Cold War. Jackson told Henry Luce that historians would view 1955 as the "year things began to get unstuck." All these things had happened because Moscow was becoming aware of its own weaknesses. One could expect further concessions in the coming months.[177] But historians have the advantage, which Jackson did not then possess, of being able to assess the second half of the year. Soviet weaknesses, which Jackson perceived, seem to have led Moscow to consolidate its position, investing itself even more heavily in the survival of the East German regime. With regard to the German question, 1955 appeared to be the year when things became almost inextricably stuck: East and West were now clearly at loggerheads over the question of reunification by means of free elections.[178]

Adenauer was thus confronted in 1955 with the limitations of West Germany's influence upon the events which would determine its future. First, Adenauer found that his ability to shape the agenda of his Western allies, though still significant, had its limits. Washington in particular had not wanted substantive discussions at Geneva I. Eisenhower, Eden, and Faure *did* placate Adenauer by tirelessly insisting upon discussion of German reunification at Geneva. Yet they refused his urgent requests that no conference take place without a settled agenda. In this instance, he did not get everything that he wanted, but did get what was most important to him.

Still, he could not have been terribly satisfied as 1956 approached. For if 1955 had demonstrated one thing, it was that even if Bonn could affect the Big Three's discussions with Moscow, it could do nothing to get Moscow to acquiesce in Bonn's German policy. In this sense, the limitations upon the Federal Republic were largely self-imposed. The more Adenauer pressed the West to refuse to deal with East Berlin, and to refuse to consider any solution which would exclude German participation in NATO, the less likely it became that the Soviets and the West could come to an agreement. *Westbindung* was paying off to the extent that Bonn's interests were taken seriously in the councils of the West. The drawback was that reunification was no closer at the end of 1955 than it had ever been.

NOTES

1. For the events surrounding EDC's death and WEU's rebirth, see especially Edward Fursdon, *The European Defense Community: A History* (New York: St. Martin's Press, 1979), 295–321.
2. For an analysis of the remarkable constitutional debate surrounding West German entry into EDC, see Karl Lowenstein, "The Bonn Constitution and the

European Defense Community Treaties: A Study in Judicial Frustration," *Yale Law Journal* 64:6 (May 1955), 805–39. The documentation of the constitutional debate is assembled in the 800,000-word collection *Der Kampf um den Wehrbeitrag* (Munich: Isar Verlag, 1952).

3. Stiftung Bundekanzler Adenauer Haus (StBKAH) III, 1 [A-C]. Letter to Churchill, 1 September, 1954.

4. Schwarz, *Die Ära Adenauer*, 247.

5. Article by Krone in *Norddeutsche Zeitung*, 9 September, 1954. ACDP, Nachlaß Krone, I-028-001/2.

6. William I. Hitchcock, *France Restored: Cold War Diplomacy and the Quest for Leadership in Europe, 1944–1954* (Chapel Hill: University of North Carolina Press, 1998), 196.

7. JFD/DDEL, White House Memoranda, Meetings with the President, 1954 [1], Box 1, Folder 11. Note also that Dulles told Adenauer on 16 September, 1954, that the United States would be willing to go ahead with interim rearming of Germany, even if the French wanted to wait until a new rearmament program was approved by the Assembly. Clearly, Dulles had had enough of French delays. JFD/DDEL, Subject Series, Box 8, Folder 13, File: Germany (2).

8. On the economic rapprochement, as well as some of its spillover into other issues, see Sylvie Lefèvre, "Vers le rapprochement des economies française et allemande (1945–1955)," *Relations Internationales* 93 (Spring 1998), 85–97. In his review of Lefèvre's subsequent book, Andrew Shennan writes of "the markedly nonlinear way" that West German recovery and integration occurred in the first ten years of peace. The beneficial results reaped by Bonn due to the death of EDC certainly support Shennan's choice of adverb and adjective. See *American Historical Review* 106:1 (February 2001), 247.

9. Ivanov, *Duait Eizenkhauer*, 239.

10. This discussion of Eisenhower's experiences at the end of World War II is based on Ambrose, *Eisenhower*, Vol. 1, 400–401.

11. Ivanov, *Duait Eizenkhauer*, 239.

12. The notes on the Eisenhower-Zhukov conversations are collected in V. Naymov, ed., *Georgii Zhukov: Stenogramma oktiabr'skogo (1957g.) plenuma TsK KPSS I drugie dokumenti* (Moscow: MFD, 2001).

13. Translations of these notes are found in *DSB* 31:807 (13 December, 1954), 902–907.

14. "Informationsgespräch," 15 November, 1945, ACDP, Nachlaß von Eckardt, I-010-007/2.

15. Soviet note of 23 October, 1954. *DSB* 31:807, 904.

16. ACDP, ibid., "Informationsgespräch."

17. *DSB*, ibid., 906.

18. Adenauer's Address to the National Press Club, 29 October, 1954, JFD/DDEL, Subject Series, International Subseries, Box 8, Folder 12.

19. Blankenhorn, 203.

20. Heinrich Krone, "Aufzeichnungen zur Deutschland- und Ostpolitik 1954–1969," in Rudolf Morsey and Konrad Repgen, *Untersuchungen und Dokumente zur Ostpolitik und Biographie*, Adenauer-Studien III (Mainz: Matthias-Grünewald-Verlag, 1967), 135. Eisenhower expressed his continued frustration with Paris in a letter

to Churchill on 14 December. Prior to French ratification of the Paris accords, the president wrote, "I am determined that we shall begin to realize some dividends on the constant pledges and pronouncements that seem to be expected of us." Boyle, *Churchill-Eisenhower Correspondence*, 182.

21. Blankenhorn, 205.

22. Grewe, 218.

23. Schwarz, *Adenauer: Der Staatsmann*, 180.

24. Blankenhorn, 206–7.

25. Telegram, Department of State to Office of the High Commissioner for Austria, 15 February, 1955, *FRUS, 1955–1957*, Vol. 5, 1.

26. Telegram, Austrian High Commission to Department of State, 26 February, 1955, ibid., 4. See also Telegram, Austrian High Commission to Department of State, 23 February, 1955, ibid., 2.

27. Wolfgang Mueller, "Stalin and Austria: New Evidence on Soviet Policy in a Secondary Theatre of the Cold War," *Cold War History* 6:1 (February 2006), 76.

28. Günter Bischof, "Österreichische Neutralität, die Deutsche Frage, und Europäische Sicherheit 1953–1955," in Rolf Steininger, Jürgen Weber, Günter Bischof, Thomas Albricht, and Klaus Eisterer, eds., *Die Doppelte Eindämmung: Europäische Sicherheit und die Deutsche Frage in den Fünfzigern* (Munich: V. Hase & Koehler Verlag, 1993), 133. On the internal power struggle within the Kremlin, and its effects on Austrian policy, see Vojtech Mastny, "Kremlin Politics and the Austrian Settlement," *Problems of Communism* 33:4 (July–August 1982), 37–51.

29. Gerhard Stourzh, *Kleine Geschichte des Österreichischen Staatvertrages* (Graz, Vienna, Cologne: Verlag Styria, 1975), 104.

30. Vladislav Zubok and Constantine Pleshakov indicate that Khrushchev in fact pushed for an Austrian settlement against Molotov's objections. The episode took place in the context of the internal battle within the Kremlin over control of Soviet foreign policy. Khrushchev thus scored a signal victory over Molotov in de-linking the German and Austrian questions. Zubok and Pleshakov, *Inside the Kremlin's Cold War*, 169–71.

31. Bischof, "Österreichische Neutralität," 155–57.

32. Adenauer prints a large portion of the TASS statement in his memoirs. See Adenauer, *Erinnerungen, 1953–1955*, 399–403.

33. Adenauer, ibid., 411–12.

34. Ibid., 413–15.

35. Eisenhower, *Mandate for Change*, 506.

36. Köhler notes that Adenauer and his aides saw Soviet compromises on Austria as directed at a "German address." Yet Köhler adds that there was no evidence that the Soviets "seriously pursued the [Austrian] plan, to also offer such a solution for Germany." *Adenauer*, 853.

37. Schwarz, *Adenauer: Der Staatsmann*, 180–81.

38. Ibid., 182.

39. NARA, Department of State Central Decimal Files, 762a.00/3-1455.

40. Memorandum of a conversation, Maier, Merchant et al., 10 March, 1955, NARA, Department of State Central Decimal File, 762a.00/3-1055.

41. Merchant had assured Krekeler, on 3 March, that he "did not foresee any complications in the hearings." Memorandum of a conversation, Krekeler and Mer-

chant, 3 March, 1955, NARA, Department of State Central Decimal File, 762a.00/3-355. The hearings before the Senate Foreign Relations Committee went as smoothly as Merchant suggested. One senator, Alexander Wiley of Wisconsin, even shared Bonn's concern that the Soviets could still try to "wreck the plans now of the Western Union [sic] and German rearmament." Dulles acknowledged that the Soviets had "held out the bait of the unification of Germany" in order to prevent German rearmament. And "they have failed." U.S. Congress. Senate. *Committee on Foreign Relations: Protocol on the Termination of the Occupation Regime in the Federal Republic of Germany* (Washington, DC: U.S. GPO, 1955), 16.

42. See Foreign Service Dispatch, HICOG to State Department, 15 April, 1955, NARA, Department of State Central Decimal File, 762a.00/4-1555.

43. Krone, *Aufzeichnungen*, 138.

44. Telegram, Conant to Department of State, 22 April, 1955, NARA, Department of State Central Decimal File, 762a.00/4-2155.

45. Krone, *Aufzeichnungen*, 136–37. Von Eckardt's memoirs provide no evidence that he had any hope for the sort of solution at which his 18 April press conference hinted. The prospect of the coming conference had caused the world, and particularly the Germans, to hope for "the great turn toward peace, toward a real peace." But "this hope in no way corresponded with reality. If one posed to the optimists the question by what compulsion or from what motive the Soviets were supposed to change their hard, hostile policy, one never received a useful answer." Von Eckardt, 364. These are not the words of one who himself possessed a useful answer.

46. Telegram, Conant to State, note 39.

47. See *Europa Archiv*, 20 May, 1955, 7573.

48. See Dispatch, HICOM to Department of State, 29 April, 1955, NARA, Department of State Central Decimal File, 762a.00/4-2955.

49. Telegram, Conant to Dulles, 23 April, 1955, NARA, Department of State Central Decimal File, 762a.00/4-2355.

50. On this point, see Raymond Aron, "Le Pari Gagné" (13 April, 1955), in Aron, *La Guerre froide*, 1374–76.

51. See memorandum of Adenauer's conversation with Dulles et al., 7 May, 1955, *FRUS, 1955–1957*, Vol. 5, 166.

52. Ibid., 119–20.

53. Boyle, *Churchill-Eisenhower Correspondence*, 185.

54. Gilbert, 396–98.

55. *Public Papers*, 1955, 351–53.

56. Eisenhower, *Mandate*, 505. It should be noted that at the above-cited press conference, Eisenhower said that "tangible evidence of Soviet sincerity" did not necessarily imply free elections in Germany. A four-power conference might take place if the Soviets gave *other* signs of their good faith. *Public Papers*, 1955, 352.

57. Anthony Eden, *The Memoirs of Sir Anthony Eden: Full Circle* (London: Cassell, 1960), 270–72.

58. Harold Macmillan, *Tides of Fortune, 1945–1955* (London: Macmillan, 1969), 584. On Eisenhower's awareness of domestic political concerns as a motivating factor in the British call for a summit, see Eisenhower, *Mandate*, 505. See also Beam, 43.

59. Kipp, *Eden, Adenauer*, 283.

60. The letters are reproduced in Peter G. Boyle, ed., *The Eden-Eisenhower Correspondence, 1955–1957* (Chapel Hill: University of North Carolina Press, 2005), 81–83.

61. *FRUS, 1955–1957*, Vol. 5, 135–36.

62. On Watson's conversation at State Department, see ibid., 136–37; for Adenauer's proposal, see 123; for U.S. statement on Germany's role, see 136.

63. Boyle, *Eden-Eisenhower Correspondence*, 83.

64. Adenauer, *Erinnerungen, 1953–1955*, 440.

65. So did the Soviets, who were equally dead set against the reunified Germany participating in NATO. The demand for *Bündnisfreiheit*, or freedom to choose alliances, seemed to many contemporary observers to be irreconcilable with the greatest possible Soviet concessions. For a thoughtful analysis of this question, see Herbert von Borch, "Glossen," *Aussenpolitik: Zeitschrift für Internationale Fragen*, 6. Jahrgang 1955, Heft 2 (February), 69–71.

66. Memorandum of a meeting at the Department of State, 23 April, 1955, *FRUS, 1955–1957*, Vol. 5, 145–46.

67. Government statements in support of rearmament are legion, and defy summary. But for a brief, accessible summary of the government's arguments from early 1955, see Press and Information Office of the German Federal Government, *The Bulletin: A Weekly Survey of German Affairs* (3:5), 3 February, 1955, 1–2. Rearmament was necessary, according to the government, for Germany's defense, freedom, and as a means of achieving reunification.

68. See Schwarz, *Die Ära Adenauer*, 259–61.

69. Letter, Conant to Livingston Merchant, Director of European Affairs, State Department, 25 April, 1955, *FRUS, 1955–1957*, Vol. 5, 147–50.

70. Aside from mentioning that he was the "point of contact" with the Western allies during preparations for the Geneva conference, Beam makes no mention of the London Working Group in his memoirs. See Beam, 43.

71. Telegram, London Working Group to Department of State, 27 April, 1955, *FRUS, 1955–1957*, Vol. 5, 151–52. As a footnote to the Eden reelection story, the British delegation to the London meetings pressed for a heads of government meeting from the beginning. The Americans "expressed grave reservations" about the idea.

72. In fact, as we have seen, the American delegation to the London Working Group was instructed to accept no proposals which envisioned German neutralization.

73. Telegram, Beam (in London) to Department of State, 28 April, 1955, *FRUS, 1955–1957*, Vol. 5, 153.

74. Telegram, Beam to Department of State, ibid., 155. On Blankenhorn's continued reference to, and rejection of, German neutralization, see Telegram, Beam to Department of State, ibid., 157. Blankenhorn noted that he was "in frequent touch" with Adenauer, and it is likely that the chancellor instructed him to emphasize this point repeatedly. The "Potsdam nightmare" may have contradicted observable fact, but it ran deep.

75. Von Eckardt, 365.

76. Not without reason did Golo Mann call Adenauer the "statesman of worry." Quoted in Frank A. Mayer, *Adenauer and Kennedy: A Study in German-American Relations, 1961–1963* (New York: St. Martin's Press, 1996), 14.

77. See Thomas Banchoff, "Historical Memory and German Foreign Policy: The Cases of Adenauer and Brandt," *German Politics and Society* 14:2 (Summer 1996), 41.

78. This is a recurring theme. Adenauer was determined to convince the West of his reliability.

79. *FRUS, 1955–1957*, Vol. 5, 153. Frank A. Mayer is correct in saying that Adenauer viewed any proposals which "acknowledged or encouraged the German division . . . [as] threats to his goal of unity." Mayer, 17. Yet in private, among the allies, he was willing to advocate a rather gradual approach to reunification himself.

80. Von Eckardt, 365.

81. See Arthur M. Schlesinger Jr., General Editor, *The Dynamics of World Power: A Documentary History of United States Foreign Policy, 1945–1973*, Vol. 1, Part 2, *Western Europe*, Robert Dallek, ed. (New York: Chelsea House, 1983), 582.

82. Boris Meissner, ed., *Moskau Bonn: Die Beziehungen zwischen der Sowjetunion und der Bundesrepublik Deutschland, 1955–1973, Dokumentation* (Cologne: Verlag Wissenschaft und Politik, 1975), 71.

83. *Public Papers*, 1955, 432.

84. *FRUS, 1955–1957*, Vol. 5, 164–65.

85. Eisenhower's letter to Eden is printed as Letter, Dulles to British Ambassador Makins, ibid., 165–66.

86. Telegram, Dulles to Department of State, 8 May, 1955, ibid., 170–71.

87. Ibid., 171.

88. Telegram, Hoover to Dulles, 8 May, 1955, ibid., 173; Telegram, Dulles to Eisenhower, 9 May, 1955, ibid., 174.

89. Hoover reported to Dulles on 9 May concerning a conversation he had had with Eisenhower. The president indicated that: "We want to give every possible consideration to helping our friends. He is cognizant of the UK position and realizes that they would like to use his name under the present circumstances even though they apparently do not expect much of a substantive nature to come out of such a conference." Ibid., 178.

90. See *DSB*, 23 May, 1955, 832–33.

91. Adenauer, *Erinnerungen, 1953–1955*, 440.

92. Telegram, summary of conversation, Adenauer and Dulles, Conant, Merchant, Robert Bowie, 8 May, 1955, NARA, Department of State Central Decimal File, 762a.00/5-855. See also *FRUS, 1955–1957*, Vol. 5, 167–70.

93. Adenauer, *Erinnerungen, 1953–1955*, 440.

94. NARA, Adenauer and Dulles conversation, cited in note 93.

95. "Programm der Sozialdemokratischen Partei Deutschlands zu den Viermächtenverhandlungen über die deutsche Wiedervereinigung," *Europa-Archiv*, 10:11/12 (5 and 20 June, 1955), 7932–36.

96. In a meeting with Conant in mid-May, the chancellor took the Social Democrats to task for their "incessant clamor for freedom of alliance," and pointedly warned that any change in American policy in Europe would mean a "decline of freedom for all European nations." Telegram, Bonn to Department of State, 16 May, 1955, NARA, Department of State Central Decimal File, 762a.00/5-1655.

97. Telegram, Bonn to Department of State, 18 May, 1955, ibid., 762a.00/ 5-1855. A week after German entry into NATO, the Soviets quickly called a conference in Poland to establish a parallel Eastern "alliance." The treaty, known as the Warsaw Pact, was quite similar to the North Atlantic treaty. See, e.g., Nation, *Black Earth*, 218–20.

98. See Adenauer, *Erinnerungen, 1953–1955*, 442–43. The chancellor's fears, as he reports it, were initially prodded by a *Newsweek* article and an ambiguous statement by Dulles.

99. *Public Papers*, 1955, 518.

100. The day before Eisenhower's press conference, the CDU Bundestag *fraktion* leader, Heinrich von Brentano, warned his fellow delegates of the dangers inherent in comparing Austria and Germany. Telegram, Bonn to Department of State, 18 May, 1955, NARA, Department of State Central Decimal File, 762a.00/5-1855.

102. Adenauer, *Erinnerungen, 1953–1955*, 443–45.

103. *Adenauer: Der Staatsmann*, 184–85. On the so-called Heusinger Plan, see 186–87; also Köhler, 859–61. Köhler observes that Adenauer was never terribly convinced himself of the utility of this plan. He is nevertheless correct in noting that the "hostility of the chancellor toward all disengagement plans would . . . have considerably lost credibility, if it were to become known" that he himself had once flirted with such an idea. For Adenauer's opposition to "disengagement," see chapter 6.

104. Telegram, Bonn to Department of State, 23 May, 1955, NARA, Department of State Central Decimal File, 762a.00/5-2355.

105. Telegram, Hoover to Bonn, London, Paris, Moscow, 1 June, 1955, NARA, ibid., 762a.00/5-2855.

106. Memorandum of Conversation, Hoover and Krekeler, 31 May, 1955, NARA, ibid., 762a.00/5-3155.

107. *Verhandlungen*, 27 May, 1955, Bd. 24:73–85, 4603.

108. See, e.g., Conant's statement in the 14 June, 1955, *Frankfürter Allgemeine Zeitung (FAZ)*. Conant remarked that "only a complete change of the status of the East bloc States would be a suitable basis of discussion for a change, as well, of the German status." As to whether the Americans would pull their troops out of Europe, the ambassador insisted that "as long as the world is divided, the Americans will leave their troops in Europe." Papers of James Bryant Conant, Pusey Library, Harvard University (JBC), Box 9, File: May–June 1955.

109. Memorandum of a Conversation, Dulles and Adenauer, 13 June, 1955, *FRUS, 1955–1957*, Vol. 5, 224–26. On Kennan's dismissal from the State Department at the beginning of the Eisenhower administration, see Kennan, *Memoirs, 1950–1963*, 168–89. Kennan must have found amusing the chancellor's impression that he was able to push aside Dulles on a question as important as Germany's future. For Adenauer's meeting with Dulles, see Köhler. Dulles was coming to the conclusion, according to Köhler, that Adenauer was "an important, but also a taxing [*anstrengender*] ally, to whose obsessions one had to listen," without necessarily putting much stock in them. *Adenauer*, 862.

110. Memorandum of a Conversation, Eisenhower, Dulles, Adenauer et al., 14 June, 1955, *FRUS*, ibid., 231.

111. Quoted in *Kölner Stadt-Anzeiger*, 18 June, 1955, JBC, Box 9, File: May–June 1955.

112. Notes on Adenauer's conversation with Eden at Chequers, 19 June, 1955, StBKAH, Handakte-Bundeskanzler, Gespräch-Aufzeichnungen I.

113. See Cioc, *Pax Atomica*, 29–31. Catherine McArdle Kelleher, *Germany and the Politics of Nuclear Weapons* (New York: Columbia University Press, 1975), 35–43.

114. See, e.g., Telegram, Bonn to Department of State, 7 July, 1955. In the assessment of the American embassy, the "overall effect of [the] exercise was to weaken govt's arguments that twelve Ger[man] divisions of great value for western defense." NARA, Department of State Central Decimal File, 762a.00/7-755.

115. Cioc, 31.

116. Memorandum, Eisenhower to Dulles, 11 June, 1955, DDEL, Whitman File, International Series, Box 15, File: Germany 1955 (2).

117. Memorandum of Discussion at the 249th Meeting of the National Security Council, 19 May, 1955, *FRUS, 1955–1957*, Vol. 5, 183.

118. Memorandum of Conversation, 20 May, 1955, ibid., 191.

119. Telegram, Department of State to London, 23 May, 1955, ibid., 194.

120. See Pach and Richardson, 109; Elmer Plischke, *Diplomat in Chief: The President at the Summit* (New York: Praeger, 1986), 292; Ambrose, *Eisenhower: The President*, 261. Ambrose notes that Dulles was so concerned about raising false hopes that he even objected to the president's suggestion that he ask all Americans to say a prayer for peace. Eisenhower ignored Dulles's warnings, and made the request. For Eisenhower's address before boarding the plane for Geneva, see *Public Papers*, 1955, 701–5. On Dulles's worries, see C. D. Jackson Log entry, 11 July, 1955, *FRUS, 1955–1957*, Vol. 5, 301–5.

121. For a more in-depth discussion of the summit, and of the goals of its individual participant nations, see Günter Bischof and Saki Dockrill, *Cold War Respite: The Geneva Summit of 1955* (Baton Rouge: Louisiana State University Press, 2000). The chapters on America and Russia, by Richard Immerman and Vladislav M. Zubok, respectively, are particularly helpful.

122. Telegram, Paris Working Group to Department of State, 9 July, 1955, *FRUS, 1955–1957*, Vol. 5, 309–11.

123. Telegram, Department of State to Paris Working Group, 10 July, 1955, ibid., 315.

124. Telegram, Tripartite Foreign Ministers Meeting to Department of State, 15 July, 1955, ibid., 319.

125. Adenauer himself was well aware of this fact. See *Erinnerungen, 1953–1955*, 468.

126. Fears that at the summit the Soviets might make some proposal with regard to Germany for which the West was not prepared had faded by this point. The presumption now was that the Soviets would not want to talk about the German issue at all. Eden suggested, on the afternoon before the conference, that the West must hold Moscow's feet to the fire on this issue. The most important issue at Geneva was, according to the prime minister, "the question of German unity and how we could help a friendly German government" while strengthening NATO. The Russians would not want to talk about Germany at Geneva. But "[w]e should do all we could to make them talk about the German problem. This was important for

Germany." Memorandum of the Conversation at the Tripartite Luncheon, 17 July, 1955, ibid., 344.

127. Grewe, 226. Grewe thought that the FRG had had more influence on conference developments at Berlin than at Geneva.

128. Ibid., 227.

129. Blankenhorn, 222; Adenauer, *Erinnerungen, 1953–1955*, 468. Adenauer and Dulles also had a secure phone line from Bern to Geneva set up in case such communication became necessary. Schwarz, *Adenauer: Der Staatsmann*, 201.

130. Von Eckardt, 370.

131. Memorandum of tripartite conversation, Geneva, 17 July, 1955, *FRUS, 1955–1957*, Vol. 5, 344, 346. Grewe remembers Adenauer having been set at ease by his report that the allies gave no indication at Geneva of any interest in neutralization. Grewe, 228.

132. *FRUS, 1955–1957*, Vol. 5, 368–70.

133. Telegram, Dulles to Department of State, 19 July, 1955, ibid., 382.

134. Telegram, Geneva Delegation to Department of State, ibid., 389–90.

135. Memorandum of Conversation between Dulles and Molotov, 19 July, 1955, ibid., 397–98.

136. Memorandum of conversation, Eisenhower, Dulles, Eden, and Macmillan, 20 July, ibid., 398–400.

137. Troyanovsky, *Cherez gody i rasstoiania*, 194. On Eden's resentments toward the United States, and its postwar primacy in the West, see Boyle, *Eden-Eisenhower Correspondence*, 18. On the desire of the United Kingdom, more generally, to retain its great power status after WWII, see, most recently, Daniel C. Williamson, *Separate Agendas: Churchill, Eisenhower, and Anglo-American Relations, 1953–1955* (Lanham, MD: Lexington Books, 2006), 1–6. Larres is particularly strong on this issue. See *Churchill's Cold War*, esp. chapter 3.

138. Telegram, Geneva Delegation to Department of State, 20 July, 1955, ibid., 405. The words are Macmillan's.

139. Telegram, Dulles to Department of State, 20 July, 1955, ibid., 403; Memorandum of conversation, Dulles and Molotov, 20 July, 1955, ibid., 419.

140. See Bulganin's comments, U.S. Delegation's record of seventh plenary session of the Geneva conference, 23 July, 1955, ibid., 498. Eisenhower responded by again asserting that the issues of German unity and European security could not be isolated from each other. He sensed, however, that "there appeared to be no reason to believe that a common ground existed" between the two camps on the German reunification issue. Due to this, he suggested that the conference move on to other agenda items.

141. Soutou, *L'alliance incertaine*, 49–50.

142. See, e.g., Ambrose, 264–65; Divine, 118–22. See also Robert I. Strong, "Eisenhower and Arms Control," in Richard A. Melanson and David Mayers, *Reevaluating Eisenhower: American Foreign Policy in the 1950s* (Urbana: University of Illinois Press, 1987), 241–66.

143. Immerman in Bischof and Dockrill, *Cold War Respite*, 54. Immerman's discussion of American pre-summit planning gives further reason to take his assessment seriously. See Immerman's *John Foster Dulles*, 140–41, in which he makes a convincing case that the president hoped for some degree of progress on arms control to come from his proposal at the summit.

148 Chapter 4

144. Hughes, 168.

145. The symbolism was not lost on Adenauer, who took the Geneva "spirit" as evidence that America and Russia were now more likely than ever to seek improved relations with each other, and thus to tacitly leave off of their agenda the question of German unity and the objections of the "troublesome old gentleman in Bonn." Geneva thus increased Adenauer's fear of a freezing of the status quo in Europe. Köhler, Adenauer, 867.

146. Nouailhat, Les États-Unis et le monde, 201.

147. Klaus Larres, "The Road to Geneva 1955: Churchill's Summit Diplomacy and Anglo-American Tension after Stalin's Death," in Larres and Osgood, The Cold War, 150.

148. Ibid., 168.

149. Zubok, A Failed Empire, 107.

150. Von Eckardt reproduces the conference directive on pages 371–73 of his memoirs.

151. Telegram, Geneva Consulate to Department of State, FRUS, 1955–1957, Vol. 5, 537.

152. Adenauer, Erinnerungen, 1953–1955, 472–73.

153. Letter, Dulles to Adenauer, 15 August, 1955, StBKAH, III, Bd. 2, [D&E].

154. Royal Institute for International Affairs, Documents on International Affairs, 1955 (London: Oxford University Press, 1958), 199–200.

155. Memorandum, Dulles to Eisenhower, 26 July, 1955, DDEL, Whitman File, Dulles-Herter Series, Box 7, File: Dulles, John Foster. July 1955.

156. Marion Gräfin Dönhoff, "Das Moskauer Ja-Wort" (22 September, 1955), in ZEIT-Geschichte der Bonner Republik 1949–1999 (Reinbek: Rowolt, 1999), 67.

157. Trachtenberg, A Constructed Peace, chapter 4. Quotes from 141–42.

158. See especially Schwarz, Adenauer: Der Staatsmann, 207–22; Schwarz, Die Ära Adenauer, 273–78; Köhler, Adenauer, 872–889; also, Besson, 192–95. For the exchange of notes between Moscow and Bonn leading to the visit, see Moskau-Bonn, 71–74, 77–81.

159. The Rapallo issue is addressed in detail by Cyril Buffet, "L'Allemagne entre l'Est et l'Ouest: Les relations germano-soviétiques au prisme de Rapallo, 1945–1991," Guerres mondiales et conflits contemporains 210 (Avril–Juin 2003), 7–18. See also Kipp's discussion of "Britische Rapallo-Ängste" in Eden, Adenauer, 83–89.

160. Telegram, Bonn to Department of State, 30 July, 1955, NARA, Department of State Central Decimal File, 762a.00/7-2855; Telegram, Bonn to Department of State, 1 August, 1955, ibid., 762a.00/7-2955.

161. See Hacke, 89.

162. Khrushchev, in his earthy way, sought to show Adenauer and the Germans that he was unimpressed by their reserve at the Moscow conference. "If our esteemed, respected partners are not ready to conduct negotiations," he told the chancellor, the Soviets "could wait—our asses aren't freezing in the wind." Khrushchev obviously sought to indicate that the Germans stood to benefit from negotiations as much as the Soviets did. Zubok and Pleshakov, Inside the Kremlin's Cold War, 180.

163. Sandrine Tesson, "La doctrine Hallstein, entre rigueur et pragmatisme (1955–1969)," *Relations Internationales* 110 (Été 2002), 222–23. On attempts to reconcile the chancellor's Moscow visit with the "Hallstein Doctrine" that was just emerging, see William Glenn Gray's excellent study of the FRG's attempts to enforce the *Alleinvertretungsanspruch* in international politics: *Germany's Cold War: The Global Campaign to Isolate East Germany, 1949–1969* (Chapel Hill: University of North Carolina Press, 2003), esp. 39–42.

164. Letter, Dulles to Adenauer, 3 October, 1955, StBKAH, III, Bd., 2, [D&E].

165. Memorandum of cabinet meeting, DDEL, Whitman File, Cabinet Series, Box 6.

166. Besson, 192.

167. Telegram, Dulles to Department of State, 3 November, 1955, DDEL, Whitman File, Dulles-Herter Series, Box 7, File: Dulles, John Foster, November 1955(2).

168. See Telegram, Dulles to Eisenhower, 4 November, 1955, ibid.

169. Memorandum, Meeting of President and Acting Secretary of State Hoover, 9 November, 1955, ibid., File: John Foster Dulles(1). According to Eisenhower, "if East Germany gets [the] independence of a free nation, the pull on the other Soviet satellites will be tremendous. The Soviets regard East Germany as the keystone of their satellite army."

170. Telegram, U.S. Delegation at Geneva to Department of State, 9 November, 1955, *FRUS, 1955–1957*, Vol. 5, 720–21. For the text of the East German-Soviet treaty, see *Documents on International Affairs, 1955*, 200–202.

171. Telegram, Dulles to Eisenhower, 7 (?) July, 1955, DDEL, Whitman File, Dulles-Herter Series, Box 6, File: Dulles, John F. November 1955.

172. Telegram, Eisenhower to Dulles, ibid.; Watson, *Molotov*, 253.

173. *Documents on International Affairs*, 1955, 69–70.

174. Unsigned article (Giuseppe Vedovato?), "Riconoscimento del Governo di Pekino contro riunificazione tedesca?" in *Rivista di Studi Politici Internazionali* 24/2 (Aprile/Giugno 1957), 187.

175. Letter, Eden to Eisenhower, 17 November, 1955, DDEL, Whitman File, Dulles-Herter Series, Box 6, File: Dulles, John Foster, November 1955(1).

176. Telegram, Dulles to Department of State, 8 November, 1955, DDEL, Whitman File, Box 6, File, Dulles, John Foster, November 1955(2).

177. Memorandum, C. D. Jackson to Henry Luce, 21 June, 1955, DDEL, Whitman File, Administration Series, Box 22, File: Jackson 1955(1).

178. On the self-imposed Soviet inflexibility with regard to the future of the GDR at this time, see Zubok, *A Failed Empire*, 108–9.

5

"The Key to World Dominance": Western Unity and the Foreign Policy Initiative, 1956

Geneva II had been a great disappointment. The Soviets rejected disdainfully the only plan for reunification that the Western governments could accept. The Geneva frustrations resulted in part from a change in emphasis in Soviet policy. With German entry into NATO, the Kremlin must have recognized what Adenauer did not: the West would never agree to neutralize Germany. Henceforth, the focus of Soviet policy would be forcing Western recognition of the status quo: that is, recognizing the division of Germany. Ideally, the Kremlin would convince all the Western capitals, including Bonn, to deal with the government in East Berlin. In this way, the Soviets could sneak recognition of the East German regime (and the other satellite governments) in through the back door. This would serve to legitimize the East German regime, and implicitly confer American recognition of the Soviet sphere. If the Soviets had their way on this, American foreign policy would help to stabilize the Soviet-sponsored regimes that Eisenhower and Dulles had pledged to roll back.

The Eisenhower administration refused to be forced into abandoning four-power responsibility for German unification. If Bonn's diplomatic flexibility was severely limited by the Hallstein Doctrine—which forbade it relations with states which recognized East Germany—the Americans refused to weaken the Potsdam declaration. Washington did not want Moscow to be able to extricate itself from its legal obligation to reunify Germany. Agreement on Germany seemed as far away as ever.

But the question remained as to whether agreements with the Soviets on issues other than German reunification were also excluded. Washington's answer to this question was less than clear. Put simply, one could not have been certain in 1956 how inflexible Western policy had become.

Moreover, international developments—and crises—in the years 1956 and 1957 brought considerable tensions within the NATO alliance. This, in turn, further complicated Western attempts to define a policy toward the Soviet Union.

It was in this context that Adenauer sought to exert his influence, and even a veto, on American policy. He wanted to be certain that Washington concluded no agreements with the Soviets which did not advance the cause of German unity—a recipe for deadlock given Moscow's commitment to the status quo. He wanted America to increase the degree of political coordination within NATO. Finally, especially after Suez, he wanted the Eisenhower administration to stop focusing on the Third World, and to pay closer attention to what really mattered: Europe. The response of the Eisenhower administration to these demands was, as can be imagined, tinged with some frustration.

"NO COMPROMISE": DISARMAMENT AND REUNIFICATION

The year began with American rejection of a Soviet initiative. On 23 January, Bulganin sent Eisenhower a letter calling for "substantially" improved relations between the two superpowers. Improving the tenor of Soviet-American relations would, Bulganin stressed, improve the chances of a disarmament agreement. This, in turn, would allow the states concerned to devote resources to more pressing matters, including improving living standards, increasing wages, and building housing. To further this end, the Russian sent a draft of a "Treaty of Friendship and Co-operation" for the president to consider.

Eisenhower's response was quick and negative. From Bonn's point of view, it could hardly have been better. Eisenhower rejected the draft treaty out of hand, noting that it duplicated agreements which America and the Soviet Union had already entered into by signing the United Nations charter. The problem, as the president saw it, was not a paucity of paper agreements, but a lack of concrete will on the part of the Kremlin to do what was necessary to reduce international tensions. Specifically, the Soviets were prolonging the German problem by refusing to deal with "the reunification of Germany by means of free elections." This, together with Soviet refusal to accept verification measures as a necessary component of an arms control agreement, left no doubt in the president's mind that now was not the time for a friendship treaty between the U.S. and the USSR.[1] Eisenhower had chosen his words well. His allies in Bonn, always fretful when Moscow and Washington engaged each other one-on-one, noted the mention of Germany. Adenauer expressed to Hoover his satisfaction with Eisenhower's letter.[2]

Not everyone was satisfied, however. The Social Democrats viewed the inclusion of the GDR in the Warsaw Pact on 28 January as a significant event which called for a response from Bonn. SPD leader Ollenhauer called on the Adenauer government and the Western powers to "take advantage of the opportunity" presented by the Bulganin letter to pursue an agreement on European security. This agreement should, of course, provide for German reunification.[3]

The government, however, remained unimpressed by the addition of East German units to the Warsaw Pact forces, and was rather dismissive of Bulganin's letter. Adenauer met with American Under Secretary of State Herbert Hoover Jr. on 4 February. At this meeting, one could detect differences in American and West German assessment of the Soviet Union's potential and motivations. Hoover thought that the Soviets were impressed by certain of their own recent successes. Their industrialization program was showing results; they had increased in military power and were "satisfied" with their own progress in the nuclear field; the switch from one-man rule to collective leadership had been relatively "trouble-free"; and Soviet propaganda had achieved some success in the nonaligned world. While he thought the Soviets might overrate themselves, he nevertheless saw "a certain danger" in their increasing "self-assurance and boldness [*Dreistigkeit*]." Hoover saw signs of this danger particularly in Khrushchev's behavior. Given Hoover's post, it is likely that his remarks represented the thinking of the State Department.

Adenauer told Hoover that he "disagreed on many points." Remarkably, Adenauer challenged Hoover on the significance of Khrushchev. He had met the Soviet leaders while in Moscow, and "he held Bulganin to be the stronger figure"! Be that as it may, the chancellor had reason to doubt the self-assurance of whomever the Soviet leaders happened to be. Both Bulganin and Khrushchev had confirmed for him that "high defense expenditures" were preventing them from dealing effectively with the considerable challenges which they now faced at home. Abroad, they also faced a great threat. China shared a long and contentious border with the Soviet Union. Khrushchev had in fact told Adenauer that the Soviets were terribly worried about the Chinese. This was a far cry from Hoover's description of a Soviet Union brimming with confidence and potentially anxious to mount new external adventures.

Not that Adenauer completely rejected the American assessment; he certainly would never deny that the Soviets posed a danger, just as Hoover had said. But to the extent that the Kremlin had gained self-confidence, the chancellor held his own Western allies responsible. And he phrased his analysis in the form of a thinly veiled rebuke of American diplomacy. The Soviets had misinterpreted the "good treatment which they received at the first Geneva Conference." Using one of his favorite metaphors for the

Soviets, he insisted that the Soviets now saw themselves as the "prodigal son," who had now been accepted back into the community of nations. When he was in Moscow, Adenauer was forced to listen to Bulganin brag about the letters which he had received from Eisenhower. Adenauer concluded that the Kremlin's new self-assurance was not a result of Russia's own strengths, but of "the mistakes and the weaknesses of the other countries." He did not need to mention the chief offender by name.[4]

Still, it is unlikely that Eisenhower's negative response to Bulganin's letter was evidence of Adenauer's veto power. The failure of the Soviets to move on the Geneva directive gave Washington sufficient reason to reject the idea of a formal "cooperation" treaty with the Soviets at this time. Why sign a cooperation treaty in the absence of cooperation? It is likely, however, that those who drafted Eisenhower's response kept German sensitivities in mind: The president twice indicated that the Soviet failure to help reunify Germany stood in the way of improved U.S.-Soviet relations.

Lines which were drawn in the latter half of 1955 continued to harden in early 1956, and it is likely that the Soviet initiative on the treaty of cooperation was motivated by Moscow's desire to gain Western recognition of the status quo in Europe. Bonn and Washington continued to be on guard against such efforts. According to the very same Hoover whom Adenauer had chastised less than a week before, America was not about to declare its acceptance of the current situation in Europe. During a speech on Germany delivered before the Foreign Policy Association, the undersecretary declared that "to be lulled into acceptance of the *status quo* is to prepare the way for the further loss of freedom."[5]

The government of West Germany certainly agreed. There could be no acceptance of the status quo. Yet many in West Germany, including some allies of the chancellor, were hard pressed at this time to explain how the policies advocated by Washington and Bonn could themselves lead to anything but reification of the status quo. In late February and early March, the SPD ratcheted up its attack on the Adenauer government for its failure to take the initiative on reunification. This in itself was not newsworthy. But the American embassy noted a significant change in the Socialists' statements. The SPD now insisted that "it is deceit or self-delusion to believe that a peacefully reunited Germany can one day become part of NATO or of the Warsaw system against the will of the other bloc." In other words, "the freedom of decision of a freely elected future all-German government will of necessity be limited."[6] As if the Eisenhower administration had needed more incentive to support Adenauer's re-election bid, the SPD now implied, in essence, that German neutralization might be a fair price to pay for unity.

More significant for the Adenauer government itself was the break with the Free Democrats which occurred in February. FDP leaders had been complaining for some time about the "authoritarian" methods according to which the chancellor ran his government, and the government's failure to satisfy them on this point certainly helped to precipitate the split, as did proposed changes in the election law which would benefit the Union Parties and diminish the FDP.[7] From the American perspective, however, what was most important was the foreign policy disputes which did so much to drive a wedge between the Union Parties and the Liberals. Thomas Dehler, justice minister in Adenauer's first cabinet and thereafter leader of the FDP, was frustrated with the government's inactivity on the reunification front. Dehler in opposition was likely, according to the German Affairs office at the State Department, "to promote a definitely nationalistic line with heavy emphasis on the need for a more flexible reunification policy."[8]

The concerns which a resurgence of German nationalism would raise need no discussion. But the other questions which Liberal and Socialist critics of the Adenauer government raised could not be easily discounted. The Federal Republic's Western allies were no more interested in Dehler's diplomatic flexibility—which conjured up images of Rapallo—than they were in the SPD's advocacy of a Germany between the alliances. Against the backdrop of such proposals, Brentano went on record, more or less, as a defender of inaction. During a speech in Frankfurt, the foreign secretary insisted that the government would rather bear the brunt of criticism for its seeming inactivity than engage in unwise reunification schemes at an "inopportune time." In words which must have been welcome in the West, he added: "We need friends if we wish to remain alive."

Having thus disposed of the neutrality idea, he went on to address the question of talks between Bonn and Moscow. Dehler advocated dialogue between the Federal Republic and the Soviet Union as an important means of breaking the diplomatic deadlock.[9] Brentano, however, thought that "diplomatic relations between Fedrep and USSR will not open any new paths." Sounding something like a caricature of himself, he added that "there can be no compromise between communism and the free world."[10]

Washington disagreed with such strong formulations. In one area in particular, that of arms control, the Eisenhower administration hoped that there could be compromise between communism and the free world. On this question, too, Adenauer had advice to give to the Americans. The chancellor may well have intended to exercise his "veto" on the question of East-West arms control in early 1956. But while considerations of West Germany's needs and interests did affect American responses to certain Soviet arms control initiatives, it was the mutually exclusive views of Washington and Moscow on verification which prevented progress on arms control in the mid-1950s.

Within the inner circles of the Eisenhower team, a seemingly unlikely advocate pressed in 1956 for the United States to take rather bold steps in the field of nuclear arms reductions. In the bureaucratic war over arms control and reduction, it was John Foster Dulles, together with his State Department, who emerged as the primary proponent of disarmament. The secretary of state thought that the time had come for the United States to clarify its position on arms control and disarmament, and to make concrete proposals in this area. Eisenhower's "Open Skies" proposal had bought time, while the president's disarmament aide Harold Stassen conducted a thorough review of America's disarmament policy. But "this period of grace [was] coming to an end."[11] The United States now had to advance real, meaningful proposals for arms control, proposals which would impress both world opinion and the leaders in the Kremlin. And Dulles considered Stassen's proposals inadequate to meet this purpose.[12] In discussions of the National Security Council (NSC), Dulles criticized Stassen's report for failing to "contemplate any appreciable reductions in armed forces and armaments" until after a vast system of inspection— involving thirty to forty thousand inspectors on the ground—was set up and in operation. If this were the American policy, Dulles noted, then "we should understand clearly that in seeking such a system we are seeking something which can never be realized." Dulles advocated control and inspection of delivery vehicles, rather than of warheads and fissionable materials as advocated by Stassen. Such controls, he thought, could be maintained with "a much smaller and less complicated system of inspection and verification."[13] The end goal of disarmament negotiations, the secretary informed Stassen, was reaching "some organic and organizational control of atomic weapons on an international basis." The world would not, Dulles argued, be content to have a well-meaning nuclear weapons state serve as a "benevolent dictator," and he thought that it would be a tragedy if Eisenhower's authority and prestige were not used as leverage to climb "at least one more rung in the ladder that led toward community control of this vast destructive power."[14]

Indicating that the urge for arms reductions had permeated the State Department beyond the cabinet level, Robert Bowie, the director of policy planning, also indicated dissatisfaction with Stassen's approach to arms negotiations. At a meeting of the NSC Planning Board in December 1955, Bowie had described Stassen's proposals as "inadequate." Bowie agreed with his superior: Stassen's proposal was fundamentally not an arms reduction proposal. It was a proposal for a system of inspection. The State Department thought that world opinion demanded more than this. The rest of the world, Bowie noted, "was not as sanguine as we seemed to be about the results of an atomic stalemate." The UN General Assembly had approved a resolution calling for disarmament *with* safeguards. The United States had to address *both* of these two points.[15]

But the State Department faced considerable resistance to its views within the administration. From the beginning, Stassen was unconvinced by arguments in favor of arms reductions. He and his team thought that "any substantial disarmament would not really be in the interest of the United States and the optimum goal should be to try to stabilize the situation at about the present level."[16] In other words, despite world opinion and the UN resolution, the United States ought to attempt to lock in the status quo. Stassen failed to explain how the United States could avoid obloquy by presenting such a disappointing proposal.[17]

Opposition to disarmament was also coming from the Department of Defense. The Joint Chiefs of Staff were concerned about the effects of any reductions in conventional forces. Army Chief of Staff General Maxwell Taylor insisted that the Army had shrunk as much as it could afford since the end of the Second World War. There was "no room left for even minor reductions in force levels." Besides, according to Taylor, the United States should make no commitments to arms reductions until a tested verification system was in place. Admiral Arleigh Burke agreed. Being unsure of Moscow's intentions, the West had to establish a thorough system of inspection before discussing arms reductions.[18] Hence, the JCS position diverged from the State Department's views even more than did Stassen's. The latter was at least willing to consider some conventional force reductions more or less contemporaneously with the establishment of a system of inspection. The Joint Chiefs did not want to *discuss* reductions until an inspection system was up and running.

But despite the lack of unanimity within the administration, some prompt decisions were necessary. The Subcommittee of the United Nations Disarmament Committee was due to meet in London beginning 19 March. Stassen, who was to head the American delegation, had to be informed as to what the American position *was*. In formally instructing Stassen, Eisenhower stressed the importance of effective safeguards and controls. The "acceptability and character" of any agreement on arms and force limitations, according to the president, depended "primarily on the scope and effectiveness of the safeguards against violations and evasions, and especially the inspection system." Stassen was to give priority to "such confidence building measures as the exchange of military blueprints, mutual aerial inspections, and the establishment of ground control posts at strategic centers." The point of departure for a system of controls and inspection was to be the president's "Open Skies" proposal made in Geneva in 1955.[19] The prerequisite set by the administration for arms reductions was, according to the best available knowledge, more than the Soviets were willing to accept.[20]

The very limited prospects of an arms reduction agreement in 1956 seem, nevertheless, to have escaped the notice of the Bonn regime. The issue of verification presents itself, in retrospect, as an insuperable obstacle to an East-West arms reduction settlement. But the Adenauer government lacked the hindsight—and perhaps insight—which would help clarify this matter. One might say that Adenauer was, in the first half of 1956, determined to exercise his veto: he intended to prevail upon his allies to reject any disarmament agreement which divorced the arms control issue from the political question of German reunification. The episode reveals a familiar pattern in Adenauer's attempts to exercise influence.

Less than a week before the opening of the disarmament subcommittee conference, Adenauer wrote to Dulles to remind him of the FRG's interest in the matters to be discussed in London. The conference discussions, he wrote, would "affect the future of Germany, whose reunification is the declared aim of the Free World."[21] In this sentence, Adenauer expressed the central linkage around which his diplomatic efforts revolved. Arms control and the German question could not be separated. In 1956, this meant specifically that there was to be no progress whatsoever on arms control unless it was accompanied by commensurate progress on the issue of German unity.

There can be no doubt that the two issues were tightly linked. The question of German unity was, for most non-Germans, fundamentally a question of European security, which East and West answered in different ways—the former by insisting upon some form of disarmed neutrality, the latter by continued *Westbindung*. Arms control was bound to be a major element of East-West discussions about European security. Without certain guarantees about the number, type, and location of the other side's weaponry, neither of the antagonistic camps was likely to pull back from the Central European line of confrontation. The two issues were connected. But Adenauer's insistence upon such a rigid connection between arms control and German reunification does not follow from this connection. His stance on this question made Adenauer—a longtime advocate of arms control—appear more hard-line than he actually was.

In Adenauer's defense, one must note that he was provoked: the West German chancellor who tirelessly advocated Franco-German rapprochement had once again to watch Paris undercut his policies. In an interview which appeared in the 6 April issue of *U.S. News and World Report*, French Premier Guy Mollet managed to call into question nearly every premise of Adenauer's foreign policy.[22] Nor was Adenauer alone. Eisenhower and his team, Mollet implied, were also making bad decisions. Mollet declared that the Western approach at Geneva was "a bad one." At the summit, the priorities of the Western foreign ministers had been German reunification, European security, and disarmament, in that order. As the new government in Paris saw it, this order was inverted. The Council of Europe had pronounced, under Mollet's leadership, that "[i]t is by beginning with disarmament that you would best advance the other questions." Trying to tie the advances on the other issues to progress on reunification was a blueprint for stalemate. Mollet admitted:

> We do not know if the Russians want the unification of Germany. It is even possible that they do not want it. But there is one certainty: If there is a chance that the Russians wish to see Germany unified, that chance can only be really envisaged in the framework of general, world disarmament. It is difficult to envisage German reunification in a period of rearmament, particularly in the center of Europe.

Moscow could never agree, in Mollet's opinion, to the reunification of a re-armed Germany in the context of the Atlantic Alliance. To avoid this blind alley, the West had to seek disarmament *first*. This would make it easier to solve the problem of European security. "And, within the framework of se-curity," the premier added, "the unification of Germany becomes easier to achieve." Given this presentation, it is difficult to see how the membership of a reunified Germany in NATO could be preserved, the West having re-solved from the start to placate the Soviets on this issue. Mollet more or less conceded this. After arms reductions had begun, the Soviets, he thought, might allow free elections in Germany. After negotiations on the matter of free elections, "the status of Germany in relation to the security organiza-tions might be changed." He was not saying, the Frenchman insisted, "that this implies a renunciation by Germany of membership in NATO. But discussion would become possible. One should not pretend at the present moment to determine right now what the future status of Germany will be." The United States, in any event, was currently placing too much em-phasis on military security. That, however, was "not the only problem in the world. If we keep talking only of security in military terms we will not win the psychological battle between East and West." Winning this battle required a change in the West's "approach" to Cold War policy.[23]

Mollet insisted that he was not out of step with France's allies. But in fact his proposals represented a "complete reversal of the western strategy up to then."[24] In particular, the idea that German unity should take a backseat to détente was new. The presumption which guided the West until that point was that the Cold War in Europe was so deeply tied to the German question that no real progress on an East-West rapprochement was possible until the antagonists had productively addressed Germany. Also new, and ominous, was the French premier's suggestion that the West might reach arms agree-ments which discriminated against Germany, while doing nothing to affect the status quo in Europe. It came as no surprise that this was not attractive to Bonn. The Foreign Office lodged a protest through the Paris embassy as soon as its relevant personnel learned of the interview. Adenauer and Bren-tano were both out of Bonn at the time; the chancellor was on vacation in

Switzerland, the foreign secretary at a spa in Bavaria. Although these were not the best circumstances for a coordinated response, the news from Paris was disturbing enough that the main players improvised a potent rebuke. Brentano himself worked on a statement to be made public by the Foreign Office. Released on 5 April, the statement declared that "disarmament and détente cannot be brought about at the expense of the most elementary freedom of the German people." No German government could accept détente if it brought with it the acceptance of Germany's bifurcation. Mixing lament with threat, Brentano added that this proscription against accepting the status quo "also determines and sets the boundaries of (*begrenzt*) the Federal Government's readiness to create the united Europe." Apparently, the West German government was not ready to discuss the unity of the European peoples with any nation which was willing to sacrifice the unity of the German people.[25]

Adenauer must have been having a rather relaxing vacation, since he learned of the Franco-German strife belatedly. When he read of the events in the papers, he reacted to the crisis by calling his foreign policy team to Ascona, Switzerland. There, he expressed his fears. The situation was "extraordinarily dangerous," the chancellor declared, because now Germany was in danger of becoming something of a bargaining chip in allied discussions with the Soviets. Yet, as one scholar notes, Adenauer "thought less of *Gesamtdeutschland* [all Germany] than about the Federal Republic," which he feared would be the object of discriminatory agreements at the London conference. West Germany thus had to insist upon the "internal connection" between disarmament and German unity.[26]

Whether the chancellor insisted upon the "internal connection" thesis more out of a desire to avoid another hurdle to the government's rearmament plans than out of solicitude for German reunification—as German historian Daniel Kosthorst implies—is impossible to say. His objections to Mollet's proposal were certainly consistent with his previously expressed intention of seeking German unification through Western strength and unity. It was nevertheless the case that 1956 was a tough year for the government's rearmament plan. The chancellor and his aides could not have looked favorably, at this time, upon a powerful allied government which proclaimed that West German rearmament stood in the way of reunification. Adenauer was getting enough of this at home.

The State Department was well aware of these difficulties. Conant telegraphed Dulles on 16 April to let him know of the CDU's concern regarding German public opinion. Krone, leader of the CDU *fraktion* in the Bundestag, had told him that the government was having trouble implementing its rearmament plan "in the face of growing uncertainty of Federal Republic population about urgency of rearmament and intentions of Western Powers toward Germany. [Krone] mentioned Mollet interview in bitter terms and said current disarmament negotiations in London had revived a number of questions in public mind such as necessity of German forces." The coming conscription debate, Krone added, was one such factor complicated by West German uncertainties. He asked that a high-level administration official—preferably Dulles or Eisenhower—strongly reaffirm current American policy on Germany. Krone, Conant noted, was uncharacteristically "distraught" over the whole issue, and conducted the discussion with an "unaccustomed overtone of exasperation that the U.S. is not giving the Federal Government expected support."[27] Such was the anxiety which the coincidence of Mollet's statement and the London conference caused in official Bonn.

Yet an analysis by the State Department's Bureau of German Affairs reveals that State was also aware of certain inconsistencies. The report quotes Adenauer as having said to the Bundestag, less than a year before, that if the Western powers addressed "controlled disarmament" right away, they would thereby "achieve a general relaxation of tension" and thus help "to bring about the reunification in peace and freedom." The document goes on to cite other instances in which the government expressed a similar willingness to accept disarmament as a step on the road to reunification.

But the bureau also conceded the real West German fear that a deal might be reached behind its back—the Potsdam nightmare. Bonn responded favorably to reassurances from Washington that détente would not be bought at the expense of German unity. And it viewed with extreme anxiety any development or event—such as the London disarmament conference—which harbored the potential for U.S.-Soviet rapprochement at the expense of Germany. This was the reason Adenauer had sent Dulles the previously cited letter concerning Germany's interest in the London discussions. It was also the reason for the "strong statements" which Bonn issued in the wake of Mollet's proposals:

> If presented with a situation in which progress seems to be being made on reducing a major cause of international tension without categorical statements of support for German unification being made simultaneously, [the German federal government] usually assert publicly that reunification must not be surrendered as the price for agreement.

If, however, the FRG's allies took pains to assure that they will not sacrifice German unity for progress on other issues, then the government was more likely to recognize that progress on disarmament may help facilitate reunification.[28] Mollet had committed a number of grave sins, but the most disturbing may have been that he did not stress his government's commitment to German unity.

Bonn thus looked to Washington for such assurance. But what was the Eisenhower administration's position on the "internal connection" thesis at the time of the London conference? And what role, if any, did Adenauer have in influencing that policy? The American position on linkage between the two issues, as articulated in various statements by Dulles and Stassen, was less rigid than the position articulated by Bonn after the Mollet interview. The Eisenhower administration *was* willing to take some—admittedly small—steps toward multilateral disarmament without insisting on commensurate progress on the reunification issue. Dulles considered this, furthermore, to be established Western policy, and was disturbed by the implication that the policy might be undergoing a transformation. But the administration's rejection of linkage seems to have applied only to the *first stage* of negotiations, after which progress on disarmament was to come more or less hand-in-hand with the settlement of "major political problems." Thus, while there were differences between the American position and the most extreme position staked out by Bonn, the difference was hardly cause for panic.

At London, the American delegation attempted to steer a course between, on the one side, Bonn's insistence on German unification in the first phase of disarmament, and, on the other side, Soviet attempts to separate the German and arms issues. On 3 April, the American delegation introduced a nonbinding draft working paper on the "first phase of a comprehensive agreement for disarmament." For "illustrative purposes," the Americans proposed a reduction of American and Soviet conventional force levels to 2.5 million. This would mean a reduction of American manpower by approximately three hundred thousand men, but was nevertheless one to one and a half million men more than called for in a Soviet draft presented on 27 March. The American draft called for the establishment of a preparatory commission to decide upon specifics of the first phase of arms reductions, and of a (seemingly) permanent Armaments Regulation Organization. The American plan, not surprisingly, focused heavily upon questions of control, verification, and transparency. Aerial observation—"Open Skies"—was, for example, to be implemented during the first phase of disarmament, and not "consider[ed]" as a "possibility" at a later stage, as the Soviet plan would have it.[29]

On 11 April, the head of the Soviet delegation to London, First Deputy Foreign Minister Andrei Gromyko, asked Stassen for clarification on the American position. Was it correct that the American proposal was "not dependent upon political settlement," but rather called for settlement of the German problem in conjunction with further disarmament measures?[30] Stassen responded that the United States thought that the German question ought to be solved "tomorrow if possible, even though we did not solve any other problem." Of course, the administration hoped to solve the German problem "concurrently with other issues." This genuflection to German unity performed, Stassen then went on to answer "yes" to

Gromyko's original question. The United States "believed we could come down to 2.5 million men without previous settlement of any of the major world problems but could not go lower unless there were some important settlements of outstanding problems." Initial progress in disarmament, Stassen added, could help improve the international atmosphere, and thus facilitate the solution of other problems. This formulation echoed the above-quoted Adenauer statement to the Bundestag, and thus presumably did not deviate from the position held by the Bonn government when it was not panicked. Stassen rejected, however, Gromyko's calls for reduction of forces by more than a million, without verification and without solution of political issues.[31]

From Washington, Dulles reaffirmed the American position that discussions on German reunification were to take place in the secondary stages of arms control discussions, and thus in the context of broader discussions on European security. In a 16 April cable to London, the secretary reaffirmed linkage between German unification and the European security issue, which had been established Western policy since Geneva. He expressed approval of the delegation's handling of this question thus far, noting that "serious dangers of discussing the relation between disarmament and reunification in connection with disarmament appears obviated." By this almost impenetrable statement, Dulles appears to have meant that the subcommittee was now free of the danger that the topic of German reunification would arise during its discussions. The implication is clearer than the original statement: the first stages of East-West arms control were to be discussed without reference to the German question. Dulles did not view the disarmament subcommittee as the proper forum for discussion of the reunification question, and was bothered by the way in which the Mollet interview—and the German reaction to it—had brought the question to the fore. British interest in discussing the issue at London, expressed by delegation leader Sir Harold Anthony Nutting, met with Dulles's stern disapproval. The secretary therefore transmitted to London a letter to British Foreign Secretary Selwyn Lloyd in which he expressed these views and reservations. He felt that allowing discussion on the connection of the two issues at the disarmament talks would be "playing into Soviet hands." If there were any thoughts of altering established policy, "of relating reunification more closely to disarmament," then this was a decision which should be made through consultations at the highest levels between the allied governments, presumably including that of the FRG. Questions relating to German unification and the corollary issue of arms limitations particular to German territory could only be solved over time. The United States simply could not accept discussions of nuclear basing restrictions or "thinning out" of forces on German territory at this stage. Given the evident differences of opinion on this issue between France and Germany, Dulles was especially anxious that the topic not be raised until the allied governments had adequate time to discuss the problem among themselves.[32]

Stassen proved willing to follow Dulles's lead. While the disarmament conference was still in session, Bulganin and Khrushchev arrived in London. The invitation had been extended in May of the previous year, and the visit of the Soviet leaders to London just happened to coincide with the disarmament conference. Still, their arrival in London at this particular moment must have provoked further hand-wringing in Bonn.[33]

The Soviets did meet informally with members of the American delegation. Khrushchev in fact raised, at a meeting with Stassen, the possibility of bilateral arms reductions in Germany. Stassen held firm to the American position, telling Khrushchev that "any agreed reduction of armed forces in Germany would be very difficult unless the German problem was solved with the reunification of Germany in freedom at the same time." This formulation of the American position was perfectly in line with Dulles's instructions of 16 April, cited above. At this stage, the United States was not willing to discuss arms limitations on German territory. And in the future, agreements upon arms reductions in Germany would have to go hand-in-hand with agreements on the status of Germany. Khrushchev, on the other hand, noted that "the Soviet Union was ready to reduce troops in Germany without waiting for a solution of the German problem."[34] As Dulles hoped, the discussions went nowhere.

But while Khrushchev expressed Moscow's concern that America was too beholden to its allies on the disarmament issue—that the "U.S. would permit even Luxembourg to stop such an agreement"—it was not Bonn, and far less Luxembourg, which prevented agreement on disarmament at London. It was, rather, the question of verification. In his talk with Stassen, Khrushchev leveled an attack on the idea of aerial observation. Washington's insistence upon aerial inspection "made the work of the subcommittee hopeless." Overflights and photography of Soviet installations were "unacceptable to the Soviet Union."[35] Yet all of the relevant documentation from the American side indicates that sufficient verification procedures were the sine qua non of the first phase of arms control from Washington's point of view. Stassen ably represented his government's position at London. But there was no overcoming this hurdle. The Soviets did not accept "Open Skies." The Americans would not relinquish it.

The reason for the failure of the London conference was obvious to Adenauer, who told West German reporters on 18 July that the London discussions had failed "because the Russians categorically rejected controls." Hyperbole aside—the Soviets had not completely rejected all possibilities for controls—the chancellor's assessment was accurate. The Russians, he thought, might genuinely want reductions of nuclear stockpiles, "but they want no controls!"[36]

In light of the above discussion, Adenauer and his government cannot be said to have exercised a "veto" over American attempts to reach an arms control agreement with the Soviets in early 1956. No doubt they *tried* to do so, after French suggestions regarding the de-linking of the arms and reunification issues. West German protests were known to Washington. But this was not enough to convince Washington to accept the most extreme formulation of the "internal connection" thesis. In the first phase of arms control talks, the Eisenhower administration wanted, primarily, to establish a set of effective verification procedures. As Dulles made abundantly clear, the Americans did not want to talk about the German question at all during this phase. This certainly seemed to contradict the position taken by Adenauer and Brentano after the Mollet interview. On the other hand, the Bonn government may well have benefited from this formulation of policy. The Americans refused even to discuss limitations on manpower and armaments in Germany at the London conference. Adenauer's coalition was in the midst of a difficult domestic battle over rearmament. Had the Western powers followed Adenauer's lead in asserting the inflexible linkage of arms control and reunification at every stage, they would have presented the Soviets with a golden opportunity to propose any number of restrictions upon German rearmament during these early disarmament talks. This would not have helped the government. By refusing at London to discuss German unification and arms control on German territory, Dulles wisely avoided giving Moscow this opportunity.

Finally, on the matter of Bonn's "veto" over disarmament agreements, one must note that any influence exerted was, in the final analysis, superfluous. The Bonn government, in this case as in others, worried about a deal behind its back. Yet this was never a legitimate possibility. First, the American insistence on verification clashed with Soviet desire that trust be the basis of any agreement. Adenauer seemed not to have appreciated the size of the chasm which separated American and Soviet thinking on the question of controls. Second, the American administration had no intention of de-linking the question of European security and disarmament from "political considerations." Dulles viewed the Western position on Germany as having been settled during the discussions leading up to the Geneva summit, discussions at which Bonn's voice was heard. His reason for refusing to engage in discussions about Germany at this time was precisely to avoid deviation from that position. Thus, no veto was necessary. That Adenauer was unaware of this might be blamed on his status as the "statesman of worry." One might also fault the lack of coordination among the Western governments for the left hand's failure to know what the right hand was doing. The events of the second half of 1956 gave emphasis to the latter explanation.

THE PROBLEM OF POLICY COORDINATION

As 1956 wore on, the German federal government increasingly felt itself besieged. Domestically, both the opposition and former allies were attacking the government's foreign and defense policies. Abroad, likewise, they perceived problems with enemies and friends. Difficulties stemming from relations with Moscow were to be expected. But the government also wondered whether it could count on its allies, and the Americans in particular, to continue supporting policies advocated by the regime in Bonn. The matters of reunification, nonrecognition of the GDR, military posture in Europe, and above all the "policy of strength" through Western unity all cropped up in this year of remarkable diplomatic activity. It almost goes without saying that Bonn grew increasingly anxious when faced with these challenges. Adenauer could not help but feel that difficulties within the alliance could be avoided if only the West would decide to coordinate its policies and actions better. He pressed this case throughout the year, reaching a fever pitch after the events in Hungary and Suez in autumn.[37]

The Eisenhower administration was faced with challenges as well, not all of which—as uncomfortable as this might have been to Bonn—directly concerned Germany. America had to lead the "free world" in conflicts around the globe, while simultaneously cutting expenditures which were undermining America's ability to sustain this leadership over the long term. As the leader of the West, America had to recognize that the Cold War was not—had never been—confined to Europe. America was a country with limited resources and an impatience with high taxes and budget deficits. Faced with this reality, and with a desire to avoid the militarization of American society, the administration had to balance the nation's external commitments with its internal realities.[38] As the Eisenhower team wrestled with these challenges in 1956, they found themselves increasingly besieged by West German complaints of neglect. Now, Washington was becoming annoyed with the West Germans.

At the heart of Bonn's importuning of Washington was the perception that the Western states were out of step with each other. Policies which Bonn considered established were now threatened by unilateral decisions, such as those of Mollet's government in Paris. A second motivating factor was the fear that the West had lost the initiative in foreign policy to the Soviets. Yet taking the initiative away from Moscow necessarily implied some deviations from established policy. The Adenauer government found this to be a difficult conundrum.

Krone recognized this difficulty back in April. The Bonn government, more than any other, was likely to suffer from the perception of stasis, as well as from the perception that it was out of step with the allies. Motivated, no doubt, by this fact, Brentano spoke of increased FRG diplomatic activity at his 13 April press conference. In response to various questions, Brentano indicated that Bonn would soon make a representation of the government's interest in reunification directly to Moscow. The FRG would also continue to propose initiatives to its Western allies.[39] Krone summarized Brentano's remarks as "Active foreign policy. Active German policy." By 16 April, Conant had already inquired of him just what Brentano's words meant. Accordingly, Krone noted that "German politicians should be careful with their remarks, if one can suspect behind them a departure from current policy."[40] The FRG had rehabilitated itself in a good measure on the basis of its reliability. Its government must not now call that reliability into question.

But it was the reliability of Bonn's allies that most concerned the West German government. NATO's failure to sufficiently address the political problems which Europe faced, and to coordinate responses, left a diplomatic vacuum which the Soviets were anxious to fill. Bonn's representative to NATO, Ambassador Blankenhorn, raised the loudest cries on this issue. As early as 3 February, he noted, friendly NATO delegates expressed concern about "the increasing passivity of the alliance." Blankenhorn shared these concerns. The alliance seemed disinclined to wrestle with the thorny question of the changes in defensive strategy necessitated by the reality of nuclear weapons. Meanwhile, the Soviets were making political inroads in Asia and North Africa. Yet on political, as opposed to military, questions, the "leading countries" often did not have clear positions for their delegates to follow.[41] Something had to be done about this.

Shortly before the North Atlantic Council was to meet, Dulles spoke to the Associated Press on, among other things, the further development of NATO. On this question, and particularly on the matter of policy coordination, Dulles was ambiguous. He acknowledged that NATO "can and should be more" than merely a political alliance, noting that the allies "have so much in common that we should be able to do more in common." He also expressed approval for statements coming out of Ottawa, Paris, and Rome which called for such an expansion of NATO's purview. But there were limits to the administration's willingness to formulate policy multilaterally. In a less noted section of the speech, Dulles hinted at the problems which lay ahead. America was a global power with global interests. NATO could not "represent the totality" of the policies of its members, Dulles said, after noting America's commitments outside of Europe. By implication, the United States would make policy toward the Pacific and the Third World as it saw fit. In addition, America would not allow requirements of alliance consultation to tie its hands. "Every NATO country," noted Dulles, "of course, has certain vital national interests that may sometimes require independent judgment. Some of us have grave worldwide responsibilities that cannot be effectively discharged unless there is a capability of prompt decision and corresponding action." NATO consultation could not be allowed to "enmesh us in a procedural web" which would prevent quick response to the moves of unfriendly powers.[42] In this speech, Dulles summed up the administration's position. Washington wanted to increase consultation and coordination in NATO, but worried that concrete agreements on consultation would limit America's flexibility to respond to Soviet moves. While Dulles clearly supported further progress in this area, it was obvious that Washington was not going to take the lead.

Nevertheless, Brentano was reportedly "elated" by Dulles's words, and wanted to raise the possibility at the Paris ministers conference of bimonthly consultations between the relevant undersecretaries, as well as proposing an emergency economic assistance fund. Dulles told ambassador Krekeler that the second proposal was not acceptable, since the "ideas behind his speech contemplated increased activity in the political area rather than the economic area."[43] But despite further statements by Dulles and others supportive of increased political cooperation,[44] West Germany's NATO ambassador was convinced that the 5–6 May NATO Ministers Conference would bring no improvements in the area of policy coordination. The larger states in the alliance, Blankenhorn observed, were patently not united on the "further development of NATO." He therefore anticipated that the conference would result only in general declarations, and no meaningful action.[45]

Meeting in Paris on the eve of the ministers conference, Brentano and Dulles met to discuss several issues of interest to the Bonn-Washington relationship. Dulles reaffirmed his commitment to the desire, expressed in the Associated Press speech, to see the "further development" of the Atlantic Alliance. Dulles, furthermore, did not see this initiative as "some new gadget to add to NATO" but rather as a "fundamental solution to problems facing the West." Increased consultation and coordination were suited, according the secretary, to help address three problems: first, the need to maintain unity in the Western camp in the face of Soviet attempts to exploit divisions between NATO countries—a problem, one might add, of particular importance to the FRG; second, the need to counter Soviet efforts in the "underdeveloped world"; and third, the difficulty faced by market economies in competition with a command economy which was not bound by the demands of costs and profits. (The last point was surprising, given Dulles's statement to Krekeler only a week before that he was not interested in discussing economic cooperation at Paris, an assertion which he reiterated the next day at a meeting with the British delegation.) Brentano, for his part, wanted to stress to Dulles the need for an initiative on the reunification question, in order to "demonstrate to the man in the street our proposal and reasons for Soviet rejection." In other words, the Bonn government was again seeking Western help in its reelection bid. The federal government needed to impress upon the West German voter that the government was doing what it could, and that the Soviets were the obstructionists. The suggestion came with a guarantee from Brentano that Bonn was not thinking in terms of bilateral negotiations with Moscow. The initiative would become an increasingly significant issue in German-American relations as the year went by.[46]

The American delegation viewed the two-day meeting with at least a tinge of apprehension. The press in the West had, they thought, built up expectations for the meeting which could not be met.[47] Toward the end of the conference, however, it was Dulles who seemed disappointed. He wrote Eisenhower on 5 May that the allies were particularly anxious to turn NATO "into an economic organization which can probably extract a little more money out of the United States." Unfortunately, America's partners were not as interested in the matter of policy coordination. Dulles found their attitude toward this problem to be characterized by "evasiveness." The notable result of this conference was the naming of the "Three Wise Men"—Foreign Secretaries Halvard Lange of Norway, Gaetano Martino of Italy, and Lester Pearson of Canada—to study the political development of NATO. The admittedly cynical Dulles, however, was afraid that the Wise Men would acknowledge the need for NATO's nonmilitary development only in "rather grudging and minimum terms that hardly are responsive to our hopes or the needs of the situation."[48]

Dulles's frustration with his allied counterparts must not have applied to Brentano, who was a reliable advocate of political consultation. On the same day that Dulles wrote the above-cited letter to Eisenhower, the West German foreign secretary spoke out vigorously in favor of efforts to increase NATO's political role. According to Brentano, it was time to "concert attitudes toward [the] Soviets and work out countermeasures." To address this need, Brentano proposed a combination of regular meetings of the undersecretaries for foreign affairs from the member nations, as well as "several" weekly meetings of the ambassadors to "discuss current political developments."[49]

Dulles brought a mixed interpretation of the Paris meeting with him to the National Security Council (NSC) session held shortly after his return.[50] He did think the Wise Men "sympathetic to the goals we have in mind." But he nevertheless noted the lack of solidarity that pervaded the meeting. America's allies were apparently interested in increased economic aid, and in the U.S. "submitting its foreign policy for review by NATO." But when it came to submitting their own policies for review, the allies had balked. The British and the French especially wanted to maintain freedom of action.[51]

From the German side, criticism of the meeting was at least as strong. Blankenhorn had predicted that nothing would come of the conference but general declarations. As he saw it, not much more than this had happened. This was particularly disturbing, given Soviet diplomatic activism. The West conspicuously lacked a "thought-out conception" of how to respond to Soviet initiatives.[52]

The impact of this lack of a thought-out, coordinated response to the Soviets was to be felt in Bonn only days after the NATO ministers meeting. Acting unilaterally, the Soviets announced a reduction of their bloated and costly military by 1,200,000 men. The announcement came as no surprise in the West; Bulganin and Khrushchev had divulged during their visit to London that force reductions of that magnitude were coming. And Brentano had already gone on record to indicate the problems that this would cause for the Adenauer government, particularly in its rearmament and compulsory service efforts.[53] Yet the announcement nevertheless caught the West flat-footed. In a memorandum dated 17 May, the German Affairs office of the State Department noted the difficulties which the proposed Soviet reductions were likely to cause for the Bonn government, and for U.S.-FRG relations. The Soviet announcement, of course, could be expected to "fortify the opposition" to Bonn's rearmament, an incessant worry of the government. Of special interest to the current discussion, however, are two other problems which might arise from unilateral Soviet force reductions. First, Moscow's move would allow the government's critics "to renew charges that the West has lost the initiative to the Soviets in the field of foreign policy." It would also cause anxiety in West Germany that "an East-West detente may be in the making on the basis of a program for general disarmament and at the expense of Germany's paramount interest in reunification."[54] The response to the Soviet reductions thus helps to clarify the connection of the two focal issues of this chapter. Many in West Germany still suffered from the Potsdam complex. The evident multilateral interest in arms control during 1956 served to exacerbate the worry that East and West might reach an agreement without German input, and thus without a second thought given to reunification. If this were to occur, Adenauer's foreign policy, and almost assuredly his government, could not weather the storm. In addition, the government was now likely to face a new barrage of criticism which asserted that the Soviets had taken the diplomatic initiative away from the West. Such considerations could only serve to strengthen Bonn's desire for increased interallied coordination—with West German input—and to convince the German federal government of the need for a new initiative on the reunification question.[55]

The above-cited document also makes clear that the State Department was aware of Bonn's difficulties. Yet events which were to follow indicate Washington's failure to satisfy Bonn's demands for inclusion and coordination. The infamous Radford Plan crisis was only the most spectacular example of this problem.[56] On 13 July, a story appeared on the front page of the *New York Times* indicating that JCS Chairman Arthur Radford was calling for a reduction in American troop strength of approximately 800,000. The fact that these cuts seemed to be a logical extension of the New Look doctrine adopted by the Eisenhower administration lent the report added credibility. And it was immediately apparent that America's forces in Europe would be hard hit by such cuts. What was less clear was whether or not the Radford Plan represented a consensus within the administration, or even among the joint chiefs.[57] What is clear is that Chancellor Adenauer chose to treat the situation as a full-blown crisis between Bonn and Washington.[58] Certainly, the contemporaneous West German debate about the length of compulsory Bundeswehr service colored Adenauer's response. The Radford Plan gave Adenauer the excuse he needed to give in to domestic pressure to reduce the proposed term of service by six months. Thus, Adenauer was able to blame the United States for forcing a decision which his military strongly opposed, but which would prove to be more popular with the German public.[59] But Adenauer's reputation as a calculating politician should not be allowed to obscure the fact that the Radford Plan came as quite a shock to him and his aides.[60] Coming only a few weeks after he had visited Washington—during which trip he had heard not a whisper of troop reductions—the publication of the plan served to emphasize both the insufficiency of intra-alliance policy coordination, and the dangers that this shortcoming brought with it.

Adenauer's failure to move the Eisenhower administration on the question of interallied policy coordination indicates the limitations of his ability to influence American decision making. To some extent, the West Germans blamed this failure on the American political season. No combined Western response to Soviet moves would be possible for the rest of the summer and into the autumn, Adenauer told a press conference on 18 July. It was now mid-July, he reminded his interlocutors. The nominations of the major party presidential candidates would come at the beginning of August. After that, America was done with foreign policy. The chancellor's press aide stepped up to second Adenauer. After the campaign began, he observed, "nothing else was any longer possible in America. . . . At that time the total war between the two camps breaks out."[61]

No doubt distractions, both domestic and foreign, prevented the administration from devoting to the coordination question the time and effort which Bonn thought it deserved. Yet there is also a more basic explanation for Washington's failure to take action on this issue. Dulles's Associated Press speech had betrayed a notable ambivalence, even if few noticed at the time. In principle, Washington—Dulles included—liked the idea of greater coordination between the allies. In practice, the administration made no serious efforts to address the question. As Dulles had said, America could not allow her hands to be tied by agreeing to submit her policies for multilateral approval. There had to be room for the Western superpower to exercise its "independent judgment."

One "independent judgment"—the administration's pursuit of the New Look at a time which was quite inconvenient for the government in Bonn[62]—was the immediate cause of the Radford Plan fiasco. Adenauer had reason to think that his American allies were making policy based on American interests without bothering to think about the implications which a New Look posture held for Washington partners. The crisis certainly damaged Adenauer's faith in the Eisenhower administration, and especially his "friend" Dulles.

So great was Adenauer's frustration with the Eisenhower administration after publication of the Radford Plan that he sent von Eckardt to America, in large measure to start building bridges to leading Democrats. Von Eckardt in fact met with Democratic presidential hopefuls Adlai Stevenson and Averell Harriman. These meetings warrant a mention, for these top Democrats told von Eckardt—and thus Adenauer—exactly what they wanted to hear. Stevenson, the eventual nominee, promised to speak out for the maintenance of "American NATO policy" in the strongest possible way, and would oppose any weakening of NATO's military strength. Harriman was even more willing to give the Germans what they wanted. Eisenhower's policy toward the Soviets was "soft," and the administration failed to reap the harvest of the "hard and decisive policy of Truman." He promised, if nominated, to "sharply attack the Eisenhower government on account of the weakness which it showed with regard to the Soviet Union." This anticipated exactly the line that the Democratic nominee of 1960 would use against Eisenhower's vice president. America must indeed be an enigma to the world every four years.[63]

But the crisis over alleged American troop reductions on the continent was, more than anything else, a symptom of the broader problem of attempting to formulate policy for an alliance of independent states. As such, it was a problem that could be managed, but never eliminated. The United States had to take into consideration the needs and demands of increasingly assertive European allies when attempting to lead NATO. At the same time, the American leadership had to balance resources available, and the public willingness to provide those resources, against the demands placed upon a *global* superpower.

Conflict within such an alliance was natural. The question was how to mitigate the effects of such conflicts. Bonn's answer was by increased multilateral cooperation on policy formulation. By this standard, American leadership of the alliance was wanting. The Eisenhower administration utterly failed to address this issue through the summer of 1956. This brought expressions of frustration from the FRG.[64] Despite its best attempts, however, the Bonn regime seemed incapable of moving the United States on this question. When it came to the related perception that the West had lost the diplomatic initiative to the Soviets, the Adenauer government was not willing to wait for Washington to act. With domestic and diplomatic needs of their own, they simply could not afford to do so.

"THE WORLD IS MOVING": THE BONN REUNIFICATION INITIATIVE

America's failure to lead the West in the direction of greater policy coordination was frustrating to America's German ally. But the perceived loss of initiative to the East brought with it greater dangers than mere conflict within the alliance. The Adenauer government had to face the West German voters in 1957, amid incessant calls by the opposition—and the Free Democrats in particular—to talk with the Soviets about reunification. Washington was well aware of these troubles. The Bonn embassy telegrammed Dulles on 12 June to inform him of the "uncertainty and malaise" in West German public opinion. This situation had resulted from German perceptions that all of the diplomatic activity in recent months had not brought reunification any closer. The unilateral Soviet arms cuts; Molotov's "resignation"; visits by Mollet and Yugoslav leader Josip Tito to Moscow; Khrushchev's "secret speech" and the resulting "de-Stalinization" campaign; and America's increased interest in the Third World; all of these developments left the "[West] Germans feeling [the] world situation moving but Germany [was] not moving with it," according to the Bonn embassy.

Particularly upsetting was a statement which Khrushchev had made to Mollet that he was not interested in allowing reunification; in Adenauer's paraphrase, "that he would rather have 17 million Germans in his hand than a united, even if neutralized Germany." Khrushchev had blatantly sought to drive a wedge between Paris and Bonn during his "conversation" with the premier, pointing out that the Soviets could easily tilt toward the Germans if France wouldn't take steps to reassure Moscow of its friendly intentions. Calling to mind the Nazi-Soviet Pact, and in this context the invasion of France by Nazi Germany that following spring, Khrushchev warned Mollet that "we are in 1939. You must decide quickly." The bind into which Khrushchev sought to lure Mollet's government also put pressure on Adenauer's, for Franco-Soviet warmth would call into question Western unity, while a Russian attempt to lure West Germans with fine words could undermine the Franco-German rapprochement upon which Adenauer had staked his European policy. This was an unwelcome distraction for a government that was still seeking to sell its security policy to the voters.

According to the Bonn embassy, the government was not panicked about its reelection prospects. Still, they expressed concern that the "optical effect of government policy would be better if chancellor seemed to show somewhat more flexibility and gave appearance of greater interest in unity problem."[65] As in 1953, the federal government needed to give voters the impression that it was doing something on the reunification front. Continued "malaise"—based on the perception that the West was passively responding to Soviet moves—would be political poison in 1957.

Brentano indicated to Dulles during their 3 May, 1956, meeting that more of the same was not good enough. Dulles wanted to make sure reunification was kept "at the forefront" of East-West relations. The issue, said the secretary, was a test of Soviet willingness to implement the free elections provision of the Geneva Summit communiqué. The West German foreign secretary politely and indirectly told Dulles that this was insufficient. Brentano said that he "hesitated to use the term initiative in connection with reunification." Yet a new, joint initiative was exactly what the situation called for. Brentano made no effort to connect this proposed reunification initiative with actual progress toward reunification. Rather, an initiative was necessary in order to show the "man in the street" how reasonable the Western proposals were, and to let him know that it was the Soviets who were continually saying "no" to reunification. According to Brentano, the general public did not understand how much flexibility the West had shown at Geneva.[66] A new initiative might raise awareness of this fact. The initiative was thus to be directed more at the West German voter than at the leaders in the Kremlin.

The Eisenhower administration stayed true to form. Unwilling to move quickly on the question of interallied policy coordination, and impatient with Bonn's questioning of U.S. security policy, Washington nevertheless lent a sympathetic ear whenever the German question threatened to undermine the CDU/CSU in their quest for reelection. The Operations Coordinating Board (OCB) of the NSC reported on 17 May that the coming Bundestag elections "can be counted on to increase the pressure in German political circles for renewed demonstrations of activity on behalf of German reunification." The OCB expected the SPD and FDP to attack Adenauer's government on this basis. Given this analysis, the West would have to reiterate "at regular intervals" allied interest in reunification; clearly, the NSC wanted to help Adenauer. Additionally, the OCB report noted that the Bonn regime would "seek some fresh Western initiative on the reunification issue prior to the 1957 elections." Underlying the discussion of this issue was a deeper concern regarding Germany's future. If the West failed to demonstrate strongly its desire for reunification, "an alienation of the Germans from the West might result." This perception of Western apathy toward "German reunification or other German interests," combined with

West German remilitarization and increasing "German dynamism," might well lead the FRG to set of on a more independent course.[67] No one wanted to see this happen.

Adenauer arrived in New York on 9 June for a visit which would take him to Washington to carry on discussions with Dulles. (The president was hospitalized on 7 June with a serious attack of ileitis.[68]) The chancellor could not have been terribly relaxed as his plane alighted. His faith in Eisenhower's commitment to established Western policies seems to have been shaken by the president's behavior during the mid-May visit of Indonesian President Sukarno.[69] The visit had been quite friendly, despite Sukarno's Cold War neutralism. At a news conference on the day before he became ill, Eisenhower went to some lengths to defend the neutrality of certain newer countries. Like the United States in its early years—and much later, one might add—these nations had adopted a policy of avoiding military alliances. This did not mean, he said twice, that they are neutral "as between right and wrong."[70] Neutrality, the leader of the free world seemed to be saying, was fine with him.

This sent shivers through Bonn. Not that there was any necessary connection between the neutrality of Indonesia and the German situation. But the American president did appear, unilaterally, to have weakened the Western proscription against neutralism. This could cause problems for his German ally, who insisted to the end that neutralism was not an acceptable path for Germany. In addition, the episode served to raise fears in Bonn that the United States was allowing its interests in the Third World to distract it from what was really important—Europe.[71] Adenauer would make this quite clear after the Suez Crisis brought the issue to a head.

On 7 June, the White house issued a clarification of the president's words, which attempted to distance Eisenhower from his apparent endorsement of neutralism. Collective security, not neutrality, was the path to security which Washington recommended.[72] The CIA's involvement in an attempt to topple Sukarno two years later, in any event, indicated that Eisenhower had not reconciled himself to the idea of "nonaligned" states.[73]

During their 12 June meeting in Washington, Dulles gave the chancellor time to vent his concerns.[74] After discussion of support costs and German rearmament, Adenauer brought up the matter of the coming elections. He stressed the political importance of foreign policy in Germany. He then made an instructive segue. According to the State Department minutes of the meeting, Adenauer said that "a matter of great importance in this connection [i.e., the domestic political ramifications of foreign policy] was the subject of German reunification or, as he preferred to call it, the liberation of 17 million people." Again, no attempt was made to disguise the linkage of Western reunification policy with the Bonn government reelection hopes. A batch of letters sent by Bulganin in recent days had Adenauer concerned. Bulganin, playing upon the unilateral troop reductions which his country had announced, called upon a number of Western governments to reduce their troop levels, particularly in Germany. This would, according to Bulganin, help facilitate reunification. The letters were a ploy, according to the chancellor, who must have held no hope at all for real progress in reunification. Reunification prospects hinged upon changes in Soviet attitudes and policies. And in Adenauer's estimation nothing at all had changed in Soviet policy since the Twentieth Party Congress. But "one could not say this to the German people."[75]

The chancellor went on to stress the importance of greater foreign policy coordination among NATO's members. As mentioned in the previous section, the chancellor was dismayed at the lack of progress on this question, which resulted in division among the allies and an inability to formulate a response to Soviet action—for example, Bulganin's recent letters—and thus contributed to the West's loss of initiative in the world arena. The new initiatives coming from Moscow in the post-Stalin period were causing problems for the alliance. Adenauer suggested to Dulles some ways of getting NATO foreign policy coordination on track: reinvigoration of the North Atlantic Council; better consultation between governments and their NATO ambassadors; an increase of the power of the secretary general; and regular meetings of high-ranking members of the foreign offices of the member states.

Dulles responded that he agreed with much of what the chancellor had said. But matters were not that easy. The situation was difficult for the United States, because "it had worldwide interests to a greater degree than other nations." Thus, while the U.S. would look favorably upon greater policy coordination, Washington "does not want this at the cost of submitting its worldwide policies to scrutiny and veto in the North Atlantic Council."[76] Dulles's statements reflect the ambivalence of an administration which saw the value of greater allied cooperation, but which nevertheless wanted to keep a free hand in foreign policy. In this regard, at least, there could be no talk of a "veto."

But Adenauer stood on firmer ground when pressing Dulles and his colleagues on the question of reunification, a question which Adenauer himself expressly linked with his government's electoral prospects. In response to Adenauer's discussion of the domestic political situation, the secretary stated that he "had to be scrupulously neutral in referring to elections in other countries." He went on to "assure the Chancellor that his sentiments of neutrality were the same as four years previously."[77] Whether he said this with a wink is not recorded in the minutes.

Adenauer's reelection was not viewed in Washington as certain, by any means. At the 15 June NSC meeting, Dulles heard from his brother what seems to have been the CIA estimate of the CDU/CSU election chances. Allen

Dulles thought that Adenauer might well be overconfident. In fact, "Chancellor Adenauer had a very tough situation on his hands in the 1957 German elections."[78] Even Conant wanted to see the Union parties win in 1957, and he could not be counted among Adenauer's greatest admirers. Late in July, Dulles received a long letter from Conant which provided the ambassador's assessment of the situation in West Germany. In this letter, Conant expressed the opinion that Adenauer's loss to an SPD/FDP coalition "would be really disastrous from an American point of view." With these two parties in power, there would be little chance indeed that the Bundeswehr would be built up in accordance with NATO plans. The criticisms of Adenauer's defense policy by Dehler and the Free Democrats may well have struck Conant as especially worrisome; he viewed "with horror" the possibility of an alliance between the FDP and the Union after the elections, and indicated that the Social Democrats would be better partners for the CDU. The severe criticism of Adenauer's foreign policy in the FRG left the government little choice, according to Conant. After talking with members of the CDU, Conant had come to the conclusion that Bonn would "go on the offensive," producing a new reunification initiative in the winter, or perhaps earlier. "From the point of view of the election which takes place in September, 1957," the ambassador added, "such timing would obviously be good politics."[79]

American support of the German initiative was vital if it were to have its desired impact. Yet Adenauer continued to be concerned that the administration in Washington was interested in pursuing its own ends, without regard to Bonn's needs. In the wake of the Radford Plan crisis, this fear focused on the question of American security planning for Europe. There were, nevertheless, signs that the West Germans had more general concerns about the way policy was made in Eisenhower's administration. And while Eisenhower's lieutenants proved willing to support the Bonn government in its diplomatic initiative, one detects signs that Washington's patience with German anxieties was wearing a bit thin.

Adenauer dispatched CDU Bundestag leader Krone to Washington in late July. The rumors of major troop withdrawals from Europe were obviously going to be the major topic of conversation. Through a briefing letter prepared by the State Department's European Affairs bureau (EUR) for Sherman Adams, who was to meet with Krone, the chief of staff learned that the Bonn government had three major objections to American troop reductions. The letter notes first that a reduction in troop strength would "imperil re-election chances for the Adenauer Government in 1957." In addition, significant manpower cuts would undermine the government's call for a buildup of twelve West German divisions. Finally, such reductions would make it far more difficult to get any progress on reunification. The latter question, as we have seen, was tied very closely with the first, both by Washington and by Bonn.[80]

These concerns weighed heavily on Krone, who was "quite excited" by reports of significant American troop reductions. According to Deputy Assistant Secretary of State Jacob Beam, however, Krone's talks in Washington had reassured him that "no actual plans to cut American forces in Europe now exist." But the State Department did not provide Krone merely with reassurances. It also let him know that the secretary was a bit put off by Bonn's constant demands for reassurance. Beam reported to Dulles that Krone "was now well aware of your feeling that the German Government was ill-advised to react so drastically to unconfirmed press reports." With this rebuke in mind, Beam thought that Krone would not press Dulles for further reassurances during their 30 August meeting, but would instead concentrate on impressing the secretary with the domestic political impact of press reports of troop reductions.[81]

But Adenauer's predilection for misgivings about his American ally continued unabated. In particular, Adenauer was from time to time struck by the odd idea that some individual, or group of individuals, had hijacked America's European policy. The chancellor was always given to the suspicion that when Eisenhower did not do what Adenauer wanted of him, there was someone acting behind the scenes, cutting the president off from information which he needed. This time, Sherman Adams was Rasputin. During a three-hour meeting with a top-level CIA representative, Adenauer expressed confidence in Dulles. But he feared that someone "was coming between" Dulles and Eisenhower. His sources indicated that Adams was the culprit. The context of the comment indicates that Adenauer was here speaking especially about America's NATO policy, and his concern that the American representatives at NATO were cut off from meaningful contact with Washington.

Adenauer's CIA interlocutor, Charles Cabell, reports telling the chancellor that this was "absolute nonsense," that Adams had nothing to do with questions of this sort, and that Dulles was in constant contact with Eisenhower on all foreign policy questions. Yet this reassurance was not enough to dispel such concerns entirely. Adenauer himself was "obviously being filled with bad info by some of his German friends both on general intelligence lines and as regards out policy and intentions." He was "badly in need," according to Cabell, of having near him an American ambassador "in whom he has confidence and in whom he can confide." In Cabell's estimation, the chancellor clearly saw his "own fate and reputation" to be inextricably bound to American policy. For this reason, he needed American help in reassuring the West German electorate that his foreign policy harmonized with that of the United States.[82] On 6 September Dulles and Conant met, and discussed "the status of Adenauer and his viewpoint and apparent misunderstanding of many of the present problems." Conant echoed Cabell's assessment that Adenauer "was getting a lot of misinformation."[83] The memorandum of this conversation does not go into any detail concerning the opinions expressed by Dulles or Conant. Yet it is obvious, nevertheless, that Washington was becoming frustrated with the chancellor's suspicions.

But the administration was nevertheless willing to help Adenauer's government in its electoral bid. This meant, in autumn 1956, support of the Bonn reunification note. The West German foreign office had prepared a lengthy note, dated 2 September, which they intended to deliver to Soviet Foreign Minister Dmitri Schepilov on 7 September. Copies were to be delivered also to the ambassadors of the other three powers which bore responsibility for German reunification. (It is perhaps worth noting that Adenauer did not intend to bring *this* question to NATO for interallied discussion.)[84] Bonn transmitted copies to London, Paris, and Washington approximately one week in advance, and sought the input of their allies on the draft.

The note began by reminding Schepilov that the Soviets themselves had indicated that the establishment of diplomatic relations between Bonn and Moscow, which had taken place one year before, was supposed to facilitate German reunification. The federal government, the note added, continued to assume that this was the desire of the Soviet Union.[85] However, the Soviets had recently taken some steps which did not seem in line with this expressed desire. In particular, the propounding of the "two Germanies" theory, and statements to the effect that German reunification was not a "pressing" issue had not helped the cause of German unity. This was regrettable. The division of Germany posed a serious risk to European security. In a line which could as well have been intended for Washington as Moscow, the note declared that even if there had been some improvements in "international tensions" since 1952, there could be no lasting peace in Europe without German reunification. Détente was not enough.

After reminding Moscow of its legal and "moral responsibility" to work toward German reunification, the note turned to Soviet objections to quick progress on reunification. The Foreign Office dismissed Soviet concerns regarding West German rearmament as misplaced. The FRG military buildup was relatively modest, and the government had renounced the right to develop weapons of mass destruction. In addition, the federal government was in favor of arms reductions, despite what Moscow might think. It simply wanted to avoid the unlinking of disarmament and reunification.

With regard to NATO, the note points to the defensive character of the alliance. Bonn, furthermore, was resolved to seek unification only by peaceful means. Nor was it clear that a reunified Germany would automatically become a member of NATO. This was up to the freely elected government of a reunified Germany to determine. And even if a reunified Germany were to choose NATO membership, a European security agreement could address Soviet worries. This future security system must, however, contain a *united* Germany. Soviet suggestions that the European security arrangement include the two German states failed to address the underlying political problems which produced conflict and instability on the Continent.

The note then went on to suggest the process by which reunification should take place. The foreign office rejected suggestions that reunification be achieved by agreement between the two German governments. The note pointed instead to the Geneva directive of 1955, and thus to four-power responsibility for reunification by means of free all-German elections. With this in mind, the note concluded with an appeal to the Soviets to do what they had repeatedly declared they would like to do: allow the Germans to decide their fate for themselves. Bonn asked Moscow for a response to the note. This, in turn, could foster dialogue which would benefit the cause of reunification.[86]

The note contained nothing new. All of its major points will be familiar to the reader by now. Beam, after reading the note, informed Dulles that it was "largely repetitive of past positions and places emphasis on the negativeness of the current Soviet position."[87] One is tempted to take this as a further sign that its wording was directed more at the West German voter than the Kremlin decision maker. But one need not draw any inferences, since the FRG embassy made this clear to the State Department. Beam informed Dulles that "[i]n order to avoid serious political losses as the result of opposition charges of inactivity on the reunification question, the Federal Government, while not anticipating any concrete results, wishes to initiate an exchange of views with the Soviet Union."[88] Beam's memorandum leaves no doubt that Washington treated the note as a CDU reelection maneuver, and not as an important step in East-West relations.

Beam urged Dulles to contact the Germans immediately, in view "of German haste to make their communication to the Soviets." Due to the fact that the note contained no surprises, it was relatively easy for the State Department to deal quickly with the matter. The European Affairs bureau (EUR) merely recommended a few changes in wording. A comparison of the State Department suggestions and the final text reveals that Bonn took these suggestions seriously. On the day that the final notes were delivered, EUR informed Dulles that "the Foreign Office made changes at least partially responsive to all our suggestions."[89]

On 11 September, EUR told the secretary that the British Foreign Office was interested in addressing to Moscow a tripartite note supporting the West German note to Schepilov. The bureau did not think that the situation called for a formal note. It was, however, important that the U.S. express to Moscow "the importance which we attach to reunification and the hope that the USSR will give careful consideration to the German Memorandum." European Affairs thus suggested that the three Western governments present oral statements to the Soviets.[90] In the end, it was decided by the three Western powers to transmit to Moscow the American, British, and French replies to the Bonn note under identical cover letters. These cover letters, in line with the suggestions of 11 September, stressed the importance of reunification and urged the Soviets to consider the West German note carefully.[91]

Such cautious punctiliousness on the part of a government which itself did not take the Bonn note seriously as a step toward reunification may seem a bit odd. It reflects, however, the seriousness with which the State Department took the real issue, Adenauer's reelection. The West German opposition, too, understood the reason behind the note. SPD press chief Fritz Heine told the American embassy on 10 September that his party "considered the note to be more for internal than for external purposes." This, of course, was true. Heine's other insight was that Adenauer had been motivated to send this note in part due to his fears of East-West détente. Adenauer, said Heine, was concerned that a fundamental agreement might be reached between the USSR and the U.S.A. on other problems without reunifying Germany."[92] While I have found no statement by Adenauer specifically indicating this as a motivation for the September note, Adenauer's fears of such an East-West deal are well established. Heine's assessment is thus quite plausible, although America's positive response to the West German initiative may have helped to lessen the chancellor's worries.

Even the SPD spokesman had to admit, moreover, that the "note was not too bad for an initial move." Perhaps it might lead to further discussion.[93] The Bonn embassy found significant evidence that the note was having its desired effect. *All parties* in West Germany had expressed "general satisfaction" with the note, and the CDU was "pleased with the favorable public reaction." The Social Democrats continued along Heine's line. The initiative, they said, was politically motivated and lacking in new ideas. It was, nevertheless, the "first step in [the] right direction."[94] The government had apparently done itself some good.

Bonn had throughout the year pressed Washington to do something about its concerns that the Western allies were out of step with each other, and that they had therefore lost the initiative in foreign policy to the Soviets. The Eisenhower administration did little about the former problem, at least in part due to concerns that increased consultation would decrease America's freedom of action. In that sense, the administration was not willing to give a "veto" over U.S. policy to Bonn, or to anyone else.

But on the second question, that of the West retaking some of the initiative in the Cold War, Washington proved willing, at least, to throw its support behind Bonn. Adenauer's government took the initiative on this issue, and Washington followed. The fact that there was nothing new in the West German note, and that not much was expected to come from it, no doubt made this decision easier. But at root lay a different cause. The Eisenhower administration always proved more willing to lend an ear to Adenauer when they believed that his domestic survival was hanging in the balance. Eisenhower's Washington was not always keen on hearing suggestions from the Germans about how to conduct alliance politics. And incessant West German complaints about American security policy actually provoked annoyance in an administration convinced of its own wisdom on this topic. But Eisenhower and Dulles were quite ready to treat Adenauer as the world's foremost expert on his own political viability. They also shared Conant's assessment that a CDU loss would be disastrous. Despite disagreements with the chancellor over NATO security policy, domestic opposition to Adenauer's rearmament policy only made this conviction stronger. Thus, when Adenauer suggested to Washington that he would need certain American actions in order to help himself politically, Eisenhower and Dulles were anxious to help.

But America's support of the Bonn initiative did not dispel the deeper anxieties which gripped the chancellor. He still feared significant unilateral reorientation of American security policy in Europe.[95] The question of allied policy coordination, which was largely responsible for the loss of initiative, remained unsolved. The United States, moreover, was giving the "impression of diminishing interest" in NATO.[96] Europe, the chancellor feared, was being superseded in Washington's thinking by the third world. This was certainly an odd complaint to make against such a Eurocentric administration.[97] But the Suez crisis provided at least superficial corroboration for this thesis.

SUEZ AND THE WESTERN ALLIANCE

The events of the autumn of 1956 have been studied exhaustively by students of international affairs. This chapter would be incomplete, however, if it failed to address its natural denouement, the crisis in Egypt and the contemporaneous suppression of the Hungarian uprising by Soviet tanks. With these events, the threads which this chapter has sought to tease apart came together again. The United States feared that it had lost the initiative to the "new" Soviet foreign policy, which was making gains in the Middle East.[98] Thus, the Eisenhower administration sought, at a very minimum, to avoid further alienating Third World opinion throughout the crisis. This brought Washington into conflict with significant NATO states, and resulted in serious strains in the Euro-American alliance.

It hardly needs to be added that policy coordination among NATO members—with the notable exception of an Anglo-French conspiracy—was almost nonexistent during these weeks.[99] All that Bonn had been warning about now came to pass in a spectacular crisis. This section does not seek to add new information to the already voluminous literature on the Suez Crisis.[100] Instead, it looks at U.S.-West German contacts after the crisis. Adenauer could not help but be affected by the events of October and November 1956. How the U.S. dealt with his importuning, after—as Adenauer saw things—failing to heed his calls for greater Western unity and cooperation, constitutes the last section of this chapter.

America's policy during the lead up to the French-English-Israeli invasion of Egypt was marked by Eisenhower's desire "to be friends with all sides."[101] In the end, the desire to avoid alienating any side resulted in strained relations with all nations involved. Throughout the episode, Cold War considerations loomed in the background. The story usually begins with Egyptian President Gamal Abdel Nasser negotiating an arms deal with Czechoslovakia.[102] Fears of Eastern Bloc inroads in a significant Arab country led to an American offer to help finance the Aswan Dam, a major public works project on the Nile. But Nasser refused to repudiate the Czech arms deal. Then in May 1956, he took what seemed in Washington to be a further step toward the East Bloc. Cairo extended diplomatic recognition to Beijing. These events, along with considerable domestic opposition to American financing of the Egyptian dam, led Dulles to withdraw the American offer.

Nasser responded by seizing, and then nationalizing, the canal. The response in Britain was immediate and furious. British Prime Minister Eden was determined that Nasser would not get away with taking over the canal. He resolved that Britain would use force to right the situation. Eisenhower was of two minds on the developing crisis. He did not want to alienate one of America's closest allies. But neither could he condone British use of force. America refused to support its NATO allies in their decision—Britain was joined by France—to use force against a Middle Eastern state.

Instead, Washington attempted to broker a diplomatic solution. Nasser, however, rejected the American proposal for internationalization of the canal. Meanwhile, the British and French, joined by the Israelis, had hatched a scheme. Israel would attack Egypt, taking the Gaza Strip and moving on the Sinai. This would give London and Paris the pretext for invading Egypt. They would land at Suez to "protect" the canal.

Israel attacked on 28 October. Eisenhower, just days away from a national election, cut his campaign short in order to focus his attention on the crisis. Washington pressed for a cease-fire. But the British and French were not interested. On 5 November, they carried out their end of the bargain, landing at Suez and beginning the conquest of the canal. The response from Moscow was both frightening and bizarre. Bulganin delivered his famous threat to use nuclear weapons if the French and British persisted. He also proposed an impossible joint U.S.-Soviet alliance to bring the war to an end. Washington responded with a threat of its own: America would use force to prevent Soviet intervention in the crisis.

The Soviet proposal of cooperation with the U.S. against Britain and France indicated their desire to press the NATO alliance to the breaking point. The administration wanted to prevent this from happening, but could not support the actions of its allies for fear of turning the rest of the Arab world toward Moscow. The president at one point declared: "I can't believe that they [the British and the French] would be so stupid as to invite on *themselves* all the Arab hostility to Israel."[103] The administration had no intention of inviting that sort of antipathy against the United States. Interests in the Third World entered Washington's considerations as much as did alliance unity. This was what Adenauer had feared would happen. Certainly, the French and British had acted outrageously, and had left Washington with few choices. The resulting injury to the Atlantic Alliance was, nevertheless, hard to heal. One American scholar concludes his study of the crisis by noting, on an up beat, that "[t]he alliance had survived the crisis."[104]

In fact, however, the alliance was bruised and battered. Köhler points out that Adenauer's "mistrust of the U.S.A. reached a new dimension during this crisis." From Rome, the Jesuit Antonio Messineo, writing the following January in the influential fortnightly *Civiltà Cattolica*, bemoaned the severity of this blow to the alliance: "it seemed that human and political motives had fallen into oblivion," including "the necessity to defend free institutions and independence."[105] The harm done to trans-Atlantic relations and the NATO alliance was felt more strongly in Europe than in the United States. Bonn could not downplay Suez as a simple "family spat," to use Eisenhower's words. Nor could the episode be dismissed as a particularly bitter dissonance between the actions of French policy makers and an American secretary of state, in the assessment of a leading scholar of Dulles and France. It was, rather, "the revelation of an absolute geopolitical rupture between the United States and France."[106]

Complicating the matter was the contemporaneous crisis in Hungary. As bad as things looked for the Western Alliance that fall, the situation in East-Central Europe looked much more perilous to Moscow. De-Stalinization had given rise to greater expectations of independence by many Hungarians, both inside and outside of the ruling elite. On 23 October, protests against the ossified government in Budapest turned into armed confrontation, and then revolution. The government of Ernő Gerő sought to assuage the public by appointing the popular reform-minded socialist Imre Nagy as prime minister. The Soviets, responding to the "imperatives of confirming the integrity of the Soviet bloc," prepared for military action while simultaneously assuring Nagy that the Red Army would evacuate his country. Feeling the pressure from the Soviet military, Nagy withdrew his country from the Warsaw Pact and appealed to the world—including the

UN and the Western powers—to guarantee Hungary's neutrality. On 4 November, the Soviets responded by launching an invasion of Hungary, which succeeded in a matter of days in suppressing the bulk of the uprising. Distracted by Suez and reluctant to confront the Soviets in their own backyard, the Eisenhower administration did not take serious diplomatic action to try to influence events. Once again, "liberation" proved to be more "principled exhortation" than active policy.[107]

Blankenhorn saw in the Suez crisis and Western inaction during the invasion of Hungary evidence of the shortcomings in NATO about which he had been complaining all year. The events of recent days "once again made perfectly clear how incomplete the political cooperation of the fifteen NATO partner states is." He feared that lack of consultation on significant questions could doom the alliance. "If we wish to maintain the alliance," said West Germany's representative to NATO, "the policies of individual powers must not present the alliance with a *fait accompli* in vital questions." Blankenhorn believed, furthermore, that if any fact had made itself clear during the crises, it was the "lack of a clear foreign policy conception in Washington."[108]

Blankenhorn proved far more ready to criticize America's actions than those of Britain, France, or Israel. In this, he was not alone. In fact, the episode helped bring about a decisive change in Franco-German relations. Policy makers in Paris quickly concluded that France would need to rely on the FRG as a continental partner, since the Anglo-American connection made the United Kingdom unreliable. In London, Eden's successor as prime minister, Harold Macmillan, nursed resentment at the way his nation had been treated by its special relation—while conceding that the United Kingdom had deceived Washington during the episode. In Bonn, meanwhile, Adenauer fretted about the damage that had been done to the Atlantic Alliance, and began to seek additional foreign backing for FRG policies. The conclusion in Bonn was striking: Germany was going to have to play a more assertive role in Western policy planning. This, in turn, called for closer relations with Paris, in order to mitigate dependence upon Washington.[109]

The chancellor's concerns were predictable, and do not require lengthy explication. Adenauer went to Paris on 6 November, in part to attempt to facilitate the rebirth of unity within the alliance.[110] Three days later, he told his cabinet that European-American relations "need to be straightened out [*bedarf einer Zurechtrüchung*]." In his estimation, the differences between the views of the American people and the Europeans were "extraordinarily large." Adenauer went on to treat his colleagues to a bilious assessment of the real threat of East-West détente. The crisis had increased Adenauer's fear that the superpowers might think of dividing the world between them. As he had told the American military governor of Cologne in 1945, America

and Russia would either go to war, or they would "come to division" of
the rest of the world. Nuclear weapons had made this choice clearer, by
making the results of war more terrifying. The alternative to war was division of the world between Washington and Moscow, and "all the other
countries mean nothing anymore." This was the real implication of the
Radford Plan, Adenauer thought, since increased reliance on the hydrogen
bomb could only make the choice faced by the superpowers starker. If the
Eisenhower administration had really reversed its position on the question
of nuclear disarmament, then it had done so because it believed that the
United States and the Soviet Union could "come to an agreement."[111] The
fact that the Americans had pursued disarmament until Soviet objections
to verification proved insurmountable seems to have been overwhelmed by
the chancellor's shock, fear, and anger.

As unrealistic as this image of Soviet-American cooperation was, the West
German government could not overcome its concerns that the "new" Soviet
diplomacy was weakening Western resolve. On 6 December, Adenauer told
Senator J. William Fulbright of his concerns regarding American public
opinion. American newspapers, he had heard, were speaking of a "golden
bridge" to the Soviets. Although he did not say this to Fulbright, such calls
for U.S.-Soviet rapprochement were certain to cause him anxieties regarding
abandonment or a "division of the world." The chancellor responded to the
"golden bridge" advocates by restating his belief in the policy of strength.
If the free world "cooperated closely," it could put enough pressure upon
the East Bloc to cause it gradually to crack. Only by such pressure could the
Soviet Union be compelled to change its foreign policy. Instead of treating
the Soviets so "nicely," the West should "let the Soviets cook in their own
juices until they again come to reason."[112]

The Bonn government could not see any substantial changes in Soviet
foreign policy. After the suppression of the Hungarian revolt, Lenz expressed his views on the new direction of Soviet policy, which allegedly
was initiated by Stalin's death and bolstered by the de-Stalinization process
initiated earlier in the year. Lenz rejected "peaceful coexistence," the buzz-
word of Soviet foreign policy, as a "magic formula." Pronouncements of a
wish to coexist with Western states could not be reconciled with the Soviet
Union's abiding desire to bring about the overthrow of those same states.
Lenz saw no evidence that the Soviet Union had altered its goal of "world
revolution."[113] If anyone had any doubts about the aims of Soviet foreign
policy, one needed only look at Hungary, Lenz wrote in the *Japan Times* at
year's end. After Suez and Hungary, Lenz concluded, there was nothing for
the West to do but draw together. The events of November indicated that
the member-states of NATO had to coordinate their policies in the future
"so that one common policy results."[114]

Blankenhorn likewise saw in the invasion of Hungary a return to the "'proven' methods of Stalinist rule." His prescription for a Western response to the crisis in Eastern Europe was the standard West German response: greater unity and cooperation among the free peoples of the West, and particularly the NATO states. Only this could help ward off the "dangerous" implications of "peaceful coexistence and the 'new look.'" Blankenhorn thus went beyond Lenz in declaring—if only to his diary—that American policy, no less than the "new look" of Moscow's diplomacy, was weakening Western unity and resolve. Blankenhorn was an admirer of Eisenhower's Democratic challenger, Governor Adlai Stevenson of Illinois. It should come as no surprise then that Bonn's NATO representative blamed Eisenhower himself for Washington's failure to lead. "Many regret that on 7 November President Eisenhower once again takes office in the White House," Blankenhorn wrote. Eisenhower was simply "not up to the responsibility, which the American world power must bear." Dulles, too, had to go. The elderly secretary had exhausted himself in the previous four years, and no longer had the energy required to lobby a reluctant president on behalf of an activist American foreign policy. Blankenhorn feared that instead of active American leadership, a second Eisenhower administration would mean a return to "atmospheric diplomacy" of the Geneva type.[115] Hungary, it seemed, was bound to a great power with an overly *active* interest in its alliance partners, while Bonn was dependent upon an ally with a very *passive* approach to intra-alliance relations.

But, like it or not, Blankenhorn was stuck with Eisenhower and Dulles. The Adenauer government attempted to use the period immediately after the Suez/Hungary episode once again to press the administration to work for alliance unity. In mid-November, Blankenhorn delivered a message from Adenauer to NATO commander General Alfred Gruenther.[116] In addition to pleading for an *increase* in American troop strength in Europe, Adenauer addressed the Suez issue. He attributed the current strains which plagued the alliance to a failure of political consultation. Adenauer was essentially saying: see, I told you so. "If we had achieved more progress in that direction some time ago," he opined, "it is doubtful if the Suez crisis would have happened." But if Adenauer thus expressed his impatience with American foot-dragging, one could also detect signs of impatience from the American side. Gruenther wrote presidential staff secretary Andrew Goodpaster that he was "considerably embarrassed to be the medium of transmission" of Adenauer's message.[117] Here, Gruenther displayed the same discomfiture as others whom Adenauer had used to circumvent Conant.

But American frustration with Adenauer was not limited to questions of procedure. Allen Dulles—whom Adenauer had previously attempted to use as a conduit to John Foster Dulles—gave voice to these frustrations in a

November meeting with Hans Globke, state secretary in the chancery. Globke again wanted to discuss the Radford Plan and, apparently, reports of American troop withdrawals from Europe. Dulles, in response, bemoaned the "ill-will and mistrust of the Federal Chancellor against the United States," which did not seem to have abated, despite American efforts to reassure Bonn. Dulles closely echoed the prior assessment of his deputy Charles Cabell, who, it will be recalled, noted that Adenauer's information came from un-named German "friends." The CIA director complained that Adenauer relied too heavily upon these "allegedly reliable" anonymous sources.[118] Obviously, Washington was growing a bit tired of Bonn's incessant complaints regarding American foreign and security policy. The fact that Adenauer's worries were based on unsubstantiated rumors only increased the frustration.

Yet the fact remained that fissures had developed in the Atlantic Alliance. Those cracks had come as a result of divergent policies toward a non-European area. This clearly exacerbated Adenauer's concern that his American allies continued to overrate the importance of Asia, the Middle East, and the United Nations, and that this distracted America from focusing on Europe. He told Fulbright of his concern that "certain circles" in the United States sought to give preference to Asia above Europe. He thought, in particular, that American interest in India was misguided. India, in his estimation, "would not become a great power any time soon."[119]

Eisenhower was largely unmoved. True to form, the president was not terribly receptive to Bonn's interventions which called for America either to change its security policy or to surrender its freedom to make policy. Responding to Adenauer's note to Gruenther, Eisenhower stressed the need to come to a peaceful settlement of the troubles in the Middle East. Clearly, this would be an American priority. With regard to NATO policy consultation on non-European matters such as these, the president was quite blunt. "I am sure you will agree," he said, "that it would be unrealistic to expect that we will be able to achieve identity of viewpoint with regard to matters outside of the NATO area." While Eisenhower, furthermore, appreciated the difficulties which rearmament posed for the Bonn regime, the U.S. had no intention of increasing the number of troops it stationed in Europe, as Adenauer had suggested to Gruenther. America already had a large percentage of its forces in Germany, the president noted. And anyway "an increase in our forces at this time would give rise to misunderstanding both here at home and abroad."[120]

The chancellor responded by pressing his case for a Eurocentric American foreign policy. The Soviets' "brutal actions" in Hungary had confirmed his opinion "that Europe remains the main target of Soviet policy and aggression." Moscow realized that control of Europe would bring in its wake control of Asia. Therefore, "in spite of all deviating maneuvers and all present assurances which she will break at a time she considers opportune," the USSR would continue to seek control of Europe. Adenauer was telling Eisenhower not to be fooled by détente moves on the part of Moscow, for their final goal remained world dominance. In an attempt to shock Eisenhower out of his complacency, Adenauer added that he believed "that the freedom of the world was never—not even in Hitler's time—so much endangered as in these years."[121]

Adenauer also raised the specter of the Nazi period in a letter to Dulles four days later. Comparing the Soviets to the Nazis, Adenauer again stressed the Soviet desire to rule the world. Even if the Soviets changed their tactics, and focused attention on this or that corner of the globe, these were nevertheless merely tactics. The Soviet goal was to control Europe. "The key to world dominance by the Russians," he told Dulles, was Europe, and not Asia. Given this Soviet aim, the West must not relax its pressure on the Soviet Union. The West had to avoid giving Moscow hope that it would be able overcome its internal and alliance troubles. So much for "peaceful coexistence."

NOTES

1. Texts of both Bulganin's and Eisenhower's letters can be found in *DSB* 34 (6 February, 1956), 191–95.

2. Conversation, Adenauer and Hoover, 4 February, 1956, StBKAH, Handakte-Bundeskanzler, Gesprächs-Aufzeichnungen I.

3. Dispatch, Bonn to Department of State, 31 January, 1956, NARA, Department of State Central Decimal File, 762a.00/1-3156.

4. Conversation, Adenauer and Hoover, 4 February, 1956, StBKAH, Handakte-Bundeskanzler, Gesprächs-Aufzeichnungen I.

5. Address by Hoover to the Foreign Policy Association, New York, 10 February, 1956, NARA, Department of State Central Decimal File, 762a.00/2-1056.

6. Telegram, Bonn to Department of State, 5 March, 1956, NARA, Department of State Central Decimal File, 762a.00/3-156.

7. See Schwarz, *Die Ära Adenauer*, 303–12.

8. Memorandum, GER (Jacques J. Reinstein) to Merchant, 2 March, 1956, NARA, Department of State Central Decimal File, 762a.00/3-256.

9. For an example of this, see Schwarz, *Die Ära Adenauer*, 304. In Dehler's estimation, talks of the type the chancellor had held in Moscow were more important than Big Four ministerial meetings.

10. Telegram, Bonn to Dulles, Report of Brentano speech, Frankfurt, 23 February, 1956, NARA, Department of State Central Decimal File, 762a.00/2-2356.

11. Letter, Dulles to Stassen, 11 December, 1955, *FRUS, 1955–1957*, Vol. 20, 240.

12. For Stassen's recommendations, see, e.g., Progress Report, Volume V, "Proposed Policy of the United States on the Question of Disarmament," 1 November, 1955, ibid., 227, 233.

13. Memorandum of Discussion at the 274th Meeting of the NSC, 26 January, 1956, ibid., 295.

14. Memorandum of Conversation, Dulles and Stassen, 29 January, 1956, ibid., 305.

15. Notes of a Meeting, NSC Planning Board, 21 December, 1955, ibid., 249. For UN Resolution 914 (X), see *Yearbook of the United Nations, 1955*, 12–13.

16. Memorandum of a Conversation, Dulles and Stassen, 30 December, 1955, *FRUS, 1955–1957*, Vol. 20, 258.

17. Dulles himself wrote Stassen to raise similar objections. If the administration were to follow Stassen's recommendations, it would open itself up to the charge that it was not really serious about arms control. Letter, Dulles to Stassen, 26 January, 1956, ibid., 287–88.

18. Memorandum of conversation, Stassen and JCS, 24 January, 1956, ibid., 276–77.

19. Letter, Eisenhower to Stassen, 10 March, 1956, ibid., 357. Only after an inspection system was working, and after its functional utility was *demonstrated* to Washington's satisfaction, would the United States be ready to begin "gradual, reciprocal reduction of armaments, armed forces, and military expenditures." Ibid., 358–59.

20. The Soviets had given no indication, up to this point, that they were willing to accept overflights of their territory. While their formal reaction to Eisenhower's surprise proposal at Geneva was cautious, Khrushchev quickly made it known that he would have none of it. During a break in the session, he told Eisenhower that he did not question his motives, "but in effect whom are you trying to fool? In our eyes, this is a very transparent espionage device, and those advisers of yours who suggested it knew exactly what they were doing. You could hardly expect us to take this seriously." Bohlen, who translated this exchange, notes that the Soviets never actually rejected the proposal, instead letting it "die of malnutrition." Bohlen, 384–85.

21. Letter, Adenauer to Dulles, 13 March, 1956, *FRUS, 1955–1957*, Vol. 20, 359.

22. Mollet had taken office in February 1956.

23. "France Tells Allies: 'Change Your Attitude,'" *U.S. News and World Report*, 6 April, 1956, 47–48.

24. Daniel Kosthorst, *Brentano und die deutsche Einheit: Die Deutschland- und Ostpolitik des Außenministers in Kabinett Adenauer, 1955–1961* (Düsseldorf: Droste, 1993), 98. Kosthorst notes that Soviet praise for Mollet's words was not long in coming. According to a State Department analysis, Soviet approval of the French proposal only served to increase German fears. See Memorandum, Edward T. Lampson (GPA) to Reinstein (GER), 11 April, 1956, NARA, Department of State Central Decimal File, 762a.00/4-1156.

25. "Mollet Assailed by West Germany," *New York Times*, 6 April, 1956, 6; Kosthorst, 98–99.

26. Kosthorst, 99.

27. Telegram, Conant to Dulles, 16 April, 1956, NARA, Department of State Central Decimal File, 762a.00/4-1256.

28. Memorandum, Lampson to Reinstein. See note 25.

29. The Soviet draft working paper can be found in *Documents on Disarmament*, 603–7. The American draft working paper is in ibid., 608–13.

30. This, in fact, is rather clearly the implication of the American working paper. Perhaps Gromyko could not believe that Washington was willing so blatantly to separate German unification from the first stage of disarmament. See especially sections 18 and 19 of the working paper in ibid., 613.

31. Letter, UN Political and Security Affairs to Assistant Secretary of State Francis Wilcox, 16 April, 1956, *FRUS, 1955–1957*, Vol. 20, 373–74. The observer from State's Bureau of International Organizations notes that Stassen was "quite careful not to hook further disarmament measures specifically to a settlement of the German problem, but to talk in terms of settling major international issues." Technically, this observation is correct. But Gromyko had asked specifically about the relationship between the German question and disarmament, and it was within this context that Stassen had made his remarks. It is, furthermore, quite likely that all those at London understood what was meant by the phrases "international issues" and "political questions." First and foremost, they referred to Germany.

32. Telegram, Dulles to London, 16 April, 1956, ibid., 375–76.

33. Blankenhorn wrote with disapproval of the proposed visit in February. The invitation had been made, Blankenhorn observed, when Eden "cherished certain illusions and hopes with regard to Soviet policy." The episode confirmed Blankenhorn's impression that Eden relied too heavily on his skills as a negotiator when formulating policy. Thus, Eden "does not have what it takes to be a prime minister." Blankenhorn, 247.

34. Telegram, London to Department of State, 25 April, 1956, DDEL, Whitman File, Administration Series, Box 35, File: Stassen, Harold E. 1956 (3).

35. Ibid.

36. Interview, Adenauer with German press, 18 July, 1956 [mistakenly labeled 1945], ACDP, Nachlaß von Eckardt, I-010-002/1.

37. For an interesting American assessment of the Adenauer government's situation and its difficulties, see "Political Developments in West Germany," a National Intelligence Estimate dated 17 April, 1956, *FRUS, 1955–1957*, Vol. 26, 78–89. According to the estimate, the FRG would continue its connections with the West, but the government would bend at some point to increasing pressure to negotiate bilaterally with the Soviets for German reunification. The estimate also noted that the government now "face[d] serious opposition from the right as well as continuing opposition from the left," due in part to Adenauer's "personal domination" of the government, and in part to his allegiance to Western policies.

38. For a lucid discussion of the Eisenhower administration and the formulation of the "New Look," see John Lewis Gaddis, *Strategies of Containment: A Critical Appraisal of Postwar American National Security Policy* (Oxford and New York: Oxford University Press, 2005), chapter 5.

39. Excerpts from Brentano's Press Conference, 13 April, 1956, *Dokumente*, III Reihe, Bd. 2, 1956, 247–48.

40. Krone, *Aufzeichnungen*, 140.

41. Blankenhorn, 246–47.

42. Statement by Dulles to the Associated Press, 23 April, 1956, *DSB* 34 (30 April, 1956), 709–10.

43. Memorandum of a Conversation, Dulles and Krekeler, 27 April, 1956, *FRUS, 1955–1957*, Vol. 26, 92–93.

44. In his statement at his departure for Europe on 1 May, Dulles said that this would be "a very important meeting because I think it is generally realized that the North Atlantic community needs to organize itself into something more than a military alliance." He thus "hope[d] and expect[ed] that at this meeting we will begin to search out new ways to express our common purposes." *DSB* 34 (14 May, 1956), 791.

45. Blankenhorn, 248–49.

46. Telegram, Paris Delegation to Department of State, 4 May, 1956, *FRUS, 1955–1957*, Vol. 26, 93–98; Telegram, Paris Delegation to Department of State, 4 May, 1956, *FRUS, 1955–1957*, Vol. 4, 55.

47. Telegram, Paris Delegation to Department of State, 5 May, 1956, *FRUS, 1955–1957*, Vol. 4, 57.

48. Letter, Dulles to Eisenhower, 5 May, 1956, *FRUS*, ibid., 75. The literature on NATO is extensive. See, e.g., Kaplan, *NATO and the United States*; Francis H. Heller and John R. Gillingham, *NATO: The Founding of the Atlantic Alliance and the Integration of Europe* (New York: St. Martin's, 1992); Ennio Di Nolfo, *The Atlantic Pact Forty Years Later: A Historical Reappraisal* (New York: Walter de Gruyter, 1991); William Park, *Defending the West: A History of NATO* (Boulder, CO: Westview, 1991). See also Ernest R. May, "The American Commitment to Germany, 1949–1955," in Lawrence S. Kaplan, ed., *American Historians and the Atlantic Alliance* (Kent, OH: Kent State University Press, 1991), 52–80; Marc Trachtenberg, "A Constructed Peace? The United States, the NATO Allies, and the Making of the European Settlement, 1949–1963," Working Papers of the Volkswagen Foundation Program in Post-War German History, No. 9: American Institute for Contemporary German Studies, German Historical Institute, 1995.

49. Telegram, U.S. Delegation at Paris to Department of State, 5 May, 1956, *FRUS*, ibid., 71.

50. On the day before this NSC meeting, Eisenhower appointed Senator Walter George as his "Personal Representative and Special Ambassador" to deal with the question of the economic and political development of NATO. See the letter of appointment in *DSB* 34 (21 May, 1956), 836.

51. Memorandum, 284th Meeting of the National Security Council, 10 May, 1956, *FRUS, 1955–1957*, Vol. 4, 78. At this meeting, Dulles also expressed concern about Adenauer's health and mental state. He thought that the chancellor was showing signs of age. As a result, "the situation was not running as smoothly in Germany as it had in the past, when Chancellor Adenauer was in full possession of his strength." Joint Chiefs of Staff Chairman Arthur Radford disagreed, however, noting that Adenauer seemed well to him. 79–80.

52. Blankenhorn, 249–50. For the the NAC communiqué which failed to meet Blankenhorn's desires, see *DSB* 34 (21 May, 1956), 836–37.

53. Memorandum, 284th Meeting of the NSC, cited in note 51, 79.

54. Memorandum, Department of State, Office of German Affairs, 17 May, 1956, NARA, Department of State Central Decimal File, 762a.00/5-1356.

55. In the Federal Republic, the opposition continued its criticism of the government's foreign policy. Dehler, for one, agreed that Bonn should take the initiative on reunification, but envisioned direct "preliminary" negotiations with Moscow for this purpose, thus diverging significantly from Adenauer's position. On the question

of increased NATO political coordination, furthermore, the FDP leader "strongly oppose[d]" this idea, which he thought would not contribute to the reduction of tensions. Despatch regarding 18 May Dehler interview with *Die Weltwoche*, Bonn to Department of State, 22 May, 1956, NARA, Department of State Central Decimal File, 762a.00/5-2256.

56. On the Radford Plan and the ensuing crisis in West German–American relations, see, e.g., Kelleher, 43–59.

57. Army Chief of Staff Maxwell Taylor was always a critic of the plan, and was thought by some to be the source of the leak. Radford himself quickly indicated that he had "not yet reached" the views which he was reported to have held. Maxwell D. Taylor, *The Uncertain Trumpet* (New York: Harper, 1959), 39–43; Kelleher, note 14, 328; see also Hans Speier, *German Rearmament and Atomic War: The Views of the German Military and Political Leaders* (Evanston, IL: Row, Peterson, 1957).

58. See, e.g., Schwarz, *Adenauer: Der Staatsmann*, 291–96; Köhler, 942–45. Köhler, who clearly thinks that Adenauer overreacted, labels the chancellor's reaction "unique," and credits Dulles for his "thorough," "well thought-out," and "sympathetic" attempts to reassure Adenauer that his worries were misplaced.

59. Speier, 212. On the Radford Plan's use as a "political excuse" for the Adenauer government's defense policy objectives and reconsiderations, see the perceptive treatment by Paul M Pittman, "A General Named Eisenhower: Atlantic Crisis and the Origins of the European Economic Community," in Marc Trachtenberg, ed., *Between Empire and Alliance: America and Europe During the Cold War* (New York: Rowman and Littlefield, 2003), 46–48.

60. Bonn's persistent attempts to gain American reassurance after the crisis indicate that more was involved than the attempt to sell a domestic necessity as alliance policy.

61. Interview, Adenauer with German Press, 19 July, 1956, ACDP, Nachlaß von Eckardt, I-010-002/1.

62. Von Eckardt reports hinting, while in America after the Radford Plan crisis, at the troubles that Western troop reductions would pose for CDU/CSU reelection hope in 1957. See von Eckardt, 453.

63. For von Eckardt's visit to America, see ibid., 451–60.

64. See, e.g., Blankenhorn, 252. West Germany's NATO ambassador complained in early October of the decline "of the political weight of the free West" due to "increasing dissonance" among leading NATO states and their "lack of a constructive, unified policy" toward the Soviets.

65. Telegram, Bonn to Dulles, 12 June, 1956, NARA, Department of State Central Decimal File, 762a.00/6-1156. Adenauer's statement is reprinted in Meissner, *Moskau-Bonn*, as is the *Le Monde* report of Khrushchev's statement, which reads: "We prefer 17 million Germans under our influence [to] 70 million reunified Germans, even if they are neutralized." 181–82. For the relevant extract of the Khrushchev-Mollet meeting, see Denis Lefebvre, *Guy Mollet: Le mal aimé* (Paris: Plon, 1992), 213–14.

66. Telegram, U.S. Delegation at NAC Ministerial Meeting (Paris) to Department of State, 4 May, 1956, *FRUS, 1955–1957*, Vol. 26, 93.

67. Ibid., 105–6.

68. See Ambrose, *Eisenhower: The President*, 322.

69. See Adenauer, *Erinnerungen, 1955–1959*, 160.

70. *Public Papers*, 1956, 554–55.

71. See Adenauer's remarks to Dulles, Memorandum of Conversation, Dulles, Adenauer et al., 12 June, 1956, *FRUS, 1955–1957*, Vol. 26, 110.

72. *DSB* 34 (18 June, 1956), 1004–5.

73. See Pach and Richardson, *The Presidency of Dwight D. Eisenhower*, 187–88.

74. "Dulles gave me the opportunity," wrote Adenauer, "to expound in detail all of my worries." Adenauer, *Erinnerungen, 1955–1959*, 162.

75. Memorandum of Conversation, Dulles, Adenauer et al., 12 June, 1956, *FRUS, 1955–1957*, Vol. 26, 107–9. For Bulganin's letter to Eisenhower, see *DSB*, 34 (20 Aug. 1956), 300–301. For the letter to Adenauer, see Meissner, *Moskau-Bonn*, 182–83. Adenauer faced tough criticism at home from those who thought Soviet policy had in fact changed somewhat. See, e.g., Telegram, Bonn to Department of State, 13 June, 1956, NARA, Department of State Central Decimal File, 762a.00/6-1356. Dulles largely agreed with Adenauer's assessment of the effects of the de-Stalinization campaign on Soviet foreign policy. A 3 April State Department press release quotes the secretary as saying that, while there have been some changes in Moscow, they still "forcibly hold East Germany detached from Germany as a whole," and maintained their domination of Eastern Europe. See *DSB* 34 (16 April, 1956), 637–38. See also the address by Deputy Under Secretary of State Robert Murphy, *DSB* 34 (30 April, 1956), 719–22.

76. *FRUS, 1955–1957*, Vol. 26, 111–12; 114–17.

77. Ibid., 114.

78. Memorandum, 288th Meeting of the NSC, 15 June, 1956, ibid., 127.

79. Letter, Conant to Dulles, 24 July, 1956, ibid., 133–38.

80. Memorandum for Goodpaster from State/EUR, 1 August, 1956, NARA, Department of State Central Decimal File, 762a.00/8-156.

81. Memorandum, EUR to Dulles, 29 August, 1956, ibid., 762a.00/8-2956. For Dulles's conversation with Krone, see *FRUS, 1955–1957*, Vol. 26, 149–51.

82. Memorandum, Cabell to Dulles, 28 August, 1956, *FRUS*, ibid., 144–49.

83. Memorandum of Conversation, Dulles and Conant, 6 September, 1956, ibid., 153.

84. It is interesting that Jacob Beam of the State Department was the first to recommend that NATO be consulted on this matter. Memorandum, EUR to Dulles, 5 September, 1956, NARA, Department of State Central Decimal File, 762a.00/9-566.

85. The Bonn regime, of course, assumed no such thing. But that is "diplomacy."

86. Meissner, *Moskau-Bonn*, 205–16.

87. Memorandum, EUR to Dulles, 5 September, 1956, NARA, Department of State Central Decimal File, 762a.00/9-556.

88. Ibid.

89. Ibid.; Memorandum, EUR to Dulles, 7 September, 1956, NARA, ibid., 762a-00/9-756.

90. Memorandum, EUR to Dulles, 11 September, 1956, NARA, ibid., 762a.00/9-1156.

91. Memorandum, EUR to Dulles, 25 September, 1956, NARA, ibid., 762a.00/9-2556. This memorandum includes as tabs all documents relevant to this transmission to Moscow.

92. Dispatch, Bonn to State, 11 September, 1956, NARA, ibid., 762a.00/9-1156.

93. Ibid.

94. Telegram, Bonn to Dulles, 15 September, 1956, ibid., 762a.00/9-1256.

95. See, e.g., Memorandum of a Conversation, Adenauer, Conant, and Donald Quarles, 10 September, 1956, *FRUS, 1955–1957*, Vol. 26, 155–61.

96. Telegram, Bonn to Department of State, 28 September, 1956, ibid., 163.

97. On Eisenhower's Eurocentrism and the Suez crisis, see, e.g., William Stivers, "Eisenhower and the Middle East," in Melanson and Mayers, *Reevaluating Eisenhower*, 194–95.

98. On Moscow's Middle East policy after Stalin's death, see Galia Golan, *Soviet Policies in the Middle East from World War II to Gorbachev* (New York: Cambridge University Press, 1990), 44–45.

99. Blankenhorn complained in his diary in early November that "neither the British nor the French government thought it necessary to inform the [North Atlantic] Council, even in passing [*andeutungsweise*] of their intentions." Blankenhorn, 255.

100. For an exhausting survey of the Suez conflict, see Keith Kyle, *Suez* (New York: St. Martin's Press, 1991). See also the useful essays in William Roger Louis and Roger Owen, *Suez 1956: The Crisis and Its Consequences* (Oxford: Oxford University Press, 1989). The most recent study of the Eisenhower administration's policy during the crisis is Cole C. Kingseed, *Eisenhower and the Suez Crisis of 1956* (Baton Rouge: Louisiana State University Press, 1995). Herman Finer's *Dulles over Suez: The Theory and Practice of His Diplomacy* (Chicago: Quadrangle, 1964) is highly critical of the secretary of state's actions during this crisis. For a more balanced assessment, see William Roger Louis, "Dulles, Suez, and the British," in Immerman, 133–58. On American economic diplomacy during the crisis, see Diane B. Kunz, *The Economic Diplomacy of the Suez Crisis* (Chapel Hill: University of North Carolina Press, 1991).

101. Ambrose, *Eisenhower: The President*, 328.

102. The following summary of American policy during the Suez crisis relies heavily on Ambrose, ibid., and Pach and Richardson.

103. Pach and Richardson, 132.

104. Ambrose, ibid., 373.

105. Köhler, *Adenauer*, 950. Messineo quoted in Carla Meneguzzi Rostagni, "Il Vaticano e la construzione europea (1948–1957)," in Ennio di Nolfo, Romain H. Rainero, and Brunello Vigezzi, eds., *L'Italia e la Politica di Potenza in Europa: 1950–1960* (Milan: Marzorati Editore, 1992), 169.

106. Boyle, *Eden-Eisenhower Correspondence*, 204; François David, "J.-F. Dulles et la France: La Crise de Suez," *Revue d'Histoire Diplomatique* 116/1 (2002), 27.

107. Bennett Kovrig, *Of Walls and Bridges: The United States and Eastern Europe* (New York and London: New York University Press, 1991), 85–102. For documentation, see Janos M. Rainer, "The Yeltsin Dossier: Soviet Documents on Hungary, 1956," in *Cold War International History Project Bulletin*, Issue 5 (Spring, 1995), 22; 24–27; Johanna Granville, "Imre Nagy, Hesitant Revolutionary," ibid., 23; 27–28; "Soviet Documents on the Hungarian Revolution," Granville, trans., ibid., 23; 29–34. A gripping study of the Hungarian Revolution that addresses the problem of liberation's rhetoric and reality is Charles Gati, *Failed Illusions: Moscow, Washington, Budapest and the 1956 Hungarian Revolt* (Stanford, CA: Stanford University Press, 2006).

108. Blankenhorn, 256–57.

109. Information on Macmillan comes from Trachtenberg, *A Constructed Peace*, 216; otherwise this paragraph follows the analysis of Soutou, *L'alliance incertaine*, 59–62.

110. Blankenhorn, 257.

111. Protocol, Adenauer's remarks at 9 November, 1956, cabinet meeting, StB-KAH, Handakte-Bundeskanzler, Gesprächs-Aufzeichnungen I.

112. Conversation, Adenauer and Fulbright, 6 December, 1956, StBKAH, ibid. Adenauer in fact saw in the suppression of the Hungarian uprising both a confirmation of his past policies, and a golden opportunity to "bet everything on the Cold War" during the coming election campaign. Köhler holds that this gamble paid off. "The consternation over Soviet actions in Hungary constituted a very important prerequisite for the electoral victory on 15 September, [1957,] apparently more than the 17th of July for the 1953 elections." *Adenauer*, 952.

113. "Statements concerning the Soviet Union," n.d. (circa November–December 1956), ACDP, Nachlaß Lenz, I-172-010, Band B I/2.

114. *Japan Times*, 29 December, 1956, ibid.

115. Blankenhorn, 258–59. Blankenhorn hoped that John J. McCloy would replace Dulles as secretary of state, but doubted that he wanted the job.

116. The West German foreign office was aware of Gruenther's opposition to cuts in troop levels. See Grewe, *Rückblenden*, 278.

117. Memorandum, Gruenther to Goodpaster, 19 November, 1956, DDEL, Whitman File, International Series, Box 15, File: Adenauer, Chancellor, 1956 (2).

118. Memorandum of conversation, Allen Dulles and Globke, 24 November, 1956, StBKAH, ibid.

119. Conversation, Adenauer and Fulbright, 6 December, 1956, StBKAH, ibid.

120. Cable, Eisenhower to Adenauer, 29 November, 1956, DDEL, Whitman File, International Series, Box 15, File: Adenauer, Chancellor, 1956 (1).

121. Letter, Adenauer to Eisenhower, 4 December, 1956, ibid. Eisenhower's response to this letter sought to be more reassuring. "I agree with you," the president told Adenauer, "that the major objective of the Soviet Union is to control all of Europe." He added that events in "other parts of the world" would not affect the "fundamental relationship of independence" which characterized the Atlantic Alliance. Cable, Eisenhower to Adenauer, ibid.

6

Toward Berlin and the
Status Quo: 1957–1958

Nineteen-fifty-seven was an election year in the Federal Republic. This fact did not, of course, interrupt the course of world events. The United States continued to devote attention to the Middle East, and Lebanon in particular, despite Adenauer's advocacy of a Europe-centered policy. Clearly, the Western superpower intended to see to its global responsibilities. But the Eisenhower administration very much wanted to see Adenauer re-elected, and was willing to help in this cause.

Most recently, the United States had lent its diplomatic support to a re-unification initiative devised in Bonn. This initiative was designed to give Adenauer the opportunity to present himself as an active campaigner for German unity, rather than to achieve progress on unification. The Soviet response, and the exchange which followed, in fact left little reason to believe that progress was at all likely. The government could not completely hide this stultification from the West German electorate, although it continued to argue that its policies were directed at reunification.

Still, 1957 in some ways echoed the previous year. The American administration had not yet given up on disarmament and continued discussions with the Soviet Union even as the election in West Germany approached. Initial evidence of increased flexibility on both sides could not have come at a worse time for the chancellor, who once again wondered about the reliability of his most important ally. Meanwhile, the Soviets indirectly raised the specter of German unreliability by launching "a small political operation," by means of a series of articles and other publications, designed to sell the citizens of the Federal Republic on the idea of a new Rapallo.[1]

The government nevertheless won a stunning victory in the September elections. For the first time, the CDU/CSU won an absolute majority in the

Bundestag. Yet sweeping re-election was no panacea for Bonn. The question of superpower disengagement in Europe had been building up all year. It came to a head in October, with Polish Foreign Minister Adam Rapacki's proposal for a withdrawal from the line of confrontation in Central Europe. This new initiative in East Bloc foreign policy, like other initiatives of the "new look" Soviet foreign policy before, left the West in a quandary, and left Bonn fretting that America would gladly back away from a potential nuclear conflict, even without progress on reunification.

Eisenhower never achieved the détente and disarmament agreements with the Soviets for which he had hoped. But while Adenauer sought throughout the 1950s to prevent Soviet-American rapprochement at the FRG's expense, it was not his intervention which brought about the steep decline in U.S.-USSR relations after 1957. The disappointing climax of the Eisenhower years was the direct result of the failure of the Soviet and American governments to resolve the basic political and security questions which plagued their relations. With his threat to sign a separate peace treaty with the East Germans, Khrushchev signaled a harder line from Moscow, in an attempt to gain recognition of the status quo. By authorizing continued surveillance overflights of Soviet territory, Eisenhower indicated America's determination to stick with "Open Skies," unilaterally if necessary. The Bonn government certainly felt the impact of the U-2 crisis. And the Berlin Crisis—which subsided in 1959, but did not end until 1961—was one of the seminal events of postwar German history. Yet the arms race and the bifurcation of Germany remained intractable problems, even for Eisenhower's successor, who resolved not to be hemmed in by the "Old Man" in Bonn. Long after Adenauer left the scene, Washington and Moscow would still be at loggerheads over these issues. Nevertheless, it is safe to say that the flaring up of the Berlin question in 1958 brought with it a decisive change in the context in which U.S.-USSR considerations of the German question took place. Lines hardened as the crisis continued, and John F. Kennedy would find it necessary to make a sweeping—and confrontational—statement of America's commitment to West Berlin. Adenauer could not have asked any more of him.

"NOT ONE IOTA": THE USSR, THE WORKING GROUP, AND THE 1957 ELECTION

The 1956 West German reunification initiative had been aimed at the domestic constituency. Adenauer and his government considered progress on reunification impossible as long as the Soviet government did not significantly change its policies. The initiative thus inaugurated an exchange between Moscow and Bonn which was no more productive than would be expected under the circumstances. Adenauer nevertheless continued to act and talk as if he were honestly seeking progress on the central question facing the German nation. To an extent, his allies were willing to go along, in part to help him in his electoral bid, but in part, also, to keep him from going too far.

The Soviets had responded to the Bonn note on 22 October. Their response was no more helpful than Bonn's note had been. Moscow placed the blame for Germany's division squarely on the shoulders of the Western allies, and decried the inclusion of West Germany in a military alliance directed against the USSR and "the other peace-loving states." The Kremlin rejected West German assurances that the alliance, and FRG membership in it, posed no threat to the USSR. No progress could be made on reunification if one ignored certain facts about the German situation. One fact was the remilitarization of West Germany. The second was the existence of two German states on the territory of the former Germany. In perhaps its most important declaration, the note claims that the situation "in Europe and in Germany itself has completely changed. Consequently, there is no longer any real basis for discussions of a reunification of Germany through the holding of all-German elections."[2] It provided merely a formal statement of what everyone already knew: The Soviets had no intention of pursuing reunification by the means set at Geneva, and were intent on using the reunification debate to press the West to recognize East Berlin. The Soviet note attracted less comment than did the swirling events in the Middle East. Yet the exchange clarified the fact that Bonn and Moscow were worlds apart on the question of reunification. Lack of progress on reunification, combined with West German concerns regarding the government's rearmament and conscription plans, provided a less than optimal beginning for a campaign year.

Without question, Washington was conscious of Adenauer's difficulties. In December 1956, the OCB took note of the "diminishing popularity of the Adenauer government." It attributed this slide to the stultification of the reunification issue and objections to conscription, as well as to a more intangible "feeling that the Chancellor has outlived his usefulness," and to the loss of popularity which always affects a government which has been in power for a long time. OCB went on to make the safe, but wrong, prediction that the Christian Democrats would not win an absolute legislative majority. It warned that a CDU-led coalition with one of the other two major parties would be "less cooperative" with the U.S. than was the current regime on rearmament, East-West relations, and "the terms which should be offered the Soviets on German reunification." In a superb example of bureaucratic understatement, OCB notes that, with a SPD-FDP government, "our difficulties would be magnified."[3] This was not a rousing call to arms to mobilize the American government to support Adenauer. But no such call was needed. The report said what everyone had accepted by then: a West German government under the leadership of anyone but the CDU would make it more difficult for the United States to see to its vital interests in Europe.[4] The implication of this conclusion was obvious.

The Adenauer government was certainly aware of this inclination on the part of Washington to help the chancellor. And it realized that Adenauer's *reliability* was the coin of the realm in alliance relations. It was nevertheless obvious that the same pressures which had motivated the Bonn note of the previous autumn were still at work. In fact, proximity to the election only made more pressing the need to counter those popularity problems to which OCB had pointed. Bonn's goal was thus to give the appearance of greater flexibility, while at the same time assuring Washington of the FRG's reliability. Krone sought to clarify this position in a conversation with Conant at the beginning of the year. The CDU parliamentary leader pointed out that the Suez/Hungary crises had spurred West German neutralist sentiment. Adenauer had attempted to counter this by painting the prospects for reunification in more optimistic colors than was his habit. Still, with the election approaching, "the chancellor would find it necessary to adopt a more flexible and less dogmatic-sounding approach to the reunification issue." This warning was meant to inoculate Washington against the fear that Bonn would strike off on its own in this election year. Krone "hastened to add" that Washington could rest assured "that the Chancellor would not change the actual basis of his policies one iota."[5] Krone wanted Washington to be aware that the "flexibility" which Adenauer would display over the course of the next eight months was all for show. The evidence suggests that Krone was being absolutely honest with the Americans. Adenauer actually considered prospects for reunification to be bleak after the Hungarian invasion. In light of recent events, the chancellor told Blankenhorn, the prospects for progress on the arms control and reunification issues had "never been poorer than today."[6]

The chancellor also remarked to Blankenhorn that the events in Hungary had raised West Germans' fears for their own security. They feared that perhaps similar developments would take place in East Germany, and then in the FRG itself. As a result, "one is today less ready than before to accommodate the Soviets in negotiations and thereby to take risks, which could lead to unforeseeable consequences."[7] It is not clear to whom Adenauer was referring here. Perhaps he should have said that *he* was less likely, as a result of the Hungarian invasion, to accommodate the Soviets. Lenz told the American embassy about unspecified polling data which showed that there had in fact been a "definite increase" in neutralist sentiment among the West German populace over the last few months. As he saw it, a large segment of the West German public was happy that the FRG had as yet no army, and worried that in the future the Germans might be dragged into conflicts like that over Hungary.[8]

The government would have to do something to respond to this sentiment within the electorate. Lenz indicated that he opposed an "appearance of greater flexibility" in Bonn's statements. Instead, he advocated that the government take a "strong line," to emphasize continuity in policy.[9] The more likely response from Bonn, however, was that which Krone had hinted at earlier in the month. The government, for purely political reasons, would have to appear more flexible than it actually was. The embassy in Bonn informed the State Department of this fact on the same day that Lenz had advocated a "strong line." While the embassy did not think that what the parties said on reunification would make very much difference in the election, it noted that the government "may be expected to show more initiative on [the] unity issue." The embassy, however, did *not* expect that Adenauer would bend on the question of the reunified Germany's freedom to choose its alliances.[10]

Bonn's Western allies were, nevertheless, concerned about the lengths to which the Bonn government might go in order to assure its re-election. This anxiety, combined with a desire to bolster the Adenauer government by giving the impression that the alliance was seeking progress on reunification, led the British, French, and Americans to agree to the creation of a Four-Power Working Group to deal with German reunification and—although Washington resisted—with arms control issues. With the next meeting of the UN disarmament subcommittee coming up before the elections, Bonn wanted to be certain that Western disarmament policy did not undercut the government. American acquiescence in this process again illustrates that Washington was willing to bend when Adenauer's future was on the line, so long as no major sacrifices were required. As Wilhelm Grewe, the FRG's representative to the Working Group, said, "the initiative for convening the working group came from us. . . . It was not hidden from the western powers that in Bonn political goals were also being pursued with this initiative; they nevertheless accepted this motive and were ready to take it into account, since they wanted and supported Adenauer's re-election."[11] No one in the Eisenhower administration ever put things this forthrightly. Yet Grewe, with these blunt words, summed up the situation; the Eisenhower administration was willing to take steps in the diplomatic sphere which aimed at influencing internal West German politics.

The West German interest in an allied working group almost certainly had its roots in the failure of the Atlantic Alliance to make progress on the question of political cooperation. The Germans had approached the French delegation at the December 1956 NATO ministerial meeting, and proposed a working group composed of representatives from the FRG,

Britain, France, and the United States. This group was to investigate the "implications of disarmament on the European situation," which presumably meant primarily the status of Germany. In addition, the group was to "review our European security proposals and to work out tactics to deal with Soviet maneuvers in this area during the coming months." Evidently, Bonn wanted no more surprises of the Radford Plan variety in an election year, nor did it want the Soviets to be able to catch the West off guard.

Paris responded favorably to this suggestion, if largely for reasons which it could not share with Bonn. According to the French delegation, the Germans had admitted that Bonn was considering a new proposal to the Soviets on reunification. This proposal foresaw the possibility for a demilitarized zone in Central Europe. The possibility of Bonn freelancing on such an important topic was, apparently, too much for the French. For this reason, Paris thought that a working group might "serve as a means of controlling the German initiative."[12] So even if Dulles had come away from the NATO meeting encouraged by "evidence of closer German relations with the British and French,"[13] the level of trust between Paris and Bonn was far from optimal.

According to the State Department's Bureau of European Affairs, the American position was that discussions of the security and disarmament issues should be kept separate (disarmament was still a topic for the UN Subcommittee, of which the FRG was not a part).[14] In addition, the United States ought to resist West German pressure to submit any new security proposal to the Soviets prior to the September elections. It would, however, be "desirable to have full discussion with the Germans of any proposals they wish to put forward."[15] Washington, then, wanted four-power consultations on European security which avoided any new proposals concerning European security. The administration also sought to divorce the topic of arms control from that of European security in discussions which included the Germans and excluded other members of the UN subcommittee.[16] One is thus left to wonder what goals Washington had for the Working Group.

The first goal, no doubt, was to help Adenauer politically. The Deputy Assistant Secretary at European Affairs (EUR), C. Burke Elbrick, said this expressly in a memorandum to Dulles. Elbrick did not think that the West Germans believed that any proposal regarding European security could make "real progress toward . . . German reunification" in the months before the election. But one could anticipate that they would "take a rather strong line that we should do something to help them before the elections." In EUR's estimation, the Working Group would provide Washington with "ways of meeting this need, which is a genuine one and should receive our sympathetic consideration."

Secondly, Washington shared Paris' concerns. Bonn desired action on the diplomatic front prior to the election. This brought with it the risk of independent West German initiatives which might be inconvenient for her allies. "Both the British and the French," noted Elbrick, "apparently regard this exercise, *as I believe we do*, primarily as one for getting an early and orderly discussion with the German Government with a view to obtaining assurance that the Germans will not go off on some uncoordinated line during their election campaign." Since the three former Western occupying powers were largely satisfied with the formulas agreed upon at Geneva, the group could serve to "smoke out what the Germans have in mind" with regard to reunification.[17]

Lenz's attempts to reassure Washington at the beginning of the year indicated the Adenauer government's awareness of this concern. In an ironic reversal of the previous autumn's developments, it was now Bonn which sought to reassure Washington of its reliability. At the end of January, Brentano sent a Christian Democrat member of the Bundestag to Washington to meet with Jacques J. Reinstein, the State Department's German desk officer. Brentano's message to State was that "the Department should be confident that German foreign policy is firm and, therefore, officials in Washington should not take alarm from reports they may read in the press concerning possible shifts in German foreign policy." Brentano said that the approaching election might make it "expedient" for government spokesmen, including the chancellor himself, to "take positions which may appear to be inconsistent with present German policy." It was Brentano's hope that State would understand that these statements would simply be expedient statements made "in the heat of the campaign." German policy remained firm.[18]

The major Bundestag debate on foreign policy at the end of January provided further evidence that the Adenauer government was not thinking in terms of new policy directions. Brentano in fact began his remarks by indicating the government's belief that reunification was not a question which could be solved outside of the context of the broader East-West conflict. And although Germans might not like this fact, it was nevertheless the case that the solution to the German question could "only be found in the framework of a [global] détente." German unity depended upon the settlement of other issues in world politics. Germany had no direct connection with some of these questions, and thus would have little influence over their solution. Reading between the lines, the foreign minister appeared to be saying that it would be fruitless for West Germany to set off on its own course in order to further the goal of reunification. This goal could only be achieved by means of a comprehensive agreement between the major powers. This was hardly a departure from established policy.

Brentano also indicated that the government was not ready to make new concessions to gain unification. No concessions were acceptable which led to a "diminishment or an endangerment" of Germany's freedom and security. The Soviet Union had to recognize that "freedom and security are not negotiable commodities [*Handelsobjekte*]." Implicitly, NATO membership was not up for negotiation. Thus, in reviewing the world situation, Brentano was led to conclude that the government had been right all along: There was "actually no real alternative" to the policy the government had been pursuing up to this point. Kurt Georg Kiesinger, the chairman of the Bundestag foreign affairs committee, reinforced the foreign minister's conclusions in a much-heckled (by the opposition) address on that same day. The fault for Germany's continued division lay not with the West, and certainly not with the government and its policies. The problem was that the Soviets had insisted on unacceptable conditions for reunification. Disarmament and neutralization, absence of free elections, and the maintenance of the "social achievements" of the GDR all appeared to be prerequisites for a settlement with Moscow. These were not acceptable to the government.[19]

The Bonn embassy took note of the debate. It was a "pure election year performance," timed to utilize Soviet brutality in Hungary to maximum effect in an attempt to "justify their [the federal government's] past policies, especially membership in NATO and rearmament." The embassy noted that neither the CDU nor the SPD had anything new to propose during the debate. In general, the government had re-emphasized its commitment to established policies, while trying to fend off accusations that it displayed "insufficient imagination and initiative on reunification."[20]

The obvious impasse in West German–Soviet relations was nevertheless a problem for the government. The sterile exchange of letters between Adenauer and Bulganin which followed the September Bonn initiative gave the impression of inflexibility on both sides. Adenauer told the Soviet ambassador in early February that relations between the two had not developed as one might have wished, and conceded that "each side bears enough blame" for the situation.[21] Bulganin's letter of 5 February continued the trend, making no new offers or concessions on the German question. The tone of the note was, however, more conciliatory than one had come to expect. Additionally, Bulganin called, in his letter, for a "decisive reorientation" in FRG-Soviet relations. The State Department simply took this newfound cordiality as evidence that the letter was written "primarily . . . to embarrass the Chancellor and to bolster the position of the SPD in the coming elections." Adenauer's reply reminded Bulganin that he and Khrushchev had told the chancellor in Moscow that the Soviet government accepted West German NATO membership as a fact. Adenauer went on to ask politely that the Russians stick with this realistic estimation.[22] If the Bonn government wanted to display its flexibility in time for the elections, it was not going to be able to do so by means of bilateral exchanges with Moscow. This fact, at least, seemed clear, and made the Four-Power Working Group that much more important.

Dulles had no objections to the Working Group, as long as it limited its purview to the issue of reunification. He told FRG Ambassador Krekeler in January that European security was not an appropriate topic for a group limited to four powers. Other nations would be affected by decisions on this topic. Thus, it would be best to limit the Working Group discussion to Germany, for which Britain, France, and the United States bore a special responsibility. He repeated this assertion to Brentano in early March. The foreign minister told Dulles that he expected a new Soviet initiative in the future. This initiative, perhaps "designed primarily for propaganda purposes," could "make some spectacular proposals within the context of the German election campaign." It was therefore important that the West be ready for this. The Working Group could prepare for potential proposals from Moscow. Dulles agreed that the West needed to prepare for "spectacular proposals" from the Kremlin. But he went on to stress the "importance that the Working Group be identified primarily with the problem of German reunification rather than that of European security, in view of the interest of many other countries in the latter question."[23]

The administration's desire to treat the disarmament, security, and reunification questions as discrete issues to be taken up in different forums reinforces German historian Detlef Felken's conclusion that American thinking on the relationship between disarmament and the German question was unclear.[24] Grewe spoke of disarmament, security, and reunification as a "package deal."[25] Even if there was, in the end, no deal, Grewe's description accurately reflects the interdependence of these questions. In the previous year, the administration had rejected Adenauer's formulation of an inextricable connection between disarmament and reunification at the first stages of arms negotiations. This did not change the fact that reunification was only imaginable as part of a European security arrangement, and that any such arrangement would have to include a comprehensive arms control agreement. America's approach to the three—discuss reunification in the Working Group, discuss disarmament with the subcommittee *without* discussing the German question, discuss security with NATO—accorded the three problems more independence than was warranted.

The American position was, as it turned out, unrealistic. The Working Group could not avoid the topics of disarmament and security, any more than Dulles himself could avoid these topics when meeting with Adenauer during the chancellor's visit to Washington in May.[26] The draft declaration hammered out by the Working Group had addressed the question of the Red Army's evacuation from the territory of East Germany in the case of reunification, a question with obvious ramifications for both the disarmament and security questions. Adenauer viewed this as one of the more important matters which he and Dulles had to address on this visit.[27] Regardless of America's wishes, no discussion of the reunification issue—even if intended primarily for internal West German consumption—could avoid the European security question.

The Working Group convened in Washington on 6 March, meeting for ten days. Meetings followed in Bonn in the middle of May and in Paris in June.[28] It released its formal statement on 29 July. In Grewe's opinion, the FRG's success in getting the three Western powers to agree to a fundamental statement on German unification at this time exceeded Bonn's expectations. (Although he admits to being disappointed that the Working Group did not then evolve into a regular forum for the discussion of disarmament.)[29] The "Berlin Declaration" was essentially a reworking of pre-established Western positions. In the declaration, the three Western powers, along with the FRG—the only government entitled to speak for all Germans—sought to lay out their position on the German question. Once again, the West reminded Moscow of the four-power responsibility for reunification, a responsibility which was "confirmed" in the Geneva directive two years before. Since Geneva, the West had not changed its position on the modality of reunification. A "freely elected all-German government" would have to be chosen by means of free, Germany-wide elections.

With regard to the security questions arising from German reunification, the four governments continued along well-established lines. "A reunified Germany may not be discriminated against," the document proclaimed, adding that German security could not be impaired by neutralization, demilitarization, or restrictions upon Germany's foreign policy. The reunited Germany had to be free to remain in NATO, if it desired to do so. The Western powers were, however, willing to give assurances that membership of a reunified Germany in the Western alliance would not confer added military advantages upon the West as a result of a pullout of Soviet troops from East Germany.

The four Western powers went on to note that reunification and a security agreement would make it easier to achieve a comprehensive disarmament agreement. "Conversely," the declaration continues, "the beginnings of a partial disarmament could contribute to settling important outstanding political problems like the reunification of Germany." Here at least, was something new: the Adenauer government had approved a statement which acknowledged that some progress on disarmament might be sought *prior to* the reunification of Germany. Adenauer's three allies sugarcoated this German concession, however, by declaring that they would enter into no disarmament agreements which prejudiced German reunification.[30]

The Berlin Declaration was thus a "ceremonial" statement, proclaiming solemnly and publicly that the three Western powers stood by their obligations.[31] The purpose of the declaration, and thus of the Four-Power Working Group, had little to do with making progress in the broad political problems which faced East and West. As Grewe had pointed out, the Germans proposed the meetings as a way of improving Adenauer's stature at home. Sympathetic to this cause, and anxious to avoid an independent election year initiative from Bonn, the Eisenhower administration proved willing to follow Adenauer's lead. In this sense, the chancellor helped formulate the administration's approach to the Soviets on the reunification question, if only in terms of presentation rather than substance; Washington's major representation to the Soviets on the European question came, in 1957, as the result of West German prodding and was a response to domestic FRG politics. It is also true that the administration went along with Bonn's linking of disarmament and reunification, at least for the purposes of the Berlin Declaration. Consideration of the disarmament and security questions went hand-in-hand with progress on the German question.[32] In this matter, too, Adenauer's influence on Washington was to be seen. Finally, the Western powers had given Adenauer something which he very much wanted, a formal statement that they would "enter into no disarmament agreement, which would stand in the way on the reunification of Germany."[33] From Bonn's point of view, the process had been something of a coup.

In fact, however, the concessions which Washington had made to Bonn were not so great, nor was Adenauer's influence so imposing. The administration wanted to help Adenauer get re-elected, and, as it had done before, it allowed the chancellor's needs to help determine what the United States said to the Soviets. Yet the chancellor had not asked Washington to do anything spectacular, nor had he sought to change the course of American policy. From the beginning, Bonn had been clear about its objectives. The government wanted something it could take home to show the voters. Washington had given its ally just that: a formal restatement of the Geneva directive, and a forthright assertion that the West would not accept the status quo in Germany in exchange for an arms agreement. The formal statement of these points in a letter to Moscow was new. But the policies which lay behind it were not.

The history of the Working Group leaves no doubt that the four members did not expect their efforts to result in concrete progress on reunification. Yet the Soviet response must have taken them by surprise. On 2 August, the Soviet Foreign Office released a bitter reply to the Berlin Declaration. The main point of the declaration, as the Soviets saw it, was to "sabotage the current [London] disarmament negotiations and to continue the Cold War" by insisting upon the connection between disarmament and German reunification. That this insistence should have surprised the Soviets was, in itself, surprising. American policy had been the same since the previous year's UN subcommittee meeting: some limited agreement

Chapter 6

on disarmament was acceptable as a first step, but further developments would have to be tied to progress on reunification. After a lengthy denunciation of Western "monopolists" and warmongers, who for nefarious reasons were pushing ahead with West German rearmament, the foreign ministry got to the crux of the problem. The Soviets still held to the "Two Germanies" thesis. America could not wish the GDR out of existence. The FRG's claim to speak for all Germans was a fiction. Real progress on reunification required a "rapprochement" (*Annährung*) between the two German governments. The German problem, Moscow declared, "cannot be solved by foreign powers behind the back of the Germans, to the detriment of the interests of one of the two German states."[34] (It is unlikely that Adenauer found this dismissal of his Potsdam fears very encouraging.) In case the Westerners had missed the point, Khrushchev told the Chamber of People's Deputies less than a week later that there was one German people, but "two German states," with different political systems, and *conflicting* domestic and foreign policies. "Whoever really wants the reunification of Germany," he intoned, "cannot ignore this."[35]

East and West were thus stuck. The major Western effort on reunification had amounted to an insistence on the Geneva formula. Moscow, in response, continued to hold to the line established on the way home from that summit: there were two Germanies, and realistic policy took account of this fact. Of course, Adenauer had not asked the West to get him out of this dead end. He instead simply wanted a statement from the West which demonstrated that Bonn and its allies were actively seeking to solve the problem. This was, in the final analysis, all that he received.

"CONTINUE OUR CURRENT POLICY": DISARMAMENT . . . AGAIN

The failure of the UN Disarmament Subcommittee to reach any sort of agreement in 1956 brought meager benefit to the West German–American relationship. The Radford Plan still rankled. Perhaps more importantly, Washington never successfully assuaged Bonn's fears that the United States was contemplating an arms control deal with the Soviets which would be detrimental to the FRG. In the context of the politics of 1957, this increasingly came to mean an arms or security deal with Moscow which left Germany divided. This section shall focus on the first of those issues, arms control. The security issue came in this year to be linked closely with the question of "disengagement" in Central Europe, and will be dealt with in the next section.

The American approach to the Four-Power Working Group revealed an uncomfortable reality. Although the Eisenhower administration did not want to call attention to this fact, it nevertheless did not view Bonn as an equal partner in the arms control debate. Arms control was a matter for the UN subcommittee, and the State Department had wanted to leave the question off the Working Group agenda. It was, as the West Germans had repeatedly noted, impossible to separate German reunification from security and arms control issues. Yet the London meetings of the subcommittee were to commence again in March, and Bonn had no control over these proceedings.[36] In addition the Soviets had, since the previous summer, indicated that they might be willing to be more flexible on the question of aerial inspection.[37] Adenauer was, throughout the year, concerned about the possibility that an arms agreement would be reached prior to the election.[38] The political fallout from such a breakthrough would be unpredictable. Britain's patent desire to cut its own defense budget only added to these fears.[39]

In his memoirs, von Eckardt recalls the fears which gripped Bonn at this point. The "greatest danger" for the FRG was a new course in American foreign policy to which Bonn was not allowed to "contribute its own ideas." Were West German policy to remain too inflexible, however, the federal government ran the risk that the U.S. and the Soviets could come to a compromise "without consideration of German interests." Von Eckardt believed that Eisenhower "thought constantly about the preservation of his popularity." For this reason, he thought that Eisenhower was seeking some sort of compromise with the Soviets, particularly in the area of arms control.[40]

Grewe expressed similar concerns. The London Subcommittee meetings, as well as whispers coming out of Paris and London,[41] brought "growing uneasiness" in Bonn. The ambassador gives in his memoirs a precise statement of the federal government's worries:

> A comprehensive disarmament agreement between East and West without prior, or at least contemporaneous, solution of the open political controversies, especially the German controversy, would have, according to the dominant interpretation [in Bonn], sealed the status quo of the division of Germany for an unforeseeable period of time.[42]

Judging by von Eckardt's and Grewe's recollections, then, the Adenauer government feared that the Eisenhower administration was so eager for a limited détente with the Soviets that they would help the Soviets cement the division of Germany. And, as they both remembered it, arms control was the main anxiety.

Lenz told the American embassy in January that he "questioned the advisability" of an American initiative on the disarmament question "at this time." Particularly in light of Hungary, a new disarmament move by the United States could only cause "confusion in the public mind."[43] No doubt, Lenz was referring primarily to the West German voters. The suppression of

the Hungarian uprising had seemed to lend credence to the federal government's interpretation of Soviet behavior. An election year was no time to
create "confusion" about this fact.

Bonn's approach to this bind was thus to attempt to maintain the linkage
of the arms and reunification questions, while at the same time, incessantly
professing the necessity for a policy of strength. As seen earlier, Adenauer's
representatives wanted Washington to know that Bonn was reliable, and
that any "flexibility" shown by the FRG toward the Soviets was electioneer-
ing. But Bonn also questioned Washington's reliability. For this reason, the
Germans repeatedly reminded their ally of the need to carry on the policy
of strength. Brentano told Dulles on 5 March that "there was no reason
to change our policies" toward the Soviets. The West, of course, had to be
ready to be flexible in responding to new Soviet initiatives, which he expected would be coming. But otherwise the West needed to "continue our
current policy with great determination."[44]

This was not simply a pep talk for its own sake. Even as the multilateral
arms control discussions were beginning in London, Bonn saw disturbing signs of "unilateral disarmament" by the FRG's allies. Adenauer wrote
Eisenhower in March that British plans to reduce conventional forces posed
a "grave threat not only to the Federal Republic but to the entire Western
Defense Community." Dulles attempted to allay German fears that America
would follow the British lead. During Brentano's visit to Washington in
March, the secretary assured the foreign minister that "our plans do not call
for any reduction in our troop strength in Germany," and that any actual
reductions in division strength would be counteracted by increasing the
number of personnel in "support units for artillery of new weapons."[45]

On a related matter, the administration decided not to press the FRG
too strongly to increase support payments for American forces stationed
in Germany. Dulles thought that West Germany could *financially* afford
to pay more. But, he and State believed, the *political* costs of seeking additional appropriations would be too high for the chancellor. The only
alternative would thus be for the United States to claim part of the money
already appropriated for payments to Britain. Given the concurrent troubles
Macmillan was having with his own defense budget, this was clearly out
of the question.[46] Eisenhower agreed that he could not press Adenauer too
hard at this point in time. Recalling that Adenauer was up for re-election,
the president thought that the chancellor was "limited in how much he
can attempt." The "real question," Eisenhower continued, "was how this
matter would affect the election."[47] The president did send a stern letter
to the chancellor, reminding him of the FRG's unexpectedly slow rearmament, and the frustration which this caused in Congress. But the president
concluded the letter by suggesting that Bonn might make a "lump-sum"
payment which could be regarded as a payment "on account," for the time

being. This approach, he added, "might provide the way out of our immediate problems." The two governments could then take up the matter again in six months, i.e., after the West German elections.[48] Eisenhower and Dulles had no intention of hurting Adenauer domestically.

What, then, about the arms control negotiations, which Bonn *did* see as a potential threat to the government's campaign strategy? The chancellor was to be in the United States from 24 to 29 May. In a letter to Adenauer on 20 May, Brentano said that he considered it very important that the German delegation in Washington emphasize the connection between disarmament and reunification. Brentano refers to Adenauer's previous success in this area, noting that due to Adenauer's "intervention" the Western powers had "made the German viewpoint into their own." He appears here to refer to Adenauer's advocacy of the "internal connection" thesis prior to the London Subcommittee conference of the previous year. Brentano believed that the time to place emphasis upon this connection had come again. The Soviets, he thought, were attempting to get an agreement with the Atlantic Alliance on nuclear armaments. This was, however, the extent of their interest in compromise. Moscow had no interest in conventional disarmament, and "even less [in] the political problems of Europe." The Soviets wanted to cement the division of Germany. They hoped to use the arms control question to this end. This could pose terrible problems for West Germany. Brentano told Adenauer that:

> If the Western Powers allow themselves to be seduced by the Soviet Union to give up this internal connection, then that would be a success of the Soviet policy and would create a very serious situation for German policy. Because such a disarmament agreement actually is based on the existing conditions. That means, thus, on the division of Germany.[49]

Brentano obviously took this visit to Washington seriously; Bonn had to maintain the bond between disarmament and reunification. It is equally obvious that he, like Adenauer's other close aides, doubted the administration's resolve to do so.[50]

At the time of Adenauer's visit to the United States, the talk within the administration focused on the question of inspection zones in Central Europe. Detlef Felken, who has studied U.S.-FRG relations at the time of the 1957 subcommittee meetings, notes that Dulles shared Adenauer's concern at this point that an inspection zone could harden the division of Germany.[51] This was exactly what Adenauer feared. The West Germans in particular were concerned about Harold Stassen, the administration's premier advocate of an inspection zone in Europe. "One expected nothing good" from Stassen, according to Grewe, who reports that Bonn was aware of Dulles's differences with Stassen on this point. Adenauer, says Grewe, was determined "energetically" to oppose any arms control ideas which would help to cement the division of Germany. In Grewe's opinion, the chancellor was "not without success."[52]

Felken agrees that the chancellor found some success in Washington, although he makes an important qualification. Dulles, as Grewe said, opposed Stassen's plan, and "appears consciously to have brought Adenauer into play here." Dulles found in the West German objection a useful "brake" to be applied to overly hurried disarmament plans for Europe. As Felken notes, Stassen certainly saw Bonn's hand here.[53]

Here, Adenauer exerted influence upon Washington. The Eisenhower administration took into consideration the political impact of inspection zone proposals upon the FRG. It is important to note, however, that opposition to Stassen's proposals was coalescing before Adenauer arrived in Washington, a fact which Felken himself notes. Dulles led the opponents. Additionally, the JCS were particularly concerned with the implications of zonal disarmament arrangements in Europe. With his newfound solicitude for the impact of American arms proposals upon Washington's allies, Radford warned Secretary of Defense Charles Wilson that the proposed zonal arrangements were "such that the strength and morale of the NATO [*sic*] would be almost immediately destroyed."[54] This statement requires no elucidation: the JCS thought some of Stassen's ideas to be not just wrong, but dangerous. Further objections were raised by the State Department. At a meeting with Stassen, Dulles and others addressed the same problem which concerned the Joint Chiefs. "In view of the effects on our NATO allies and the complexity of the multinational interests involved," the participants agreed that the East European zone of inspection should be treated separately from the question of the inspection zones for North America and the Soviet Union. The establishment of European zones, furthermore, should "be handled in a way allowing Europeans to have a full voice in the development of the position."[55] Adenauer could not have said it better himself.

While in Washington, Adenauer certainly sought to gain reassurance—both for himself and for West German voters—that no steps on disarmament which affected Germany would be taken without the FRG's input. Elbrick wrote Dulles on the eve of Adenauer's arrival that the chancellor, while in Washington, would seek public statements to that effect. The West German government, according to Elbrick, still worried that they had "no firm and clear assurance that an agreement will not be made on disarmament which will result in a relaxation of tension on the basis of the status quo."[56] None of this would have come as surprise to the secretary. Dulles, nevertheless, briefed Eisenhower on the same point. The secretary of state urged Eisenhower to "assure him [Adenauer] that we will do nothing in the disarmament field which would prejudice the reunification of Germany."[57]

Adenauer departed from Washington with both public and private assurances that he could keep his Potsdam nightmare on the shelf. The Four-
Power Working Group was preparing the Berlin Declaration, which, as seen
in the previous section, committed the four allies to take no steps toward
disarmament which would "prejudice German reunification." Adenauer
and Dulles discussed the declaration on 26 May.[58] But that discussion focused on the specific wording of the declaration. The principle had already
been established by the working group. The joint communiqué issued at
the end of Adenauer's visit provided another assertion of the "connection,"
this time at the highest levels. The communiqué mentioned European security and reunification in the same breath. Both Washington and Bonn
wanted disarmament, and hoped that first steps toward disarmament
would lead to further progress in East-West negotiations. Progress would
come, they hoped, both in arms control and in the "settlement of outstanding major political problems, such as the reunification of Germany." Any
comprehensive disarmament settlement, they declared, "must necessarily
presuppose a prior solution of the problem of German reunification."[59]
German unity was not simply connected inextricably with arms control and
European security; it was in fact a *precondition* of any significant arms-and-
security settlement.

These, then, were the public statements by which Washington confirmed
the tight linkage between disarmament and reunification. The chancellor
had obviously gone to Washington in part to gain such public statements
by which Washington confirmed his policies. As can be readily imagined,
the chancellor and his associates also sought *private* assurances that the
London talks would do nothing to undercut West Germany's policy, and
thus its government. True to form, the Eisenhower administration gave such
assurances. Also true to form, Adenauer and Brentano were not convinced.
During a long meeting with Dulles on 28 May, Adenauer pointedly referred
to the importance of his re-election for the Western allies. He noted that:

> if the proposals to be made at London could be used for propaganda purposes
> and if it could be portrayed that steps were being taken in the disarmament
> field without laying a basis for political settlements, this would have a very
> serious effect on the German elections. He said he frankly could see no chance
> for the Government.

Dulles supposed that he "must have failed to make his point clear" on this
question—a very generous assessment, given his incessant attempts to ap-
pease the chancellor. Dulles thus took another shot at reassuring the Germans. It was American policy, he told them, to get the NATO allies more
involved in the arms control discussions. When issues such as German

reunification arose in connection with arms control, the Americans thought that the allies had the right, "indeed, the responsibility" to participate.

Responding now to questions from Brentano, Dulles stressed again that the United States would not impose any disarmament settlement on Germany. "The United States could not think for Germany," so Germany would have to think for itself. As to the London talks, Dulles implied that these concerned only the first stage of disarmament. The United States—despite the wishes of Governor Stassen—had no intention of agreeing to inspection zones, arms limitations, or ground controls in Europe at this time. When these questions *did* arise in the following stages, Washington intended to consult fully with the affected countries. Again Brentano expressed his concerns, and again the secretary insisted that current American proposals "did not involve areas where the problem of freezing the political situation was at issue."[60] At a meeting on the same day, the president likewise sought to reassure Adenauer that the United States would not "take up in any international conference any matter in which one of our allies is concerned [or] take decisive action on it without the consent of that ally."[61]

Adenauer thus left Washington with concrete assurances that the U.S. would not address controls and restrictions which directly affected Germany in this phase of the subcommittee talks. He also learned that the United States had every intention of including the West Germans if and when discussions turned to these issues. Yet hardly had the chancellor unpacked his bags when word came to him—via the French, he said—of a new proposal from Stassen which indicated that the arms negotiator intended to "sell out" to the Soviets.[62] He treated American Consul General Elim O'Shaughnessy to a diatribe against this proposal and other statements by Stassen which were "in complete contradiction" to what Dulles had promised him in Washington. Despite Eisenhower's and Dulles's assurances, the Americans seemed ready to come to terms with the Soviets on European disarmament in the first phase. Now "it would look as if he had been duped" by the Americans. This would be devastating to his re-election campaign. Ironically, O'Shaughnessy, who had to suffer through this tongue-lashing, had come to the chancellor for the purpose of sharing with him a telegram from Dulles, in which the secretary firmly restated the reassurances which he had given to Adenauer in Washington. Dulles responded to the report of this interview by immediately dispatching a cable to Adenauer. In this message, Dulles noted that Stassen's proposals had been unauthorized and did not reflect American policy. Again, he told the chancellor that the U.S. would do nothing which Adenauer "might deem detrimental to German reunification," and that Washington had no intention of presenting Bonn with "any fait accompli."[63] Dulles had acted quickly to prevent the issue from turning into another Radford Plan crisis. Still, he may well have asked himself just how many times he needed to say the same thing before Adenauer and his aides would accept it.

But whether or not Adenauer accepted administration assurances, it was nevertheless clear that he had gotten most of what he wanted in Washington. The U.S. would not consider issues directly affecting German unity or security in the first phase of arms negotiations. And when later negotiations did concern Germany, Washington would make no decisions without Bonn's approval. If the Soviets wanted an agreement which solidified Germany's bifurcation, then they would have to take that up with the FRG. In a sense, of course, this implied a veto: no agreements concerning Germany without West German input and approval.

But when it comes to the more immediate question addressed by Felken—did Adenauer significantly influence U.S. arms control policy during the spring of 1957?—the issue is a little murkier. Adenauer unquestionably pressed hard on this issue. As Felken implies, his efforts may have stiffened Dulles's already stiff spine. As seen in chapter 5, however, Dulles's opposition to the idea of dealing with Germany during the first phase of disarmament was nothing new. Nor were his differences with Stassen a big surprise. These, too, had become clear in 1956. In addition to Dulles, the Joint Chiefs opposed Stassen's ideas. In order, then, to conclude that Adenauer had significantly reduced American flexibility in the subcommittee talks, one would have to argue that Stassen could have overcome the objections of the State Department and the Pentagon. This would indeed be a hard case to make. Perhaps, then, it is best not to put too fine a point on the argument: Adenauer gave a nudge to those who already agreed with him. This was certainly an accomplishment. But it was not a veto.

The reassurances which he had received were nevertheless useful to Adenauer during the campaign. Making repeated references to the London talks in his campaign speeches, the chancellor was able to stress the importance of Western unity in negotiations with the Soviets. This had been one of the keynotes of his foreign policy since 1949, and Washington had done nothing to undercut him in this election year. Throughout the campaign, Adenauer continued to stress the themes of Western unity in the face of the Soviet challenge. Hand-in-hand with this theme went the call for "reliability" on the part of the FRG. If the SPD were to win, then NATO, *Westbindung,* and the strong foreign policy which could bring arms reductions and other benefits would be forfeit. His policies would lead to arms reductions. But "one must have patience."[64]

The London talks produced no results which undermined Adenauer's campaign plans. In fact, the talks produced no results at all. Admittedly, the Americans kept one eye on German sentiment at all times during the subcommittee meetings. Dulles himself went to London in late July to take

charge of the American delegation. In a letter to Adenauer, he explained
that he "remembered well the degree of trust in the U.S. that you expressed
in relation to this matter." Given the Bonn government's reliance on the
U.S., Dulles "wanted personally to be sure that nothing might occur here
which would be embarrassing to you."[65]

As the election drew nearer, however, Adenauer had less and less to
fear from London. The questions of inspection zones and a nuclear test
ban proved to be insurmountable. On 27 August, the head of the Soviet
delegation, Valerian Zorin, delivered an angry broadside against the West.
In order to "deceive public opinion," Zorin believed, the Western powers
were "playing a double game." They were cynically using the subcommittee
discussions to camouflage their real intention, which was to go ahead with
a military buildup. The West had placed a further roadblock on the path to
disarmament when they presented the Soviets with the Berlin Declaration.
Moscow thought linkage of the reunification and disarmament issues was
likely to delay progress on both. Of course, this was what the Western powers seemed to want.[66] In all this, there was nothing new. Zorin's accusations
and objections had all been heard often enough before.

The tone of his remarks, nevertheless, indicated how poorly the talks had
gone. By late August, there was no sign of the optimism which had caused
the West German chancellor so much worry earlier in the year. The subcommittee sputtered along for a few days, before adjourning indefinitely on
6 September. In the estimation of the Bonn embassy, the breakdown of the
London talks, together with other evidence of a tougher line from Moscow,
seemed to "strengthen [the] position of government parties." Adenauer had
been saying all along that the danger posed by Moscow had not abated despite the "new look" in Soviet diplomacy. In light of what appeared to be a
new hard line coming from Moscow, West German voters might recognize
that Adenauer had a point, after all.[67] The London talks, then, did the CDU
no harm. And, if the American embassy's analysis was right, their failure
might have done it some good.

EASTERN EUROPE, GERMANY,
AND THE DISENGAGEMENT QUESTION

This study begins at a time when hopes for change and flexibility in international politics were high. It ends with the reinforcement of the status quo
in Central Europe. The Soviet "peace offensive" and Washington's desire
for a limited détente together created a new atmosphere for East-West diplomacy. Both Stalin's successors and Truman's thought that by 1953 the
time was right to channel some of the competition between the two blocs
into negotiation. The result was—on the European question—five years

of diplomatic activity without much palpable achievement. The two blocs were unable to resolve the outstanding, interrelated questions of European security, arms control, and German unification. To continue along this path, Moscow knew, would only further reinforce "the integrity of the Federal Republic and West Berlin."[68] Faced with this likelihood, Moscow opted in 1958 for a departure from previous policy.

German historian Waldemar Besson is correct in saying that the disengagement discussion of 1957–1958 "offered the last chance to prevent the final consolidation of the status quo before the onset of the atomic stalemate of the Great Powers."[69] For this reason—and because of the caustic debate which broke out in the United States over the issue—the disengagement question has attracted a fair amount of attention from German and American scholars.[70] A relatively brief discussion here, then, should serve as a link to the troubling developments of 1958, when the failure of disengagement brought significant changes in Soviet policy, and changed the nature of East-West diplomacy on the German question.

As Besson suggests, the disengagement debate occurred against the background of the approaching nuclear stalemate. The growth of the nuclear arsenals of both superpowers, combined with improved delivery capacity, made conflict between the blocs more dangerous with every day that passed. Increased vulnerability to nuclear annihilation gave both superpowers an incentive to avoid unnecessary risks, and to avoid threatening the other's vital interests. The superpowers would thus need to come to some implicit understanding of where lines were drawn. Since both the U.S. and the USSR viewed Germany as a vital interest, this development threatened to cement Germany's division.

Then, too, there was the question of Eastern Europe. The suppression of the Hungarian uprising had not eradicated "national communism"—communism in Eastern Europe with a nationalist flavor and a certain degree of independence from Moscow—although it had certainly indicated its limitations. Most significantly, Polish "national communism," under the leadership of First Secretary Władysław Gomułka, seemed to go hand-in-hand with a certain amount of autonomy in foreign policy.[71] The fact that the East's major disengagement initiative came from this regime, and not from Moscow, made it more difficult to dismiss out of hand.

The Eisenhower administration accepted the idea that the Gomułka regime represented something new in Eastern Europe. So too did Bonn, even if cautiously. In a conversation at the American embassy in Bonn on 23 January, State Secretary of the Chancery Globke spoke of the recent election in Poland. While hardly a free and fair election, Globke nevertheless "considered that any progress toward national Communism in the Soviet bloc is preferable to the former situation, where the satellite regimes were completely subservient to Moscow." He explained that Bonn had to be very careful in its incipient relations with Warsaw. Strong signs of a German-Polish rapprochement "would be regarded with the utmost suspicion" by Moscow. And Bonn did not want to do anything "which would jeopardize that degree of independence which Gomułka appears to have obtained thus far."[72]

The European Affairs bureau at State agreed that Poland had achieved a "relative degree of independence from Soviet control and domination." Predictably, Warsaw was more autonomous in domestic than in foreign policy. Nevertheless, even in foreign affairs, "the Poles continue to show some independence," particularly in Gomułka's failure to applaud Soviet actions in Hungary. All of this made for the "most important development in the Soviet bloc, since Tito's expulsion [from the Cominform] in 1948, in the direction of U.S. national interests."[73] Allen Dulles argued the case for American economic aid to Poland in April, pointing out the need to support Gomułka, and to give the impression to Poles that he could successfully "expand the area of independent action" which Poland had gained from Moscow.[74] By May, the State Department was considering the possibility of a "radical revision" of America's Polish policy since Gomułka's rise the previous October. The new Polish regime was "a subversive influence in the Bloc," which the United States wished to encourage.[75]

But this solicitude for Polish independence did not in any way imply that Bonn and Washington would respond positively to a disengagement proposal which had its origins in Warsaw. Piotr Wandycz has convincingly demonstrated that Poland did in fact have a role in drafting the plan which its foreign minister, Adam Rapacki, first sketched out on 2 October, 1957. In fact, it appears that Warsaw took the lead on this proposal, which Rapacki then had to sell to Moscow.[76] More recent scholarship in fact indicates that the Polish government viewed the plan as a step in asserting some independence in Polish foreign relations: Poland would not sit by passively while Ulbricht and Khrushchev imposed a German policy on the other Warsaw Pact nations. The plan was thus "an important confidence-builder for the Polish government."[77]

But for Bonn and Washington, the issue was less the plan's parentage than its implications. Rapacki suggested the creation of a nuclear weapons free zone in Central Europe, encompassing both German states, Poland, and Czechoslovakia.[78] This arrangement would preclude the stationing of nuclear warheads in West Germany and thus clearly serve the interests of the Soviet Union.[79] By this time, the Eisenhower administration had decided in favor of equipping NATO forces with intermediate-range ballistic missiles (IRBMs), a rather clear step toward the nuclearization of NATO's forces in Europe.[80] Particularly troubling for Moscow was America's haste to provide the Bundeswehr with weapons systems which could deliver either conventional or nuclear payloads.[81] The similarity of Rapacki's proposals and Moscow's desire for a nonnuclear Germany were too obvious to overlook.

Hardly had the United States and FRG gotten around to ignoring Rapacki's speech when the nuclear stalemate mentioned by Besson moved one giant step forward.[82] On 4 October, the Soviets launched the first artificial Earth satellite, Sputnik. According to one perceptive scholar of nuclear affairs, the Sputnik launch ushered in the "nuclear epoch," a period of about six years during which "the danger of nuclear war was much on the public mind."[83] This was a shocking display of Soviet ballistic missile capabilities. America now seemed vulnerable as it never had before, and Americans, for the first time, had to view themselves as "candidates for annihilation." Adenauer, meanwhile, gave thanks to God—in his words—for Sputnik, which he hoped would shake the Americans out of their "lethargy."[84] Eisenhower and certain members of the scientific community attempted to play down the significance of Sputnik, and thus to allay the fears of the American public.[85] But the administration had only limited success, and concern about a "missile gap" worked its way into the psyche of the American voter. In other parts of the world, the pull of the U.S. model may also have been weakened, since Americans could no longer boast a clear lead over the "socialist world" in applied sciences.[86]

While the American administration reacted skeptically to Sputnik— Eisenhower did not believe that the launching of the satellite significantly altered the strategic balance—there was disturbing evidence that Moscow intended to press its advantage. In a background paper prepared by EUR for the December NATO Heads of Government meeting, the State Department pointed to this problem. Since Sputnik, the paper observed, Moscow had "clearly implied that the West (and particularly the United States) must accept the status quo and the legitimacy of the [Eastern] bloc (including East Germany) as a precondition for any lasting East-West accommodation." The Soviets thought that American recognition of their sphere would strengthen the position of the East European communist regimes.[87] It appeared that the Kremlin was anxious to exploit its October surprise in order to force recognition of the European status quo on a panicked America.

Still, the Eisenhower administration refused to be shaken by Sputnik, or tempted by Rapacki, into giving up its goals of rearming West Germany and building up NATO's nuclear sword. America's initial failure to respond to Rapacki's proposal demonstrated the administration's distaste for Soviet—or Soviet-sponsored—disengagement plans. The Rapacki Plan, as Felken notes, was not a particularly good deal for NATO. It would have denied to NATO the means by which to counter superior Soviet force levels on the Continent, and would have "favored in this manner the stabilizing of a military power imbalance," which NATO nuclear strategy had sought to rectify. In addition, Rapacki had not offered any progress on the reunification issue. In fact, the plan was based upon recognition of the status quo, and, by implication, of the two Germanies thesis.[88] As such, the plan could generate concern in Bonn. But it was hardly likely to engender much excitement in the West.

While the Rapacki Plan gave Adenauer further opportunity to fret, it was a disengagement proposal put forth by an American which upset official Washington. With George Kennan's Reith Lectures in November and December 1957, the American attitude toward disengagement shifted from disinterest to open hostility. Kennan recounts his lectures—broadcast over the BBC—in his memoirs, and speaks of the "chagrin and remorse" with which he recalls the entire episode.[89] He had reason to regret the firestorm which his words ignited. But since his third lecture contradicted Washington's and Bonn's policies, proclaiming that they would never result in German reunification, it is hard to imagine why he did not anticipate a virulent negative reaction.

In addressing Germany, Kennan declared that the problem of Europe's division could not be settled without the settlement of the German problem. And the Soviets could not look sympathetically on any solution which left American or other Western armed forces in West Germany. Moscow could not be expected to withdraw from the GDR without the promise of a "compensatory withdrawal of American armed power from the heart of the continent." The implication was obvious: "So long . . . as it remains the Western position that the hands of a future all-German government must not be tied in any way in the matter of Germany's future military engagements, I see little hope for any removal of the division of Germany at all." The West had to accept the Soviet position. A reunified Germany could not be a member of NATO.

Leaving the specifics to the "planners," Kennan nevertheless thought that the West should display greater flexibility in its negotiating stance with the Soviets, and put the onus for rejection of reunification squarely upon them. Addressing the question of Western European security, Kennan doubted that a withdrawal of American and other NATO forces from the "heart of Europe" would threaten the West. He thought that American thinking on this question rested on certain "distortions" and false assumptions. When these were cleared away, perhaps Washington would recognize the value of disengagement. Finally, Kennan advised the Bonn regime that it just might want to agree to maintain some of the "social achievements" of the GDR as a condition for reunification. It would be foolish, he said, to let "vindictiveness, intolerance, or political passion block the road to reunification."[90] In his next lecture, Kennan questioned the Western reliance on nuclear weapons and suggested an end to the policy of first use, which, in light of NATO's conventional inferiority, would clearly cause problems.[91]

Thus the former policy planner had, in the Reith Lectures, used a high-profile forum to cast doubt upon the very basis of the West's German and security policy. "My punishment was not long in coming," Kennan wryly observed.[92] The originality of Kennan's thinking was not always accompanied by an equal measure of good political sense. If Kennan found the negative reaction to the Reith Lectures to be "a traumatic experience," it is nevertheless difficult to imagine his suggestions receiving a friendly response in Adenauer's Bonn or Eisenhower's Washington.[93]

Bonn's reaction to Kennan's neutralization and disengagement proposals was severe and adamant. The Adenauer regime sought to discredit Kennan's ideas, to make "a laughing stock" of his proposals. The chancellor and his advisers had no use for disengagement schemes, either of the Kennan or the Rapacki variety. They were particularly disturbed by the idea of a withdrawal of American forces from Europe.[94] Grewe summed up the government's attitude on disengagement in his study of postwar West German foreign policy. Proposals for an atomic weapon–free zone in Central Europe, he wrote, were designed to bring about "a new solution of the European security problem on the basis of the status quo, i.e., especially on the basis of the continuing division of Germany."[95] Should it have come as any surprise, then, if Brentano concluded that "Whoever says such things is no friend of the German people"?[96]

In the United States, the primary opponent of Kennan's proposal was Dean Acheson, formerly Truman's secretary of state, and a man who had no great love for the Eisenhower administration. But he, like the administration, considered Kennan's proposals unrealistic, foolish, and even dangerous. He wanted, furthermore, to make the world aware that Kennan's positions were not those of the Democratic Party. In a 12 January, 1958, press release which garnered wide attention, Acheson opined that Kennan had never really grasped power relationships, but rather he took a "rather mystical attitude toward them."[97] The Eisenhower administration was clearly in full agreement with Acheson's criticisms of Kennan. Dulles wrote Acheson to thank him for the service he had rendered by replying to the Reith Lectures, which, he thought, undermined American policy abroad. Politics, as they say, makes strange bedfellows, and Acheson even joked that his wife was thinking of leaving him, since he had received such a positive letter from Dulles.[98]

Acheson expounded on his criticism of disengagement in the pages of *Foreign Affairs* that April. Disengagement in Germany would do little to affect the basic conflict between the United States and the Soviet Union, he wrote. It would, rather, be followed by American withdrawal from Europe as a whole, and perhaps from other areas as well. But it strained credulity to assert that the Soviet Union would actually pull *its* forces out of Eastern Europe, knowing full well that this would mean the demise of Soviet-sponsored governments in that area. They wanted no more Hungaries. Neutralization of Germany, furthermore, would almost certainly result in an "accommodation" between Germany and its Russian neighbor. The current generation of policy makers had strong memories of the Nazi-Soviet Pact of 1939. Acheson reminded them of the danger that history would repeat itself. He favored, instead, a policy of strength. A "strong, united Europe," together with U.S. and UK forces, could meet the challenges of the Cold War. Neutralization of Central Europe, coupled with a retreat of American power, could not.[99]

Meanwhile on the Rhine, the West German government was doing its best to combat disengagement proposals. In a message to Adenauer on 8 January, Bulganin attempted to breathe new life into the Rapacki Plan by giving it the Kremlin's imprimatur. The Soviet regime, Bulganin wrote, saw no reason to put off consideration of the Polish proposal. The Czechs, Poles, and East Germans had already agreed to the inclusion of their territories in an atomic weapons–free zone. Now it was up to the German federal government to do the same.[100] Adenauer responded on 20 January that he was "disappointed" by Bulganin's letter. Rapacki's plan did not go to the heart of the problem. The question facing East and West was not the *location* of atomic weapons, but the matter of controlling their production. He also "regretted" that the Soviets seemed to be trying to drive a wedge between the FRG and its Western allies, by continually pointing to the dangers of German rearmament.[101] In short, Adenauer's official response to the Soviet proposal was to shrug it off. At best, the Rapacki Plan did not address the basic issues in East-West security. At worst, the Soviets were attempting to exploit the disengagement issue to cause a rift in the Atlantic Alliance.[102]

Brentano also found the proposal unappealing. Disengagement proposals all had one thing in common, he said in the government's 23 January statement on foreign policy. All of these proposals sought "the recognition of the status quo by the West." This, furthermore, meant nothing other than ignoring the question of German reunification, and thus the fundamental political problem which had "poisoned" the atmosphere of international relations since 1945. It was incomprehensible to the foreign minister that Moscow should propose that reification of this unjust status quo could become the basis for a satisfactory settlement between East and West.[103] This was long-accepted West German policy. The division of Germany was a fundamental cause of the Cold War. No solution to the conflict was possible, thus, without reunification. Nuclear weapons were a symptom of the problem, and not its basic cause. And the Rapacki Plan was silent on the question of German unity. Therefore Bonn, like Washington, thought it could only do more harm than good. The SPD leadership was far more receptive to the plan, though this brought criticism from Willy Brandt, the newly elected mayor of West Berlin and a rising star in the party.[104]

As Gaddis suggests, both East and West saw new moves toward reunification as risky at this point.[105] This certainly accounts for the severity of American and West German responses to the Reith Lectures. Kennan's proposals,
if enacted, would strike at the heart of NATO security policy. As surety,
Kennan could only offer his instinctive belief that the Soviets would not
exploit the situation to their own strategic advantage. This was inadequate.
Kennan's proposals, however, were not the official policy of the American
administration or—as Acheson took pains to demonstrate—of the opposition. The Rapacki Plan, on the other hand, was adopted, if not actually
sired, by Moscow. This plan also threatened to undercut Western defense
strategies, without even pretending to overcome Germany's division. Instead, it offered a prolongation of the status quo. One cannot imagine why
Bonn or Washington would have agreed to such a plan. If disengagement
was the last chance to overcome German division, as Besson said, then it
was a long shot from the beginning.

ULTIMATUM ON BERLIN

The East-West thaw during the 1950s had been inaugurated by Stalin's
death and the Soviet peace offensive. With the "Chance for Peace" speech,
Eisenhower had sought to show American interest. During this period,
the United States and the Soviet Union resumed contacts at the foreign
ministers level, and succeeded in resolving the dispute over Austria. This
period of détente reached its high point in the summer of 1955, when the
heads of government from Moscow, London, Paris, and Washington met
at the Geneva summit. Not since Potsdam, exactly ten years before, had
the American president and the Soviet premier met face to face. The major
result of Geneva was its "spirit." This atmospheric development nevertheless represented an improvement over U.S.-Soviet diplomacy as it had been
conducted up to that point.

But the promise of Geneva was never fulfilled. The Soviet leadership had
indicated that this would be so as they stopped in East Berlin on their way
back from the summit. In propounding the "two Germanies" thesis, the
Soviets called on the West to accept the division of Germany as the basis
for a European settlement. This position was unacceptable to the United
States, and to its German ally, both of which continued to insist upon the
Geneva directive as the only acceptable approach to the German problem.
The Geneva Spirit could not bridge this gap.[106]

Throughout the period, the United States had to balance its interest in
improved relations with the Soviets with the interests of its ally in Bonn.
The Adenauer foreign policy was predicated upon the existence of East-West

hostility and a more-or-less imminent threat from the Soviet Union. It was this hostility, this threat, which justified West German rearmament, and which called for the FRG to bind itself tightly to the free Western world. The Eisenhower administration had its problems with Adenauer. But it never wavered from its conviction that continued CDU rule was in America's best interest. For this reason, Eisenhower and his lieutenants sought to aid the chancellor whenever they believed his political future was in question. This relationship culminated in Adenauer's smashing election victory in September 1957, which gave the CDU/CSU an absolute majority in the Bundestag.

But there was little time to celebrate. The détente had been winding down, after its 1955 high point, when the Soviet premier brought it to an abrupt end. On 27 November, 1958, Khrushchev made the startling announcement that the occupation of Berlin must end. If six months hence there had been no change in Western policy, the Soviet Union would sign a separate peace treaty with the GDR. This would effectively end four-power control of Berlin. The three Western occupiers would then have to negotiate with the East Berlin regime, if they wanted continued access to their sectors.[107] Moscow was effectively telling the West that it had half a year to accept the "two Germanies" thesis and, thus, to ratify the status quo. The West could do so willingly now, or Moscow could force them to do so the following May.[108]

Whatever the intricacies of politics within the Kremlin or the Warsaw Pact, it is clear that the opening of the Berlin Crisis was the final nail in the coffin of the détente of the 1950s, which, in any event, had been gravely ill since shortly after Geneva. The first thaw in American-Soviet relations since the onset of the Cold War had failed to set aside the burning question of the postwar European settlement. Khrushchev therefore decided to force a settlement. In so doing he closed one chapter in the triangular German-Soviet-American relationship, and opened another.

NOTES

1. Cyril Buffet, "L'Allemagne entre l'Est et l'Ouest: Les relations germano-soviétiques au prisme de Rapallo, 1945–1991," *Guerres mondiales et conflits contemporains* 210 (April–June 2003), 10–11. The French in particular were susceptible to a "complexe de Rapallo," according to Chantal Metzger. "Dossier: Les deux Allemagnes dans la guerre froide," in *Guerres mondiales*, ibid., 4.

2. Meissner, *Moskau-Bonn*, 220–26.

3. Progress Report on NSC 160/1, 5 December, 1956, *FRUS, 1955–1957*, Vol. 26, 184.

4. The Bonn embassy, however, doubted that an SPD victory would change German foreign policy to an "extent dangerous to [the] West," although they expected

ning

that the socialists would put increased emphasis on reunification. Telegram, Bonn to State, 25 January, 1957, *FRUS, 1955–1957*, Vol. 26, 197.

5. Despatch, Bonn to State, 4 January, 1957, NARA, Department of State Central Decimal File, 762a.00/1-457.

6. Blankenhorn, 263.

7. Ibid., 262.

8. Despatch, Bonn to State, 25 January, 1957, NARA, Department of State Central Decimal File, 762a.00/1-2557.

9. Ibid. On Lenz's opposition to the more flexible policy, see also Telegram, Bonn to Dulles, 21 January, 1957, NARA, Department of State Central Decimal File, 762a.00/1-2157.

10. Telegram, Bonn to State, 25 January, 1957, *FRUS, 1955–1957*, Vol. 26, 194–98. The analysis added that the SPD was in a very strong position, and that its chances of entering the next government were "almost even" (197). It is therefore especially surprising that the embassy did not think the positions which the parties staked out on reunification would have much impact in the coming months.

11. Grewe, 292.

12. Memorandum, EUR to Dulles, 10 January, 1957, NARA, Department of State Central Decimal File, 762a.00/1-1057. Tab B to this document, which apparently contains information about this West German plan, is unfortunately not in the State Department files.

13. Memorandum of a conference, Eisenhower and Dulles, 15 December, 1956, *FRUS, 1955–1957*, Vol. 4, 165.

14. It is interesting, in this context, that Adenauer indicated on 14 January—through his spokesman—that the "Federal Government could not comment on question of relationship between conventional and atomic disarmament at present, when powers concerned were considering how to proceed with disarmament negotiations at the U.N." Telegram, Bonn to State, 14 January, 1957, NARA, Department of State Central Decimal File, 762a.00/1-1457.

15. Memorandum, EUR to Dulles, 10 January, 1957; see note 12.

16. See, e.g., Memorandum, EUR to Dulles, 17 January, 1957, NARA, Department of State Central Decimal File, 762a.00/1-1757. EUR notes that disarmament must be kept separate from the security question, because Canada, although a member of the UN Subcommittee, was not to be represented in the Working Group. Also, the West Germans "have no special claim to a preferred role in disarmament, and have neither the position nor the competence to deal with most of the issues" which would arise.

17. Memorandum, EUR to Dulles, 5 February, 1957, NARA, Department of State Central Decimal File, 762a.00/2-557. Emphasis added.

18. Memorandum, EUR to Dulles, 31 January, 1957, ibid., 762a.00/1-3157.

19. *Verhandlungen*, Bd. 34, 10 January–31 January, 1957, 10640–59.

20. Telegram, Bonn to Dulles, 2 February, 1957, NARA, Department of State Central Decimal File, 762a.00/2-257.

21. Memorandum of meeting, Adenauer and A. A. Smirnov, 8 February, 1957, StBKAH, Handakte-Bundeskanzler, Gesprächs-Aufzeichnungen I.

22. For Bulganin's 5 February letter, see Meissner, *Moskau-Bonn*, 233–37. For Adenauer's 27 February response, see ibid., 237–40. For the State Department analysis

of Bulganin's letter, see Memorandum, EUR to Dulles, NARA, Department of State Central Decimal File, 762a.00/2-1157.

23. Memorandum of a conversation, Dulles, Brentano et al., *FRUS, 1955–1957,* Vol. 26, 213–14.

24. Felken, *Dulles und Deutschland,* 444.

25. Grewe, 290.

26. As Grewe told Reinstein on 19 June, "the core of the reunification problem was at the present time the subject of disarmament. He [Grewe] thought it was unrealistic that the Working Group try to deal with reunification without discussing the relationship of reunification with disarmament." Memorandum of a conversation, Grewe and Reinstein, 19 June, 1957, NARA, Department of State Central Decimal File, 762a.00/6-1957. During his May visit, Adenauer stressed to Eisenhower the importance of maintaining the connection between the arms control and reunification issues. See Köhler, 953.

27. See, e.g., Memorandum of a conversation, Adenauer, Dulles et al., 26 May, 1957, *FRUS,* ibid., 259–61. Adenauer, *Erinnerungen, 1955–1959,* 309.

28. Editorial note, *FRUS, 1955–1957,* Vol. 26, 219.

29. Grewe, 296.

30. For the text of the Berlin Declaration, see Meissner, *Moskau-Bonn,* 283–85. An English-language draft is in NARA, Department of State Central Decimal File, 762a.00/7-257.

31. See Felken, 443.

32. Grewe does not take credit for the American change of heart on this position, noting that the Western powers had been "gradually distancing themselves from this position" for two years. Grewe, 296.

33. Meissner, *Moskau-Bonn,* 284.

34. Meissner, *Moskau-Bonn,* 287–92. The vitriol which the letter directed at Adenauer and his government must be seen in the context of the upcoming election.

35. Ibid., 292.

36. The subcommittee held its first meeting of the year on 18 March, and its last on 6 September. See Editorial Note, *FRUS, 1955–1957,* Vol. 20, 464.

37. Dulles even told Adenauer in May that he thought the Soviets might be interested in some sort of limited arms control agreement. Records, Meeting of Adenauer and Dulles, Department of State, 27 May, 1957, StBKAH, Handakte, Gesprächs-Aufzeichnungen I.

38. See Felken, 437–40.

39. This was the year in which the British would move toward a "New Look" of their own. The new defense minister, Duncan Sandys, would institute a policy "reflecting greatly reduced reliance on manpower and a strong declaratory emphasis on Britain's burgeoning nuclear deterrent." Martin S. Navias, *Nuclear Weapons and British Strategic Planning, 1955–1958* (Oxford: Oxford University Press, 1991), 134. On the Sandys White Paper, see ibid., 134–87.

40. Von Eckardt, 476.

41. See Franco-British draft note in *Europa-Archiv* 15:4 (February 1960), 116–19.

42. Grewe, 296–97.

43. Despatch, Bonn to Department of State, NARA, Department of State Central Decimal File, 762a.00/1-2557.

44. Memorandum of a conversation, Brentano, Dulles et al., *FRUS, 1955–1957,* Vol. 26, 213.

45. Memorandum of a conversation, Brentano, Dulles, et al., 5 March, 1957, ibid., 215–17; Letter, Adenauer to Eisenhower, 23 March, 1957, ibid., 221.

46. Memorandum, Dulles to Eisenhower, 27 March, 1957, DDEL, International Series, White House, Office of the Staff Secretary, Box 6, File: Germany—Volume I of III (1) [February 1956–March 1957].

47. Memorandum of a conference with the president, 2 April, 1957, DDEL, File: Germany—Volume I of III (2). At this meeting, the question of troop withdrawals from Europe arose. It seems worth noting that Radford quickly spoke up, insisting that "we should let our allies know" if the administration decided to cut American troop strength. The general, apparently, had learned his lesson.

48. Letter, Eisenhower to Adenauer, 12 April, 1957, *FRUS, 1955–1957,* Vol. 26, 227–29.

49. Arnulf Baring, *Sehr Verehrter Herr Bundeskanzler! Heinrich von Brentano im Briefwechsel mit Konrad Adenauer, 1949–1964* (Hamburg: Hoffmann und Campe Verlag, 1974), 213.

50. At a 15 May press conference, Adenauer said that the government would accept "unconditionally" any arms agreement that came out of the London talks. It was nevertheless clear that his government harbored concerns about the sub-committee's deliberations. Telegram, Hamburg consulate to Dulles, 16 May, 1957, NARA, Department of State Central Decimal File, 762a.00/5-1657.

51. Felken, 440. For Stassen's May 1957 disarmament proposal, see *FRUS, 1955–1957,* Vol. 20, 504–10.

52. Grewe, 297.

53. Felken, 440–41.

54. Memorandum, JCS to Wilson, 22 May, 1957, *FRUS, 1955–1957,* Vol. 20, 542. On Dulles's skepticism regarding arms reduction agreements in Europe more generally, see Kenneth Osgood, *Total Cold War: Eisenhower's Secret Propaganda Battle at Home and Abroad* (Lawrence: University Press of Kansas, 2006), 198–99.

55. Informal Record of Meeting, Dulles, Stassen, Nixon et al., *FRUS,* ibid., 548.

56. Memorandum, Elbrick to Dulles, 23 May, 1957, ibid., 250.

57. Memorandum, Dulles to Eisenhower, 24 May, 1957, ibid., 257.

58. Memorandum of a conversation, Adenauer and Dulles, 26 May, 1957, ibid., 259–61.

59. Eisenhower, *Public Papers, 1957,* 420–23.

60. Minutes of a Meeting, Adenauer, Brentano, Dulles et al., 28 May, 1957, *FRUS, 1955–1957,* Vol. 20, 266–79.

61. Memorandum of a conversation, Adenauer, Brentano, Eisenhower, Dulles et al., 28 May, 1957, ibid., 282.

62. Presumably Adenauer was referring here to a draft arms control proposal presented by Stassen on 9 May. The focus of this proposal was aerial inspection zones, as well as arms reductions which might occur in the Russian, North American, and European zones of inspection. Particularly disturbing may have been reports of Stassen's proposal for "parallel inclusive reductions of armaments and armed forces," that would include force reductions and arms-deployment limitations in Europe. *FRUS, 1955–1957,* Vol, 20, 504–10.

63. Telegram, Bonn to State, 5 June, 1957, ibid., 604–7; Telegram, Department of State to Bonn, ibid., 608–9.

64. See Adenauer campaign speeches: Kiel, 5 July, 1957; Nuremberg, 7 July; Bonn, 6 August, ACDP, Nachlaß von Eckardt, 010-001/1.

65. Telegram, Dulles to Bonn, 31 July, 1957, *FRUS, 1955–1957*, Vol. 20, 672. See also Felken, 450.

66. For the text of Zorin's speech, see *Documents on Disarmament, 1945–1959*, Vol. 2, 849–68.

67. Telegram, Bonn to Dulles, 9 September, 1957, NARA, Department of State Central Decimal File, 762a,00/9-957. In addition to the failure of the subcommittee talks, the embassy offered as evidence of a harder line from Moscow the announcement that the Soviets had tested a ballistic missile, the latest Soviet note on reunification, and Soviet aid to Syria. For the unhelpful Soviet note of 7 September, see Meissner, *Moskau-Bonn*, 305–10. For Soviet policy toward Syria, see Golan, *Soviet Policies in the Middle East*, 140–41.

68. Besson, *Die Außenpolitik der Bundesrepublik*, 209.

69. Ibid., 208.

70. See Pöttering, 134–83; Besson, 203–9. On the SPD and disengagement—and the Eisenhower administration's lack of interest in the Socialists' ideas on this topic—see especially Grabbe, *Unionspareien, Sozialdemokratie*, 245–50. On the Rapacki Plan, see Piotr Wandycz, "Adam Rapacki and the Search for European Security," in Craig and Loewenheim, *The Diplomats*, 289–317. On Adenauer's response to the Polish foreign minister's proposal, see Schwarz, *Adenauer: Der Staatsmann*, 382–84. Especially important is Hanrieder's incisive discussion of the paradoxes of Bonn's reunification policy, which the disengagement debate helped to bring out. He observes that "without an abating of East-West tensions neither side could afford to allow unification on the opponent's terms, yet an accommodation between East and West made it likely that the German status quo would get not only a tacit but a legal blessing." Thus, a series of "connected paradoxes" faced Bonn. Reunification seemed to require East-West détente, but the prospects for détente were dependent upon acceptance of the status quo in Europe, and hence the division of Germany. *Germany, America, Europe*, 164–65.

71. On Polish "national communism" under Gomułka see, e.g., Norman Davies, *God's Playground: A History of Poland*, Vol. II (New York: Oxford University Press, 2005), 440–45.

72. Despatch, Bonn to State Department, 24 January, 1957, NARA, Department of State Central Decimal File, 762a.13/1-2457. On the 20 January Polish elections, see Davies, 585–87.

73. Memorandum, Beam to Dulles, 23 March, 1957, *FRUS, 1955–1957*, Vol. 25, 593–94.

74. Memorandum, Allen W. Dulles to John Foster Dulles, ibid., 611.

75. State Department Discussion Paper, Relations with Poland, May 1957, DDEL, White House Central Files, Confidential File, Subject Series, Box 47, File: State, Department of (May 1957), (1).

76. For Rapacki's speech to the UN General Assembly, see *Dokumente zur Deutschland Politik*, III. Reihe, Band 3/1957, 1681–1686. On Warsaw and Moscow, see Rosenberg, *Soviet-American Relations*, 178.

77. Sheldon Anderson, *A Cold War in the Soviet Bloc: Polish–East German Relations, 1945–1962* (Boulder, CO: Westview Press, 2001), 204–5. Anderson has utilized declassified records from, among other sources, the Polish Communist Party's Central Committee and the Polish foreign office.

78. Wandycz, 296–97.

79. John Lewis Gaddis has suggested that Soviet documentation demonstrates that the purpose behind the Rapacki Plan was to "undercut the position of the West German government." It thus was not a "serious move toward disengagement." Gaddis, *We Now Know*, 138. Gaddis cites a Cold War International History Project Conference Paper, "The Soviet Union and the Politics of the Rapacki Plan," delivered in Essen in June 1994 by Beate Ihme-Tuchel.

80. See Dulles's remarks at NSC meeting, 12 December, 1957, *FRUS, 1955–1957,* Vol. 4, 215.

81. On the internal West German debate about Adenauer's nuclear policy in 1957, see Cioc, *Pax Atomica,* particularly 75–91.

82. Dismissal of the Rapacki Plan was not, however, universal in the West. The U.K. government under Macmillan felt compelled to respond seriously to the Polish ideas, "despite the risk of serious damage to Anglo-German relations." John P. S. Gearson, *Harold Macmillan and the Berlin Wall Crisis, 1958–62* (New York: St. Martin's Press, 1998), 27.

83. Michael Mandelbaum, *The Nuclear Revolution: International Politics Before and After Hiroshima* (London and New York: Cambridge University Press, 1983), 218.

84. Lawrence Freedman, *The Evolution of Nuclear Strategy* (New York: St. Martin's Press, 1983), 139; Gregor Schöllgen, *Die Aussenpolitik der Bundesrepublik Deutschland* (Munich: C. H. Beck, 2001), 48.

85. On Eisenhower's response to Sputnik and the crisis which followed, see Robert A. Divine, *The Sputnik Challenge: Eisenhower's Response to the Soviet Satellite* (Oxford and New York: Oxford University Press, 1993).

86. On the main early proponent of the "missile gap," Senator Stuart Symington, see ibid., 178–83; On the global perception of Sputnik's significance, see most recently Steven Wagner, *Eisenhower Republicanism: Pursuing the Middle Way* (DeKalb: Northern Illinois University Press, 2006), 110.

87. "Summit" Meeting with Soviets, Background Paper for December 1957, NATO Heads of Government Meeting, DDEL, Subject Series, Confidential File, Dwight D. Eisenhower—Records as President, White House Central Files, Box 47, File: NATO(6).

88. Felken, 458–59.

89. George F. Kennan, *Memoirs: 1950–1963* (Boston: Little, Brown and Co., 1972), 243.

90. George F. Kennan, *Russia, the Atom, and the West* (London: Oxford University Press, 1958), 33–50; Nouailhat, *Les États-Unis et le monde,* 206–7.

91. Kennan, 244–49.

92. Kennan, 249. Kennan notes that Adenauer had spoken out against neutralization at the May NATO Council meeting, caustically adding that "I, ignoring his great authority, had spoken in favor of neutralization."

93. Ibid., 255.

94. Hans-Gert Pöttering, *Adenauers Sicherheitspolitik: Ein Beitrag zum deutsch-amerikanischen Verhältnis* (Düsseldorf: Droste Verlag, 1975), 158–60.

95. Wilhelm Grewe, *Deutsche Außenpolitik in der Nachkriegszeit* (Stuttgart: Deutsche Verlags-Anstalt, 1960), 379.

96. Kennan, 250.

97. See Douglas Brinkley, *Dean Acheson: The Cold War Years, 1953–1971* (New Haven, CT, and London: Yale University Press, 1992), 80–81.

98. Ibid., 83–84.

99. Dean Acheson, "The Illusion of Disengagement," *Foreign Affairs*, Vol. 36, No. 3 (April 1958), 371–82. After looking over a proof of the article, Kennan wrote Acheson that he had rarely "seen error so gracefully and respectably clothed." Letter, Kennan to Acheson, 20 March, 1958, Acheson Papers, Yale University, Box 17, file 222. A less glib rejoinder appeared in *Foreign Affairs* in early 1959. See Kennan, "Disengagement Revisited," *Foreign Affairs*, Vol. 37, No. 2 (January 1959), 187–210. Harrison points to the "strong and conservative effect" that the Hungarian uprising had upon the Kremlin leadership. *Driving the Soviets*, 88.

100. Meissner, *Moskau-Bonn*, 322.

101. Ibid., 327–32.

102. For Adenauer, disengagement "meant nothing other than a new attempt by the Soviet Union to cast doubt upon the equal rights of the Federal Republic within the western camp." Besson, 204–5.

103. Meissner, *Moskau-Bonn*, 332–33.

104. Wolfgang Schmidt, "Die Wurzeln der Entspannung: Der konzeptionelle Ursprung der Ost- und Deutschlandpolitik Willy Brandts in den fünfziger Jahren," *VfZ* 50/4 (October 2003), 554.

105. Gaddis, *We Now Know*, 138.

106. The Berlin Crisis, on the other hand, could do so, at least to some extent. On the rather sudden display of flexibility by both Washington and Moscow after the outbreak of the crisis, see especially McAdams, *Germany Divided*, 44–49. McAdams notes that at negotiations following the 1959 Geneva foreign ministers conference, the Americans "bandied about proposals—to the evident horror of some West German observers—that were geared toward meeting the Soviet Union's demands halfway." On West German distrust of the Eisenhower administration during this period, see, e.g., Köhler, 149–69, particularly 162–66.

107. *Documents on International Affairs*, 1958, 146–64.

108. As Ulam notes, the Warsaw Pact gave the Soviets a hedge against any possible Western attempt to retain access to West Berlin by force. An attack on the GDR was an attack upon all the signatories of the pact, and thus would be considered an attack on Russia. *Expansion and Coexistence*, 619–20.

7

"The Strongest Weapon Is Unity": Berlin, 1958–1960

Dwight D. Eisenhower was the first president to be covered by the Twenty-Second Amendment to the U.S. Constitution, which his fellow Republicans had pushed through in order to prevent any future Democrat from dominating the executive for two decades. Even without the heart attack and stroke that befell him during his terms in office; even absent the strong desire of his wife to get out of Washington; even absent the importuning of his ambitious vice president, Eisenhower would have been compelled to leave the conclusion of the Berlin drama to his successor.

Not so Konrad Adenauer. As the old general prepared to pack his bags for Gettysburg (a fine location for an old general, one must admit), his German counterpart, twelve years his senior, had no immediate plans to take up golf or memoir-writing. The crisis over Berlin caused him much anxiety, and helped further to impel him to seek a closer relationship with Paris. The French president at the time, Charles de Gaulle, was a willing partner in this effort. And Adenauer, being Adenauer, was not inclined to leave foreign policy—toward Paris, Washington, or anywhere else that mattered—to any of the callow youths who hoped to succeed him. *Der Alte* was determined to see that his key policies were firmly institutionalized prior to his retirement. This would prevent any successor from reversing the major decisions that he had made about the Federal Republic's future. One had to wait for the right time.

But since the years 1949 to 1960 were years of near constant challenges that demanded a response from Bonn, the "right time" for Adenauer's departure never came. As has been said of FDR (the president whose longevity in office had inspired the Twenty-Second Amendment), Adenauer's conception of the Federal Chancellorship was himself in office.

This, at least, was *Adenauer's* conception. Others disagreed with the equation of the officeholder and the office. Within his own governing coalition, he faced opposition to his continuance in office into the new decade. But no member of the Union was willing to challenge Adenauer for leadership, and the Old Man proved more than a match for his FDP critics.[1] As a result, Adenauer remained in the chancery until 1963, thus outlasting not only the Eisenhower administration, but the crisis over Berlin.

This chapter takes the story of the U.S.-FRG alliance to the end of the "Ike Age." Bonn's turbulent relationship with Eisenhower's young successor has been ably covered elsewhere. I shall thus focus more narrowly upon the impact of the Berlin Crisis on U.S.–West German relations until the pause of 1959. An international history of the crisis, from Khrushchev's ultimatum until the construction of the Berlin Wall, would itself take (or, to be hopeful, *will take*) the historian who writes it a full volume. Excellent recent work has been conducted on various aspects of this event, and scholars working in newly available East Bloc documents have added significantly to our understanding of the tremendous, multilateral messiness of this episode. It is to these that one must turn to begin understanding the state of historical scholarship on this crisis.[2]

Some years ago, Oxford Medievalist Maurice Keen wrote that defining the beginning and the end of the Middle Ages was largely dependent upon the perspective of the individual historian. "The problem of defining such a period as the Middle Ages," he wrote, "is not that of finding limits which can be justified on all grounds, but ones which are justifiable."[3] This study begins in 1953, which is quite "justifiable": In 1953, Eisenhower assumed office; Stalin departed office and, in fact, Earth; and Adenauer faced the challenge of reelection. I have set the end at 1960, since Eisenhower's departure from office coincides with the abeyance of the Berlin issue. In January 1961 Eisenhower's successor entered office with a predisposition against Adenauer, a sentiment that was soon reciprocal. Kennedy would have to face the gravest East-West crises yet, over Berlin and then Cuba. Both of these episodes greatly strained America's leadership of the Atlantic allies. Neither is a topic for this study.

WHY WAS THERE A SECOND BERLIN CRISIS?: NOVEMBER 1958

The second Berlin Crisis was initially launched by Khrushchev, beginning on 10 November, 1958. Unlike other crises of the Cold War era—say the crisis in Vietnam that the Johnson administration would find itself wrestling with in summer 1965—this was not an issue that developed over time, and thus defies attempts to fix a beginning date. In fact, in a follow-up note given over to the West on 27 November, Khrushchev had even proclaimed an end date for the crisis that he had loosed: The three Western powers had 180 days before the Soviets would unilaterally cede their final occupation rights to the GDR government. Were it to come to this France, the United Kingdom, and the United States would be forced to decide between de facto recognition of the GDR, or de facto abandonment of West Berlin. Atlantic Alliance policy making from this point forward revolved around the question of how to avoid being presented with this dilemma by 27 May.

Eisenhower and Dulles responded to the challenge with a sustained effort directed at achieving this goal. The effort was marked by firm but prudent policy toward the Soviet Union, and unflagging diplomacy within the alliance. Christian Bremen has observed that, throughout the crisis over Berlin, the president's primary objective was the maintenance of alliance unity.[4] American policy making during these months reveals an administration that was run from the top, at least when issues of this significance were at stake. Eisenhower wanted to confront the Soviet Union with a cohesive NATO. If this were achieved, he reasoned, Moscow would not risk outright military confrontation. Trans-Atlantic policy would succeed if the Atlantic allies could agree on a response to the Soviet challenge, and show the East a solid front. One therefore did not need to treat the crisis as the prelude to World War III. Nor did Khrushchev's six-month timetable have to be treated as a final ultimatum. United, the West could avoid ceding the initiative to Moscow. What was required was patience, firmness, and unity. As he said at his 11 March, 1959, news conference, "let's not make everything such a hysterical sort of a proposition. We ought to keep our steadiness."[5]

Because the episode began with a statement and a time limit from Khrushchev, Westerners inside and outside of government naturally sought first to understand what was behind Khrushchev's provocative maneuver. This required educated guesses based on limited information. Writing about the crisis nine years on, Adenauer made certain to stress the fact that he had been busy in the previous years with study of Russia and its history. In addition, and rather tellingly, he believed the "Russian mentality" was comprehensible only to people "who had lived among them for a long time, or on the other hand to people, like us, who were forced to live under a dictatorship." One notes that this category excludes the Anglo-Americans. He did not think that Khrushchev was seeking a military confrontation; "A war was of no use to him" (*Er konnte keinen Krieg gebrauchen*). And he thought that the premier might be acting largely for domestic consumption, since the XXI Party Congress was approaching. But with dictatorships, one never knew. A dictatorial regime might always be driven to a military confrontation with other states on the basis of "some sort of reason of domestic politics."[6] Again, one never knew.

The primary question that policy makers had to ask is the question with which scholars have had to wrestle ever since: Was Khrushchev's bombshell of a proclamation the aggressive act of a confident superpower, or a defensive act by a government that worried about its grip on its empire? The question does not necessarily demand an either/or answer: If the proclamation was aimed, as Eisenhower thought, at splitting the Western allies, then Soviet actions might with reason be called "offensive." Yet the motivation might have stemmed from domestic political worries, as Adenauer suggested, or from a perception that Moscow's dominance over Eastern Europe was growing shaky. Then too, the likelihood that the Americans might equip the Bundeswehr with nuclear weapons no doubt caused worries.

William Taubmann has done very significant work in the published and archival Soviet sources. And the picture he paints makes clear that the driving force behind the crisis was Khrushchev himself. According to Mikoyan, Khrushchev did not even clear his remarks with his Presidium colleagues.[7] Nor had he sought analysis from the Foreign Ministry regarding the likely Western response to his unilateral renunciation of the postwar settlement for Europe.[8]

Aleksandr Fursenko and Timothy Naftali have helped to clarify the odd tone and content of Khrushchev's second statement, which came on 27 November. This statement has always been perplexing in that it seemed to present the West with a furiously worded ultimatum that foresaw unilateral Soviet abrogation of Potsdam as the only alternative to Western recognition of the GDR. Yet it also set a rather long time limit of six months for a satisfactory response, and indicated that West Berlin might become a "free city" rather than being gobbled up by the East. What was the point of a diplomatic *coup de main* that gave the opponent half a year to devise a response? And why, of all things, issue an ultimatum granting a concession before discussions had begun?

The message was mixed, Fursenko and Naftali conclude, because the second note was drafted as a compromise between two factions within the Presidium. They add, pointedly, that it "is hard to imagine an ultimatum as a compromise for any government."[9] It was no easier to imagine at the time, and Washington and Bonn were left guessing about the motivations behind this highly unorthodox initiative. Fursenko and Naftali do not portray a Soviet Presidium that broadly shared Khrushchev's belief that a solution of the German problem had to come before summer. Rather, they present a CP leadership and Moscow foreign ministry that was rather placid about the German question until Khrushchev's seizure of the issue. As late as October:

> there seemed to be no particular crisis brewing, nor was there any pressure at that moment from the Kremlin for action. There was time before West Ger-

many acquired nuclear weapons, if that ever happened. There was also time to manage whatever economic difficulties were experienced by East Germany.

The result was, according to Fursenko and Naftali, an "elegant nonpolicy" that the foreign ministry crafted in order to kick the can down the road a bit. The diplomats, if given control of German policy, would have suggested that great inhibitor of decisive action: the four-power conference.[10]

But why, then, should the premier have chosen to turn the languid fall into a feverish winter? Taubmann's explanation emphasizes questions of prestige. As Khrushchev saw it, his status and his nation's reputation were on the line by the end of 1958. From January through May, Khrushchev angled quite openly for an invitation to Washington. He made it (almost painfully) clear, on numerous occasions, both public and back-channel, that he wished to sit down with Eisenhower. He perceived that he needed some sort of diplomatic triumph to buttress support for his leadership within the Party Presidium. Troyanovsky, Khrushchev's foreign affairs aide, adds his perception that Khrushchev was seeking, at this point, to "prove that Molotov and the others were wrong and that he, not they, belonged on top." He also feared the loss of personal prestige that would follow the nuclear arming of West Germany, should Russia under his leadership do nothing to seek to stop it.[11]

Concern for Moscow's leadership of the international communist bloc provided an additional incentive to get stalled negotiations over Germany and arms control off the dime. As the ex officio leader of the communist world, Khrushchev presented a rather limited résumé of accomplishments in the East-West struggle since he had sat down with the leaders of the bourgeois powers in Geneva. It was no secret that questions had surfaced in Beijing about his management of Cold War high politics. Nor had he vanquished his critics within the Kremlin, as Hope Harrison notes in her first-rate international history of the troubled Soviet–East German relationship. When those critics challenged him to show what peaceful coexistence had brought, what could he say? "[H]e had not signed any major agreements with the Western Powers; and in spite of his recognition of the FRG, he had still not obtained Western recognition of the GDR."[12] Khrushchev had reason to think that he needed a victory. Solving the German Problem—within six months and to the advantage of his German allies—was the triumph that he needed. Although the point is debatable, Gerhard Wettig seems to be correct in his analysis that Khrushchev's goals were broader than simply forcing Western recognition of the GDR, since the status quo in West Berlin was for him a "cancerous growth" that would have to be removed at some point.[13]

Khrushchev thus desired a settlement of the German questions on terms favorable to his regime, and himself. The question of timing—why late

1958?—came down to Khrushchev's concern for the stability of the East German regime, and, closely related to this, to Ulbricht's haranguing of Moscow. In Harrison's assessment, Khrushchev sought, during the crisis that he launched, "to involve the West in the matter of the stabilization of the GDR."[14] By fall 1958—and in stark contrast to the sanguinary position of the Soviet Foreign Ministry at the time—"a sense of urgency was developing among the East German leaders."[15] The patent economic failure of the GDR, when compared with the "Economic Miracle" next door; the unrest among the East German public; the steady flow of talented and educated East Germans into the FRG; the perception that a nuclear-armed Adenauer regime was likely in the near future—all of these concerns weighed on Ulbricht and his colleagues. Ulbricht thus pressured the Soviet leadership to do something to mitigate the problem of continuing regime instability.[16] Getting the West out of Berlin was to be an important step in solidifying the East Berlin regime's hold on power, and thus the USSR's hold on Eastern Europe. Khrushchev can be said to have acted defensively, in the sense that he saw his actions as likely to preserve a threatened asset.

Marc Trachtenberg has written that the primary reason that the Soviet Union chose to challenge the West on Berlin was fear over the progress of West German rearmament. The Soviets were aware that the other three former occupying nations were fundamentally status quo powers: The United States, France, and the United Kingdom were willing to accept the continued division of Europe, and of Germany, so long as the Soviets did not seek to move the line of demarcation westward. But the Bonn regime was another matter. If West Germany became militarily powerful, then it could begin to act out on its own, challenging the Soviet Union—perhaps even for control of the East Zone. The Soviets feared, above all, a nuclear-armed FRG. The question of Bundeswehr nuclearization "lay at the heart of Soviet policy during the Berlin crisis." An assertive FRG, no longer restrained by its great power patrons—this was the nightmare that threatened to overturn the basic premises of Soviet postwar security policy. Trachtenberg's analysis was shared, at least to some extent, by the State Department in early 1959.[17]

Soviet documentation that has become available since Trachtenberg wrote these words does not support the argument that the Soviet leadership *in general* was motivated by the fear of West German power when the decision was made to challenge the West on Berlin. The documentation consulted by Fursenko and Naftali does suggest a strong level of concern in Moscow regarding German nuclearization in principle. But Adenauer seems to have deceived the Soviets, including the usually perceptive Mikoyan, about his approach to acquisition of nuclear warheads. This appears to have led the Kremlin leadership to believe, throughout 1958, that it had some time to convince *der Alte* to reverse course.[18] It is not clear how long Adenauer could have continued portraying himself as undecided, particularly since his government had secretly asked the United States for battlefield nuclear warheads in the previous year. But the timing of Khrushchev's ultimatum appears to have been the result of East German pressure, and Khrushchev's fear for the survivability of that regime. As A. James McAdams has observed, the sensational nature of Khrushchev's November ultimatum can distract from the fact that "over an extended period between 1955 and 1957 Soviet officials barely mentioned the [Berlin] issue in their contacts with the West."[19] Ulbricht, on the other hand, was importuning Moscow on the Berlin issue, and his efforts may well have been decisive in Khrushchev's timing.

DIPLOMACY OF LOW EXPECTATIONS: BONN, WASHINGTON, AND ALLIED UNITY—DECEMBER 1958–APRIL 1959

The Eisenhower administration was quite strikingly of one mind during the run of Khrushchev's ultimatum: Allied unity had to be maintained. A show of resolve would send the desired signal to Moscow, with which confrontation was avoidable as long as the Allies acted as if they were willing to fight over Berlin.[20] But even if a united front were to be had—which was questionable from the beginning—this would be just half of the diplomatic balancing act that Eisenhower and Dulles set for themselves. They would need to avoid the perception that the united West was presenting the Kremlin with an ultimatum of its own, namely, peace or war over Berlin. There was a great difference between being "willing to fight" and having any desire to do so. Eisenhower insisted that shows of Western resolve be coupled with a diplomatic approach that left the Soviets a face-saving way to back down.[21] As Stephen Ambrose observes, the president's approach during the crisis was marked by an unwillingness to act as if there were a crisis.[22] Thus, he sought to create an atmosphere in which neither side appeared to make concessions under duress.

More striking than the agreement within the administration concerning the need for Allied unity was the near-superhuman effort by Dulles to achieve this unity. The secretary had perhaps grown used to encountering the adjectives "well-traveled" and "peripatetic" in his press clippings. But from December through February, Dulles acted as if the four Western powers could be held together by means of diplomatic exertion alone. In horrible pain due to a return of his stomach cancer, and with months to live, Dulles returned to Washington from Mexico in the early days of December. He entered the hospital to undergo tests, but left his doctors behind to fly to Paris for a scheduled NATO Council meeting. With only weeks of active service remaining, he continued his diplomatic consultations until he was no longer able.[23] From his hospital bed, he continued to urge unity and "no concessions" upon Macmillan, when the prime minister visited in March.[24]

Bonn agreed wholeheartedly on the matters of unity and refusal to make concessions while the threat from Moscow was still operative. Hans-Peter Schwarz begins his thorough discussion of Adenauer's actions during the crisis by observing the extreme caution with which the chancellor had sought to handle the Berlin issue. The divided Berlin was, in his view, "a political time bomb"; the situation was "so precarious that any change of status would be unworkable."[25] He thus continued to insist upon the long-established formulas for East-West negotiations concerning Germany's future. This meant that the Berlin issue could not be settled independently of the entire German Question. This issue, in turn, was inextricably linked to the security situation in Europe.[26] This approach had not led to progress in the past years. But insisting on this course could slow down demands from within West Germany, and within the NATO alliance, for a settlement of the Berlin matter.

In this sense, Adenauer hoped that the result of Allied unity would be delay: Hold off the mercurial Russian premier, and throw proposals at him, in the hope that the 27 May deadline would pass without incident. In the words of a State Department official, the goal was to find a way of "talking the Berlin crisis to death."[27] In the meantime, Adenauer insisted, Western unity would keep Khrushchev at bay. The Soviets would not fight a war over Berlin, and were now engaged in a "colossal bluff."[28] The Soviets would relent, in due course. But until the Kremlin relented, Adenauer would do all in his power to convince his people to stand firm. Heinrich Krone's summary of Adenauer's 7 December speech in West Berlin provides a synopsis of his public declarations through the six months:

> The [27 November] note must first be disposed of before there can be negotiations. Berlin and the West are indissolubly connected. The Western Powers have given their word, and they keep their word.[29]

Bonn's policy depended upon *reliable* allies. Under no circumstances could the chancellor, his government, or the West German populace give the impression of anything other than unity.

The stakes were high, and for no one more than for the Germans themselves. If an East-West war resulted from the Berlin Crisis, Germany would be its first battlefield. The FRG was now relying on the American nuclear deterrent in a more immediate way than ever before.[30] Adenauer's predictable anxiety about American reliability was, as a result, overblown during the crisis. Dulles in particular provoked Adenauer's Potsdam nightmares when his public statements seemed to call into question first the Western refusal to deal with East German officials as "agents" of the Soviet occupying power, and later on the matter of reunification by free elections. Hope Harrison makes the important observation that Dulles backed away from his agent-theory statement immediately, going so far as to tell the press that "we would in these matters be largely guided by the views of the Federal Republic of Germany." But the damage was done. Once again, the shades of the Rapacki Plan haunted the Chancery. In mid-January, Adenauer wrung his hands before his assembled aides: "The West is growing weak. Even Dulles."[31]

January was the low point for Adenauer for another reason. It was then that Mikoyan traveled to Washington to talk with U.S. leaders. On 17 January, he was received by Eisenhower. Adenauer was unaware that Khrushchev's Berlin initiative had caused a split within the Presidium. Thus he was unaware that Mikoyan was anything but Khrushchev's trusted emissary, sent to drive a wedge between Washington and Bonn. Rather, he and Khrushchev decided on his visit primarily to ease *Soviet* anxieties over the crisis. Mikoyan was to sound out Eisenhower on the question of a summit.[32] His arrival in Washington was much less the result of a continuing diplomatic offensive, and much more an indicator of second thoughts in Moscow. Cooler heads, if not prevailing in the Presidium, were at least being heard.

Not so in Bonn, where the Mikoyan visit set off a new round of speculation, both within and outside of the government. For Felix von Eckardt, Mikoyan's departure for America indicated that diplomacy between East and West "was proceeding at full speed" (*lief auf Hochtouren*), pointedly adding that America's German allies "were not told much about what was discussed [with Mikoyan] in Washington." Nor were the policy makers in Bonn alone in their assessment of the reason for Mikoyan's visit. The British Foreign Office also concluded that Mikoyan's visit was a sign that the Soviets were ready, in fact anxious, to conduct serious negotiations then and there in Washington. Unlike the Germans, however, the British were rather enthused by the prospect of Soviet-American negotiations. So enthused, in fact, that an aide-mémoire given to the German Affairs desk by the UK embassy on 13 January expressly delegated to the Eisenhower Administration the authority to conduct negotiations with Mikoyan on behalf of London.[33]

Wilhelm Grewe, now serving as Bonn's ambassador in Washington, was given the task of expressing his government's concern regarding the appearance that Mikoyan's visit would produce, especially after the poorly worded statement by Dulles on elections and German unification. Dulles, not for the first time, clarified what he had said, and how it had been "misinterpreted or exaggerated." He then gave Grewe quite a strong set of reassurances that he could report back to the chancery. The Mikoyan talks would not "lead to any change [in] U.S. policy," and the American people were not going to allow themselves to "be fooled" by the cosmopolitan Old Bolshevik. Dulles added that he had made it clear to Mikoyan that "we were not planning to negotiate with him."[34] How much more reassurance could the Germans need?

The question must remain open as to whether Adenauer was incapable of trusting his most important ally when so much was at stake; or whether, conversely, the Americans did not do enough to assure him that they would not negotiate behind his back. It is not possible to estimate what degree of reassurance would have sufficed in this case. The fact of his doubt remains. On 26 January, he told Krone that the Soviets had plans to expand their power westward through Europe, but that "America . . . does not sufficiently appreciate this danger." After the Berlin Crisis and the construction of the Wall, his assessment was unchanged. Statesmen who "knew Russia" were not likely to be surprised by Kremlin actions. "But sometimes I worry that in the United States one does not know the Russians even today." Americans still engaged in "wishful thinking" toward the Soviets; the eighty-seven-year-old German added with a laugh that self-deceptive optimism "is always the sign of youth."[35] One scholar has recently said that Adenauer:

> Followed every step of Allied diplomacy with embittered suspicion, fearful that at any moment the Western Allies might find some agreement with the Soviets that called into question his unification policy or the fundamentals of West German security.[36]

This description accurately portrays Adenauer's mood at its lowest ebb.

Still, his thinking on the Allies and their role in the crisis was anything but static. He was most concerned when Mikoyan was actually talking to the British and Americans without any German oversight, or when other Western governments gave the impression that the West's position on the Berlin and German issues was more flexible than he believed it to be. Thus, January was bleak. But he was always capable of drawing distinctions between allied governments. Sometimes, his allies made it easy for him to do so.

Far more provocative than Mikoyan was Macmillan, whose actions during the crisis caused Adenauer to rally 'round the flag—in this instance, the *American* flag. His distrust of Eisenhower and Dulles was doing him no good in Washington. Dulles was growing irritated with his German friend and the constant care and feeding that he required. The decision by Macmillan to take an independent, conciliatory approach to Moscow brought Adenauer, Eisenhower, and Dulles together in a very clear, and perhaps reassuring, manner. The Americans and the Germans both considered the prime minister's decision to travel to Moscow in February to be foolish and dangerous. Both agreed that a united Allied front was indispensable at this time. Only the unity of the NATO alliance could deter the Soviets from taking risky steps forward. Indeed, Bonn viewed the deterrent power of the united West as the most important factor in preventing World War III from breaking out *in Germany*.

Bonn interpreted signs that an important ally was wobbling as playing right into Soviet hands, since it was widely assumed that Khrushchev had stoked the crisis in order to cause just such a split. Even worse, London's weakness in the knees might embolden the Soviets to provocative action— action that posed, to use an overworked adjective in this case quite literally, an existential threat to the German people. After the passage of so many years, Macmillan's approach to the crisis appears rather reasonable. But his actions were not taken after the passage of years, but then and there, at a time when London's German ally was seeking solidarity.

In late January, Dulles told Defense Secretary Neil McElroy that "the British are falling apart." The perception arose, understandably, that the London government was cracking under the pressure of potential war with the Soviets over the technical question of access rights to Berlin. Christian Bremen makes a convincing case, however, that British actions and statements during these critical weeks were largely in keeping with British policy goals. The division of Germany was a "satisfactory situation," and in any event unification was not likely to come in the medium term. It therefore made a good deal of sense to seek to dispose of specific issues and flashpoints— Berlin being one—by agreement with the Soviets. This would greatly reduce the chances of war, which no one wanted. And such an approach would allow the West, in the words of a Cabinet resolution, to "work towards a new attempt to reach agreement between the great Powers [*sic*] on a political and economic settlement in Europe."[37] Here again was Churchill's "percentages plan" from the wartime "Tolstoy" discussions: East and West could live peacefully, as long as they could agree on who got what.

That this sort of policy planning—rather than panic in the face of crisis—lay behind Macmillan's diplomatic gesture was in no way reassuring. It was, in fact, the negation of Adenauer's stated policy for Germany's future, and a repudiation of the CDU/CSU foreign policy. The Adenauer government thus had little choice but to trust in the Americans, who alone had the capacity to prevent the West's German policy from veering wildly off course. The hope was that Bonn could use its leverage with the U.S. to derail its least reliable ally.

Eisenhower, Dulles—even Congress—*never considered* relinquishing rights in West Berlin. One can find no clearer statement of resolve than Dulles's *"*Thinking Out Loud" note of late January 1959. The document bears no date. But since it was a response to UK Foreign Secretary Selwyn Lloyd's paper of the same name, given to Dulles on the 23rd, it can be taken to represent the American secretary of state's thought as of the end of January. The secretary begins by expressing doubt about the willingness of the Western European public to "permit the governments to risk launching a land operation merely to keep open the Western access to Berlin." The doubt came with good reason, since Selwyn Lloyd had told Dulles in his note that the British people would not support war in order to force the Soviets to continue as the juridical occupiers of East Germany. Dulles granted that access rights seemed a "minor" matter. But by continually advancing such minor issues that were not "worth" fighting over, "very great Soviet gains could be made . . . in stages and degrees." If, furthermore, the Soviets were able to compel "us" (whether "us" meant the United States or the major Western powers is unclear) to recognize the government of the GDR, the result would be a serious loss of morale among West Berliners, and, probably, most West Germans. Thus, a solution to the Berlin issue on Soviet terms could only "expose the lack of willpower in the Western alliance and encourage further pressures."[38]

At the end of the standoff, Western rights in Berlin had to be maintained. West Berlin was the virtual "superdomino," to use William Burr's telling description: "If it fell, the impact would reverberate throughout the Western system."[39] The implications of such a development were *predictable*: none of America's allies could count on mutual security agreements—and *unpredictable*: would West Germany seek an agreement with the Warsaw Pact, or take up position as a loose canon on the European deck? Neither was acceptable. Viewed in this way, postwar American security policy was only as secure as the Potsdam framework for Berlin. The consequences of allowing the Soviets to settle the question via *diktat* were unthinkable. Dulles, quoting an earlier Foreign Office aide-mémoire, summed up his view: "It is, of course, essential that we should show absolutely no weakness in our determination to uphold our rights in relation to Berlin and to make it plain to the Russians that we would if necessary be prepared to risk a general war in support of these rights." Eisenhower expressed the same resolve, with terms from one of his escapist hobbies: cards. "Khrushchev should know that when we decide to act, our whole stack will be in the pot," he said in December, with metaphorical language that reinforced his belief that Moscow was "bluffing."[40] As Gerhard Wettig has shown, Khrushchev initially assumed that the American administration would behave in what he considered a rational manner, and would not risk nuclear war over West Berlin access rights. Thus, despite the Kremlin's "official thesis" that the Americans were dangerous "war mongers," Khrushchev was certain that they would in fact "shy away from a war."[41] Thus it was important that the Americans made this point loud and clear, and not just to reassure Bonn, but also to clarify this matter for Moscow.

As noted earlier, Dulles made a valiant attempt to keep up the appearance of Western unity, as well as to mitigate the damage that Macmillan's initiative might do to Anglo-German relations. It was a hard slog for an ill but determined diplomat. Adenauer was unsure of Macmillan's motives for breaking ranks. But the chancellor elicited from the British embassy that Macmillan (in Schwarz's paraphrase) "would like to negotiate at any price, because he fears, or alleges that he fears, a war." Adenauer also suspected that domestic politics drove Macmillan and Selwyn Lloyd: The Tories could expect the peace offensive to assist them in the elections later that year. This, however, was the *only* advantage that the British could expect from the initiative. Schwarz describes Adenauer as "furious," and casting the Sceptred Isle as "Perfidious Albion." The chancellor did not consider it a coincidence that Macmillan and Selwyn Lloyd had rushed in to fill the leadership gap that had opened with the progressive incapacitation of the dying Dulles.[42]

From Adenauer's perspective this act of lèse-majesté—committed against a Republican from a republic—was compounded by London's failure to consult ahead of time with the Allies. Thus with *him*. This was the great sin for Adenauer: When Germany's future was at stake, his allies had to consult Bonn, and, equally important, let the German people know that Bonn was being consulted. He reported some weeks later that he had made some sharp, rather caustic comments to British Ambassador David Steel—one of his favorites, it should be added—when Steel informed Adenauer in January of Macmillan's decision to go to Moscow. "Paris is certainly worth a Mass, and I do understand that one likes winning elections; but 7 to 10 days for an election trip—that's a bit much."[43] The damage done to Anglo-German relations by the falling-out in early 1959 was not easily repaired.

Nor was the Anglo-American bond, the most special of all "Special Relationships," left unscathed by events. In Washington at the beginning of March, von Eckardt wrote Adenauer to tell him what he had learned of American attitudes toward the British intervention. He reported that the press coverage of Macmillan's adventure was more or less as negative as that of the non-Socialist newspapers in the FRG. In addition, his conversation with Dulles had left no doubt about the secretary's views on the matter. Yet one had to proceed under the assumption that the "maintenance of Anglo-Saxon solidarity . . . is and indeed also will remain the basis of the U.S.A.'s policy."[44] And in fact, there was no rupture between Thames and Potomac—certainly nothing along the lines of the bitterness that had followed the Suez fiasco.

Yet the frequent exchange of civil correspondence between "Ike" and "Harold" before, during, and after the latter's Moscow visit betrayed the president's frustration. On 24 February, for example, Eisenhower damns with faint praise Macmillan's fundamental reasoning for the trip: "Presumably the conversations which you and [Khrushchev] are carrying on should be producing a better atmosphere" for East-West negotiations. Eisenhower immediately goes on to say, "by his own words [Khrushchev] has no apparent interest in such a development." Perhaps the president's desire to "maintain Anglo-Saxon solidarity" explains why he did not simply say: "You're wasting our time, Harold." He ends his note by implying that Macmillan's excursion was going to make it tough for him at that day's press conference, and by adjuring the prime minister to remember that the West "is a unit" during this crisis. So "we are not going to be divided or defeated by threats."[45] Eisenhower was diplomatically proper toward Macmillan. But he made little effort to hide his conviction that Macmillan was hurting the West by his efforts.

Fortunately for both Dulles's diplomacy and Adenauer's health a new regime in neighboring France brought a strong, reliable personality to the Western diplomatic team. The newly elected President Charles de Gaulle was not the type to crack under military threat, as some in London were thought to have done. De Gaulle had been serving as crisis-premier until November 1958, when French voters made him the first president of the Fifth Republic. Adenauer reached out immediately to the Frenchman, who expressed a desire to meet in the near future. The two statesmen were on the final day of a late November two-day mini-summit when Khrushchev delivered his ultimatum. The crisis only served to increase the conversation's perceived significance, and the two appear to have reached what Daniel Koerfer called a "tacit understanding" (*stille Übereinkunft*). De Gaulle "showed uncompromising toughness with regard to Berlin." For his part, Adenauer would accept the Gaullist approach toward the construction of a European community.[46] This approach would hold the United Kingdom at arm's length. But after the damage done to Anglo-German relations during the Berlin Crisis, this presented much less of a problem for Adenauer. Indeed, his growing doubts about the "Anglo-American" bloc led him all the more to seek a close alignment across the Rhine. Especially after Dulles's death, his concerns regarding the reliability of his Anglophone allies impelled the "arch-civilian" chancellor to seek the company of the man known simply as "the General."[47] By early March, Adenauer had enough confidence in de Gaulle to wonder aloud if he should propose to Paris that it represent the Federal Republic's interests at the next East-West summit![48] It had been a whirlwind courtship.

Americans often think of de Gaulle as a main source of friction in the Atlantic Alliance. But at this point, the Eisenhower administration valued his calm certitude and hard-nosed approach to discussions with the Soviets. Rather, it was Adenauer who was trying the patience of some in Washington during the first part of 1959. The primary complaint was the inflexibility that the Bonn government showed in its approach to potential negotiations with the Soviets. The problem arose from a basic difference on a fundamental question, and thus might have done significant damage to German-American amity, had the Eisenhower team been less capable, or Khrushchev more so. Adenauer "wished unconditionally to prevent any change in the western German policy, whereas Eisenhower sought a solution to the Berlin problem."[49] The chancellor was set foursquare against any decoupling of the Berlin question from the broader German Question, even on a provisional, tactical level. Eisenhower and company, however, were quite willing to come to some sort of understanding with the Soviets that would defuse the current crisis, as long as it did not prejudice Western rights in West Berlin. Adenauer, and some of his aides, could see no compromise solution that avoided at least tacit recognition of the Ulbricht regime. This was initially unacceptable to them. If the Atlantic Allies began to deal directly and officially with what Adenauer still dismissively labeled "Pankow," the edifice of his "German policy" would collapse. Hallstein Doctrine, *Alleinvertretungsanspruch*, reunification through a policy of strength: Nothing would be tenable after the Alliance accepted—even unofficially and grudgingly—the right of Ulbricht to speak for 18 million Germans. The Union-led government would also become untenable, in the opinion of its leader.

No question it was a predicament. The Eisenhower team had decided at the beginning of the crisis to take no steps that would suggest a willingness to recognize the GDR. Dulles, however, took a lawyerly approach to the question of interaction with East Berlin. Bremen conveys the secretary's approach, as he articulated it to Grewe, among others: Dulles's conclusion as an experienced international lawyer was that representatives of Western governments could engage in a range of contacts with East German officials without implicitly recognizing the regime. This interpretation may have been "legalistic," an adjective favored by Dulles's detractors. Yet this legalism "opened up to Dulles greater possibilities for maneuver." The Allies could take a pragmatic course in dealing with East Germany without undermining Adenauer's policies or standing.[50] After all, the United States had dealt directly with officials from the PRC when the Korean War made this necessary. No one thought this marked the end of the American nonrecognition policy toward the Beijing regime.[51] Despite Adenauer's complaints, the two governments agreed completely on the end goal. The difference was that Eisenhower and Dulles sought to act pragmatically throughout the crisis. Dulles no doubt had primarily himself to blame for the common impression that he was a rigid and ideological Cold Warrior. But in the case of Berlin, the Dulles of caricature and cliché is noticeable largely by his absence.

The approach taken by Eisenhower and Dulles required from the key Allies both firmness in resolve *and* flexibility in approach. The British let Washington down on the former. Eisenhower and Dulles exerted steady, backstage pressure to persuade the Germans of the latter. Ironically, the Americans had concluded what Macmillan complained of all along, namely, that Adenauer and the men around him were too rigid on the matter of Berlin. Unlike Macmillan, however, they chose to keep this conclusion out of the public debate.

As winter gave way to spring, Dulles gave way to Christian Herter, who served first as acting secretary and after 15 April as secretary. Cancer had forced Dulles to resign. Herter started to show his frustration with German intransigence while Dulles was still officially secretary of state. He complained to Brentano in March about the German role in the four-nation Working Group that had been convened in London to coordinate policy for an East-West foreign ministers conference set for the following May. The FRG had staked out a position on negotiations with Moscow that was "almost completely negative." It was not clear to Herter what the basis for discussion with the Soviets could be, if the West adopted Bonn's line. He thus suggested to Brentano that he would like to "as soon as possible to receive from the Federal Government a more precise basis for action (*Arbeitsgrundlage*)." America's ambassador in Bonn, David K. E. Bruce, expressed to the German delegation the concern that it would be "unpleasant" if the Working Group were to arrive at a compromise set of instructions, only to have the government in Bonn reject it.[52] Getting Brentano to agree was quite enough of a challenge. The State Department was presumably not anxious to run the chancellor's gauntlet.

The task nevertheless fell to Bruce. The ambassador caught up with Adenauer at his vacation spot in Lombardy. There he had a long conversation with the chancellor, during which he "explained to him frankly" how difficult it was for the Germans in the Working Group to negotiate under perpetual threat of a Chancery veto. Adenauer could hardly have missed the point: he was making life unpleasant for the other three delegations as well. It was high time for a bit of flexibility. At home, the CDU's former junior partner, the Free Democratic Party, was also attacking him for his inflexibility in the realm of *Ostpolitik*.[53] And because the *West German government* had itself been allowing East German stamps on inter-German commercial papers—while obstinately refusing even to discuss allowing GDR stamps on transit documents of the FRG's allies—the Adenauer government had opened itself up to criticism on this very matter.[54] How perfidious was Albion, really, in refusing to go to the brink of nuclear war over this issue? German-German passport stamping was acceptable, but life and death hung upon whose stamps adorned British documents? It was quite a lot to ask, even of a friend.

The West German government had to deal with the pressure to be more "flexible" and "creative." Because a simple "*Nein*" was not an option,

Adenauer had begun in the first week of January to discuss with his most trusted aides a plan that would address the perception of inflexibility. Anxiety still hung in the air: If Bonn did not take steps that seemed reasonable to its allies, it might yet find them willing to impose their own solution. He spoke with Krone on 6 January about an idea that, with some tweaking, developed into the so-called Globke Plan. Adenauer envisioned an East-West agreement that would put off reunification "for years," if it were stipulated that it was not feasible now; that would leave the East under the SED regime, and the West in NATO; and to find a way to engage in "conversations with a view to humanizing conditions in the Zone [i.e., the GDR]."[55] By the last of these propositions Adenauer had in mind an end to religious persecution by the SED regime, as well as a freeing up of travel between the two Germanies.

The details of a plan that never bore fruit are of limited interest. What the plan says about Bonn's thinking on the German Question and the Berlin Crisis are rather more significant. For Adenauer and his inner circle were in fact willing to make concessions on several of the major issues. What was required by Bonn was that the formulation of an "interim solution," to use Adenauer's phrase, would stress the adjective—*interim*. The Federal Republic—at least as long as the Union-led coalition held sway—would never agree to a formalized, permanent division of Germany. Nor would they support any Allied decision that suggested formal recognition of "Pankow." In Adenauer's eyes, the second of these would be taken to imply the first. "*De jure* recognition of the GDR [*sic*] could never be demanded from the German people," he told Bruce in March.[56] But that left de facto recognition. Could that be asked, if not demanded, of them? And what would that mean for Adenauer's reunification policy?

Reunification was not going to occur at any time in the foreseeable future. The Globke Plan did not provide the impetus for an East-West agreement. The division of Europe was not formalized until the 1970s. But it helped break the logjam in Bonn. Globke and Krone now recognized, as Schwarz puts it, that the "orthodox German policy" would be "thrown overboard" with acceptance of the Globke line. In Krone's summary: "accepting that Pankow exists, that one cannot count on reunification in the foreseeable future, and that therefore the main thing that we must [see to] for the present is an improvement in the internal, human conditions in the Zone."[57] Since this was much the same as Adenauer told Bruce in the following month, it is a fair assumption that the federal government now had a new German policy. Adenauer told Macmillan that the "ultimate goal of German unification could not, of course, be explicitly abandoned," but perhaps could be cast as "a light at the end of what might be a very long tunnel." On 18 March, the American embassy in Bonn was able to forward a summary of the changed stance articulated that week by the chancellor, who expressed a willingness to grant de facto recognition to the GDR under the right conditions.[58]

This was a useful development, bringing, as it did, Bonn's policy more in line with realities as they presented themselves in Europe. And since at this time both superpowers refused to recognize regimes that were actually exercising sovereignty over parts of China and Korea, it would not have come with good grace to say to the West Germans that "it's about time." The trouble for the West came when the details of this new policy direction had to be worked out, and worked out in the same contentious, dangerous, multilateral environment that had given rise to the change.

But that torch was passed to the Kennedy administration. The Berlin Crisis of the Eisenhower years did not end so much as fade out. The Allied strategy had aimed at discouraging the Soviets from unilaterally "solving" the problem of divided Berlin. As a consequence, the West was united in its determination to get discussions on Berlin out from under the ultimatum that Khrushchev had delivered. Eisenhower and Adenauer were in complete agreement that the West would give not one inch as long as the Soviet threat was still valid. The method of implementing this strategy was for a united West to play rope-a-dope with the Kremlin. They would give no provocation, but also would make no concession on specific issues. And they would keep the talking going until the six months were up. Khrushchev could continue to fulminate and insult, should that continue to be a hobby. (It did.) But eventually he would have to decide between making good his threats and being clearly labeled the aggressor, or simply taking what he could get and moving on to another topic. In Taubmann's words, "if the Western allies stood still, the Soviets faced an unpleasant choice between taking military action or backing down."[59] (Khrushchev was, thus, faced with the unpleasant option that caused John Kennedy to institute "Flexible Response" two years later: Escalation or surrender did not provide sufficient options in times of crisis.)

In this case, a concession on the adversary's primary desideratum worked quite well. The West gave the Soviet premier a foreign minister's conference in Geneva. The conference provided a way for Khrushchev to save face without having to do what he said he would do—either get a peace treaty or end the occupation. He could now step off the bus before it went over the cliff. Although the foreign ministers made no progress on specific issues, Eisenhower decided in March that conditions had improved sufficiently to warrant a summit meeting in the summer. The U.S. embassy in Moscow passed word of this on to Gromyko on 26 March.[60] Khrushchev now had the summit he so desperately craved. Thus 27 May came and went. It was not a day for Khrushchev to bury the West, but rather a day for the West to bury Dulles, who had days before lost his battle with cancer. Adenauer was moved by the loss, and moved again when he was told that a grain dish he had sent to help with stomach pain was the last meal that his friend had eaten.[61]

The study of international affairs can breed cynicism, and national leaders who have rarely met and barely tolerated each other are often in the habit of calling each other "friend." But the connection between Dulles and Adenauer was perhaps as close as this sort of relationship can be. Both men shared a conviction that communism posed a fundamental threat to the existence of the West. Both were known, and mocked, for decrying "godless" and "atheistic" communism. But both were concerned that the survival of Western pluralistic liberalism depended upon their decisions and actions. The experience of Germany's recent National Socialist past made this threat more real than it perhaps is to those who today write about the immediate postwar years.

Both were also inflexible, rather distant men, who often did not trust those working around them: Dulles doubted the loyalty of capable State Department hands, while Adenauer periodically suspected that his Foreign Office was seeking to sabotage his policies. Both were born during the time of the chancellor who united Germany, at a time when their nations were building railways. Both served at the pinnacle of power when Germany was divided, and missiles could cross oceans. This may help explain why neither was as creative or flexible in solving problems as one might have hoped. The Kennedy team would come into office viewing both as dinosaurs, and regret only that Adenauer had not followed Dulles into political extinction—Berlin's youthful, dynamic mayor Willy Brandt was more to their liking.[62]

But the relationship between the two men proved to be a significant factor in the success of the Allied response to Berlin. Perhaps *no one* could have reassured Adenauer during this turbulent time that his nation was going to be consulted with, and not dictated to. But Adenauer appeared to trust Eisenhower's foreign secretary more than he did his own during these critical months. Adenauer, depending on the situation, could express frustration with, or anger toward, Dulles. But as Grewe astutely points out, in which of Adenauer's relationships would this *not* have been the case?[63] In fact, those men who worked most closely with Adenauer—and who thus had firsthand knowledge of how difficult a character he could be—were not likely to dismiss talk of friendship between the two.[64]

Tallying the impact of the Berlin Crisis on the German-American relationship, one is struck by the fact that so little damage was done. American annoyance with Adenauer's suspicious ways and unconventional approach to diplomacy increased. But no significant worsening of the relationship was to come until the next administration took over from Eisenhower and Herter. Both weathered the storm with prestige and fundamental principles intact. This was in no way predictable. Still, Herter was less patient with Adenauer than Dulles had been. American frustration with the Old Man only grew stronger in the coming years. Adenauer was more right than he knew when he said of Dulles: "He was one of Germany's most loyal and reliable friends."[65] Germany has not seen another American like him since.

The documentary evidence on the Kremlin's actions during the Berlin Crisis remains limited—some memoirs written by officials with competing agendas; some, but not all, of the relevant documentation from Soviet-era archives; the reminiscences of Khrushchev to his son; and a few other sources as of this writing. These materials have clarified a number of questions. Yet it is probably prudent to avoid drawing overly firm conclusions based on research that is by force of circumstance spotty. The Soviet side of this story remains blurry today, and historical narratives should take this into account. They should also reflect that in 1958 and 1959, Soviet actions were barely comprehensible.[66]

In Umberto Eco's labyrinthine novel *The Name of the Rose*, the protagonist, a crime-solving friar, seeks to find the pattern behind a series of murders in a fifteenth-century monastery. He unravels the riddle to his satisfaction, only to find that the murderer in fact was not acting according to a plan. Rather, he was all along responding to Friar William's ongoing theorizing. Perhaps the most fascinating revelation to come from the scholarship of Taubmann, Harrison, Fursenko and Naftali, Wettig, and others who have worked with newly available Soviet materials is that the leaders of the Western powers may well have been in a situation like that of the fictional Friar William of Baskerville.

Confronted with a crisis, they sought to divine the rationale behind the terms and timing of Khrushchev's diplomatic challenge. Yet Khrushchev himself does not seem to have had anything that deserves the label "plan," and much of his early action was, in any event, taken in response to infighting within the Kremlin. Add to this the fact that the American, British, and French did not know that Adenauer had successfully deceived the Soviets about Bundeswehr nuclearization, or that Khrushchev was baldly lying to his East European allies about Soviet strategic capabilities.[67] Between the important unknowns and the "known" untruths, one wonders that things worked out rather rationally, if anticlimactically. By April, as we have seen, Khrushchev was looking for a way out. When it was offered by the West, he jumped at the offer, with the result that he had raised the threat of a cataclysm over Berlin, before settling for the status quo ante.

It is a good thing that the storylines of *The Name of the Rose* and "The Crisis over Berlin" diverge at this point. Eco's novel ends with a confrontation between the friar and a murderous monk that brings about an apocalyptic conflagration, forever sundering the link between word and world. In the Middle Ages, it was still possible to keep even such epistemological calamities limited. Fortunately, the decision makers in this Cold War narrative were not set on making a postmodernist point, and settled for something much more mundane than the flaming finish that might have been.

NOTES

1. For a recent summary of this issue, see Geoffrey K. Roberts, *German Electoral Politics* (Manchester: Manchester University Press, 2006), 78–79.

2. On U.S. policy during the Berlin Crisis, and especially on the strategic/nuclear issue, see esp. Trachtenberg, *Constructed Peace*, chapter 7, and *History and Strategy*, chapter 5. On German-German relations, see McAdams, *Germany Divided*, chapter 2. On Soviet policy, and Khrushchev's decisions and critics, see Taubman, *Khrushchev*, chapters 15 and 16. For the British side, see Gearson, *Harold Macmillan and the Berlin Crisis*. On France, see P. Maillard, *De Gaulle et le problème allemand* (Paris: Oeil, 2001).

3. Keen, *The Pelican History of Medieval Europe* (London: Penguin, 1968), 11.

4. Christian Bremen, *Die Eisenhower-Administration und die zweite Berlin Krise 1958–1961* (Berlin: Walter de Gruyter, 1998), 220. Bremen's study is an exhaustively researched, meticulous treatment of administration policy during the crisis, in the tradition of rigorous German historiography. My treatment of American policy is deeply indebted to his work.

5. See Peter Boyle, *Eisenhower* (London: Pearson, 2005), 133.

6. Adenauer, *Erinnerungen, 1955–1959*, 454–57; *Teegespräche*, 1955–1958, 304. The Communist Party Congress was set to convene on 21 January, 1959.

7. Taubmann, *Khrushchev*, 398–99. Harrison, however, has doubts that the Presidium members and other officials were as out of the loop as Mikoyan suggests. Harrison, *Driving the Soviets*, 107.

8. Aleksandr Fursenko and Timothy Naftali, *Khrushchev's Cold War: The Inside Story of an American Adversary* (New York: W. W. Norton, 2006), 196.

9. Fursenko and Naftali, 207.

10. Fursenko and Naftali, 191–92.

11. Taubman, *Khrushchev*, 400–403.

12. Hope M. Harrison, *Driving the Soviets*, 97.

13. Gerhard Wettig, *Chruschtschows Berlin-Krise 1958 bis 1963: Drohpolitik und Mauerbau* (Munich: R. Oldenbourg Verlag, 2006), 34.

14. Harrison, *Driving the Soviets*, 96.

15. Fursenko and Naftali, *Khrushchev's Cold War*, 191.

16. See Harrison, *Driving the Soviets*, esp. 104–5.

17. Trachtenberg, *A Constructed Peace*, 251–54. In preparing for a possible conference with the Soviets, State Department planners also considered it possible that the Soviets were motivated by fear of Bundeswehr nuclearization, although this

was not viewed as Khrushchev's primary motivation for setting his deadline. See 12 March, 1959, "Working Paper: Elements of a Western Position at a Conference with the Soviets," prepared for Four-Power Working Group discussions at Paris. Foy D. Kohler Papers (Hereafter FKP), University of Toledo, Collection 036, Box 80, Folder 14: "Germany 1958–1959."

18. Fursenko and Naftali, 186–89.

19. McAdams, *Germany Divided*, 29.

20. For an early assessment based on declassified American documents that are now available to scholars, see William Burr, "Avoiding the Slippery Slope: The Eisenhower Administration and the Berlin Crisis, 1958–1959," *Diplomatic History* 18/2 (Spring 1994), 117–205. Quoted on p. 118.

21. Bremen makes this case quite convincingly. *Die Eisenhower-Administration und die zweite Berlin-Krise*, 69, 112.

22. Ambrose, *Eisenhower*, Vol. 2, 511.

23. For a harrowing summary of Dulles's travels and travails, see Immerman, *John Foster Dulles*, 190–95.

24. "Memorandum of Conversation," Macmillan, Selwyn Lloyd, Eisenhower, and Dulles, 20 March, 1959, *FRUS, 1958–1960*, Vol. 8, 512–15.

25. Schwarz, *Adenauer: Der Staatsmann*, 467. See also Adenauer, *"Wir haben wirklich etwas geschaffen,"* 1184.

26. The record is rife with such statements by the chancellor. See, for instance, his off-the-record conversation with British journalists in late January 1959. Adenauer, *Teegespräche, 1959–1961*, esp. 5–11.

27. Hillenbrand to Merchant, 9 January, 1959. Quoted in Bremen, 124.

28. *Teegespräche*, ibid., 11. This is doubtless what one would expect him to say to the jittery British and their government. Yet his constant repetition of the theme suggests that he in fact based his analysis of the crisis on the belief that Khrushchev would not choose war.

29. Krone, *Tagebücher, Erster Band, 1945–1961* (Düsseldorf: Droste, 1995), 320.

30. Felken makes this point in *Dulles und Deutschland*, 479.

31. Harrison, *Driving the Soviets*, 118; Schwarz, *Adenauer: Der Staatsmann*, 474, 500; Krone, *Tagebücher*, (16 January, 1959), 325.

32. Mikoyan, *Tak Bylo*; Harrison, 116–17; Taubmann, *Khrushchev*, 409.

33. Von Eckardt, *Ein unordentliches Leben*, 551; UK Embassy (Washington) to GER, "Aide-Memoire," 13 January, 1959. FKP, Box 80, Folder 14: "Germany 1958–1959."

34. Telegram, State to Bonn Embassy (15 January, 1959), *FRUS*, ibid., 267–69.

35. Krone, *Tagebücher*, ibid., 328; Philip C. Brooks, "Interview with Dr. Konrad Adenauer," 10 June, 1964 (1966), Harry S. Truman Library, 15–16.

36. Gray, *Germany's Cold War*, 96.

37. Bremen, *Die Eisenhower-Administration und die zweite Berlin-Krise*, 149–51.

38. "Thinking Out Loud by John Foster Dulles," n.d., *FRUS*, ibid., 292–93. See also Bremen, ibid., 143.

39. Burr, ibid., 180.

40. Dulles, "Thinking Out Loud," 294; Ambrose, *Eisenhower: The President*, 503.

41. Wettig, *Chruschtschows Berlin-Krise*, 37.

42. Schwarz, *Adenauer: Der Staatsmann*, 475, 488–89; Köhler: *Adenauer: Eine politische Biographie*, 1022. Grewe also believed that "The absence of Dulles was clearly

very helpful for the Britons." *Rückblenden,* 391. See also Richard Aldous, *Macmillan, Eisenhower, and the Cold War* (Dublin: Four Courts Press, 2005), 71.

43. Krone, *Tagebücher, Erster Band,* 31–32. The idiom concerning Paris refers to the decision by Henry of Navarre, in 1593, to renounce Protestantism in order to gain the French throne. *"Paris vaut bien une messe,"* he declared in explaining his decision: "Paris is well worth a Mass." Whether Adenauer meant to conjure for Steel images of England's subsequent diplomatic isolation under Elizabeth I may never be known.

45. Adenauer, *Teegespräche,* 1959–1961, 20–21.

45. E. Bruce Geelhoed and Anthony O. Edmonds, eds., *The Macmillan-Eisenhower Correspondence, 1957–1969* (New York: Palgrave, 2005), 217–18. See also Geelhoed and Edmonds, *Eisenhower, Macmillan, and Allied Unity, 1957–1961* (New York: Palgrave, 2003), 65–69. The authors confirm Adenauer's suspicions that Macmillan was interested in using the "peace issue" in the 1959 Commons elections.

46. Köhler: *Adenauer: Eine politische Biographie,* 1010.

47. I owe this last observation to Pierre Maillard's *De Gaulle et le problème Allemande: Les leçons d'un grand dessein* (Paris: F.-X. de Guibert, 2001), 174. So strong was his civilian streak that Adenauer is reported to have disdained the use of the term "strongbox" or "safe" in his office, since the German term *Panzerschrank*—literally "armored cabinet"—carried echoes of Hitler's tanks.

48. Krone, 337. Krone reminded his enraptured leader that the partnership with France should only be undertaken with the understanding of the Americans.

49. Bremen, 116.

50. Ibid., 77–78.

51. Memorandum of Conversation, Dulles and Grewe (17 November, 1958), *FRUS,* ibid., 78–79.

52. Grewe, ibid., 399.

53. Telegram, Bonn Embassy to State (26 April, 1959), *FRUS,* ibid., 644; Irving, *Adenauer,* 177.

54. Bremen, 217.

55. Krone, 327.

56. Schwarz, ibid., 480, 484. Schwarz details the history of the Globke Plan in the intervening pages. Because this is a paraphrase of Adenauer's words, it is not clear from the text if he, himself, slipped in using the name GDR.

57. Krone, 329; see also Schwarz, ibid., 482.

58. Memorandum of Conversation, Macmillan, Selwyn Lloyd, Eisenhower, and Dulles (20 March, 1959), *FRUS,* ibid., 513; Telegram, Bonn Embassy to Secretary of State, 18 March, 1959, FKP, Box 80, Folder 14: "Germany 1958–1959."

59. Taubman, 209.

60. Editorial Note, *FRUS,* ibid., 532. See also Immerman, *John Foster Dulles,* 194–95.

61. Schwarz, ibid., 502.

62. On Dulles's initial reception as secretary among the professional Foreign Service, see Foy D. Kohler, "John Foster Dulles Oral History," Princeton University Library project, FKP, Box 22, Folder 27: "John Foster Dulles Oral History Transcript and Correspondence, 1965–1967," esp. 4–7.3.

63. Grewe, ibid., 381.

64. See, for example, the memoirs of Adenauer's secretary, Anneliese Poppinga, "*Das Wichtigste ist der Mut*": *Konrad Adenauer—die letzten fünf Kanzlerjahre* (Bergisch Gladbach: Gustav Lüge Verlag, 1994), 94–97; 121. Adenauer was not sentimental about his relationship with Dulles. He was always clear that statesmen could be friends only to the degree that they could agree on the important strategic issues. By this definition, Dulles was indeed a close friend of the chancellor, who worried terribly about his replacement by Herter.

65. Schwarz, ibid., 502.

66. Although David Reynolds is surely correct in stating that Khrushchev "really wanted . . . an invitation to the United States," which he received as a result of the post-crisis negotiations. *Summits* (Philadelphia: Basic Books, 2007), 171.

67. Fursenko and Naftali, 199.

Bibliography

ARCHIVAL SOURCES

Archiv der Christlich-demokratische Politik (Sankt Augustin/Bonn, Germany)

Nachlass Theodor Blank
Nachlass Felix von Eckardt
Nachlass Heinrich Krone
Nachlass Otto Lenz

Eisenhower Presidential Library (Abilene, Kansas, U.S.A.)

Dwight D. Eisenhower, Papers as president of the United States
Sherman Adams Records; Robert B. Anderson papers; Robert Cutler papers; Eleanor Lansing Dulles papers; John Foster Dulles papers; Gordon Gray papers; Christian A. Herter papers; C. D. Jackson papers; Neil H. McElroy papers; Walter Bedell Smith papers; Harold Stassen papers, 1953–1957
Oral Histories
White House Office, Cabinet Secretariat: Records, 1953–1960
———. Office of the Special Assistant for Disarmament (Harold Stassen): Records, 1955–1958.
———. Office of the Special Assistant for National Security Affairs (Robert Cutler, Dillon Anderson, and Gordon Gray): Records, 1952–1961.
———. Office of the Staff Secretary: Records of Paul T. Carroll, Andrew J. Goodpaster, L. Arthur Minnich, and Christopher H. Russell, 1952–1961.

National Archives and Records Administration
(College Park, Maryland, and Washington, D.C., U.S.A.)

State Department Central Decimal File
Papers of the Policy Planning Staff (State Department)

Pusey Library, Harvard University (Cambridge, Massachusetts, U.S.A.)

Papers of James Bryant Conant

Seeley G. Mudd Manuscript Library, Princeton University
(Princeton, New Jersey, U.S.A.)

Allen W. Dulles Papers
John Foster Dulles Papers
Livingston T. Merchant Papers

Stiftung Bundeskanzler Adenauer Haus (Rhöndorf, Germany)

Handakte Bundeskanzler

Ward M. Canaday Center, University of Toledo (Toledo, Ohio, U.S.A.)

Foy D. Kohler Papers

Yale University Library (New Haven, Connecticut, U.S.A.)

Papers of Dean G. Acheson

PUBLISHED PRIMARY SOURCES, MEMOIRS, AND DOCUMENTS

Acheson, Dean. "The Illusion of Disengagement," *Foreign Affairs* 36/3 (April 1958), 371–82.
———. *Present at the Creation: My Years in the State Department* (New York: W. W. Norton, 1969).
Adenauer, Konrad. *Erinnerungen*, Three Volumes (Stuttgart: Deutsche Verlags-Anstalt, 1965, 1966, 1968).
———. *Teegespräche*, 1950–1954 (Berlin: Siedler Verlag, 1984).
Aron, Raymond. (Georges-Henri Soutou, ed.). *Les articles de politique internationale dans Le Figaro de 1947 à 1977*, Vol. I, *La Guerre froide (Juin 1947 à mai 1955)* (Paris: Éditions de Fallois, 1990).

Baring, Arnulf. *Sehr verehrter Herr Bundeskanzler! Heinrich von Brentano im Briefwechsel mit Konrad Adenauer, 1949–1964* (Hamburg: Hoffmann und Campe Verlag, 1974).

Beam, Jacob. *Multiple Exposures: An American Ambassador's Unique Perspective on East-West Issues* (New York: W. W. Norton, 1978).

Blankenhorn, Herbert. *Verständnis und Verständigung: Blätter eines politischen Tagebuchs, 1949 bis 1979* (Frankfurt am Main: Verlag Ullstein, 1980).

Bohlen, Charles. *Witness to History, 1929–1969* (New York: W. W. Norton, 1973).

Boyle, Peter E. *The Churchill-Eisenhower Correspondence, 1953–1955* (Chapel Hill: University of North Carolina Press, 1990).

Buchstab, Günter, ed. *Adenauer: "Es mußte alles neu gemacht worden." Die Protokolle des CDU-Bundesvorstandes, 1950–1953* (Stuttgart: Ernst Klett Verlag, 1986).

Bundesministerium für Gesamtdeutsche Fragen. *Dokumente zur Deutschlandpolitik, 1953–1957*.

The Bulletin: A Weekly Survey of German Affairs.

Clay, Lucius D. *Decision in Germany* (Garden City, NY: Doubleday, 1950).

Conant, James B. *My Several Lives: Memoirs of a Social Inventor* (New York: Harper and Row, 1970).

Eden, Anthony. *The Memoirs of Sir Anthony Eden: Full Circle* (London: Cassell, 1960).

Eisenhower, Dwight D. *The White House Years*, Two Volumes (Garden City, NY: Doubleday, 1963, 1965).

Fursenko, A. A., ed. *Prezidium TsK KPSS. 1954–1964.* Vol. 1, *Chernovie protokol'nie zapisi zasedanii. Stenogrammi* (Moscow: Rosspen, 2003).

Great Britain. Parliament. *Parliamentary Debates: House of Commons, Official Report (Hansard).*

Grewe, Wilhelm. *Rückblenden, 1976–1951* (Frankfurt am Main: Propyläen, 1979).

Herzfeld, Hans. *Berlin in der Weltpolitik, 1945–1970* (Berlin: Walter de Gruyter, 1973).

Hughes, Emmet John. *The Ordeal of Power: A Political Memoir of the Eisenhower Years* (New York: Athenaeum, 1963).

Jahn, Hans Edgar. *An Adenauers Seite: Sein Berater erinnert sich* (Munich: Albert Langen Georg Müller Verlag, 1987).

Kennan, George F. "Disengagement Revisited," *Foreign Affairs* 37:2 (January 1959), 187–210.

———. *Memoirs, 1950–1963* (Boston: Little, Brown, 1972).

———. *Russia, the Atom, and the West* (London: Oxford University Press, 1958).

Kennedy, John F. "A Democrat Looks at Foreign Policy," *Foreign Affairs* 36:1 (October 1957).

Kroll, Hans. *Lebenserinnerungen eines Botschafters* (Cologne: Kiepenheuer und Witsch, 1967).

Krone, Heinrich. "Aufzeichnungen zur Deutchland- und Ostpolitik 1954–1969," in Rudolf Morsey and Konrad Repgen, eds. *Untersuchungen und Dokumente zur Ostpolitik und Biographie*, Adenauer-Studien III (Mainz: Matthias-Grünewald Verlag, 1967).

———. *Tagebücher, Erster Band, 1945–1961* (Düsseldorf: Droste, 1995).

Lenz, Otto. *Im Zentrum der Macht: Das Tagebuch von Staatssekretär Lenz* (Düsseldorf: Droste, 1989).

Macmillan, Harold. *Tides of Fortune, 1945–1955* (London: Macmillan, 1969).

———. *Riding the Storm, 1956–1959* (New York: Macmillan, 1971).

Meissner, Boris, ed. *Moskau-Bonn: Die Beziehungen zwischen der Sowjetunion und der Bundesrepublik Deutschland, 1955–1973, Dokumentation* (Cologne: Verlag Wissenschaft und Politik, 1975).

Mikoyan, Anastas. *Tak Bylo: Razmyshleniya o Minuvshem* (Moscow: Vagrius, 1999).

Naumov, V., ed. *Georgii Zhukov: Stenogramma oktyabr'skogo (1957g.) plenuma TsK KPSS I drugie dokumenti* (Moscow: MFD, 2001).

"Programm der Sozialdemokratischen Partei Deutschland zu den Viermächtenverhandlungen über die deutsche Wiedervereinigung," *Europa-Archiv* 10:11/12 (5 and 20 June, 1955), 7932–36.

Public Papers of the Presidents of the United States. Dwight D. Eisenhower. 1953–1960 (Washington: USGPO, 1958–1961).

Royal Institute for International Affairs. *Documents on International Affairs.*

Schlesinger, Arthur M., Jr., gen. ed. *The Dynamics of World Power: A Documentary History of United States Foreign Policy, 1945–1973*, Vol. 1, Part 2, "Western Europe," Robert Dallek, ed. (New York: Chelsea House, 1983).

Taylor, Maxwell D. *The Uncertain Trumpet* (New York: Harper, 1959).

Troyanovsky, Oleg. *Cherez gody i rasstoiania: Istoriya odnoi sem'i* (Moscow: Vagrius, 1997).

United Nations. *Yearbook of the United Nations.* 1955.

U.S. Arms Control and Disarmament Agency. *Documents on Disarmament.* 1945–1959.

U.S. Congress. Senate. Committee on Foreign Relations. *Protocol on the Termination of the Occupation Regime in the Federal Republic of Germany* (Washington: USGPO, 1955).

U.S. Department of State. *Bulletin.* 1953–1960.

———. *Foreign Relations of the United States.* (Various volumes, 1952–1960.)

Von Borsch, Herbert. "Glossen," *Aussenpolitik: Zeitschrift für Internationale Fragen* 1955:2 (Februar), 69–71.

Von Eckardt, Felix. *Ein unordentliches Leben* (Düsseldorf: Econ-Verlag, 1967).

Verhandlungen des Deutschen Bundestages. 1953–1960.

PERIODICALS

Current Digest of the Soviet Press
The Economist (London)
Keesing's Contemporary Archives
Life
Neue Zürcher Zeitung
The New York Times
Rivista di Studi Politici Internazionali
The Times (London)
U.S. News & World Report

SECONDARY SOURCES

Aldous, Richard. *Macmillan, Eisenhower, and the Cold War* (Dublin: Four Courts Press, 2005).

Ambrose, Stephen E. *Eisenhower*, Two volumes (New York: Simon and Schuster, 1983, 1985).

Anderson, Sheldon. *A Cold War in the Soviet Bloc: Polish-East German Relations, 1945–1962* (Boulder, CO: Westview Press, 2001).

Arend, Anthony Clark. *Pursuing a Just and Durable Peace: John Foster Dulles and International Organization* (Westport, CT: Greenwood Press, 1988).

Banchoff, Thomas, "Historical Memory and German Foreign Policy: The Cases of Adenauer and Brandt," *German Politics and Society* 14:2 (Summer 1996).

Bandulet, Bruno. *Adenauer zwischen West und Ost: Alternativen der deutschen Aussenpolitik* (Munich: Weltforum Verlag, 1970).

Bark, Dennis L., and David R. Gress. *A History of West Germany, Volume 1: From Shadow to Substance* (Oxford: Blackwell, 1993).

Baring, Arnulf. *Außenpolitik in Adenauers Kanzlerdemokratie* (Munich: R. Oldenbourg, 1969).

Bell, Coral. *Negotiation from Strength: A Study in the Politics of Power* (London: Chatto and Windus, 1962).

Besson, Waldemar. *Die Aussenpolitik der Bundesrepublik: Erfahrungen und Maßstabe* (Munich: R. Piper and Co Verlag, 1970).

Bischof, Günter, and Stephen E. Ambrose, eds. *Eisenhower: A Centenary Assessment* (Baton Rouge: Louisiana State University Press, 1995).

Blumenwitz, Dieter, Klaus Gotto, Hans Maier, Konrad Repgen, and Hans-Peter Schwarz. *Konrad Adenauer und seine Zeit: Politik und Persönlichkeit des ersten Bundeskanzlers*, Two volumes (Stuttgart: Deutsche-Verlags-Anstalt, 1976).

Bowie, Robert R., and Richard H. Immerman. *Waging Peace: How Eisenhower Shaped an Enduring Cold War Strategy* (New York: Oxford University Press, 2002).

Boyle, Peter G., ed. *The Eden-Eisenhower Correspondence, 1955–1957* (Chapel Hill: University of North Carolina Press, 2005).

———. *Eisenhower* (London: Pearson, 2005).

Bremen, Christian. *Die Eisenhower-Administration und die zweite Berlin Krise 1958–1961* (Berlin: Walter de Gruyter, 1998).

Brinkley, Douglas. *Dean Acheson: The Cold War Years, 1953–1971* (New Haven, CT: Yale University Press, 1992).

Bruce, Gary. *Resistance with the People: Repression and Resistance in Eastern Germany, 1945–1955* (Lanham, MD: Rowman & Littlefield, 2003).

Buffet, Cyril . "L'Allemagne entre l'Est et l'Oest: Les relations germano-soviétiques au prisme de Rapallo, 1945–1991," *Guerres mondiales et conflits contemporains* 210 (Avril–Juin 2003), 7–18.

Casey, Steven. "Selling NSC-68: The Truman Administration, Public Opinion, and the Politics of Mobilization," *Diplomatic History* 29/4 (September 2005), 655–90.

Cioc, Mark. *Pax Atomica: The Nuclear Defense Debate in West Germany during the Adenauer Era* (New York: Columbia University Press, 1988).

Clemens, Clay. *Reluctant Realists: The Christian Democrats and West German Ostpolitik* (Durham, NC: Duke University Press, 1989).

Cohen, Warren I. "China Lobby," in Alexander DeConde, et al., eds., *Encyclopedia of American Foreign Policy* (New York: Scribner's Sons, 2002), 185-91.

Coleman, David G. "Eisenhower and the Berlin Problem," *Cold War Studies* 2/1 (Winter 2000), 3-34.

Cook, Don. *Forging the Alliance: NATO: 1945-1950* (New York: William Morrow, 1989).

Creswell, Michael. *A Question of Balance: How France and the United States Created Cold War Europe* (Cambridge, MA: Harvard University Press, 2006).

David, François. "J.-F. Dulles et la France: La Crise de Suez," *Revue d'Histoire Diplomatique* 116/1 (2002).

Davies, Norman. *God's Playground: A History of Poland*, Vol. II (New York: Oxford University Press, 2005).

DeSantis, Vincent P. "Eisenhower Revisionism," *Review of Politics* 38:2 (April 1976), 190-207.

Diedrich, Torsten. *Der 17 Juni 1953 in der DDR: Bewaffnete Gewalt gegen das Volk* (Berlin: Dietz Verlag, 1991).

Di Nolfo, Ennio. *The Atlantic Pact Forty Years Later: A Historical Reappraisal* (Berlin: Walter de Gruyter, 1991).

Di Nolfo, Ennio, Romain H. Rainero, and Brunello Vigezzi, eds., *L'Italia e la Politica di Potenza in Europa: 1950-1960* (Milan: Marzorati Editore, 1992).

Divine, Robert. *Eisenhower and the Cold War* (Oxford: Oxford University Press, 1981).

———. *The Sputnik Challenge: Eisenhower's Response to the Soviet Satellite* (Oxford: Oxford University Press, 1993).

Dönhoff, Marion, Helmut Schmidt, and Theo Sommer. *Zeit—Geschichte der Bonner Republik, 1949-1999* (Reinbeck bei Hamburg: Rowohlt, 1999).

Döring-Manteuffel, Anselm. *Die Bundesrepublik Deutschland in der Ära Adenauer: Außenpolitik und innere Entwicklung, 1949-1963* (Darmstadt: Wissenschafltische Buchgesellschaft, 1983).

Eisenberg, Carolyn Woods. *Drawing the Line: The American Decision to Divide Germany, 1944-1949* (Cambridge: Cambridge University Press, 1996).

Ekiert, Grzegorz. *The State against Society: Political Crises and Their Aftermath in East Central Europe* (Princeton, NJ: Princeton University Press, 1996).

Felken, Detlef. *Dulles und Deutschland: Die amerikanische Deutschlandpolitik, 1953-1959* (Bonn: Bouvier Verlag, 1993).

Filitov, A. M. "SSSR i GDR: god 1953-i," *Voprosy Istorii* (7/2000).

———. "SSSR i germanskii vopros: Povorotnye punkty (1941-1961 gg.), in N. I. Egorova and A. O. Chubar'ian, eds., *Kholodnaya voina. 1945-1963 gg.: Istoricheskaia retrospektiva* (Moscow: Olma Press, 2003).

Finer, Herman. *Dulles over Suez: The Theory and Practice of His Diplomacy* (Chicago: Quadrangle, 1964).

Fogarty, Michael P. *Christian Democracy in Western Europe, 1820-1953* (Notre Dame, IN: University of Notre Dame Press, 1957).

Freedman, Lawrence. *The Evolution of Nuclear Strategy* (New York: St. Martin's Press, 1983).

Fursdon, Edward. *The European Defense Community: A History* (New York: St. Martin's Press, 1979).

Fursenko, Aleksandr, and Timothy Naftali, *Khrushchev's Cold War: The Inside Story of an American Adversary* (New York: W. W. Norton, 2006).

Gaddis, John Lewis. *Strategies of Containment: A Critical Appraisal of American National Security Policy during the Cold War*, Revised Edition (New York: Oxford University Press, 2005).

———. *The United States and the End of the Cold War* (New York: Oxford University Press, 1992).

———. *We Now Know: Rethinking Cold War History* (Oxford: Oxford University Press, 1997).

Gati, Charles. *Failed Illusions: Moscow, Washington, Budapest and the 1956 Hungarian Revolt* (Stanford, CA: Stanford University Press, 2006).

Gatzke, Hans W. *Germany and the United States: A "Special Relationship?"* (Cambridge, MA: Harvard University Press, 1980).

Gavín, Victor. "France and the Kafkaesque Politics of the European Defense Community," *Cardiff Historical Papers*, 2007/2.

Gearson, John P. S. *Harold Macmillan and the Berlin Wall Crisis, 1958–62* (New York: St. Martin's Press, 1998).

Golan, Galia. *Soviet Foreign Policies in the Middle East from World War II to Gorbachev* (Cambridge: Cambridge University Press, 1990).

Gor'kov, Yu. A. "Besedy G. K. Zhukova i D. Eizenchauera na Zhenevskom Soveshchanii 1955 g.," *Novaia i Noveishaia Istoriia* 5/1999, 98–114.

Gotto, Klaus, Hans Maier, Rudolf Morsey, and Hans-Peter Schwarz, eds. *Konrad Adenauer: Seine Deutschland- und Außenpolitik, 1945–1963* (Munich: Deutscher Taschenbuch Verlag, 1975).

Grabbe, Hans-Jürgen. *Unionsparteien, Sozialdemokratie und Vereinigte Staaten von Amerika, 1945–1966* (Düsseldorf: Droste Verlag, 1983).

Granieri, Ronald J. *The Ambivalent Alliance: Konrad Adenauer, the CDU/CSU, and the West, 1949–1966* (New York: Berghahn Books, 2003).

Granville, Johanna. "Imre Nagy, Hesitant Revolutionary," *Cold War International History Project Bulletin*, Issue 5 (Spring 1995), 23; 27–28.

———. Trans. "Soviet Documents on the Hungarian Revolution," *Cold War International History Project Bulletin*, Issue 5 (Spring 1995), 23; 29–34.

Grenstein, Fred. *The Hidden-Hand Presidency: Eisenhower as Leader* (New York: Basic Books, 1982).

Grewe, Wilhelm. *Deutsche Aussenpolitik in der Nachkriegszeit* (Stuttgart: Deutsche Verlags-Anstalt, 1960).

Guhin, Michael A. *John Foster Dulles: A Statesman and His Times* (New York: Columbia University Press, 1972).

Hacke, Christian. *Weltmach wider Willen. Die Außenpolitk der Bundesrepublik Deutschland* (Stuttgart: Klett-Cotta, 1988).

Haftendorn, Helga. *Deutsche Außenpolitik zwischen Selbstbeschränkung und Selbstbehauptung, 1945–2000* (Stuttgart: Deutsche Verlags-Anstalt, 2000).

Harrison, Hope. *Driving the Soviets up the Wall: Soviet-East German Relations, 1953–1961* (Princeton, NJ: Princeton University Press, 2003).

———. "New Evidence on Khrushchev's 1958 Berlin Ultimatum," *Cold War International History Project Bulletin*, Issue 4 (Fall 1994), 35–39.

———. "Soviet-East German Relations after World War II," *Problems of Post-Communism* 42:5 (September–October 1995), 9–17.

———. "Ulbricht and the 'Concrete Rose': New Archival Evidence on the Dynamics of Soviet-East German Relations and the Berlin Crisis, 1958–1961," *Working Paper No. 5*, Cold War International History Project (May 1993).

Heller, Mikhail, and Aleksandr Nekrich. *Utopiia u Vlasti: Istoriia Sovietskogo Soiuza s 1917 goda do nashikh dnei*, Part 2 (Frankfurt am Main: Interchange, 1982).

Hershberg, James C. "'Explosion in the Offing': German Rearmament and American Diplomacy, 1953–1955," *Diplomatic History* 16:4 (Fall 1992), 511–49.

———. *James B. Conant: Harvard to Hiroshima and the Making of the Nuclear Age* (New York: Alfred A. Knopf, 1993).

Hiscocks, Richard. *The Adenauer Era* (Philadelphia: J. B. Lippincott, 1966).

Hitchcock, William I. *France Restored: Cold War Diplomacy and the Quest for Leadership in Europe, 1944–1954* (Chapel Hill: University of North Carolina Press, 1998).

Hoopes, Townsend. *The Devil and John Foster Dulles* (New York: Little, Brown, 1973).

Immerman, Richard H., ed. *John Foster Dulles and the Diplomacy of the Cold War* (Princeton, NJ: Princeton University Press, 1990).

———. *John Foster Dulles: Piety, Pragmatism, and Power in U.S. Foreign Policy* (Lanham, MD: Rowman & Littlefield, 1998).

Irving, Ronald. *Adenauer* (London: Pearson, 2002).

Ivanov, R. F. *Duait Eizenkhauer: Chelovek, Politik, Polkovodets* (Moscow: IPO Poligran, 1998).

Junker, Detlef, ed. *The United States and Germany in the Era of the Cold War, 1945–1990: A Handbook*, Volume 1, 1945–1968 (Cambridge: Cambridge University Press, 2004).

Kaplan, Lawrence S. *American Historians and the Atlantic Alliance* (Kent, OH: Kent State University Press, 1991).

———. *NATO and the United States: The Enduring Alliance* (Boston: Twayne, 1988).

Kastner, Jill Davey Colley. "The Ambivalent Ally: Adenauer, Eisenhower, and the Dilemmas of the Cold War, 1953–1960" (PhD Dissertation, Department of History, Harvard University: 1999).

Kelleher, Catherine McArdle. *Germany and the Politics of Nuclear Weapons* (New York: Columbia University Press, 1975).

Kingseed, Cole C. *Eisenhower and the Suez Crisis of 1956* (Baton Rouge: Louisiana State University Press, 1995).

Kipp, Yvonne. *Eden, Adenauer und die deutsche Frage: Britische Deutschlandpolitik im internationalen Spannungsfeld, 1951–1957* (Paderborn: Ferdinand Schöningh, 2002).

Kisatsky, Deborah. *The United States and the European Right, 1945–1955* (Columbus: Ohio State University Press, 2005).

Kissinger, Henry. *Diplomacy* (New York: Simon and Schuster, 1994).

Kleinmann, Hans-Otto. *Geschichte der CDU, 1945–1982* (Stuttgart: Deutsche-Verlags-Anstalt, 1993).

Kleßmann, Christoph, and Bernd Stöver, eds. *1953—Krisenjahr des Kalten Krieges in Europa* (Cologne: Böhlau Verlag, 1999).

Knight, Amy. *Beria: Stalin's First Lieutenant* (Princeton, NJ: Princeton University Press, 1993).

Koch, Peter. *Konrad Adenauer: Eine politische Biographie* (Reinbeck bei Hamburg: Rowohlt, 1985).

Koenen, Gerd. *Der Russland-Komplex: Die Deutschen und der Osten 1900–1945* (Munich: C. H. Beck, 2005).

Köhler, Henning. *Adenauer: Eine politische Biographie* (Frankfurt am Main: Propyläen, 1994).

Kosthorst, Daniel. *Brentano und die deutsche Einheit: Die Deutschland- und Ostpolitik des Außenministers in Kabinett Adenauer, 1955–1961* (Düsseldorf: Droste, 1993).

Kovrig, Bennett. *Of Walls and Bridges: The United States and Eastern Europe* (New York: New York University Press, 1991).

Kramer, Mark. "The Early Post-Stalin Succession Struggle and Upheavals in East-Central Europe: Internal-External Linkages in Soviet Policy Making," *Journal of Cold War Studies* 1–3 (1999), 3–55; 3–38; 3–66.

Krieger, Wolfgang. *General Lucius D. Clay und die amerikanische Deutschlandpolitik 1945–1949* (Stuttgart: Klett-Cotta, 1988).

Kyle, Keith. *Suez* (New York: St. Martin's Press, 1991).

Lamézec, Yann. "Les relations franco-britanniques et l'échec de la C.E.D.: Le point de vue français (mai 1952–août 1954)," *Revue d'Histoire Diplomatique* 120/1 (2006), 29–60.

Large, David Clay. *Germans to the Front: West German Rearmament in the Adenauer Era* (Chapel Hill: University of North Carolina Press, 1996).

Larres, Klaus. *Churchill's Cold War: The Politics of Personal Diplomacy* (New Haven, CT: Yale University Press, 2002).

Larres, Klaus, and Torsten Oppeland, eds. *Deutschland und die USA im 20. Jahrhundert: Geschichte der politischen Beziehungen* (Darmstadt: Wissenschaftliche Buchgesellschaft, 1997).

Larres, Klaus, and Kenneth Osgood, eds. *The Cold War after Stalin's Death: A Missed Opportunity for Peace?* (Lanham, MD: Rowman & Littlefield, 2006).

La Serre, Françoise de, et al. *Les Politiques étrangères de la France et de la Grande-Bretagne depuis 1945: L'inévitable adjustement* (Paris: Presses de la Fondation Nationale des Sciences Politiques, 1990).

Lee, Sabine. "Perception and Reality: Anglo-German Relations during the Berlin Crisis 1958–1959," *German History* 13:1 (1995), 47–69.

Lefebvre, Denis. *Guy Mollet: Le mal aimé* (Paris: Plon, 1992).

Lefèvre, Sylvie. "Vers le rapprochement des economies française et allemande (1945–1955)," *Relations Internationales* 93 (Printemps 1998).

Leffler, Melvyn F. *A Preponderance of Power: National Security, the Truman Administration, and the Cold War* (Stanford, CA: Stanford University Press, 1992).

———. *For the Soul of Mankind: The United States, the Soviet Union, and the Cold War* (New York: Hill and Wang, 2007).

Litván, Györgi, ed. *The Hungarian Revolution of 1956: Reform, Revolt and Repression, 1953–1963* (London: Longman, 1996).

Louis, William Roger. *Suez 1956: The Crisis and Its Consequences* (Oxford: Oxford University Press, 1989).

Lowenstein, Karl. "The Bonn Constitution and the European Defense Community Treaties: A Study in Judicial Frustration," *Yale Law Journal* 64:6 (May 1955), 805–39.

——, ed. *Just Another Major Crisis?: The United States and Europe since 2000* (Oxford: Oxford University Press, 2008).

Lundestad, Geir. *"Empire" by Integration: The United States and European Integration, 1945–1997* (New York: Oxford University Press, 1998).

Maelstaf, Geneviève. *Que Faire de L'Allemagne? Les responsables français, le statut international de l'Allemagne et le problème de l'unité allemande, 1945–1955* (Paris: Imprimerie Nationale, 1999).

Maier, Charles S. "Privileged Partners: The Atlantic Relationship at the End of the Bush Regime," in Geir Lundestad, ed., *Just Another Major Crisis?: The United States and Europe since 2000* (Oxford: Oxford University Press, 2008).

May, Ernest. "'Who Are We?' Two Centuries of American Foreign Relations," *Foreign Affairs* 73 (March/April 1994), 134–38.

——. "The American Commitment to Germany, 1945–1955," *Diplomatic History* 13:4 (Fall 1989).

Mayer, Frank A. "Adenauer and Kennedy: An Era of Distrust in German-American Relations?" *German Studies Review* 17:1 (February 1994), 83–104.

——. *Adenauer and Kennedy: A Study in German-American Relations, 1961–1963* (New York: St. Martin's Press, 1996).

McAdams, A. James. *Germany Divided: From the Wall to Reunification* (Princeton, NJ: Princeton University Press, 1993).

McKeever, Porter. *Adlai Stevenson: His Life and Legacy* (New York: William Morrow, 1989).

Medvedev, Roy. *Let History Judge: The Origins and Consequences of Stalinism* (New York: Columbia University Press, 1989).

Medvedev, Zh. A. "Zagadka Smerti Stalina," *Voprosy Istorii* 1 (2000), 83–91.

Melanson, Richard A., and David Mayers. *Reevaluating Eisenhower: American Foreign Policy in the 1950s* (Urbana: University of Illinois Press, 1987).

Metz, Stephen. "Eisenhower and the Planning of American Grand Strategy," *Journal of Strategic Studies* 14:1 (March 1991), 49–71.

Miard-Delacroix, Hélène. *Question nationale allemande et nationalisme: Perceptions françaises d'une problématique allemande au début des années cinquante* (Paris: Presses Universitaires du Septentrion, 2004).

Miscamble, CSC, Wilson D. *From Roosevelt to Truman: Potsdam, Hiroshima, and the Cold War* (New York: Cambridge University Press, 2007).

Morsey, Rudolf, and Konrad Repgen. *Adenauer-Studien I* (Mainz: Matthias-Grünewald-Verlag, 1971).

Mueller, Wolfgang. "Stalin and Austria: New Evidence on Soviet Policy in a Secondary Theatre of the Cold War," *Cold War History* 6:1 (February 2006), 63–84.

Müller-Roschach, Herbert. *Die Deutsche Europapolitik, 1949–1977: Eine politische Chronik* (Bonn: Europa Union Verlag, 1980).

Naimark, Norman. *The Russians in Germany: A History of the Soviet Zone of Occupation, 1945–1949* (Cambridge, MA: Belknap Press/Harvard University Press, 1995).

Nation, R. Craig. *Black Earth, Red Star: A History of Soviet Security Policy, 1917–1991* (Ithaca, NY: Cornell University Press, 1992).

Newman, Kitty. *Macmillan, Khrushchev, and the Berlin Crisis, 1958–1960* (New York: Routledge, 2007).

Ninkovitch, Frank A. *Germany and the United States: The Transformation of the German Question since 1945* (Boston: G. K. Hall, 1988).

Nouailhat, Yves-Henri. *Les États-Unis et le monde au XXe siècle* (Paris: Armand Colin/Masson, 1997).

Osgood, Kenneth. *Total Cold War: Eisenhower's Secret Propaganda Battle at Home and Abroad* (Lawrence: University Press of Kansas, 2006).

Ostermann, Christian. "New Documents on the East German Uprising of 1953," *Cold War International History Project Bulletin,* Issue 5 (Spring 1995), 10–21.

———. *Uprising in East Germany, 1953* (New York: Central European University Press, 2001).

Pach, Jr., Chester, and Elmo Richardson. *The Presidency of Dwight D. Eisenhower* (Lawrence: University Press of Kansas, 1991).

Park, William. *Defending the West: A History of NATO* (Boulder, CO: Westview, 1986).

Parmet, Herbert. *Eisenhower and the American Crusades* (New York: Macmillan, 1972).

Patterson, James T. *Mr. Republican: A Biography of Robert A. Taft* (Boston: Houghton Mifflin, 1972).

Petelin, B. V. "Konrad Adenauer: Patriarch germanskoi politiki," *Novaia i noveishaia istoriia* 3 (2006).

Plischke, Elmer. *Diplomat in Chief: The President at the Summit* (New York: Praeger, 1986).

Poppinga, Anneliese. *"Das Wichtigste ist der Mut": Konrad Adenauer—die letzten fünf Kanzlerjahre* (Bergisch Gladbach: Gustav Lüge Verlag, 1994).

Pöttering, Hans-Gert. *Adenauers Sicherheitspolitik 1955–1959: Ein Beitrag zum deutsch-amerikanischen Verhältnis* (Düsseldorf: Droste Verlag, 1975).

Pulzer, Peter. *German Politics, 1945–1995* (Oxford: Oxford University Press, 1995).

Rabe, Stephen G. "Eisenhower Revisionism: A Decade of Scholarship," *Diplomatic History* 17:1 (Winter 1993), 97–115.

Rae, Nicole. *The Decline and Fall of the Liberal Republicans: From 1952 to the Present* (Oxford: Oxford University Press, 1989).

Rainer, Janos M. "The Yeltsin Dossier: Soviet Documents on Hungary, 1956," *Cold War International History Project Bulletin,* Issue 5 (Spring 1995).

Reynolds, David. *Summits: Six Meetings That Shaped the Twentieth Century* (New York: Basic Books, 2007).

Riklin, Alois. *Das Berlin Problem: Historisch-politische und völkerrechtliche Darstellung des Viermächtestatus* (Cologne: Verlag Wissenschaft und Politik, 1964).

Ritter, Gerhard, and Merith Niehauss. *Wahlen in Deutschland 1946–1991: Ein Handbuch* (Munich: Verlag C. H. Beck, 1991).

Roberts, Geoffrey K. *German Electoral Politics* (Manchester, UK: Manchester University Press, 2006).

Ruane, Kevin. "Agonizing Reappraisals: Anthony Eden, John Foster Dulles and the Crisis of European Defence, 1953–54," *Diplomacy & Statecraft* 13/4 (December 2002), 151–85.

Schmidt, Wolfgang. "Die Wurzeln der Entspannung: Der konzeptionelle Ursprung der Ost- und Deutschlandspolitik Willy Brandts in den fünfziger Jahren," *Vierteljahrshefte für Zeitgeschichte* 51:4 (Oktober 2003), 521–63.

Schoonover, Thomas. "It's Not What We Say, It's What We Do": The Study and Writing of U.S. Foreign Relations in the United States," Newsletter, Society for Historians of American Foreign Relations 31:2 (June 2000).

Schulz, Klaus-Peter. *Adenauers Gegenspieler: Begegnungen mit Kurt Schumacher und Sozialdemokratie der ersten Stunde* (Freiburg: Verlag Herder, 1989).

Schwartz, Thomas A. *America's Germany: John J. McCloy and the Federal Republic of Germany* (Cambridge, MA: Harvard University Press, 1991).

——. "The Berlin Crisis and the Cold War," *Diplomatic History* 21:1 (Winter 1997), 139–48.

——. "The United States and Germany after 1945: Alliances, Transnational Relations, and the Legacy of the Cold War," [1995 Bernath Lecture] *Diplomatic History* 19:4 (Fall 1995), 549–68.

Schwarz, Hans-Peter. *Adenauer, Der Staatsmann* (2nd Edition), Two volumes (Munich: Deutscher Taschenbuch Verlag, 1994).

——. *Die Ära Adenauer, Gründerjahre der Republik, 1949–1957*, Volume 2 of Karl Dietrich Bracher, Theodor Eschenberg, Joachim C. Fest, and Eberhard Jäckel, gen. eds., *Geschichte der Bundesrepublik Deutschland* (Stuttgart: Deutsche-Verlags-Anstalt, 1981).

——. "Adenauer und Europa," *Vierteljahrshefte für Zeitgeschichte* 27:4 (Oktober 1979), 471–523.

——, ed. *Konrad Adenauers Regierunsstil* (Bonn: Bouvier Verlag, 1991).

Shennan, Andrew. (Review of Sylvie Lefèvre [author]). "*Les relations économiques franco-allemandes de 1945 à 1955: De l'occupation à la cooperation*," *American Historical Review* 106:1 (February 2001), 247.

Soutou, Georges-Henri. *L'alliance incertaine: Les rapports politico-stratégiques franco-allemands, 1954–1996* (Paris: Fayard, 1997).

Speier, Hans. *German Rearmament and Atomic War: The Views of the German Military and Political Leaders* (Evanston, IL: Row, Peterson, 1957).

Spicka, Mark E. *Selling the Economic Miracle: Economic Reconstruction and Politics in West Germany, 1949–1957* (New York: Berghahn Books, 2007).

Steininger, Rolf, Jürgen Weber, Günter Bischof, Thomas Albricht, and Klaus Eisterer, eds. *Die Doppelte Eindämmung: Europäische Sicherheit und die Deutsche Frage in den Fünfzigern* (Munich: V. Hase und Kohler Verlag, 1993).

Stourzh, Gerhard. *Kleine Geschichte des Österreichischen Staatsvertrages* (Graz: Verlag Styria, 1975).

Sugar, Peter F., gen ed., Péter Hanák, assoc. ed. *A History of Hungary* (Bloomington: Indiana University Press, 1990).

Suri, Jeremi. *Henry Kissinger and the American Century* (Cambridge, MA: Belknap/ Harvard University Press, 2007).

Tesson, Sandrine. "La doctrine Hallstein, entre rigueur et pragmatisme (1955–1969)," *Relations Internationales* 110 (Summer 2002), 219–34.

Trachtenberg, Marc, ed. *Between Empire and Alliance: America and Europe during the Cold War* (Lanham, MD: Rowman & Littlefield, 2003).

——. "Constructed Peace? The United States, the NATO Allies, and the Making of the European Settlement, 1949–1963," *Working Papers of the Volkswagen Foundation Program in Post-War German History*, No. 9: American Institute for Contemporary German Studies, German Historical Institute, 1995.

——. *A Constructed Peace: The Making of the European Settlement, 1945–1963* (Princeton, NJ: Princeton University Press, 1999).

——. *History and Strategy* (Princeton, NJ: Princeton University Press, 1991).

Unsigned essay (Giuseppe Vedovato?) "Riconoscimento del Governo di Pekino contro riunificazione tedesca?" *Rivista di Studi Politici Internazionali* 24:2 (Aprile/Giugno 1957), 187–94.

Vaïsse, Maurice, Pierre Mélandri, and Frédéric Bozo. *La France et l'OTAN, 1949–1996* (Armées: Éditions Complexe, 1996).

Von Rauch, Georg. *Geschichte der Sowjetunion* (Stuttgart: Alfred Kröner Verlag, 1990).

Von Sternberg, Wilhelm. *Adenauer: Eine deutsche Legende*, Second edition (Berlin: Aufbau, 2005).

Ulam, Adam. *Expansion and Coexistence: Soviet Foreign Policy, 1917–1973*, Second edition (New York: Praeger, 1974).

Wagner, Steven. *Eisenhower Republicanism: Pursuing the Middle Way* (DeKalb: Northern Illinois University Press, 2006).

Wall, Irwin. *The United States and the Making of Postwar France, 1945–1954* (New York: Cambridge University Press, 2002).

Watson, Derek. *Molotov: A Biography* (New York: Palgrave, 2005).

Wettig, Gerhard. *Bereitschaft zu Einheit in Freiheit? Die sowjetische Deutschland-Politik, 1945–1955* (Munich: Olzog Verlag, 1999).

——. *Chruschtschows Berlin-Krise, 1958–1963: Drohpolitik und Mauerbau* (Munich: R. Oldenbourg Verlag, 2006).

——. *Stalin and the Cold War in Europe: The Emergence and Development of East-West Conflict, 1939–1953* (Lanham, MD: Rowman & Littlefield, 2007).

Wetzlaughk, Udo. *Die Alliierten in Berlin* (Berlin: Verlag Spitz, 1988).

——. *Berlin und die deutsche Frage* (Cologne: Verlag Wissenschaft und Politik, 1985).

Weymer, Paul. *Adenauer* (New York: Dutton, 1957).

Wiggerhaus, Norbert, and Roland G. Foerster. *Die westliche Sicherheitsgemeinschaft: 1948–1950* (Boppard am Rhein: Harald Boldt Verlag, 1988).

Wighton, Charles. *Adenauer: A Critical Biography* (New York: Coward-McCann, 1964).

Williamson, Daniel C. *Separate Agendas: Churchill, Eisenhower, and Anglo-American Relations, 1953–1955* (Lanham, MD: Lexington Books, 2006).

Winand, Pascaline. *Eisenhower, Kennedy, and the United States of Europe* (New York: St. Martin's Press, 1996).

Wunderlin, Charles E. *Robert A. Taft: Ideas, Tradition, and Party in U.S. Foreign Policy* (Lanham, MD: Rowman & Littlefield, 2005).

Zubok, Vladislav. *A Failed Empire: The Soviet Union in the Cold War from Stalin to Gorbachev* (Chapel Hill: University of North Carolina Press, 2007).

Zubok, Vladislav, and Constantine Pleshakov. *Inside the Kremlin's Cold War: From Stalin to Khrushchev* (Cambridge, MA: Harvard University Press, 1996).

Index

Acheson, Dean, 222–23
Adams, Sherman, 123
Adenauer, Konrad: advocates German reunification, 61, 173–82, 198–99, 200; uses American influence in Atlantic Alliance, 120; and appearance of influence in alliance, 26, 46, 47, 62–64, 78, 87, 127, 130, 162, 199; and Austria, 106, 110, 116; and "autocratic" methods, 107; and Berlin Crisis (1958–1959), 233ff; Berlin Foreign Ministers Conference, 83–86; and Blankenhorn, 46; on British troop reductions, 210; in Bundestag foreign policy debate (1955), 124; CDU, leadership of, 232; and Churchill, 31, 42, 43–45, 61, 98; on collective security, 102; concerns about Eisenhower, 39, 46, 60, 122–24, 152, 213; and Council on Foreign Relations, 30; and de Gaulle, 244; and disarmament, 40, 126, 206, 209, 215; Draper's assessment of, 42; on Dulles, Allen, 187–188; Dulles, John Foster, relationship with, 13–15, 60, 102, 122, 133, 172, 249–50. *See also*

Dulles, John Foster: Adenauer, friendship with; and Eden, 120; on Eisenhower, 13, 60; elections (1953), 4, 22, 25–26, 28, 58, 61, 67, 69–71, 81–82; elections (1957), 173–74, 197–98, 202, 213, 215, 224; Eurocentric policy, advocates, 197; on European Defense Community, 12, 14, 41, 68; and FDP, 232; flexibility of, 200, 203, 210, 246–47; and Mendès-France, Pierre, 99; on German neutralization, 120, 123, 221; Globke Plan and, 247; historical memory of, 116; Hungary and, 200–201; June 17, response to, 60–61; and Kennedy, 232, 240; and Korea, 27; and "liberation," 60; and Macmillan, 243; media and, 29–30; misunderstands American policy making, 124; on Mollet proposal, 161; and NATO, 10–11, 97, 116–17, 126, 135; on Nazi period, 189; on negotiations with the Soviets, 38–41, 43, 46–47, 58–59, 61, 66–67, 69, 103, 108, 113–15, 119–20, 125, 164–65; on nuclear weapons and the Soviets,

269

Ollenhauer, Erich, 76, 105–6
"Open Skies" proposal, 156, 162, 165, 198
Operations Coordinating Board (OCB), 174, 199–200
O'Shaugnessy, Elim, 214
Ostpolitik, 246

peace offensive, Soviet, 19 ff
Petelin, B. V., 76
Pleven, René, 11
Potsdam Agreement, 35, 162, 242
Prague Coup (1948), 7

Raab, Julius, 104
Radford, Adm. Arthur, 128; "Radford Plan," 171, 214–15
Rapacki, Adam. *See* Rapacki Plan
Rapacki Plan, 218–20, 223; and Bulganin, 222
Reinstein, Jacques J., 203
Reith Lectures. *See* Kennan, George: Reith Lectures of
Rhee, Syngman, 9
Riddleberger, James, 64–65
Roosevelt, Franklin D., 6, 231

Salisbury, Harrison, 20
Salisbury, Lord, 66, 71
Schumacher, Kurt, 76
Schwarz, Hans-Peter, 106, 135, 238
Schwartz, Thomas A., 4, 7
Semyonov, Vladimir Semyonovich, 64
Social Democratic Party (SPD), 153; on Adenauer's perceived inflexibility, 108; and American political aid to Adenauer, 74; and Bundestag foreign policy debate, 204; on Soviet flexibility, 108
Socialist Unity Party (SED), 57, 59, 247
Soutou, Georges-Henri, 22
Soviet Union: American relations with, 3; and division of Germany,

158–59; French relations with, 173; NATO, FRG entry into, 104–5; NATO, opposition to, 101. *See also specific topics*
Sputnik, 219
Stalin, Joseph, 9, 57; and Berlin blockade, 2; death of, 15, 19, 59
Stassen, Harold: and arms control, 126, 156, 211; and Dulles, 164; and Gromyko, 162–63
State, U.S. Department of: Policy Planning Staff (PPS), 33
Steel, David, 243
Stevenson, Adlai, 187
Stimson, Henry, 6
Suez Crisis, 152, 175, 182–89; Blankenhorn on, 185
Sukarno, Achmed, 175
summits: Geneva (1955), 128–33, 153, 223; Paris (1960), 4

Taft, Robert: and doubts about NATO, 10, 46; Republican Party, 13
Taubmann, William, 234–35, 248
Taylor, Maxwell, 157
Tito, Josip, 139, 173, 218
"Tolstoy" discussions. *See* Churchill, Winston: and "Tolstoy" discussions
"Treaty of Friendship and Co-operation," 152
Troyanovsky, Oleg: on East-West relations, 21; on Berlin foreign ministers conference, 81
Truman, Harry S., 4, 7; and German policy, 13
Twenty-Second Amendment, 231
"Two Germanys" policy, Soviet, 179, 220, 223

U-2 crisis, 198
Ulbricht, Walter, 59, 218; during Berlin Crisis (1958–1959), 236, 245
United Nations, 121, 152, 157, 188

About the Author

Steven J. Brady teaches history at the University of Notre Dame, where he is a faculty fellow of the Nanovic Institute for European Studies. He has published a number of essays and reviews on U.S.-German relations, and on Vatican diplomacy. He lives in South Bend, Indiana, with his wife and three children.